# SELECTED READINGS IN THE
# HISTORY OF LIBRARIANSHIP

# SELECTED READINGS
# IN THE HISTORY
# OF LIBRARIANSHIP

By
JOHN L. THORNTON, F.L.A.

*Librarian, St. Bartholomew's Hospital Medical College*

*Second Edition*

LONDON
THE LIBRARY ASSOCIATION
1966

*A mirror for librarians*, First edition (Grafton), *1948*
*Classics of librarianship*, First edition (Library Association), *1957*

*Second edition, published 1966*
*by the Library Association*
**7 Ridgmount Street, Store Street,**
*London, W.C.1.*

Set in 11 point 'Monotype' Bembo (Series 270)

*Made and printed in England by*
STAPLES PRINTERS LIMITED
*at their Rochester, Kent, establishment*

# Contents

5

**6**                      CONTENTS

# Illustrations

# Preface

THIS selection is based on *A mirror for librarians*, published by Grafton & Co. in 1948, and *Classics of librarianship*, issued by the Library Association in 1957, both of which were subtitled *Selected readings in the history of librarianship*. Both books have been out of print for some time, and the suggestion from the Library Association that a new edition of the *Classics* was required, prompted me to tender the obvious idea of preparing a combined new edition. All the selections have been retained, but many of the biographical sketches have been revised, and additional references have been incorporated. A few librarians are represented for the first time in this edition.

The idea behind the initial collection of material for this volume was the selection of representative writings of men who have influenced the development of librarianship, together with the presentation of brief 'thumb-nail' portraits, and references for further reading. Living authors have been excluded, but I have endeavoured to pick out eminent librarians and persons interested in the development of libraries who have contributed in some significant way to the benefit of their profession. Many have been completely forgotten except by the few enthusiasts delving into the history of librarianship; others, even of this century, may suffer the same fate when their colleagues and contemporaries fade away. But it is well to remember that modern librarianship did not evolve overnight, but has its roots far back through the ages. The writings of book-lovers and librarians of the past can convey to us their thoughts on many problems that are still with us, and their solutions were in many instances as temporarily effective as are our own.

Any selection must obviously be a personal one, and although I have taken advantage of suggestions for inclusion, I have probably omitted persons who should have been included, and included some whose work or personalities appealed to me more than they might to others. I do not apologize, but can only hope that every reader will find something stimulating.

Some librarians have achieved recognition for the systems they built up, for their personalities, or for their influence on the development of contemporary librarianship, yet wrote nothing that can be read today with profit. It is then next to impossible to select material for reprinting, and readers will appreciate that some of those represented in this collection are selected for their personalities and their influence on the profession rather than for their writings here reproduced. Not all the selections can be major contributions to library literature, and some are presented as being typical of their authors rather than as epoch-making writings. Some mirror the library world of the period; some are classics that will never age; most represent the thoughts of some of our predecessors who, looking into the future, built our present.

I must express my grateful thanks to members of the staff of the Library Association Library for their great assistance extending over many years. Without the facilities made freely available by this and other libraries I could not have gained access to the wide range of literature perused for the compilation of this volume. Also to those who have provided me with answers to queries, and assisted me in the selection of material.

I desire to express my thanks to the following publishers, etc., for permission to quote extracts from books and periodicals: A. C. McClurg & Co. (Kirkwood and Lipsius); Houghton, Mifflin & Co. (Naudé); Yale University Press (Putnam); Williams and Wilkins Co. (W. W. Bishop); School Library Association (Esdaile); Cassell and Co. Ltd. (Greenwood); the H. W. Wilson Company (Dana); Bibliographical Society (M. S. R. James, Mason, and Ogle); Paul B. Hoeber, Inc. (MacAlister); Literary Executors and H. K. Lewis (Osler); Clarendon Press, Oxford, the late G. W. Wheeler, Esq., and Bodleian Library (Bodley); Miss D. M. Norris (Alcuin); F. W. Faxon Co. (Green); *The Times*, Mrs. F. A. Akenhead and Mrs. M. Hankey (Nicholson); Lake Placid Club Education Foundation (Dewey); U.S. Office of Education (Billings, Cutter); Library Association (Axon, Bray, Briscoe, Brown, Garnett, Minto, Nicholson, Pitt, Prideaux, Stewart and Wright); *Libri* (Barnard); Mrs. Berwick Sayers and *Library Review* (Sayers).

For permission to use photographs I am grateful to the following: Ashmolean Museum, Oxford (Dee); Bodley's Librarian (Bodley); American Library Association (Billings, Cutter and Dana); Cambridge University Library (Bradshaw); Elliott and Fry, Ltd. (Osler); and Miss Evelyn K. Green (Wheatley). Also to Dr. F. N. L. Poynter and *Medical History* for the loan of the block of the portrait of W. J. Bishop, and to the Department of Medical Illustration, St. Bartholomew's Hospital, for photographic work. I am indebted to Miss Yvonne Hibbott for assistance in the preparation of the manuscript.

JOHN L. THORNTON

*Wembley, February* 1966

# CHAPTER I

# The History of Librarianship

"If history teaches us anything, it is that life is a constant succession of turning points, each in some sort a legacy of the past, and none of them more decisive in reality than any of the others."

RAYMOND IRWIN.

IT is an astonishing fact that the history of most subjects tends to be neglected until it becomes an examination subject. Yet a knowledge of what has happened in the past is essential if we would progress into the future, avoiding the mistakes of our predecessors, adopting methods that have proved successful, and pursuing paths that have been blazed for our guidance, with the object of extending them farther towards our goal. Librarianship can still be compared to a vast unchartered country that demands exploitation to the full. We must study the maps of previous explorers, extend and correct them, but in leaving more signposts we must always be grateful to the pioneers who guided our initial efforts.

Modern librarianship is the conglomeration of the work of many men and women extended over several centuries. Not only librarians, but people from many other professions have contributed towards this development, and the further we delve into the history of the subject, the more we appreciate the fact that our inheritance has gradually evolved by the activities, for better or worse, of numerous individuals and various groups of people, many of whom have disappeared into complete obscurity. This disregard of the work of our predecessors has been fostered by undue emphasis on the present, as if we were initiating a new movement which will henceforth be dated from our era. In fact, the roots go very deep, the trunk supporting the branches has been well-established for a considerable period, and we may consider ourselves fortunate if we can add one perpetual leaf to the tree that is older than Porphyry.

The history of a subject should form the basic ingredient of its study. It need not be intensive, but should commence as a general survey of the entire field, with a closer look at the most significant events, and the more prominent personalities associated with them. In librarianship, this enables one to respect the antiquity of our calling, to appreciate the gradual advance (and sometimes decline) of various movements and techniques, and to base our future on sound foundations. We can take advantage of past experience, and learn from the mistakes of others instead of repeating them. Sympathy with the past is the difference between a bare professional existence and the full significance of being part of one's profession.

In recent years greater interest has been taken in the history of librarianship, mainly because it has become an examination subject. This has revealed a dearth of literature on the subject, for in the past there was little encouragement to produce books that could not prove commercial propositions. Edward Edwards' *Memoirs of libraries*, 2 vols., 1859, contains a wealth of historical material, and entailed years of research, yet it cannot be said to have proved a financial success. Ernest A. Savage[1] has described the circumstances leading to the writing of two remarkable pieces of research. James Duff Brown persuaded a publisher to ask Savage to write a short history of libraries, which was published in 1908 as *The story of libraries and book collecting*. One edition was sold in this country, and the book was reprinted many times in the States, but the royalties did not cover the author's expenses. The editor of Methuen's Antiquary Books then commissioned Savage to write *Old English libraries*, 1911, but fifty favourable reviews resulted in an income that failed to cover the expenses entailed in writing a very scholarly work. "No more library history," said Savage, who further suggests that "the study of library history must be subsidized and supervised." Fortunately Ernest A. Savage later produced several historical articles, and his *A librarian's memories*, 1952, is a mine of personal information on many of the major characters in librarianship in the first half of this century.

Several valuable historical studies have appeared in recent years from the pens of Raymond Irwin and W. A. Munford,[2] and the subject has also received great stimulus as the result of lectures at University College, London, and by the formation of the Library History Group of the Library Association. The latter has already been involved in the production of *Annals of the Library Asscociation, 1877–1960*, 1965, and has planned a bibliography of library history.

The subject has also been invoked by candidates preparing theses for the School of Librarianship at University College, London, and for the Library Association. A vast amount of research remains to be done. Histories of individual libraries of the past and present; of groups of libraries in particular areas, or covering particular subject fields; of library movements, and particular phases of library activities; of local parish, village, town and country, national and international library

---

[1] Savage, Ernest A. Casual amateur in bibliography. *Library Association Record*, 65, 1963, pp. 361–365.
[2] See General References, pp. 397 and 398–399.

activities; of social and economic factors influencing the development of libraries; of library literature and associations; of education for librarianship; of reading habits, types of literature, bibliography in all its aspects, and the host of subjects that combine to make librarianship a fascinating profession. We cannot hope to master all these topics in a lifetime, but must skim the surface, foster our particular interests, exploit material to which we have ready access, and contribute our mites to the history which is not only a record of the past, but which is still being made.

This brings us to the fundamentals of history. These are not merely records of dates of foundation of libraries and the opening of branches; of the initiation of gatherings of librarians to form associations; of the passing of Library Acts'of Parliament; of the publication of cataloguing codes and classification schemes; of the introduction of new techniques and modifications thereof; and of the publication of significant books on the subject. These are important, but they have been brought about by librarians and others, many of whom have devoted their lives to the advancement of librarianship within their respective fields. Some librarians spend most of their lives in one library attending to routine, and leaving the system much as they found it. Others introduce improvements, and are in turn succeeded by others who 'modernize', and practically obliterate all traces of their predecessors. A comparative few extend their activities beyond the walls of their own institutions, and influence a wider field. They attend meetings, join in discussions, serve on committees and councils, lecture and write to the benefit of librarianship. Some of these may glory in the sound of their own voices, and attain power that brings support for varying reasons from those without ideas of their own, or those readily influenced by oratory. This has sometimes resulted in measures being introduced that have proved detrimental to the profession. Potential "cogs in the wheel" may become "spanners in the works", and the profession has always suffered from a minority of people wielding power who have spurned change, or who have introduced measures that have proved detrimental to librarianship. A common fault in all spheres of life is insistence that the majority is always right, and must prevail. This can result in the obliteration of advanced views put forward by an enlightened minority; in the stifling of the ideas of specialist interests; and in the potential ability of the less experienced to overrule their superiors in length of service. Librarianship has experienced all these, for librarians are not immune to the tactics of the politician – the powerful speech from the platform to the readily hypnotized audience that will accept even weak arguments rather than think for itself.

Many librarians who were prominent in the profession while alive have been quickly forgotten after death. Some have outlived their contemporaries, and have not even achieved adequate obituary notices. These are seldom adequate, for they are usually written in a hurry, and even if factual, rarely contain criticism of even the most outrageous subjects. The Library Association some years ago recorded the voices of eminent librarians. It also collects portraits and biographical material, and might also compile bibliographies of the writings of those who have contributed to the development of librarianship. We would welcome a comprehensive "Biographical dictionary of librarianship" incorporating full details of the lives, appointments and publications of librarians of the past, with supplements published at regular intervals. This would prove a significant contribution to the history of librarianship.

Biographies of great librarians are needed, but sufficient suitable material is difficult to trace; it is also quite a problem to find a publisher, as there has not been a large enough market for this type of book. The American Library Association published Lydenberg's biography of John Shaw Billings in 1924 in an edition of one thousand copies. Forty years later several hundred copies were still available.[1] Although libraries purchase this material, few individuals do so, and there is a marked decline in the purchase of books by students of most subjects, this despite the fact that an allowance for books is made in their grants. The publication of a work depends largely upon the potential market, and commercial publishers seldom entertain the publication of an edition of a thousand copies. Fortunately the Library Association has encouraged this type of book, and several biographies of librarians have been commissioned. An outstanding example is W. A. Munford's *Edward Edwards, 1812–1886*, an invaluable, well-documented study of a remarkable personality, published by the Library Association in 1963. The author succeeded in unearthing a great deal of new material, but many librarians have left little upon which comprehensive biographies can be based. This is one reason why diaries should be preserved, the memoirs of librarians be printed, and the observations of friends, relatives, descendants and associates be recorded as soon as possible.

The following pages contain brief details of fifty librarians and others who have contributed in one way or another to the history of librarianship, followed by extracts from their writings, with references to sources of additional information. They represent a personal selection made as the result of extensive study of the literature of librarianship made over more than thirty years. History is a fascinating subject, and should not, as so often happens, be left for the years following retire-

[1] Rogers, Frank Bradway. John Shaw Billings: 1838–1913. *Library Journal*, 88, 1963, pp. 2622–2624.

ment. It can prove an interesting recreation, and if in the course of study one can produce something contributing to that history, one can become part of it. Much remains to be done; the field is vast, and comparatively unexplored. Retirement may never come, or the inclination may fade before the opportunity arises. History is but one person's interpretation of events of the past, and research on the subject can never be finalized until every possible source has been fully exploited, and interpreted without bias. The events of today will be the history of tomorrow, and fifty years from now our successors will look back at our professional activities just as we survey the librarianship of half a century ago. Our efforts will then appear just as primitive and antiquated as do those of our predecessors, but we trust that our contributions to the development of librarianship will be appreciated as links in a chain extending far into the past, and, we hope, as far again into the future.

# CHAPTER 2

# Alcuin of York (735–804)

"Europe had sunk abruptly into a slough of ignorance and illiteracy, but in every generation there were a few patient souls to keep the light of knowledge burning."

RAYMOND IRWIN.

LIBRARIANS frequently fail to appreciate the antiquity of their calling, and of library routine methods. The latter are as old as libraries, and have changed surprisingly little with the passing of the centuries. As in modern times, certain characters stand out above their fellows as persons who have contributed to the advancement of their craft, and a prominent figure connected with early libraries existed in Alcuin.

Alcuin (also known as Albinus, Albin and Ealhwine) was born in York in or about 735, and was educated there under Archbishop Egbert and his successor Ethelbert. The Cathedral School there was one of the foremost of the period, and Alcuin later assisted in the school, and in 778 became headmaster. He was a great favourite of Ethelbert and travelled extensively with him on the Continent. On returning from Rome in 781 Alcuin met Charles the Great in Parma, and was invited by him to move to Aachen. With the consent of his own king, Alfwald, and of Eanbald I, the new Archbishop of York, Alcuin quitted the school at York and went to reside with Charles the Great, who made him head of two monasteries. Alcuin greatly influenced Charles in political, theological and educational matters, planning several schools which he organized on the lines of the school at York. He also wrote many letters to prominent personalities of the period, the surviving letters being of great historical importance. Alcuin also wrote several commentaries and treatises on the scriptures, biographies, poems and songs. His collected works were published by Duchesne in 1617, and by Frobenius in 1777.

Alcuin remained in France for the remainder of his life except for a visit to England from 790 to 792, and supervised the education of the royal family. He also became involved in political disputes, and in 796 Alcuin withdrew to Tours, where the school had declined, but he soon restored it to its former greatness, replenishing the library of St. Martin's with books borrowed from England, and with copies made in the scriptorium at York. In 1739 St. Martin's possessed 272 manuscripts, many of which, together with those from other local churches, found their way into the Public Library of Tours.

Alcuin does not appear to have been a great scholar, but he excelled both as teacher and administrator. He set an example to his contemporaries by his saintly life, and by his momentous achievements. His simple epitaph at St. Martin's read: "Here doth rest the lord Alchuuin the Abbat, who died in peace on the fourteenth of the Kalends of June. When you read, O all ye that pass by, pray for him and say, The Lord grant unto him eternal rest."

Librarians remember Alcuin chiefly for his influence on the development of the library at York and for his metrical catalogue, which it has been suggested was compiled at Tours. The library was rich in Latin, Greek and Hebrew authors, some of whom are named in Alcuin's verses.

### REFERENCES

Browne, G. F., Bishop of Bristol. *Alcuin of York: lectures delivered in the Cathedral Church of Bristol in 1907 and 1908*, [etc.], London, [etc.], 1908.
*Dictionary of National Biography*, Vol. 1, pp. 239-240.

## ALCUIN'S METRICAL CATALOGUE

"Traditit ast alio caras super omnia gazas
   Librorum nato, Patri qui semper adhaesit,
   Doctrinæ sitiens haurire fluenta suëtus:
   Cujus si curas proprium cognoscere nomen,
   Fronte sua statim praesentia carmine prodent,
   His diversit opes diversis sortibus; illi
   Ecclesiae regimen, thesaurus, rura, talenta:
   Huic sophiae specimen, studium, sedemque, librosque,
   Undique quos clarus collegerat ante Magister,
   Egregias condens uno sub culmine gazas.
   Illic invenies veterum vestigia Patrum,
   Quidquid habet pro se Latio Romanus in orbe,
   Graecia vel quidquid transmisit clara Latinis:
   Hebraicus vel quod populus bibit imbre superno,
   Africa lucifluo vel quidquid lumine sparsit.
   Quod pater Hieronymus quod sensit Hilarius, atque
   Ambrosius Praesul, simul Augustinus, et ipse
   Sanctus Athanasius, quod Orosius edit avitus:
   Quidquid Gregorius summus docet, et Leo Papa:
   Basilius quidquid, Fulgentius atque coruscant,
   Cassiodorus item, Chrysostomus atque Johannes,

Quidquid et Althelmus docuit, quid Beda Magister,
Quae Victorinus scripsere, Boëtius; atque
Historici veteres, Pompeius, Plinius ipse
Acer Aristoteles, Rhetor quoque Tullius ingens.
Quid quoque Sedulius, vel quid canit ipse Juvencus.
Alcuinus et Clemens, Prosper, Paulinus, Arator,
Quid Fortunatus, vel quid Lactantius edunt.
Quae Maro Virgilius, Statius, Lucanus, et Auctor
Artis grammaticae, vel quid scripsere Magistri
Quid Probus atque Focas, Donatus, Priscianusve,
Servius, Euticius, Pompeius, Comminianus.
Invenies alios per plures, lector, ibidem
Egregios studios, arte et sermone Magistros,
Plurima qui claro scripsere volumine sensu:
Nomina sed quorum praesenti in carmine scribi
Longius est visum, quam plectri postulet usus.''

Loosely translated as:

"There shalt thou find the volumes that contain
All of the ancient fathers who remain;
There all the Latin writers make their home
With those that glorious Greece transferred to Rome;
The Hebrews draw from their celestial stream,
And Africa is bright with learning's beam.
Here shines what Jerome, Ambrose, Hilary, thought
Or Athanasius and Augustine wrought.
Orosius, Leo, Gregory the Great,
Near Basil and Fulgentius coruscate.
Grave Cassiodorus and John Chrysostom
Next Master Bede and learned Aldhelm come,
While Victorinus and Boethius stand
With Pliny and Pompeius close at hand.

Wise Aristotle looks on Tully near.
Sedulius and Juvencus next appear.
Then come Albinus, Clement, Prosper too,
Paulinus and Arator. Next we view
Lactantius, Fortunatus. Ranged in line
Virgilius Maro, Statius, Lucan, shine.
Donatus, Priscian, Probus, Phocas start
The roll of masters in grammatic art.
Eutychius, Servius, Pompey each extend
The list. Comminian brings it to an end.

There shalt thou find, O reader, many more
Famed for their style, the masters of old lore,
Whose many volumes singly to rehearse
Were far too tedious for our present verse."

From Norris, Dorothy May. *A history of cataloguing and cataloguing methods, 1100–1850,* [etc.], 1939, pp. 8–10.

# CHAPTER 3

# Richard De Bury (1287–1345)

"In books I find the dead as if they were alive; in books I foresee things to come; in books warlike things are set forth; from books come forth the laws of peace. All things are corrupted and decay in time. Saturn ceases not to devour the children that he generates: all the glory of the world would be buried in oblivion, unless God had provided mortals with the remedy of books."

RICHARD DE BURY.

THE *Philobiblon*, generally attributed to Richard de Bury, is one of the most remarkable books in the literature of librarianship. Completed six hundred years ago, it contains much shrewd advice and information that remains of value even today, the modern English translation being a most interesting document.

Richard de Bury, son of Sir Richard Aungevile, was born on January 24th, 1287, near Bury St. Edmunds, Suffolk, and was educated at Oxford. He became tutor to Prince Edward of Windsor, and upon the latter's accession to the throne as Edward III, was honoured with many political appointments. In 1322 Richard de Bury became Chamberlain of Chester, and Edward III made him Clerk of the Privy Seal. He was also sent in 1330 and 1333 as ambassador to the Pope, and upon one of these visits met Petrarch. In 1333 Richard became Dean of Wells, and a little later, Bishop of Durham; when he died in 1345 he was buried in that Cathedral.

The authorship of *Philobiblon* has been doubted, but apparently no better claim to it has been laid than the activities of Richard de Bury. Ernest C. Thomas's edition of the work was compiled from twenty-eight manuscripts and several printed editions, and apparently Thomas did not doubt the authorship of the book until his edition was being printed. His attention was then drawn to a note on Richard de Bury by one of his contemporaries which threw doubt upon his character, but certainly does not prove that de Bury was not the author of *Philobiblon*.

Richard de Bury died in debt, some of his books being sold to satisfy his creditors, but he is said to have owned more books than all the other English bishops put together. He had a library at each of his residences, and spared no effort to increase his collection, even acquiring books from abroad. The *Philobiblon* is probably the only book written by de Bury, and the work is described in the final paragraph as having been completed "in our manor-house of Aukland on the 24th day of January in the year of our Lord one thousand three hundred and forty-four."

There have been several printed editions of *Philobiblon*, and numerous manuscripts of it also exist, all of which are recorded in the remarkably fine edition prepared in honour of Sir Basil Blackwell's seventieth birthday, and edited by Michael Maclagan. This contains the Latin and English texts, with biographical and bibliographical introductions. Editions were printed at Cologne, 1473; Spires, 1483; Paris, 1500; Oxford, 1598 and 1599, edited by Thomas James; Frankfurt, 1610 and 1614; Leipzig, 1674; Helmstadt, 1703; London, 1832; Paris, 1856; Albany, 1861; London, 1888, edited by E. C. Thomas, followed by numerous editions, and translation into German, Italian, Polish, Spanish, etc.

## REFERENCES

*Philobiblon. Richard de Bury. The text and translation of E. C. Thomas. Edited with a foreword by Michael Maclagan*, Oxford, 1960. This contains the Latin and English texts, with a biographical introduction (pp. xi–xxxvii), and a bibliography of printed editions of manuscripts (pp. xxxvii–lxxiii).

*The Philobiblon of Richard de Bury, Bishop of Durham, Treasurer and Chancellor of Edward III. Edited and translated by Ernest C. Thomas*, [etc.], 1888. Contains Latin text followed by modern English version; biography (pp. xi–xlvii); bibliography of printed editions and MSS.; and references to original material. Thomas's translation also appeared in The King's Classics Series as *The love of books. The Philobiblon of Richard de Bury, newly translated into English by E. C. Thomas*, 1902.

## Richard de Bury's Philobiblon

In books I find the dead as if they were alive; in books I foresee things to come; in books warlike affairs are set forth; from books come forth the laws of peace. All things are corrupted and decay in time; Saturn ceases not to devour the children that he generates; all the glory of the world would be buried in oblivion, unless God had provided mortals with the remedy of books. Alexander, the conqueror of the earth, Julius the invader of Rome and of the world, who, the first in wars and arts, assumed universal empire under his single rule, faithful Fabricius and stern Cato, would now have been unknown to fame, if the aid of books had been wanting. Towers have been razed to the ground; cities have been overthrown; triumphal arches have perished from decay; nor can either pope or king find any means of more easily conferring the privilege of perpetuity than by books. The book that he has made renders its author this service in return, that so long as the book survives the author remains immortal and cannot die, as Ptolemy declares in the Prologue to his Almagest: He is not dead, he says, who has given life to science.

[pp. 161–162]

. . . .

Finally, we must consider what pleasantness of teaching there is in books, how easy, how secret! How safely they lay bare the poverty of human ignorance to books without feeling any shame! They are masters who instruct us without rod or ferule, without angry words, without clothes or money. If you come to them they are not asleep; if you ask and inquire of them, they do not withdraw themselves; they do not chide if you make mistakes; they do not laugh at you if you are ignorant. O books who alone are liberal and free, who give to all who ask of you and enfranchise all who serve you faithfully! by how many thousand types are ye commended to learned men in the scriptures given us by inspiration of God! For ye are the mines of profoundest wisdom, to which the wise man sends his son that he may dig out treasures: Prov. 2. Ye are the wells of living waters, which father Abraham first digged, Isaac digged again, and which the Philistines strive to fill up: Gen. 26. . . . Ye are the golden vessels of the temple, the arms of the soldiers of the Church, with which to quench all the fiery darts of the wicked, fruitful olives, vines of Engadi, figtrees that are never barren, burning lamps always to be held in readiness – and all the noblest comparisons of scripture may be applied to books, if we choose to speak in figures.

[pp. 163–165]

. . . .

From what has been said we draw this corollary welcome to us, but (as we believe) acceptable to few: namely, that no dearness of price ought to hinder a man from the buying of books, if he has the money that is demanded for them, unless it be to withstand the malice of the seller or to await a more favourable opportunity of buying. For if it is wisdom only that makes the price of books, which is an infinite treasure to mankind, and if the value of books is unspeakable, as the premises show, how shall the bargain be shown to be dear where an infinite good is being bought? Wherefore, that books are to be gladly bought and unwillingly sold, Solomon, the sun of men, exhorts us in the *Proverbs: Buy the truth*, he says, *and sell not wisdom.*

[p. 169]

. . . .

Almighty Author and Lover of peace, scatter the nations that delight in war, which is above all plagues injurious to books. For wars being without the control of reason make a wild assault on everything they comes [sic] across, and lacking the check of reason they push on without discretion or distinction to destroy the vessels of reason.

(pp. 191–192]

. . .

In sooth we cannot mourn with the grief that they deserve all the various books that have perished by the fate of war in various parts of the world. Yet we must tearfully recount the dreadfull ruin which was caused in Egypt by the auxilliaries in the Alexandrian war, when seven hundred thousand volumes were consumed by fire. These volumes had been collected by the royal Ptolemies through long periods of time, as Aulus Gellius relates. What an Atlantean progeny must be supposed to have then perished: including the motions of the spheres, all the conjunctions of the planets, the nature of the galaxy, and the prognostic generations of comets, and all that exists in the heavens or in the ether! Who would not shudder at such a hapless holocaust, where ink is offered up instead of blood, where the glowing ashes of crackling parchment were encarnadined with blood, where the devouring flames consumed so many thousands of innocents in whose mouth was no guile, where the unsparing fire turned into ashes so many shrines of eternal truth?

[pp. 193–194]

. . .

But in truth infinite are the losses which have been inflicted upon the race of books by wars and tumults. And as it is by no means possible to enumerate and survey infinity, we will here finally set up the Gades of our complaint, and turn again to the prayers with which we began, humbly imporing that the Ruler of Olympus and the Most High Governor of all the world will establish peace and dispel wars and make our days tranquil under his protection.

[pp. 196–197]

. . .

Moreover, we had always in our different manors no small multitude of copyists and scribes, of binders, correctors, illuminators, and generally of all who could usefully labour in the service of books. Finally, all of both sexes and of every rank or position who had any kind of association with books, could most easily open by their knocking the door of our heart, and find a fit resting-place in our affection and favour. In so much did we receive those who brought books, that the multitude of those who had preceded them did not lessen the welcome of the after-comers, nor were the favours we had awarded yesterday prejudicial to those of to-day. Wherefore, ever using all the persons we have named as a kind of magnets [sic] to attract books, we had the desired accession of the vessels of science and a multitudinous flight of the finest volumes.

[p. 206]

.    .    .    .

To him who recollects what has been said before, it is plain and evident who ought to be the chief lovers of books. For those who have most need of wisdom in order to perform usefully the duties of their position, they are without doubt most especially bound to show more abundantly to the sacred vessels of wisdom the anxious affection of a grateful heart. Now it is the office of the wise man to order rightly both himself and others, according to the Phœbus of philosophers, Aristotle, who deceives not nor is deceived in human things. Where-fore princes and prelates, judges and doctors, and all other leaders of the commonwealth, as more than others they have need of wisdom, so more than others ought they to show zeal for the vessels of wisdom.

[p. 224]

.    .    .    .

Books delight us, when prosperity smiles upon us; they comfort us inseparably when stormy fortune frowns on us. They lend validity to human compacts, and no serious judgements are propounded without their help. Arts and sciences, all the advantages of which no mind can enumerate, consist in books. How highly must we estimate the won-drous power of books, since through them we survey the utmost bounds of the world and time, and contemplate the things that are as well as those that are not, as it were in the mirror of eternity. In books we climb mountains and scan the deepest gulfs of the abyss; in books we behold the finny tribes that may not exist outside their native waters, distinguish the properties of streams and springs and of various lands; from books we dig out gems and metals and the materials of every kind of mineral, and learn the virtues of herbs and trees and plants, and survey at will the whole progeny of Neptune, Ceres, and Pluto.

[p. 229]

Extracts from *The Philobiblon of Richard de Bury, Bishop of Durham, Treasurer and Chancellor of Edward III. Edited and translated by Ernest C. Thomas, [etc.], 1888.*

# CHAPTER 4

# Dr. John Dee (1527–1608)

"Whereby your Highness shall have a most notable library, learning wonderfully be advanced, and passing excellent works of our forefathers from rot and worms preserved, and also hereafter continually the whole realm may (through your Graces goodnes) use and enjoy the whole incomparable treasure so preserved."

JOHN DEE.

ALTHOUGH known as the collector of a private library, which he estimated to contain "neere 4,000" items, of which 1,000 were MSS., John Dee has received little recognition as a contributor to librarianship, yet if his idea had come to fruitation he would be honoured as the founder of the State National Library.

John Dee was born on July 13th, 1537, and educated at Chelmsford Grammar School and St. John's College, Cambridge. He graduated B.A. in 1546, and was elected a Fellow of Trinity College. He travelled on the Continent before proceeding to M.A., and then once more travelled abroad. He was a student at Louvain in 1548, visited Paris University, and appears to have acquired a doctorate during this period, returning to England in July, 1550. He became established as mathematician, astronomer and astrologer, and when Queen Mary came to the throne he calculated her nativity, casting a horoscope for her sister, Princess Elizabeth. He was later accused of treason, but discharged by the dreaded Star Chamber.

On January 15th, 1556, he presented a "Supplication"[1] to Queen Mary, "for the recovery and preservation of ancient writers and monuments", but we are not aware that it received any consideration whatsoever from the Queen. Dee wanted to collect together the remnants of literature remaining from the dissolution of the monasteries, and to procure copies of treatises from the larger European libraries. This was almost fifty years before the opening of the Bodleian Library, and nearly two hundred years before the foundation of the British Museum.

When Queen Elizabeth came to the throne she was Dee's patron for many years, and it appears strange that he did not submit his "Supplication" to her, but perhaps he considered the opportunity had

[1] The original manuscript, badly damaged by fire, is in the British Museum (Cott. MS. Vitell. C. vii. f. 310); a later MS. copy is also housed there (Add. MS. 4630. f. 1).

slipped away. He wrote many books, and collected together a large library, much of which was destroyed when a mob raided his house at Mortlake. Dr. John Dee died in December, 1608, his efforts to tranmute base metals into gold having proved as unsuccessful as his attempt to collect together the literature of his period for the benefit of scholars. (Portrait, Plate 1.)

### REFERENCES

Dee, John. *Autobiographical tracts of Dr. John Dee, Warden of the College of Manchester.* Edited by James Crossley, for the Chetham Society, 1851 (*Chetham Society*, O.S. 24, *Miscellanies*, Vol. 1.)

*Dictionary of National Biography*, Vol. 14, 1888, pp. 271–279.

James, Montague Rhodes. Lists of manuscripts formerly owned by Dr. John Dee. With preface and identifications. *Supplement to Transactions of the Bibliographical Society*, 1921.

Smith, Charlotte Fell. *John Dee, 1527–1608*, [etc.], 1909.

Thornton, John L. Dr. John Dee and his scheme for a national library. *Medical Bookman and Historian*, 2, 1948, pp. 359–362.

## A SUPPLICATION TO Q. MARY, BY JOHN DEE, FOR THE RECOVERY AND PRESERVATION OF ANCIENT WRITERS AND MONUMENTS.

### To the Queenes most excellent Majestie.

In most humble wise complaining, beseecheth your Highnes, your faithful and loving subject, John Dee gentleman, to have in remembrance, how that, among the exceeding most lamentable displeasures, that have of late happened unto this realm, through the subverting of religious houses, and the dissolution of other assemblies of godly and learned men, it hath been, and for ever, among all learned students, shall be judged, not for the least calamity, the spoile and destruction of so many and so notable libraries, wherein lay the treasure of all Antiquity, and the everlasting seeds of continual excellancy within this your Grace's realm. But, albeit that in those dayes many a pretious jewel and ancient monument did utterly perish (as at Canterbury did that wonderful work of the sage and eloquent *Cicero de Republica*, and in many other places the like) yet if, in time, great and speedy diligence be shewed, the remanents of such incredible store, as well of writers theologicall, as in all other liberal sciences, might be saved and recovered: which now in your Grace's realm being dispersed and scattered, yea and many of them in the unlearned men's hands, do still yet (in this time of reconciliation) dayly perish; and perchance of purpose by some envious person enclosed in walls, or buried in the ground, to the great injurie of the famous and worthy authors, and the pitifull hindrance of the learned in this your Highnes realme: whose travailes, watchings, and pains might greatly be relieved and eased; for that such doubts and points of learning, as much cumber and vex their heads, are most pithyly in such old monuments debated and discussed. Therefore your said suppliant maketh most humble petition unto your Majestie, that it might stand with your good will and pleasure, such order and meanes to take place, as your said suppliant hath devised for the recovery and continuall preservation of all such worthy monuments, as yet are extant, either in this your Graces realm of England, or else where in the most part of all Christendome. Whereby your Highness shall have a most notable library, learning wonderfully be advanced, and passing excellent works of our forefathers from rot and worms preserved, and also hereafter continually the whole realm may (through your Graces goodnes) use and enjoy the whole incomparable treasure so preserved: where now no one student, no nor any one college, hath half a dozen of those excellent jewels, but the whole stock and store thereof drawing nigh to utter destruction and extinguishing, while here and there by private mens negligence (and sometimes malice) many a famous and excellent author's book is rent, burnt, or suffered to rott and decay. And your said suppliant is so much the more willing to move this suit unto your Highnes, for that by his said device your Graces said library might in very few yeares most plentifully be furnisht, and that without any one penny charge unto your Majestie, or doing injurie to any creature. Finally in the erecting of this your Library Royall, your Grace shall follow the footsteps of all the famous and godly princes of old time, and also do like the worthy Governors of Christendome at these dayes: but far surmounting them all both in the store of rare monuments, and likewise in the incredible fruit, which of this your Highnes act will follow ere it be long. The merit whereof shall redound to your Majesties honorable and everlasting fame here on earth, and undoubtedly in heaven highly be rewarded; as knoweth God, Whom your said suppliant most heartily beseecheth long to preserve your grace in all prosperity. Amen.

Articles concerning the recovery and preservation of the ancient monuments and old excellent Writers: and also concerning the erecting of a Library without any charges to the Queens Majestie, or doing injury to any of the Queens Highnes subjects, according to the tenor and intent of a supplication to the Queens grace in this behalf exhibited by John Dee, Gentleman. A.1556, the xv day of January.

1. *Imprimis*, the Queen's Majesties commission to be granted for the

seeing and perusing of all places within this her realm, where any notable or excellent monument may be found, or is known to be. And the said monument or monuments so found and had by the said Commissioner then, of the former possessor in the Queens Majesties name to be borrowed, and so nevertheless to be restorable to the said former possessor after such convenient time, wherein of every such monument one fair copy may be written, if the said former possessor be disposed to have the said monument or monuments again: and thereupon either he or his assignes do at the said Library (the place whereof is by the Queen's grace to be appointed) demand the said monument or monuments by bill assigned with the hand of the said Commissioner, wherein both the name or names of the said monument or monuments is or are particularly expressed, and also the convenient time for the said restitution prescribed.

2. That it may be referred to my Lord Cardinal's Grace and the next Synod to conclude an order for the allowance of all necessary charges, as well toward the riding and journeying for the recovery of the said worthy monuments, as also for the copying out of the same, and framing of necessary stalls, desks, and presses, meet for the preservation and use of the said monuments in the Queens Majesties Library aforesaid.

3. That the said Commission be with speed dispatched for three causes especially: first, lest after this motion made, the spreading of it abroad might cause many to hide and convey their good and ancient writers (which nevertheless were very ungodly done, and a certain token, that such are not sincere lovers of good learning). Secondly, that by the travail of these three months, February, March, and April next going before the Synod, in May next appointed, the said Synod may have good proof, whereby to conjecture, how this matter will take success. And thirdly, upon the said trial of three months, the proportion of the charges in riding and writing may the better be weighed, what they will in manner amount to.

4. A meeting place to be forthwith appointed for the said monuments to be sent unto, untill the said Library may be made apt in all points necessary; and that in this said place, before or at the Synod-time, the said monuments may be viewed and perused, according to the pleasure of my Lord Cardinals Grace and the said next Synod.

5. Finally, that by furder device of your said suppliant, John Dee (God granting him his life and health), all the famous and worthy monuments, that are in the notablest Librarys beyond the sea (as in

Vaticana at Rome, S. Marci at Venice, and the like at Bononia, Florence, Venice, &c.) shall be procured unto the said Library of our soveraign Lady and Queen, the charges thereof (beside the journeying) to stand in the copying of them out and the carryage into this realm only. And as concerning all other excellent authors printed, that they likewise shall be gotten in wonderfull abundance, their carriage only into this realme to be chargeable.

From *Autobiographical Tracts of Dr. John Dee, Warden of the Collegehof Manchester.* Edited by *James Crossley*, for the Chetham Society, 1851, pp. 46–79 (*Cisetham Society*, O.S. 24, *Miscellanies*, Vol. 1). Also printed in Hearne, Thomas. *Johann. Glastoniensis Chronica, sive historia de rebus Glastoniensis*, [etc.], Oxford, 1726, Vol. 2, pp 490–495.

# CHAPTER 5

# Sir Thomas Bodley (1545–1613)
## and
# Dr. Thomas James (1573? –1629)

"I concluded at the last to set up my staffe at the Librarie-dore in Oxon; being throwghly persuaded that, in my solitude and surcease from the common-wealth-assayers, I coulde not busie myselfe to better purpose then by redusing that place (which then in every part laye ruined and wast) to the publique use of studients."

THOMAS BODLEY.

THE Bodleian Library, Oxford has for centuries been the Mecca for scholars from all over the world. Its antiquity, and the fact that it is maintained up to date by means of copyright privilege render it of primary significance, and its foremost position is almost entirely due to the efforts of one man. Sir Thomas Bodley planned the restoration of Duke Humphrey's Library, personally supervised every detail of its reconstruction, and made provision for its future development. He carefully considered every minute detail connected with the organization and furnishing of the library, and as his letters indicate, put the collection foremost in his thoughts, never missing an opportunity to solicit gifts, and taking great pains to acquire literature from abroad, if it could not be purchased in England.

Sir Thomas Bodley was born at Exeter on March 2nd, 1545, and was educated at Geneva and Magdalen College, Oxford. Between 1576 and 1580 he travelled in Italy, France and Germany, and from 1585 to 1596 he was envoy to Denmark, France and Holland. In the following year Bodley married a rich widow, and retired from diplomatic life. On February 23rd, 1598, he wrote to the Vice-Chancellor of Oxford University, offering to restore Duke Humphrey's Library, the letter being reproduced below (pp. 38–39). He immediately began collecting books, seeking gifts from all possible donors, and sending agents to the book marts on the Continent. He later ventured even farther afield, asking the Consul of Aleppo to procure volumes in Arabic, Syriac, Persian and Turkish (see p. 43). With the rapid accumulation of books it became necessary to appoint a custodian, and in 1601 Dr. Thomas James became the first Keeper of the Library. Bodley, however, strictly reserved to himself the right to make all decisions respecting library matters, and the correspondence between Bodley and James is of great interest. James was not permitted even to marry without Bodley's permission (see pp. 33–34), and it is probable that had James been given a free hand he would have made an even better librarian than he was permitted to be.

In 1604 Bodley was knighted, and in the following year the first catalogue of the Library, compiled by James, was printed. The Keeper was also instrumental in obtaining from the Stationers' Company the grant of one copy of every book issued by a member of the Company, which came into effect in December, 1610.

It is not generally known that Bodley's London residence was "The Great House" within the precincts of St. Bartholomew's Hospital where he lived from 1599 to 1612. The house was a three-storey building with a courtyard, garden and a long gallery with five large windows and four chimneys. In this gallery Bodley arranged his books before they were carried to Oxford. Lady Bodley died in this house in 1611, and was buried in the parish church of St. Bartholomew-the-Less, where there is a tablet to her memory on the north-east wall of the nave. Sir Thomas also died there on January 28th, 1613, but was buried in Merton College Chapel, Oxford, bequeathing the greater part of his property for the benefit of his Library.

Thomas James was educated at Winchester and New College, Oxford, where he pursued theological studies, and in fact retained his interest in theology throughout his life. He prepared an edition of Richard de Bury's *Philobiblon*, which was published at Oxford in 1598 and 1599. James was Keeper of the Bodleian from 1601 until his resignation in 1620, and did not spare himself to enhance the value of the Library. He presented his private collection to the Library, secured numerous valuable gifts, compiled two printed catalogues of the Bodleian, issued in 1605 and 1620 respectively, and also compiled a subject catalogue, which is still available in manuscript form and represents an early outstanding example of this type of catalogue.

James' activities were strictly supervised and greatly restricted by Bodley. He was not permitted to shelve manuscripts and printed books separately, and he also disapproved of alphabetical arrangement under broad headings; but Bodley's permission was necessary before the minutest detail was made an accomplished fact. The letters exchanged between the founder and the keeper are of great interest, painting a vivid picture of their relationship, and certain of them are here reproduced.

## REFERENCES

*Letters of Sir Thomas Bodley to Thomas James. . . . Edited . . . by G. W.* Wheeler, Oxford, 1926.

*Letters of Sir Thomas Bodley to the University of Oxford, 1598–1611. Edited by G. W. Wheeler,* Oxford, 1927.

*Letters addressed to Thomas James, first Keeper of Bodley's Library. Edited by G. W. Wheeler,* Oxford, 1933.

Macray, William Dunn. *Annals of the Bodleian Library, Oxford. . . . Second edition, [etc.],* Oxford, 1890.

*Pietas Oxoniensis in memory of Sir Thomas Bodley, Knt., and the foundation of the Bodleian Library,* [Oxford], 1902. Contains biography of Bodley, genealogy, chief gifts to the Bodleian after his death, lists of librarians and sub-librarians, bibliographical list of printed catalogues; also, portraits of Bodley, Humphrey Duke of Gloucester, Archbishop Laud, John Selden, Bishop Richard Rawlinson, Francis Douce, Thomas James, *etc.* The portrait of Bodley is reproduced as Plate 2.

Power, Sir D'Arcy. Sir Thomas Bodley's London house. *Bodleian Quarterly Record,* 8, No. 90, Summer, 1936.

*Trecentale Bodleianum. A memorial volume for the three hundredth anniversary of the public funeral of Sir Thomas Bodley, March 29, 1613,* Oxford, 1913. Contains his autobiography written in 1609, his letter offering to refound the University Library, extracts from his will, *etc.*

## Letters of Sir Thomas Bodley to Thomas James

### Letter 9

Sir, The general liking of the Librarie doth greatly content me: and faine I would answear their desires, which would haue it frequented, out of hand: but so many cheires, as shall be requisit, can not soddainly be made, nor many thinges more perfourned, which apperteine vnto the place, and the bookes, and to the dignitie and state of an action begonne with so great expectation. The necessitie of hauing casements, will soone appeere heereafter, and they may be quickly had. But I am of opinion, that when this present heat, which is very vnusual, shall be slaked, there will be little cause, to complaine this twelue moneth. I pray yow keepe a note, of the bookes that are double, and lette me haue it, with the Catalogue, which I desire should be written as your owne, with placing the fol$^o$. bookes by themselues in the Alphabet, and then the 4$^{to}$ & c. I doe not thinke that yow shall finde, aboue one or two bookes of a sort, that are double, being newe bought. But among M$^r$ Gents, there were diuers newe bound, which may seeme newe bought, when I had the same before, not knowing what bookes he would giue in his later gifte: whereby thei felle to be double. Howbeit we shall haue time enough and meanes, to make them away with very litle losse: and my desire is, that yow would be very sparing, in acquainting others, with suche bookes: or with any other imper-fection, in this first collection. I would willingly vnderstand, what

PLATE I

DR. JOHN DEE

(1527 – 1608)

(From the painting in the Ashmolean Museum, Oxford,
by kind permission of the Director)

PLATE 2

SIR THOMAS BODLEY
(1545 – 1613)

(From the oil-painting in the Bodleian Library,
by kind permission of Bodley's Librarian)

fault is founde with the cheines. For I knowe thei will catche, but yet lesse than any, that I haue seene. At my departure from Oxford, last, M^r Vicechancellour did promise, that I should haue the copies of suche letters as should be written to Sir Io. Fortescue, and the B. of Hereford, which I pray yow procure and send vnto me: and signifie withall, by whome and when they shall be sent. I would also vnderstand to whome it was resolued, that the Vicechancellours should addresse their particular letters of thankes, in the Vniuersities name: which importeth very muche, for the encouraging of other gentlemen, to be done with good respect. I would intreat yow, to speake to M^r Principal, to send me a note what volumes are superfluous, and what is wanting in Menochius workes. Likewise at your good leasure, I would request a catalogue of euery one of their bookes, which were procured there by yow in the Vniuersitie, to witte of M^r Ridleis M^r Drapers, the schoolemasters of Winton, your brothers & c. to the end I may put them downe orderly on my register. My hope was and is that the greatest part of our Protestant writers will be given: but whether they be or no, they shall all be had, before the place be frequented. I pray yow be not weery of writing often to me. For the good disposition of all thinges in the Librarie doth greatly depend vpon our continual correspondence. And thus for the present I bidde yow hartely adieu.

       Your affectionat fast frind

            Tho. Bodley.

Iuly 22. London. [1601].

I pray yow remember to send me an example of their handes, whose writing yow commended vnto me, at my being in Oxon.

                    [pp. 9–11]

.    .    .    .

## LETTER 14

Sir, Concerning your letter of the 8. of this moneth, I haue not nowe the leasure, so to answear it all, as ether I am desirous, or some pointes thereof require. But yet if yow please, to weigh that litle that I write, with a ballance of a staied and vntroubled judgement, I doe not doubt but I shall giue yow very good satisfaction. And first where yow wonder at my suddaine flatte denial of your continuance in that place, if so be yow should be maried: I did wonder as muche, to see yow come vpon the suddaine, when I was ready to depart, and require to be resolued, what yerely stipend yow might trust to: because yow meant, as yow saied, to resign your felowship very shortly, and might determine withall, to take a wife: for whiche your state would haue neede, of 40$^{li}$ stipend at the lest. This your abrupt and vntimely demaund, with vnusual termes and wordes, did seeme to me so very strange, as I complained vnto yow, of your ouer late proposal, of a mater of that weight, when I was ready to begonne. Howbeit mine answear I am sure, was frindly and considerat. That yow should alwaies be assured of 20$^{li}$ from me, and that in time I made no question of raising it further to 20 or 30 more: wherof notwithstanding, I could not as yet giue any assurance. But for the point of your marriage, I might by no means yelde vnto it: holding it absurd in yow or in any, for sundrie great respectes: nether did I, as I signified, see any necessitie of giuing ouer your fellowship. . . .

Thus wishing to that humour which bredde the subject of this letter, all the purging that may be, and your self all the good that your hart can desire, I betake both yow and all your actions, to Gods good direction.

your vnchangeable frind<br>Tho. Bodley.

From Burnham.   Sept. 11 [1601].

[pp. 17–18, 21]

.    .    .    .

LETTER 46

Sir, I am very glad to heare of Sir Io. Fortescues comming thither: whome I knowe yow will welcome, according to his dignitie, and desert to that place. Yow shall doe best, in my judgement, to be so short, as he may not conceaue it, to be muche premeditat: which will make so muche more for your owne commendation. Howbeit I could wishe, that the ioiners did returne, out of hand, for the sooner finishing for those shelues. For their worke in that place, is no ill sight to Sir Io. or to any. I pray yow hasten your mans writing of my Catalogue: the want wherof in good perfection, both hath and will trouble me not a litle. And if yow please to send me a note of the principal bookes in fol$^{o}$. printed in Italy, Paris, or Lions, of those which yow haue lately collected to be wanting in the Libr. I will presently conuey it, to Io. Bille, who is nowe in Paris. I would onely haue suche as are printed in those places, or els where therabout, and not all in fol$^{o}$. that yow haue gathered, but some of the principal, for the more expedition, of your copieng of them out. As touching your Frankford Catalogues, there is a bigge volume in 4$^{o}$. printed, conteining all from the yere 64. to 92. There is likewise an other from that time, to 1600. in 4$^{o}$. printed by Henningus. These are bothe to be had at Nortons.

But I thinke it is the later that you require: wherof I pray yow send me worde and I will conuey it with my next letter. Wherewith at this present I bidde yow adieu.

your assured ever
Tho. Bodley.

London.   Aug. 27 [1602].

[pp. 52-3]

.     .     .     .

## LETTER 47

Sir, I knowe not what is meant by the note, which I haue returned heerewith: but, as I doe suppose, it crept in with the rest vnwares to your self. Your Catalogue hath onely bookes in lawe and Physicke, because, as I imagine, yow haue gathered none of the other 2. faculties. By the cariar yow shall receaue your Franckf. Catalogue, and likewise a glasse of the best inke, that I can presently find. I shall request yow, that in writing the names of the Autours to be fixed at the headdes of the Deskes, yow would with your penne expresse your letters as full as yow can. For it chaunceth, by reason of sundrie letters but half drawen, when your paper taketh not the inke, which causeth obscuritie. I pray yow pardon my curiositie in these trifles: for that I am desirous, as neere as I can to meete with all exceptions. My trust is in yow, that my Catalogue shall be written out of your man with all expedition: for that without it, I am no body. If yow can not finde paper large and good enough, to write the tables of the deskes, I thinke it shall not skille, if 2. sheetes of some other paper, then roial, be pasted netely together: which may be done, as I suppose, without any blemishe. Which is all that I haue worth the signifieng presently: wherupon I am to bidde yow most hartely a Dieu.

your euer assured
Tho. Bodley.

London.   1. Sept. [1602].

Lest the cariar should refuse the cariage of your glasse of inke, my man made him beleue it was a glasse of distilled water: and suche yow must aske for.

[pp. 53-4]

.     .     .     .

## LETTER 92

Sir, I will be at the charge of printing the Catalogue, and so I pray yow signifie to Mr Barnes, with whome, for the price, I will accord, at my comming to Oxon: praieng him the while to prouide suche newe chaces, and rulers, with all other necessaries, as that worke shall require: to the end the Catalogue may be printed assoone as is possible. The next weeke, God willing, I will send away my bookes, and purpose my self, to be with yow shortly after: a which time we shall agree vpon the Letter, and all thinges els in doubt. I pray yow send me Bacon, and as for Hadrianus ioned with him, he shall be returned bound with some other. Yow forgotte to send me word as touching the chestes to be placed in the windowes for the vse of the smaller bookes, what length, depth, and bredth thei may be of, and what number of books yow thinke they may conteine: wherin I shall request yow to vse the aduise of M^r Principal Hawley in special, and to commend me most hartely vnto him. I would receaue your answear by the first the next weeke, for that I purpose therupon to send some wenscotte with my bookes. Yow must neede aduenture to send 2 or 3 letters to Io Cheinman, by seueral messengers, whereby some one may com to his handes. Commend me most hartely to your brother.

your euer assured<br>Tho. Bodley.

London.   Iunij 13. [1604].

[pp. 97–8]

·      ·      ·      ·

LETTER 142

Sir, I haue sette downe in Englishe, the effect of a speeche, which I should desire might be vsed to the king. I haue written it in hast, and without curiositie, for your vnderstanding onely: and so as yow may adde or diminishe, change or interpose what yow thinke good. For I haue onely sette downe the roughe draught, which yow may refine, if yow like it. If I chaunce to see your brother before the cariar depart, I will conferre with him about it. To my iudgement, it will fitte your person and the place very well, being written in pure latin, and gracefulle deliuered. The lending of any booke out of the Librarie may be assented to by no meanes: neither is it a mater that the Vniuersitie or Vicechancelour are to deal in. It can not stand with my publike resolution with the Vniuersitie, and my denial made to the B. of Glocester, and the rest of the interpreters in their assemblie in Christ-churche, who requested the like at my handes, for one or two bookes. I pray yow therefore, whensoeuer yow shall talke with D. Blincowe, or any other that may happen to make the like request, to intreat them to pardon me, being altogether bent, sins thinges haue bin setled in the Librarie to obserue all orders as strictly as may be. The booke required is but litle, and may soone be perused in the Librarie it self, which I doe not doubt, by D. Blincowe will consider, and excuse my precisnesse in obseruing an order so much approued by others, and vrged still by my self. With Sir Tho. Lakes I will deale to that effect as yow desire: but to speede yow of that, which may be for your purpose, till this businesse about the kinges comming be ouerpast, I for my part shall not haue the leisure to deuise. For it requireth more enquirie, and information of thinges then yow doe happely thinke on as yet. Howbeit in time conuenient for it, you shall be sure I will endeuour, what I can for your good, by my self and by my frindes, in any respect.

your affectionat frind

Tho. Bodley.

London. Iuly 26. [1605].

[pp. 147–8]

. . . .

LETTER 231

Sir, The speeche goeth heere, that sins St. Thomas Eue, the Librarie doore hath continued shutte: which is highly disliked of all that vuderstand it: but of no man more, than of my self: because many doe imagine, that the abuse is committed, with my toleration. Whereupon they doe descant, that whensoeuer God shall calle me, that whole Institution will quickly goe to wracke: which vndoubtedly will minister much occasion of repentance, among all sortes of persons, that haue bin contributours. In which regard I can not choose, but request yow for heerafter, to alter your course (which nowe I heare is too common) in taking that liberite. For my meaning was euer, and so it is, I am sure, of the whole Vniuersitie, that still there should be that accesse, for students to that place, as was formerly allowed by the ancient statutes: which neuer permitted so large vacations. And although in som regardes, they were held ouer strict, yet as neere as is possible, they must needes be obserued: which I will alwaies endeuour, and yow will second me I hope, as I shall alwaies be

your louing and very assured frind.

Tho. Bodley.

Fulham. Ian. 3. [1613].

[pp. 230–1]

From *Letters of Sir Thomas Bodley to Thomas James, First Keeper of the Bodleian Library.* Edited with an Introduction by *G. W. Wheeler,* Oxford, 1926.

## BODLEY'S LETTERS TO THE UNIVERSITY OF OXFORD

### LETTER I

### [To the Vice-Chancellor]

Sir although you know mee not, as I suppose, yet for the farthering of an offer, of evident vtilitie, to your whole Vniuersity, I will not be to scrupulous, in craving your assistance. I haue bin alwaies of a mind, that yf god of his goodnesse, should make mee able to doe any thing, for the benefit of posteritie, I would shew some token of affection that I haue evermore boarne, to the studies of good learning. I know my portion is too slender, to performe for the present, any answerable act, to my willing disposition: but yet to notifie some part of my desire in that behalf, I haue thus to deale. Where there hath bin heretofore a publike library in Oxford: which you know is apparent, by the rome it self remayning, and by your statute records I will take the charge and cost vpon me to reduce it again to his former vse: and to make it fitte, and handsome with seates, and shelfes, and Deskes, and all that may be needfull, to stirre vp other mens benevolence, to helpe to furnish it with bookes. And this I purpose to beginne, assoone as timber can be gotten, to the intent that you may reape, some spedie profitt of my proiect. And where before as I conceaue, it was to be reputed, but a store of books of diuuese benefactors: because it never had any lasting allowanc[e], for augmentation of the number, or supplie of bookes decaied: whereby it came to passe, that when those that were in being, were ether wasted or embezeled the whole foundation came to ruine: to meete with that inconvenience, I will so provide heereafter (if god doe not hinder my present designe) as you shall be still assured of a standing annual rent, to be disboursed every yere in buing of bookes, in officers stipends, and other pertinent occasions with which prouvision, and some order for preservation of the place, and of the furniture of it, from accustomed abuses, it may perhaps in tyme to come, proue a notable treasure for the multitude of volumes: an excellent benefit for the vse and ease of students: and a singuler ornament in the Vniuersity. I am therefore to intreat you, because I will doe nothing without their publike approbation, to deliuer this that I have signified in that good sort, that you thinke meete: and when yow please to lette me knowe, their adceptation of my offer I will be redy to effect it, with all convenient expedition. But for the better effecting of it, I doe desire to be informed whether the Vniuersity be sufficiently qualified by licence of Mortmaine, or other assurance to receaue a farther grant of anye rent or anuetie, then they doe presently enioy. And if any instrumentes be extant, of the auncient donations to their former library, I would with their good liking, see a transcript of them: and likewise of such statutes, as were deuised by the founders, or afterwarde by others for the vsage of the bookes. Which is now as much as I can thinke on, wherevnto at your good leasure, I would request your frendly answere. And yf it lie in my abilitie, to deserue your paines in that behalf, althoug[h] wee be not yet acquainted you shall find me very forward.

ffrom London ffeb: 23. 1597.

your affectionat frend

Tho. Bodley.

[pp. 4-5]

. . . . .

LETTER 6

[Endorsed] To the right worshipfull my very special good frind M$^r$ Doctour Riues Vicechancelour of the Vniuersitie of Oxon.

Sir, I knowe there be many, that faine would haue me hasten, their free accesse vnto the Librarie: whiche hath bin euer my endeuour, to perfourme assoone as might be. I did onely first desire, that by some sightly shewe of bookes, the place might receaue the greater grace and reputation, and thereby minister more contentment to students and strangers. For I haue euer bin persuaded, that the better credit it carieth, for stoare and worthe of bookes, the sooner most men will be drawen, not onely to affect it, but to aduaunce and enriche it, with some of their best and rarest Autours: aswel to manifest their loue vnto to Vniuersitie, as to bring suche a place of publike studie, to a state of singularitie. And although in that respect I doe not rest as yet satisfied, with this quantitie of bookes, that I haue gathered already: yet because I am vnwilling, that the hope of hauing more, should stoppe the vse of these in being, to the preiudice perhaps, of many mens profiting in their priuat studies, I would intreat yow therefor nowe, to acquaint the Vniuersitie with my full resolution, which is, if they be so contented, to sette the Librarie open for students to frequent it, before the next Act. But as there can be litle hope of either good vsage, or long continuance, of any Fundation of that nature, without orders and statutes for the gouernment of it: so I can not but make bolde, to recommend the same in earnest wise, to their effectual consideration. I could easely coniecture (suche hath bin their wonted fauour) that they will willingly conforme their maner of proceeding, to what proiect soeuer I shall deliuer, yet knowing, as I doe, mine owne insufficiencie, for a mater of that moment, I will by no meanes vndertake, to contriue it of my self. Onely this I doe desire they may vnderstand, that because it is an Action whiche concerneth me neerer, then any one whosoeuer, and therefor driueth me to meditat more seriously vpon it, I will nowe impart vnto them, and from time to time heerafter, what to me in my iudgement, seemeth meete to be ordeined: referring it still whatsoeuer I shall signifie, to be reformed, reiected, or accepted, as they shall finally determine. As nowe for the present, my opinion is this, that before they goe about to establishe statutes for continuance, it would auaile very muche, to make proofe beforehand, for one whole yere, howe all thinges will be guided by the practise of some fewe, of their ancient orders: and then after to goe forward, vpon a deeper inspection into all inconueniences, with a perfecter plotte of gouernment. For I see that diuers constitutions, whiche were carefully deuised for the vse of the former Librarie, may well be reuiued, and receaued againe as authentical and good, with some litle alteration. They are all recorded, as I take it, in their publike Statut bookes, of whiche to serue the present turne, I haue noted these to be the chiefest. First, assoone as the rowme was replenished with bookes, before that Libertie would be graunted, for any to frequent it, there was a special day assigned, and committies deputed, for taking an othe of euery Graduat, and of as many besides, as by Licence were allowed to studie in that place. The Forme of that othe is expressely there sette downe, with this addition to it, that euery Graduat alwaise after, at the time of his Admission, should take the same precisely. Whether nowe the like againe, may be thought a fitte othe, to be publikely ministred (wherunto for my self I doe very muche incline) or whether it may suffice, that they have sworen already in general termes, to obserue all the statutes of the Vniuersitie, I leaue to them to be discussed; whiche I make no doubt they will perfourme, so as nowe euery Graduat, aswell as heerafter, may hold himself thereby religiously tied, to tender the safetie and good of the Librarie. An other meete point for them to decide, is touching the qualitie of those persons to whome it shall be lawfull, to enioie the freedome their [sic] of studie. There was a Limitation in the former Decrees, permitting it onely vnto Graduates, and to the sonnes of Lordes of the Parliament house: but enioining withall that no Batcheler Graduat, excepting Batchelers of Diuinitie, and Licentiates in euery Facultie, might studie in the Librarie, without their habites and hoodes: vnless they had formerly taken the degree of a Master, or procured a Dispensation from the Congregation house. This Limitation, I suppose, (submitting my opinion to their reformation) may be suffered still to stand in force: but with some further qualification, That any gentleman stranger, may haue libertie to enter, so he come accompanied with a Graduat, or some other that is sworen, and will answear on his othe, for suche as come with him. For I doubt very muche, it would be reputed a defectiue constitution, if when persons of Nobilitie and eminent calling, with a great many others of merit and worthe, shewe themselues so bountifull, in helping to furnishe their stoarehouse with bookes, there should be no prouiso made, for their accesse vnto the place. Wherupon I could wishe in my slender discourse, when any gentleman of sort, shall at any time request, for his furtherance in some studie, to come in of himself, aswell as with another, and like as euery Graduat, to become a freeman of the Librarie, that his licence then should passe by the way of a Grace, and that there should be no refusal, without some cause of great exception: but alwaies with condition that he shall frame himself to take the accustomed othe, or promise to keepe it on his Honor if his dignitie and state, shall require that preeminence. Furthermore, there is somewhat nowe at first, to be duly considered, in that which of ancient [time] was decreed, about the Election, Function, and Stipend of the Librarie Keeper: on whose fidelitie and care they are chiefly to relie, for the managing of this businesse. But as touching his Election, I must become an humble suitour to the Vniuersitie, that they will ratifie the choise, which I haue made already: ouerforwardly perhaps, as not of any right belonging vnto me: but yet forced vnto it, for many vrgent occasions, whiche craued as soone as my manual workes were finished, the present assistance of a diligent Keeper: so as then I admitted Mr James of New College, vpon special presumption of their fauorable liking, of whomsoeuer I should constitut: but of him in particular, for his honestie, and learning, and singular abilitie, to acquite himself of such a charge: besides his manifold desertes, in the publike late occasions of the Vniuersitie. And for the duties apperteining to his Office and Function, although some of them be specified in the old Decrees, yet are they most of suche a kinde, as according to the time, and state of thinges present, and the discrepant nature of this newe Institution, must either be reformed, or vtterly made voide: as there must for other causes be diuers newe ordeined. Which will be then perfourmed best, when by one yeres obseruation, they shall be able to discerne, where abuses may haue entrance, and what statutes to sette downe for their timely preuention. In the meane while I should thinke it might content, for this yeres trial, to tie the Keeper no further, by virtue of his othe, then according to the forme already prescribed, to be faithfull in his custodie, and diligent in opening and shutting the Librarie: referring him for his houres and daies of intermission, and for his maine direction in all other seruices, to that which certaine persons appointed vnto it, by publike consent, shall aduise him for the time. For suche I would request the Vniuersitie to delegat, and I will

willingly ioine my travels to theirs, whereby to grownde my course
of dealing, vpon a surer fundation then mine owne onely liking.
Lastly for the stipend, whiche was alotted in time past, to the Keeper
for his seruice, by the gifte, as I remember, of King Henry the fourth,
it is a mater, in my opinion, to be aduisedly thought on, howe it
should be nowe disposed. For were it so, as I haue heard, that it was
conferred on the Reader of the Lady Margarites Lecture, vpon the
dissolution of the former Librarie: sith there is at this present an other
newe a foote, I can not readily conceaue, howe it can be well with-
drawen, from the vse assigned for it, in the first Donation. But being
vtterly ignorant, howe that mater hath bin caried, I leaue it to them,
to decide as they please. For that which I doe vtter, is all in respect,
of the excessiue paines and cumbers, whiche will light vpon the Keeper
and will vndoubtedly deserue a farre greater stipend, then the summe
of twentie poundes, which is all as yet by my designe, that is to be
defalked from the annual rent of one hundred markes, prouided for
the Librarie. Howbeit I haue no meaning, neither is it a thing, that I
could accord, to haue any part of it on the soddaine, deducted from
the pension of the present Reader: but onely that heerafter it may be
conuerted, when his reading is expired, to the purposes first intended.
And when that resolution is publikly taken, I will both for the Reader
and Keepers contentation, vntil this Readers place be vacant, disbourse
euery yere the twentie pounds, together with the summe of his
ancient allowance. This is all in effect that I will recommend to their
present consultation, whiche may suffice, I doe not doubt, for this
yeres vsage of the Librarie: although I knowe that for heerafter, there
must a formal booke be drawen, both of these and other statutes,
concerning the recept, custodie, and imploiment of the publike
reuenue, and of that whiche is conferred of beneuolence vpon it: and
for the annual choise of Ouerseers, to take the Keepers Account of
bookes, to suruey their defectes, for their bindinges, cheininges,
placinges, and to enquire of all abuses: of whiche pointes in like sort,
when the time shall be for it, I will be carefull to deliuer my priuat
conceat: but still with that respect, that my duty requireth, in reseruing
a power and authoritie to them, to alter all that I propose, as they by
their experience, shall finde there is occasion. And thus without other
ceremonie, then earnest intreatie, that yow will not sticke to pardon
my necessarie length of writing, and when the time shall be for it, to
make report of the tenour to the Vniuersitie, I bidde yow very hartely
and happely farewell.

your very assured frind

Tho. Bodley.

From London
    Marche 27. 1602.

[pp. 11-14]

## LETTER 15

To the right wor<sup>ll</sup> M<sup>r</sup> Doctor Singleton vicechancellor of the vniuersitie of Oxon.

Sir About some three yeares past, I made a motion heere in London to M<sup>r</sup> Paule Pindar Consull of the Company of the Englishe Marchantes at Aleppo a famous port in the Turkes dominions: that he would vse his best meanes, to procure me some bookes in the Syriacke Arabicke, Turkishe and Persian tongues, or in any other language of those Esterne nations: bycause I make no doubt but in processe of time, by the extraordinarie diligence of some one or other student they may bee readily vnderstoode, and some speciall vse made of theire kinde of learninge in those partes of the worlde. And where I had a purpose to rembourse all the charge, that might growe there-vpon he sent of late vnto me twentie severall volumes in the foresaid tongues and of his liberall disposition hath bestowed them freely on the Librarie. They are manuscriptes all (for in those cuntries they haue no kinde of printing) and were valued in that place at a verie highe rate. I will send them, er be longe, praying you the whyle, to notifie so much vnto the vniuersitie and to move them to write a letter of thankes which I will finde meanes to convey to his handes, being lately departed from London to Constantinople. Whether the letter be indited in Latin or Englishe it is not much materiall, but yet in my conceite it will doe best to him in Englishe. . . .

London 1611° Novemb. 5th                          Tho. Bodley.

Sir   M<sup>r</sup> Pindars bookes treat of different maters in sundrie sciences as M<sup>r</sup> James hath lately learned of a Persian, Secretarie to the Persian Ambassador Sir Robert Shirley from whose mouthe he hath taken notes of the subject of as many of them, as the Persian vnderstoode.

[pp. 21–2]

From *Letters of Sir Thomas Bodley to the University of Oxford, 1598–1611. Edited by G. W. Wheeler*, Oxford, *for private circulation*, 1927.

# CHAPTER 6

# Justus Lipsius (1547–1606)

> "Lipsius himself is indeed more interesting than most of his imitators, for he did clothe the bare bones of his subject with a little flesh, while his successors for the most part contented themselves with summarising his facts."
>
> RAYMOND IRWIN.

JUSTUS LIPSIUS, or Joest Lips as he was known in his native Belgium, was born on October 18th (or possibly November 15th), 1547, at Overyssche, near Brussels, and became a student at Louvain University. In 1567 he published *Variarum lectionum libri tres*, and then went to Rome, where he spent two years in the study of manuscripts. His *Antiquarum lectionum libri quinque* appeared in 1575, and Lipsius occupied many years travelling extensively in Europe. He taught at Jena, Cologne, Louvain and Antwerp, before becoming professor of history at Leyden, which chair he occupied for eleven years. Lipsius prepared editions of Seneca, Tacitus (which went into five revised editions) and many scholarly works. In 1590 he went to Mainz, but finally settled at Louvain as professor of Latin in the Collegium Buslidianum, and died there on March 23rd (or April 24th), 1606.

Lipsius was "inconsistent with regard to religious beliefs", being now Jesuit, now Lutheran, now Calvinist, now Romanist, but he published the first history of libraries in the modern sense of the word, searching original Latin, Greek and Hebrew sources for the material. Entitled *De bibliothecis syntagma*, the book was first published at Antwerp, 1602, with a second edition at Helmstadt, 1620, and a third at Antwerp in 1629. It also appeared in Lipsius' *Opera ominia*, 1610–1630, 1637 and 1675, and a French version by Gabriel Peignot in his *Manuel bibliographique*, Paris, 1800. The English translation by John Cotton Dana, from which the following extracts are taken, contains a misprint on the title-page. This reads "Translated from the second edition . . . 1607", but the translator's note and an advertisement in the book give the date as 1602. This is also given in the introductory note as the date of the *first* edition, with the second dated 1620. Lipsius had been dead fourteen years when this appeared, so that Dana's translation is probably from the *first* edition, 1602.

Lipsius deals with Egyptian, Greek and Roman libraries, his material having been copied wholesale by later writers. He recognized that his work was but an introduction to the subject, and the last three chapters are here reproduced.

REFERENCES

Anderton, Basil. A stoic in his garden. *The Library*, 3rd Ser., 7, 1916, pp. 291–303. Contains translation of part of second book of Lipsius' *De constantia*, Leyden, [*c.* 1584].)
*Encyclopaedia Britannica*, 14th edition, Vol. 14, p. 172. (Numerous references to additional biographical sources.)

## LIPSIUS ON THE HISTORY OF LIBRARIES

I have gone rapidly over the early history of libraries and have mentioned those of which time has not destroyed all records. As to what I have written, I must confess that it is but a trivial mention of a great subject,—as the old saying goes, "a drop of water out of a full bucket". Yet I have said enough, perhaps, to act as an incentive or to serve as an example.

I shall add a few words on the decoration of libraries and the arrangement of their books.

From Isidore I learn that the more experienced architects did not think that the ceilings of libraries should be gilded, or that the floors should be made of any Carystian marble; this because the glitter of gold is rather tiring to the eyes, while the green of Carystian marble rests them.

This is good advice from whomever it may have come. True it is, as my own experience proves, that a brilliant light is disturbing to the attention and makes writing difficult: and green is a colour which seems to rest and refresh eyes.

Boethius adds something further to this subject of decoration, when he says, in his book on *Consolidation*, "The walls were decorated with ivory and glass". Does he mean the walls of the room itself? It would seem so, for the bookcases or shelves were not placed against the walls, in which case the ornamentation of the latter would not have been seen, but were set out in the room, just as they are in most public libraries to-day. Glass cut in squares, circles, ovals, and rhomboids were used like marble tiles, to ornament the walls, though oftener the arches and the ceilings. Pliny says in his *Natural History*, book xxxvi, "Tiles made of earth they transformed into glass and put on the arches; and this is a recent invention". It was, then, still a novelty in the time of Nero and Seneca. Yet Seneca speaks of it as a common thing, in letter lxxxvi, on baths, where he says, "Unless the arch is covered with glass". On this point consult my work on the baths of the Romans.

That it was also used on the walls, Vopiscus, as well as Boethius shows when he says in speaking of Firmus, "The house appears to have been covered over with squares of glass, with bitumen and other material between the squares". I think the bitumen was here used to fasten the squares of glass to the wall, and not to join them to each other. The joints between the pieces of glass were more appropriately covered with ivory, as Boethius seems to say they were. Ivory was placed also on the bookcases themselves; whence the phrase "ivory library", in the Pandects. Seneca mentions bookcases made of cedar and ivory.

Common sense and the general fitness of the thing of course make it plain that there were bookcases in libraries; I would add the fact that the cases were numbered. Vopiscus so indicates when he says, "The Ulpian library has the elephant book in the sixth case". Whether by "elephant" he means made of ivory or of the skin of an elephant, I cannot say. The old scholiast in commenting on this phrase, from Juvenal, "Hic libros dabit et forulos" (This one will furnish you with books and cases), gives as an equivalent phrase, "Armaria, bibliotheca" (A library and the books in it). I think the word *foruli* (pigeon-holes), as here used, properly means either compartments in the shelves, "nests" for the books, following Martial's use of the word; or, in Seneca's use of it, separate little cases for them. Sidonius speaks of these cases and of other things found in libraries. "Here," he says, "is an astonishing number of books and you would think yourself in a library and could see the shelves (*plutei*) of the grammarians; or the seats (*cunei*) of Athenaeus; or the lofty bookcases (*armaria*) of the booksellers." *Plutei* are the sloping tables on which books were placed for reading; *cunei*, the rows of seats, as explained in Athenaeus; and *armaria*, bookcases, generally wide and tall, as I have shown. These last Cicero seems to call *pegmata* in a letter to Atticus.

A most appropriate method of decorating a library, one which ought to be imitated by us to-day but unhappily is not, is that of placing in it and near their writings the statues or busts of great authors. How delightful it must have been to the readers to see them, and how stimulating to the mind! We all wish to become familiar with the features and the general appearance of great men, with those material bodies in which dwelt their celestial spirits, and, lifting our eyes from their books, here they are before us! You could read the writings of Homer, Hippocrates, Aristotle, Pindar, Virgil, Cicero, and others, and at the same time feast your eyes upon the counterfeit presentment of each one. Again I say, a most beautiful custom, and why, Most Illustrious Friend, do we to-day not imitate it, under your leadership? This idea seems to have originated with the Romans—not every good thing, after all, has come from the Greeks! Pliny is of this opinion. "Nothing," he says, speaking in his most happy vein, "is more delightful than to have knowledge of the face and bearing of the authors one reads. Asinius Pollio, at Rome, apparently originated this idea of placing statues in libraries; the same Asinius who was the first, by founding a free library, to make the wisdom of mankind free to all. Whether the kings at Alexandria and Pergamum, who showed great zeal in the founding of libraries, had done the same before, I find it impossible to learn." So it seems, as I have said, that Asinius was the originator of the idea; and Pliny says that he placed in a library, the first public one opened in the city (not, in the world, as some absurdly render the phrase), the statue of a living man, Marcus Varro, the first person to have that honour. Afterwards the same distinction was shown to others, either through courtesy or because it was justly due them; for example, to the poet Martial, who boasted that Stertinius wished to place a statue of him in his library. But for the most part this honour has been reserved for the dead, and for those who have, by common consent, proved their greatness.

Pliny says, "A certain custom, now just established, ought not to be passed by in silence. I refer to the fact that they place in libraries, not only the statues in gold, silver, or bronze of those whose immortal souls may be said to be speaking there through their books, but also the statues of those whose books are not there; and even imaginary statues of those of whom no portraits have been preserved." He calls the custom a new one, meaning that it originated with Pollio. He says also that these statues of the dead were for the most part made of metal. I would add that they were also made of plaster, in which they were easily duplicated for private libraries. Juvenal says, "Though you may find everywhere busts of Chrysippus in plaster".

Indeed I think the portraits were sometimes paintings, and that perhaps they placed portraits at the beginnings of books. Seneca says, "Those exquisite works of highest genius, illustrated with the portraits of their authors". Suetonius says of Tiberius, "He placed their writings and their portraits in the public libraries among the old and accepted authors". And Pliny in his letters remarks, "Herennius Severus, a most learned man, is very desirous to place in his own libraries the statues of Cornelius Nepos and Titus Atticus". So, according to these two writers, both statues and portraits were used. Pliny also says in speaking of Silius Italicus, "He owned many villas in these same places, and in them he had many portraits; moreover, he not only owned them, he almost worshipped them, especially the portrait of Virgil". Vopiscus says of Numerian that a certain oration of his was held to be so eloquent that it was decided that a statue be made of him as an orator, not as emperor, and placed in the Ulpian library with this inscription: "To Numerian, Emperor, the greatest Orator of his time". Sidonius, justly boasting of a statue erected to himself in the same place, says, "Nerva Trajan has seen fit to place an enduring statue of me, in honour of my writings, among other authors in both libraries". By "both libraries" he means that his statue was set up in the Greek as well as in the Latin library.

Small portraits or statues were, it seems, often placed on brackets projecting from the cases or shelves on which stood the works of the writers they represented. I quote a line from Juvenal, "And bids the bust of Cleanthes guard the shelf on which his works repose".

The same custom is referred to in the distich which was inscribed on a bust of Virgil: "No harm can come to a poet who is honoured by having both his verse and his bust upon the library shelf"; meaning that he has attained to lasting fame who lives both in his books and in his sculptured likeness. Note also the seals or medallions above the shelves referred to by Cicero in a letter to Atticus. In Cicero's day they ornamented libraries with statues of the gods as well as of authors.

I have nothing further that seems worth saying on this subject of libraries, except a few words about their use. If they stand empty, or with only an occasional visitor; if students do not frequent them and make use of their books, why were they ever established, and what are they save that "idle luxury in the garb of scholarship" to which Seneca alludes? The Alexandrian kings saw to it that there were students to make use of their library, for they built near it a Museum, so called because it was, so to speak, a temple of the Muses, in which it was possible to follow the Muses, to cultivate the humanities, free from all cares, even from the labour of providing food and lodging, since the students in it were supported from the public funds. How admirable an institution! Strabo gives us the best description of it:

"Part of the royal palace is a Museum, in which one may stroll or sit at ease, with a great hall, in which men of letters, who are members of the Museum, hold meetings and take their meals together. Moreover, this college, as we may call the Museum organization with its students, has a foundation or common fund for its support; and a priest, who is president of the Museum, formerly appointed by the kings of Egypt, but at the present time by the emperor."

He says this was part of the royal palace. Doubtless the kings wished it to be near their own apartments that they might have at hand the learned men who were its inmates, and converse with them when they pleased; thus acquiring knowledge and training their minds. It had porticoes and exedras, the former being more for the exercise of the body, the latter for the training of the mind, as in them

PLATE 3
GABRIEL NAUDÉ
(1600 – 1653)

PLATE 4

DR. THOMAS BRAY

(1656 – 1730)

the students gathered, conferred, and held discussions. There was also a hall, where they ate together. Philostratus says the same thing in speaking of Dionysius, who was, he writes, "received into the Museum"; and then adds, "The Museum is the Egyptian banquet-hall of learning which brings together all the men of letters from all parts of the world".

Note particularly the words, "all the men of letters from all parts of the world", for even if not to be taken literally they shew that the number was very large and the expense very great. Timon the satirist calls our attention to the same points when he says, in his satirical and carping way, "Many people are supported at public expense in Egypt the populous, that they may idly browse among books and quarrel over them in the cave of the Muses". Athenaeus, commenting on this passage, says, "Timon spoke of the Museum as a cave or cage, thus making sport of the philosophers maintained there, as if they were so many rare birds".

Athenaeus, we see, calls them philosophers; but Strabo uses the more general phrase, "men of letters and savants"; and no doubt scholars of every sort were admitted. Strabo puts special stress on the word "men", showing that boys and youths and those beginning their studies were not taught in the Museum, as they would be in a similar place to-day; but that admittance was rather a reward for erudition already attained, an honour rightly earned. At Athens, following a similar custom, those who deserved the honour were supported in the Prytaneum at public expense.

What think you of that, O Prince of to-day? Does not the wish rise within you to establish again this noble custom?

Continuing Strabo's account of the Museum: he says a priest was appointed to manage its affairs, who was selected by the kings or emperors. The position must have been of great dignity, and one which it was thought the emperor himself should fill. One may ask if the emperor did not appoint all the officials? Philostratus seems to imply that he did, when he says, speaking of Dionysius the sophist, "The Emperor Hadrian appointed him satrap or governor of many people, and named those who shall receive public honours, and those also who should be maintained at public expense in the Museum". Again, speaking of Polemon, he says, "Hadrian made him a member of the Museum, where he lived at public expense". Let me add that, though I have not so indicated in my translation, Philostratus uses in the phrase I have quoted a word meaning "circle", from which it would seem that members were admitted in a certain order and in proper turn, some even being chosen before any vacancy had occurred. These no doubt waited in confidence and entered in due course, in the order of their appointment. A like custom prevails to-day among princes in conferring favours.

Athenaeus throws light on this matter of appointments to the Museum by the emperor when he says that a certain poet, Pancrates, very cleverly praised Hadrian's favourite, Antinous, and that the emperor delighted with the subtle flattery, ordered the poet to be supported free of expense at the Museum.

So much for the reports of Strabo and others on the Museum and its management.

Let me add that the inmates of the Museum by no means lived therein an idle and useless life (how could they, being men who were dedicated, as it were, to public service?), but were diligent in writing, in arguing, and reciting their own works. Spartianus testifies to this in his remark about Hadrian, to the effect that he propounded questions to the savants in the Museum at Alexandria, and in turn answered those they presented to him.

Let me note that Suetonius says that the Emperor Claudius added a second Museum to the original one and ordered that certain books be read there every day, and

I close,

O Most Illustrious Ruler, with the wish that you, a descendant of great men and born to do great things, may long continue in that work, worthy of the highest praise, which you have already begun,—the work of encouraging the production of books and the cultivation of the liberal arts among men, and so make your name for all time revered.

To you, John Moretus, because of the friendship which has bound together for now these many years you and our Plantin—alas, now no more!—and all his family and myself,—to you, I say, I entrust the printing and the publishing of this my Outline of the History of Libraries: to you and to no one else. And this my wish and will I thus declare in accordance with the law laid down by the great Emperor and the Kings.

Justus Lipsius

From *A brief outline of the history of libraries*, by *Justus Lipsius*. *Translated from the second edition* (Antwerp, the Plantin Press, John Moretus, *1607* [sic. *1602*] *the last from the hand of the author*, by *John Cotton Dana*, Chicago, 1907. (*Literature of libraries in the seventeenth and eighteenth centuries. V. Edited by John Cotton Dana and Henry W. Kent.*), pp. 95–121.

# Chapter 7

# John Durie (1596–1680)

"It is true that a fair Librarie, is not onely an ornament and credit to the place where it is; but an useful commoditie by itself to the publick; yet in effect it is no more than a dead Bodie as now it is constituted, in comparison of what it might be, if it were animated with a publick spirit to keep and use it, and ordered as it might bee for public service."

JOHN DURIE.

JOHN DURIE (Dury, or Drury) was a Scotsman by birth, his grandfather being John Durie (1537–1600), a monk of Dunfermline and an adherent of John Knox. This ancestor married Marion, daughter of Sir John Marjoribanks, and the second of their three sons was Robert, who became the father of the John Durie under consideration. Robert Durie was also a minister, and for attending a prohibited meeting of the General Assembly was banished from the country. He went to Holland with his large family, and became the first minister of the Scottish Church at Leyden. John was sent to a friend at Sedan to be educated for the ministry, and continued his studies at Leyden, and later at Oxford. In 1628 John Durie was appointed minister of Elbing, in West Prussia, and became associated with Dr. Godeman in attempting to reconcile the Lutherans and the Reformed Churches. This business brought him to England, and he made an extensive tour of the Continent from 1631 to 1633. Upon returning to England Durie was ordained, and created a chaplain to the King, but continued to travel widely. In 1645 he married an Irish lady, the aunt of Lady Catherine Ranelagh; their only child, Dora Katherina, married Henry Oldenburg the scientist.

In 1649 Bulstrode Whitelock was appointed keeper of the King's medals and library, and the following year John Durie was appointed his deputy. Durie settled down to study librarianship, and sent two letters on the subject to Samuel Hartlib, who wrote a preface, and published the work as *The reformed library-keeper: with a supplement to The reformed school, as subordinate to colleges in universities*, London, 1650. Durie was of the opinion that librarianship was becoming worthy of recognition as an independent profession, and that the librarian should be not merely custodian and distributor of books but a missionary of culture. He also demanded adequate salaries for librarians, and the second letter repeats the gist of the first in more flowery language.

Appended to the tract is a short account in Latin of the Duke of Brunswick's library at Wolfenbüttel.

Durie wrote about fifty books and tracts, but his political views caused him to leave the country after four years as a librarian. At the Restoration his letters pleading for an interview were disregarded, and following further extensive travels in Germany he died in 1680.

John Durie's tract was reproduced in *The Library* of 1892, and was also included in the series *Literature of libraries in the seventeenth and eighteenth centuries*, edited by Dana and Kent, but this latter series was limited to 250 copies, with twenty-five on large paper. Durie's views remain interesting, despite the fact that they were published three hundred years ago, for has not Richard Garnett described him as "the first who discovered that a librarian had a soul to be saved"?

## REFERENCES

Garnett, Richard. Librarianship in the seventeenth century. *Library Chronicle*, 1, 1884, pp. 1–7; also in Garnett's *Essays in librarianship and bibliography*, 1899, pp. 174–190.

Granniss, Ruth Shepherd. Biographical sketch, in *The reformed librarie-keeper, or, two copies of letters concerning the place and office of a librarie-keeper*, by John Drury, Chicago, 1906. (*Literature of libraries in the seventeenth and eighteenth centuries. Edited by John Cotton Dana and Henry W. Kent.*)

John Durie's *Reformed librarie-keeper* and its author's career as a librarian. *The Library*, 4, 1892, pp. 81–89.

## DURIE ON THE REFORMED LIBRARIE-KEEPER

The Librarie-Keeper's place and office, in most countries (as most other Places and Offices both in Churches and Universities) are lookt upon, as Places of profit and gain, and so accordingly sought after and valued in that regard; and not in regard to the service, which is to bee don by them unto the Common-wealth of Israel, for the advancement of Pietie and learning; for the most part men look after the maintenance, and livelihood settled upon their Places, more then upon the end and usefulness of the emploiments; they seek themselves and not the Publick therein, and so they subordinate all the advantages of their places, to purchase mainly two things thereby viz. an easie subsistence; and som credit in comparison of others; nor is the last much regarded, if the first may bee had; except it bee in cases of strife and debate, wherein men are over-heated: for then indeed som will stand upon the point of Honor, to the hazard of their temporal profits; but to speak in particular of Librarie-Keepers, in most Universities that I know; nay indeed in all, their places are but Mercenarie, and their emploiment of little or no use further, then to look to the books committed to their custodie, that they may not bee lost or embezeled by those that use them, and this is all. I have been informed that in Oxford (where the most famous Librarie now extant amongst the Protestant-Christians is kept), the settled maintenance of the Librarie-Keeper is not above fiftie or sixtie pound *per annum;* but that it is accidentally, *viis et modis* sometimes worth an hundred pound: what the accidents are, and the waies by which they com, I have not been curious to search after; but I have thought, that if the proper emploiments of Librarie-Keepers were taken into consideration as they are, or may bee made useful to the advancement of Learning; and were ordered and mainteined proportionally to the ends, which ought to bee intended thereby; they would bee of exceeding great use to all sorts of Scholars, and have an universal influence upon all the parts of Learning, to produce and propagate the same unto perfection. For if Librarie-Keepers did understand themselves in the nature of their work, and would make themselves, as they ought to bee, useful in their places in a publick waie; they ought to becom Agents for the advancement of universal Learning: and to this effect I could wish, that their places might not bee made, as euerie-where they are, Mercenarie, but rather Honorarie; and that with the competent allowance of two hundred pounds a year, som emploiments should bee put upon them further then a bare keeping of the books. It is true that a fair Librarie, is not onely an ornament and credit to the place where it is; but an useful commoditie by itself to the publick; yet in effect it is no more then a dead Bodie as now it is constituted, in comparison of what it might bee, if it were animated with a publick spirit to keep and use it, and ordered as it might bee for public service. For if such an allowance were setled upon the emploiment as might maintain a man of parts and generous thoughts, then a condition might bee annexed to the bestowing of the Place; that none should be called there-unto but such as had approved themselves zealous and profitable in som publick waies of Learning to advance the same, or that should bee bound to certain tasks to bee prosecuted towards that end, whereof a List might bee made, and the waie to trie their abilities in prosecuting the same should be described, least in after times, unprofitable men creep into the place, to frustate the publick of the benefit intended by the Doners towards posteritie. The proper charge then of the Honorarie Librarie-Keeper in an Universitie should bee thought upon, and the end of that Imploiment, in my conception, is to keep the publick stock of Learning, which is in Books and Manuscripts, to increas it, and to propose it to others in the waie which may bee most useful unto all; his work then is to bee a Factor and Trader for helps to Learning, and a Treasurer to keep them, and a dispenser to applie them to use, or to see them well used, or at least not abused; and to do all this, first a *Catalogue*, of the Treasurie committed unto his charge is to bee made, that is all the

Books and Manuscripts, according to the Titles where-unto they belong, are to bee ranked in an order most easie and obvious to bee found, which I think is that of Sciences and Languages; when first all the Books are divided into their *subjectam materiam* whereof they Treat, and then everie kinde of matter subdivided into their several Languages; and as the Catalogue should bee so made, that it may alwaies bee augmented as the stock doth increas; so the place in the Librarie must bee left open for the increas of the number of Books in their proper Seats, and in the Printed Catalogue, a Reference is to bee made to the place where the Books are to bee found in their Shelvs or repository. When the stock is thus known and fitted to bee exposed to the view of the Learned World, then the waie of Trading with it, both at home and abroad, is to bee laid to heart both for the increas of the stock, and for the improvement of it to use. For the increas of the stock both at home and abroad, correspondencie should bee held with those that are eminent in everie Science, to Trade with them for their profit, that what they want and wee have, they may receiv upon condition, that what they have and wee want, they should impart in that facultie wherein their eminence doth lie; as for such as are at home eminent in anie kinde, becaus they may com by Native right to have use of the Librarie-Treasure, they are to be Traded withal in another waie, viz. that the things which are gained from abroad, which as yet are not common, and put to publick us should bee promised and imparted to them for the increas of their private stock of knowledge, to the end that what they have peculiar, may also bee given in a requital, so that the particulatities of gifts at home and abroad, are to meet as in a Center in the hand of the Librarie-Keeper, and hee is to Trade with the one by the other, to caus them to multiplie the publick stock, whereof hee is a Treasurer and Factor.

Thus hee should Trade with those that are at home and abroad out of the Universitie, and with those that are within the Universitie, hee should have acquaintance to know all that are of anie parts, and how their view of Learning doth lie, to supplie helps unto them in their faculties from without and from within the Nation, to put them upon the keeping of correspondencie with men of their own strain, for the beating out of matters not yet elaborated in Sciences; so that they may bee as his Assistants and subordinate Factors in his Trade and in their own for gaining knowledg: Now because in all publick Agencies, it is fit that som inspection should bee had over those that are intrusted therewith, therefore in this Factorie and Trade for the increas of Learning, som tie should bee upon those Librarie-Keepers to oblige them to carefulness.

I would then upon this account have an Order made that once in the

year the Librarie-Keeper should be bound to give an Account of his
Trading, and of his Profit in his Trade (as in all humane Trade Factors
ought, and use to do to their principals at least once a year), and to this
effect I would have it ordered, that the chief Doctors of each facultie
of the Universitie should meet at a Convenient time in a week of the
year to receive the Accounts of his Trading, that hee may shew them
wherein the stock of Learning hath been increased for that year's
space; and then he is to produce the particulars which he hath gained
from abroad, and laie them before them all, that everie one in his own
facultie may declare in the presence of others that which hee thinketh
fit to bee added to the publick stock, and made common by the
Catalogue of Additionals, which everie year within the Universities is
to be published in writing, within the Librarie itself, and everie three
years (or sooner as the number of Additionals may bee great, or later,
if it bee smal) to be put in Print and made common to those that are
abroad. And at this giving up of the accounts, as the Doctors are to
declare what they think worthie to bee added to the common stock of
Learning, each in their Facultie; so I would have them see what the
Charges and Pains are whereat the Librarie-Keeper hath been, that for
his encouragement and extraordinarie expenses in correspondencies
and transcriptions for the publick good may bee allowed him out of
some Revenues, which should be set apart to that effect, and disposed
of according to their joint consent and judgment in that matter. Here
then hee should be bound to shew them the Lists of his correspondents,
the Letters from them in Answer to his, and the reckoning of his
extraordinarie expense should bee allowed him in that which hee is
indebted, or hath freely laid out to procure Rarities into the stock of
Learning. And because I understand that all the Book-Printers or
Stationers of the Common-wealth are bound of everie Book which is
Printed to send a Copie into the Universitie Librarie; and it is impossible
for one man to read all the Books in all Faculties, to judg of them what
worth there is in them; nor hath everie one Abilitie to judg of all
kinde of Sciences what everie Author doth handle, and how
sufficiently; therefore I would have at this time of giving accounts the
Librarie-Keeper also bound to produce the Catalogue of all the Books
sent unto the Universitie's Librarie by the Stationars that Printed them;
to the end that everie one of the Doctors in their own Faculties should
declare, whether or no they should bee added, and where they should
bee placed in the Catalogue of Additionals; for I do not think that all
Books and Treaties, which in this age are Printed in all kindes, should
bee inserted into the Catalogue, and added to the stock of the Librarie,
discretion must be used and confusion avoided, and a cours taken to
distinguish that which is profitable from that which is useless, and

according to the verdict of that Societie, the usefulness of Books for the public is to bee determined; yet because there is seldom anie Books wherein there is not somthing useful, and Books freely given are not to bee cast away, but may bee kept; therefore I would have a peculiar place appointed for such Books as shall bee laid aside to keep them in, and a Catalogue of their Titles made Alphabetically in reference to the Author's name with a note of distinction to shew the Science to which they are to bee referred. These thoughts com thus suddenly into my head, which in due time may be more fully described, if need bee, chiefly if, upon the ground of this account, som competencie should bee found out and allowed to maintein such charges as will bee requisite towards the advancement of the Publick good of Learning after this manner.

From John Durie's *Reformed librarie-keeper* and its author's career as a librarian. *The Library*, 4, 1892, pp. 85–89.

# Chapter 8

# Gabriel Naudé (1600–1653)

"For certainly there is nothing which renders a Library more recommendable, then [sic] when every man findes in it that which he is in search of, and could no where else encounter; this being a perfect Maxime, That there is no Booke whatsoever, be it never so bad or decried, but may in time be sought for by some person or other."

GABRIEL NAUDÉ.

GABRIEL NAUDÉ was born in Paris on February 2nd, 1600, and was educated at Paris University. After graduating M.A., he turned to the study of medicine. In 1620 he published his first political pamphlet, and two years later was appointed librarian to President Henri de Mesmes. Naudé continued the study of medicine, and in 1626 went to Padua, but was recalled after a brief period by the death of his father. The year 1631 saw Naudé in Rome, where he was librarian successively to Cardinals Bagni and Barberini. Richelieu recalled him to Paris as his librarian, but when Richelieu died, Naudé was engaged by Mazarin to form a library. For five years Naudé travelled extensively collecting books, but following Mazarin's fall from power his library was sold in 1652. Naudé purchased the medical items for 3,500 livres, and went to Sweden, where he succeeded Isaac Vossius as librarian to Queen Christina. Within a year, however, he was on his way back to Paris, Mazarin having been reinstated, but Naudé died at Abbeville on July 29th, 1653, before reaching his objective.

In his will Naudé left the medical collection to Mazarin, who purchased the remainder of Naudé's extensive library. Queen Christina, who had purchased numerous MSS. at the forced sale of Mazarin's library, now returned them, as did many other purchasers. By 1660 Mazarin had amassed 45,000 volumes, which he bequeathed to the Collège Mazarin, the State later taking it over.

Gabriel Naudé wrote extensively on politics, on magic and on the Rosicrucians, and his *Advis pour dresser une bibliotheque*, Paris, was written as early as 1627, and appeared in 1644 in an edition which is supposed to have been revised by the author, but was actually reprinted verbatim. It was reprinted in 1646 and 1668, a Latin translation by J. A. Schmidt appearing in 1703. John Evelyn was in Paris when the 1644 edition appeared, and admiring it, he made the translation which was published in 1661.

Printers at Oxford lost Evelyn's original manuscript, and he was displeased with the book when it did appear. Under the date November 16th, 1661, he wrote in his Diary, "I presented my translation of *Naudaeus concerning libraries* to my Lord Chancellor, but it was miserably false printed". Evelyn presented a copy of the book to Pepys, who records in his Diary for October 5th, 1665: "I abroad to the office, and thence to the Duke of Albemarle, all my way reading a book of Mr. Evelyn's translating, and sending me as a present, about gathering a library, but the book is above my reach"!

Copies of Evelyn's translation are rare, and the Riverside Press edition with a foreword by John Cotton Dana is also difficult to acquire, only 400 copies having been printed for sale. This edition was published at Cambridge, Massachusetts, in 1903, and is an exact replica, with certain corrections, of the 1661 edition.

Gabriel Naudé probably never practised medicine, but found his vocation as a librarian. Circumstances hindered his efforts to collect together a monumental library on behalf of Cardinal Mazarin, but his little book gives us some idea of the character of an eminent book-lover who can justly be numbered among the great librarians of the past. (Portrait, Plate 3.)

## REFERENCES

Courtney, Joseph W. Gabriel Naudé. *Annals of Medical History*, 6, 1924, pp. 303–311.

Granniss, Ruth Shepard. Biographical sketch. In Naudé, Gabriel. *News from France; or, A description of the library of Cardinal Mazarin; preceded by the surrender of the library (now newly translated)*. Two tracts, Chicago, 1907. (*Literature of libraries in the seventeenth and eighteenth centuries*. Edited by John Cotton Dana and Henry W. Kent), pp. 9–39.

Keynes, Sir Geoffrey. John Evelyn as a bibliophil. *The Library*, 4th Ser., 12, 1932, pp. 175–193.

Lindsay, David Alexander Edward, *27th Earl of Crawford and Balcarres*. Gabriel Naudé and John Evelyn: with some notes on the Mazarinades. *The Library*, 4th Ser., 12, 1932, pp. 383–408.

Morin, Georges. Un médecin bibliothécaire: Gabriel Naudé (1600–1653). *Paris-médical*, 1929, i, pp. 136–141.

Naudé, Gabriel. *Advice on establishing a library*. With an introduction by Archer Taylor, Berkeley & Los Angeles, 1950.

Rice, James V. *Gabriel Naudé, 1600–1653*, Baltimore, [etc.], 1939. (Johns Hopkins Studies in Romance Literature and Languages, Vol. XXXV.) Select bibliography of the writings of Naudé (39 items), pp. 125–127.

Smith, George. Gabriel Naudé: a librarian of the seventeenth century. *Library Association Record*, 1, 1899, pp. 423–431, 483–493.

## NAUDÉ ON ERECTING A LIBRARY

And in earnest, if we finde it not strange that *Demetrius* made a shew and Parade of his Artillery, vast and prodigious Machines; *Alexander* the Great of his manner of encamping; the Kings of *Ægypt* of their Pyramides; nay *Solomon* of his Temple, and others of the like: since

*Tiberius* well observes it in *Tacitus, cœteris mortalibus in eo stare consilia quid sibi conducere putent, principum diversam esse sortem, quibus omnia and famam dirigenda:* How much ought we then to esteem of those, who have never sought after these superfluous inventions, and, for the most part, unprofitable; well judging and believing, that there was no expedient more honest and assur'd, to acquire a great reputation amongst the people, than in erecting of fair & magnificent *Libraries,* to devote and consecrate them afterward to the use of the Publick? As true is it, that this Enterprise did never abuse nor deceive those who knew how to manage it well, and that it has never been judg'd of such consequence, that not only particular persons have made it successeful to their own advantage, as *Richard de Bury, Bessarion, Vincentius Pinelli, Sirettus, Henry de Mesme* your Grandfather of most happy memory, the English Knight *Bodley,* the late President *Thuanus,* and a world of others; but that even the most ambitious would still make use of this, crown and to perfect all their glorious atchievements, as with the Key-stone of the Arch, which adds lustre & ornament to all the rest of the Edifice. And I produce no other proofs and testimonies of what I say, than those great Kings of *Ægypt,* & of *Pergamus, Alphonsus* of *Arragon,* Matth. Corvinus, & have all of them had a particular affection, and sought (amongst the almost infinite number of Monarchs and Potentates, which have also practis'd this Stratogem) to amass great numbers of Books, and erect most curious and well furnisht Libraries: not that they stood in need of other subjects of recommendation and Fame, as having acquir'd sufficient by the Triumphs of their great & signal Victories; but because they were not ignorant, that those persons, *quibus sola mentem animosque perurit gloria,* should neglect nothing which may easily elevate them to the supream and Sovereign degree of esteem & reputation.

[pp. 11–14].

. . . .

I shall only adde then, for the result of all these reasons, and of many other; that it is easier for you to conceive, than 'tis for any other to expresse it, that I pretend not hereby to engage you in a superfluous & extraordinary expence, as being not at all of their opinion, who think Gold and Silver the principal nerves of a Library, and who perswade themselves, (esteeming Books only by the price they cost) that there is nothing good to be had but what is dearly purchased. Yet, neither is it my designe to perswade you, that so great a provision can be made with a shut purse, and without cost; very well knowing that the saying of *Plautus* is as true on this occasion, as in many others, *Necesse est facere sumptum qui quaerit lucrum:* but to let you see by this present Discourse, that there are an infinity of other expedients, which a man may make use of with a great deal more facility and lesse expence, to attain at last, the scope which I propose to you.

[pp. 17–18].

.          .          .          .

In order to this, you must by no means omit, and neglect to cause to be transcrib'd all the Catalogues, not only of the ancient or modern, publike or private, with us, or amongst strangers; but also of the *Studies* & *Cabinets*, which for not being much known, or visited, remain buried in perpetual silence: A thing which will no way appear strange, if we consider four or five principal reasons, which have caused me to establish this propssition. The first whereof is, That a man can do nothing in imitation of other Libraries, unlesse by the means of their Catalogues he have knowledge of what they contain. The second, For that they are able to instruct us concerning the Books themselves, the place, the time, and the form of their Impression. The third, Because that a minde which is generous and nobly born, should have a desire and an ambition to assemble, as in one heap, whatsoever the others possesse in particular, *ut quæ divisa beatos efficiunt, in se mixta fluant.* The fourth, For that by this means, one may sometimes do a friend service and pleasure; and when we cannot furnish him with the Book he is in quest of, shew and direct him to the place where he may finde some Copie, a thing very feasible by the assistance of these Catalogues. Finally, Because it is altogether impossible, that we should by our own industry, learn, and know the qualities of so vast a number of Books, as it's requisite to have, it is not without reason, that we follow the judgements of the most intelligent and best versed in this particular, and then to deduce this Inference; Since these Books have been collected and Purchas'd by such and such, there is reason to believe, they deserv'd it for some circumstance unknown to us: And in effect, I may truly say, that for the space of two or three years, that I have had the honour to meet sometimes with *M. de F.* amongst the Book-sellers, I have frequently seen him buy Books so old, ill bound, and wretchedly printed, that I could not chuse, but smile and wonder together, till that he being afterwards pleas'd to tell me the cause and the circumstances for which he purchas'd them; his reasons seemed to be so pertinent, that I shall never otherwise think, but that he is a person the best versed in the knowledge of Books, and discourses of them with more experience and judgement, than any man whatsoever, not only in *France*, but in all the world besides.

[pp. 22–24].

.          .          .          .

But you, my Lord, who have the reputation of knowing more then [sic] can be taught you, and who deprive your self, of all sort of contentments, to enjoy, & plunge your self, as it were, in the pleasure which you take in courting good Authors; to you it is that it properly attains, to possess a Bibliotheque, the most august, and ample, that hath ever been erected: to the end that it may never be said hereafter, that it was only for want of a little care which you might have had, that you did not bestow this Piece upon the Publique; and of your self, that all the actions of your life had not surpassed the most heroick exploits of the most illustrious persons. And therefore I shall ever think it extreamly necessary to collect for this purpose all sorts of Books (under such precautions, yet, as I shall establish) seeing a Library which is erected for the publick benefit ought to be universal, but which it can never be, unlesse it comprehend all the principal Authors that have written upon the great diversity of particular Subjects, & chiefly upon all the Arts & Sciences; of which, if one had but considered the vast numbers which are in the *Panepistemon* of Angelus Politianus, or in any other exact Catalogue lately compiled: I do not at all doubt, but that you will be ready to judge by the huge quantity of Books (which we ordinarily meet with in Libraries) in ten or twelve of them, what number you ought to provide, to satisfie the curiosity of the Readers upon all that remains. And therefore I do nothing wonder, that *Ptolemy* King of *Ægypt* did not for this purpose collect one hundred thousand Volumes, as *Cedrenus* will have it; not four hundred thousand, as *Seneca* reports; not five hundred thousand as *Josephus* assures us; but seven hundred thousand, as witnesse, & accord, *Aulus Gellius*, *Ammianus Marcellinus*, *Sabellicus Volaterran*. Or that *Eumenes* the son of *Attalus* had collected two hundred thousand; *Constantine* a hundred and twenty thousand: *Sammonicus* (*Præceptor* to the Emperour *Gordian* the younger) sixty thousand. *Epaphroditus*, a simple Grammarian only, thirty thousand. And that *Richard* of *Bury*, *Monsieur de Thou*, and Sir *Tho. Bodley* have made so rare a provision, that the Catalogues only of either of their Libraries do amount to a just Volume. For certainly there is nothing which renders a Library more recommendable then [sic] when every man findes in it that which he is in search of, and could no where else encounter; this being a perfect Maxime, That there is no Booke whatsoever, be it never so bad or decried, but may in time be sought for by some person or other.

[pp. 30-33].

. . .

The fourth is, to retrench & cut off all the superfluous expenses, which many prodigally and to no purpose bestow upon the binding and ornaments of their Books, and to employ it in purchasing such as they want, that so they may not be obnoxious to that censure of *Seneca*, who handsomely reproaches those, *Quibus voluminum suorum frontes maxime placent titulique;* & this the rather, that the binding is nothing but an accident & form of appearing, without which (at least so splendid and sumptuous) Books become altogether as useful, commode & rare; it becoming the ignorant onely to esteem a Book for its cover; seeing it is not with Books, as it is with men, who are onely known and respected for their robes and their clothes, so that it is a great deal better, and more necessary, for example, to have a good quantity of Books, well & ordinarily bound, than to have a little Chamber or Cabinet full of washed, gilded, ruled, and enriched with all the manner of nicity, lux and superfluity.

[pp. 100–101].

.  .  .  .

The seventh point, and which seems absolutely necessary to be treated of after the precedent, is that of the *Order* and *Disposition* which Books ought to observe in a *Library;* for without this, doubtless, all inquiring is to no purpose, and our labour fruitless; seeing Books are for no other reason laid & reserved in this place, but that they may be serviceable upon such occasions as present themselves; Which thing it is notwithstanding impossible to effect, unless they be ranged, and disposed according to the variety of their subjects, or in such other sort, as that they may easily be found, as soon as named. I affirm, moreover, that without this Order and disposition, be the collection of Books whatever, were it of fifty thousand Volumes, it would no more merit the name of a *Library*, than an assembly of thirty thousand men the name of an Army, unlesse they be martially in their several quarters, under the conduct of their Chiefs and Captains; or a vast heap of stones and materials, that of a *Palace* or house, till they be placed and put together according to rule, to make a perfect and accomplished structure.

[pp. 122–123].

.  .  .  .

After all which it shall be very requisite to make two *Catalogues* of all the Books contained in the Library, in one whereof they should be so precisely dispos'd according to their several *Matters* and *Faculties*, that one may see & know in the twinkling of an eye, all the Authors which do meet there upon the first subject that shall come into ones head; and in the other, they should be faithfully ranged and reduced under an *Alphabetical* order of their *Authors*, as well to avoid the buying of them twice, as to know what are wanting, & satisfie a number of persons that are sometimes curious of reading all the works of certain Authors in particular.

[pp. 150–151].

From *Instructions concerning erecting of a library: presented to my lord the President de Mesme. By Gabriel Naudeus, P., and now interpreted by Jo. Evelyn, Esquire,* Cambridge [Mass.]. *Printed for Houghton, Mifflin & Company, at the Riverside Press,* 1903.

# CHAPTER 9

# Rev. James Kirkwood (circa 1650–1708)

'And it is not to be expected, that any man can advance or improve any Act of Science to a full Degree, till first he have a full and comprehensive Knowledge of all that hath been written and discovered of that Subject before him: and therefore compleat and free Libraries are absolutely necessary for the Improving of Arts and Sciences, and for Advancing of Learning amongst us.'

JAMES KIRKWOOD.

SCOTLAND has given birth to numerous prominent benefactors of librarianship, and even in the seventeenth century several of her sons were active in an endeavour to provide literature for the people, or for select groups. James Kirkwood and Samuel Brown in particular fostered the love of reading, made good literature available to a public cut off from the large towns, and sowed the seeds of interest in public libraries.

James Kirkwood was born about 1650 at Dunbar, Scotland, graduating M.A. at Edinburgh University in 1670. In the year 1690 Kirkwood corresponded with the Hon. Robert Boyle concerning the ignorance of the Gaelic people of scripture and general literature, freely distributing copies of the Bible to those too poor to purchase them. In 1699 appeared his anonymous pamphlet *An overture for founding and maintaining of bibliothecks, in every paroch throughout the Kingdom . . . humbly offered to the present assembly*,[1] which suggested that parish ministers should deposit their books to form the nucleus of parish libraries, the local schoolmaster acting as librarian. Four catalogues of each collection were to be written out, one each for the minister, the presbytery, the library and the central depôt at Edinburgh. The minister was to receive the value of his books by means of an annual tax on the income of the parish, and every good book published was to be purchased. Kirkwood even visualized the setting up of a printing press for the publication of established classics and new works. The year 1702 saw the appearance of his second pamphlet, *A copy of a letter anent a project for erecting a library in every presbytery or at least county in the Highlands, [etc.]*, and two years later (March 29th, 1704) the General Assembly passed "An act anent libraries in the Highlands,"

[1] Privately reprinted as *Proposals made by Rev. James Kirkwood in 1699, to found public libraries in Scotland. . . . With introductory remarks by William Blades*, 1889.

followed by further legislation in 1705, 1706 and 1709. Kirkwood wanted to see a library in every county in the Highlands founded by public and private benefactions. Books were to be loaned to approved preachers, school-masters and students, every borrower depositing a quarter more than the value of the book, as shown in the catalogue, as security. Books were to be retained no longer than six weeks, and a half-yearly inspection was to be made by the Presbytery.

Many libraries were founded, but they suffered badly from neglect, most having completely disappeared by 1826. Kirkwood is believed to have founded a library for clergy in the Highlands in 1699. On March 4th, 1703, he was elected a corresponding member of the Society for Promoting Christian Knowledge, on March 11th of that year reading before the Society *Letters and papers from Mr. Kirkwood relating to the erection of lending libraries in the Highlands.*

James Kirkwood anticipated by many years the public demand for literature, and his object failed mainly because education must precede the desire for increased knowledge. He lived in advance of his contemporaries, and although the torch he kindled to all intents and purposes flickered out, his project was obviously a forerunner of the county library movement. In the year 1708 he died, bequeathing his books to the Presbytery of Dunbar.[2]

## JAMES KIRKWOOD ON PAROCHIAL LIBRARIES IN SCOTLAND

I. Books are so vastly multiplied, and do so encrease dayly, that most part of Students either want Money to buy any moderat Collection of them; or 2 *ly.* they want Convenience to keep them, for Books are very troublesome to Transport from place to place; or 3 *ly*, they have not them in due time, while they are young and free from Cares; for after a man is settled in the World, then the Cares of his Family, and the Affairs of his Calling, do so take up his Mind, that he can have no time nor heart to study. 4. The Money that is bestowed upon Books must be looked upon as lost; and this certainly is a great Discouragement. 5. Many Books which a Student shall happen to buy, will after perusal, be found little worth, at least for his purpose, whereby he is lamentably disappointed, and loseth both his Money and time. 6. We live at much distance from these famous Towns, where most part of Books are Printed, that there are many useful new Books Printed which we never hear of, and these we hear of, cannot be brought home to us without great Expenses and Trouble. 7. Although a Student had all the Advantages that can be reasonably

[2] See reference at end of chapter.

expected in one man, yet he cannot Acquire all the Books in the World, that may relate to the Subject he studies; and so he will still be uneasie and suspicious, that there may be something worth his Knowledge in these Books he wants. And it is not to be expected, that any man can advance or improve any Act or Science to a full Degree, till first he have a full and comprehensive Knowledge of all that hath been written and discovered of that Subject before him: and therefore compleat and free Libraries are absolutily necessary for the Improving of Arts and Sciences, and for Advancing of Learning amongst us.

For effectuating of this, and for remeding all the fore-named Inconveniencies, it is modestly conceived with submission to better Judgments, that the Founding and Maintaining of Bibliothecks in every Paroch within this Kingdom, will be a most effectual means, for thereby a Student will have compleat Libraries within a few Miles of the place where he shall happen to reside, out of which he may easily furnish himself from time to time, of all sorts of Books fit for his purpose without Money, and that in his youth, while he hath health and strength to Study, and is free from the cares of the World, neither can he be troubled with useless Books, seeing he may presently return them to the Bibliotheck and take others; and Lastly, These Libraries in a few years, being furnished, not only with all the valuable and usefull Old Books in any Art or Science, but also with all the valuable New Books, so soon as ever they are heard of or seen in the World, as will clearly be demonstrat afterwards.

The Method and particulars which I think necessary for this Founding and Maintaining of Bibliothecks in every Paroch throughout this Kingdom are these.

1st. A convenient place in every Paroch must be set a part, and fitted for keeping of Books.

2 ly. Every present Minister must give in all his Books, to the Bibliotheck of his own Paroch, at the sight of the Heretors of the Paroch, who shall cause rank them conform to their volumes, and shall cause take exact Alphabetical Catalogues of them, with the place where, and the time when they are printed, of which Catalogues, there must be four principal Coppies subscribed by the Minister and Heretors of each Paroch; whereof one Copy shal be kept by the Minister, as an obligation upon the Paroch till he be payed for his Books, another shall be kept by the Heretors in a little Chist in the Bibliotheck, that it may be an obligation upon the Keeper of the Bibliotheck, to be answerable for all these Books; the third must be kept in the Bibliotheck openly, that any Heretor of the Paroch, or Minister of the Presbyterie may get a double of it when they please;

and the fourth Copy shall be sent to the principal Library at *Edinburgh*, to [be] kept there for several uses.

3 *dly*. For avoiding all debates and difficulties, that may arise between Heretors and Ministers in valuing these Books, it will be fit that some Ministers and Heretors be appointed to draw out a general Catalogue of all the Books in the Kingdom, out of those particular Catalogues that shall be sent in to *Edinburgh* from every Paroch, and to set a certain price upon each Book; which general Catalogues with the price affixed to each Book, shall be Printed and distributed through every Paroch of the Kingdom, conform to which Catalogue, the Books in every Paroch shall be valued: or there may be laid down some general rules for valuing of Books at so much *per* Sheet, and so much for Binding.

4 *tly*. When any Minister shall die, or be removed from one Kirk to an other, then he or his Heirs or Assigneys, shall have right to all the Stipends of that Paroch to which he gave in his Books, ay and while he be payed of their full value conform to the Catalogue: and the Ministers of the Presbytery shall supply that Kirk during that time, but if the Paroch cannot conveniently want a minister so long, then the succeeding Minister shall want such a proportional part of the Stipend as shall be thought fit, which shall be payed yearly to the first Minister, his Heirs or assigneys, till the full value of his Books be payed.

5 *thly*. Where the Kirks are vacant, the Ministers of the Presbyterie with the Heretors of the Paroch, shall have power to bestow all the vacant Stipends of that Kirk, upon such Books as they shall think most fit and necessary for the Bibleotheck[1] of that Kirk.

6 *thly*. Each Presbyterie shall endeavour to be a compleat Library, within it self, that is, they shall endeavour to have one Copy at least of every valuable Book extant in some one Bibliotheck or other within their bounds; wherefore it will be necessary that all the Ministers in one Presbyterie, compare their Catalogues, and consider of what Books they have more Coppies than are needful amongst them, and what Books they think useful; of which they have no Coppies at all, that they may exchange the Books they have for those they want, conform to the value set on each Book by the general Catalogue.

7 *thly*. The keeper of the Bibleotheck, who may be the Reader or School-master of the Paroch, must find caution to the Minister and Heretors, to be faithful in keeping the Books, and in preserving them from all inconveniences; and he shall not lend out any Book but to

---

[1] This word is also spelled "Bibliothek" in Kirkwood's book, and is here copied as printed. [J. L. T.]

an Heretor of the Paroch, or to a Minister of the Presbyterie, or to such persons residing within the Paroch as shall find sufficient caution for all the books they get out of the Library, and he shall take obligations from them all, that they shall restore the Books in good condition, and within such a set time as may be sufficient for reading the Book, but within one Moneth at farthest; that so an Heretor may not defraud the rest of the use of any Book. And for preventing the imbazling the Books of thir Libraries, it is fit there be a note written upon the reverse of the Title page, and on the last leaf of each Book Subscribed by the Minister, declaring that the Book belongeth to the Bibleotheck of such a Paroch, so that wherever any Book shall be found wanting the Title page and the last leaf, it may be suspected to be stollen from the Libraries, and so may be confiscat to their use.

8 *thly*. It will be convenient that there be a Book binder in every Presbyterie, to bind all the Books that belong to that Presbyterie, for which end he must be provided with a House, and all the Instruments fit for his Trade, and with some small Stipend yearly to maintain him; and then whatsoever Books he shall bind he shall be payed only for the materials, but nothing for his work; or the keepers of the Bibleothek or Ministers Servants may be taught to bind Books, and may easily bind all the new Books that shall be given in to that Library in Sheets.

9 *thly*. It will be convenient that all the Bibliothicks in the Kingdom observe the same method of ranking and placeing their Books: which method may be to rank the Books according to their name and number, in the general Catalogue, which name and number must be written upon a piece of paper, and battered to the back of the Book, or to some leaf of it, that it may be easiely seen and read, by any person that comes into the Bibliothick, that so Ministers or Students, when they shall happen to remove from one Paroch or Bibliothick to another, they may not be at a loss where to find any Book, for by this method they will presently know in what place every Book should stand.

These are all the particulars which I think necessary for the present for founding of Bibliothicks in every Paroch, but for the maintaining and promoting these it will be necessary further, that.

10 *thly*. One Moneths Cess to be payed yearly, to be settled as a Fond for buying and Printing, all such Books New or Old, as shall be judged valuable and usefull to be distributed through the Kingdom, and every Bibliotheck in the Kingdom shall get a Copy of every Book that shall be printed: the one half of this Moneths Cess must be payed by the Heretors conform to the proportions of their Stipends.

11 *thly*. This Money or Fond must be entrusted to some honest

Person or Persons, who shall therewith Erect a Printing-House, and Paper Manufactory, and shall maintain a Correspondence with all the Printing presses abroad throughout *Europe*, and shall bring home some Coppies of all the Books that shall be Printed, as soon as possible, and shall Reprint all such Books whether New or Old, as shall be judged fitting, or worthy to be distributed through the Kingdom, and they shall be oblidged to give up Accompts how the Money is bestowed, from time to time to such Ministers and others, as shall be appointed to receive, and examine the same.

12 *thly*. A Commission of the General Assembly must be appointed, to Revise all the New Books that are brought home from time to time, and to give some short Account of them in Print, or to employ such persons as they shall judge most fit for that Work: and to Revise all the Old Books, and to determine what Books shall be Printed every Moneth, and to receive and examine the Printers Accompts.

This is a method which I think will be both easie and effectual for establishing and promoting of Bibliothecks in every Paroch throughout this Kingdom, neither do I foresee any material Objection, that can be made against any particular Article of it.

[pp. 25–41]

. . . .

You may remember, That I had some Discourse with you, when I was in *Scotland;* About Libraries for the *Highlands*, at which time also I shewey [*sic*] you a Schem, about ordering the Libraries. . . . The great examples of Charity, which this Kingdom afford, particularly in what concerns Libraries for the Plantations have animated and disposed me to fall to work, and to try what may be done for those in our Native Country, who need such helps and encouragements as much as any. I need not say much about the Reasons for this Undertaking. The Printed Paper which I send you, will show how great and important they are, and it is likely, your own knowledge and observation, will furnish you with others.

I thought fit to mention the kinds of Books which we intend to purchase; That they who give Books, and not Money may know what sort of Treatises we aim at, and may not put us off with trash. As for Popish Books and perhaps some others likeways, tho they be not fit for the weaker sort of People; yet for the Library of a Divine they are convenient and necessary, that so they be the more able to deal with the Adversary. I suppose no body of any discretion or Learning will question this.

[pp. 61–63]

It would be of some advantage to this design, if you and some others of the Ministry, would write to some Ministers of the Presbyterian way, at *London* to move them to concurr in this Affair: And if to all this were added some endeavours in *Scotland*, to procure some Books, or Money to buy them, we might then hope to get Libraries erected in Each Presbytry-Seat of the *Highlands*, and perhaps for *Orkney* and *Zetland*, whose need of Books is likeways apparent.

[pp. 65–66]

AN ACCOUNT OF A DESIGN ABOUT ERECTING SOME LIBRARIES IN THE HIGHLANDS OF SCOTLAND, FOR THE USE CHIEFLY OF MINISTERS AND PROBATIONERS

The Reasons for setting on foot this Design are:

I. The great scarcity of Books among the Ministers in those Parts, some of them hardly having so many as are worth twenty shillings.

II. The small Provision many of them have in the *Highlands* (tho in other parts of the Kingdom, Ministers are for the most part, much better provided for) so that very few of them can spare anything out of their poor livings towards the purchasing of Books.

III. The great industry of the *Romish Missionaries* amongst them makes it necessary for them to be tolerably provided with such Books, as may enable them to encounter their Adversaries.

IV. The gross ignorance of the People in those parts, together with some late endeavours to seduce the Inhabitants of the Isle of *Hirta* into a state of Heathenism, make it very necessary that they should be provided with such Treatises as prove the Truth of the Christian Religion.

V. The Excellent Parts and Capacities of the Ministers generally throughout the *Highlands;* as they invite generous and charitable Persons to afford them what assistance they can, in this kind; so they give good ground to expect much fruit from such a Charity.

VI. As such Libraries will be of extraordinary Advantage to the Ministers, so they will be greatly useful to such young men as intend for the Sacred Office, who cannot acquire any tolerable measure of necessary and useful knowledge, unless they are furnish'd with a sufficient number of good Books.

VII. To all which must be added their great distance from all such places where they might either buy or borrow such Books as are useful to them.

To Answer in part the above-mention'd Design, it is intended, to have one Library in each County of the *Highlands*; except where there are but few Parishes, in which case, one Library is at first to serve two or three Counties: Their Number may be afterwards increased as Encouragement is given.

The Money or Books which shall be given may be put into the hands of M$^r$. *Taylor* a Bookseller at the Ship, or of M$^r$. *Robinson* at the Golden Lion in St. *Paul's* Church-yard, who will give the Benefactors a note of what Money or Books shall be intrusted to them.

[pp. 73–76]

Extracts from *Two tracts on the founding and maintaining of parochial libraries in Scotland*. By *James Kirkwood*, Chicago, 1906. (Dana, John Cotton, and Kent, Henry W. *Eds*. *Literature of libraries in the seventeenth and eighteenth centuries. IV.*)

# CHAPTER 10

# Dr. Thomas Bray (1656–1730)

"To his further influence in spreading the idea of lending libraries may partly be ascribed the formation and development of library societies which was so remarkable a feature of the eighteenth century both in England and America."

GEORGE SMITH.

CERTAIN of the libraries established by Dr. Bray, and by his "Associates" still exist as monuments to the activities of a great man, who foresaw the enormous possibilities of the development of libraries in isolated areas almost two hundred years before the field was really cleared for the establishment of county libraries. Although Bray's libraries were intended primarily for the clergy, he widened their scope and was directly responsible for the foundation of numerous libraries both in this country and abroad.

Thomas Bray was born at Marton, Shropshire, in 1656, attending school at Oswestry before entering Hart Hall, Oxford, to study theology. In 1699 he went to Maryland, three years after he had been appointed Commissary of that colony, and he proposed that parochial libraries should be provided there for the use of ministers. Later, Bray planned to establish a lending library in every deanery throughout England and Wales. He established libraries at Gravesend, Deal and Plymouth for the use of clergy awaiting embarkation at those ports. In 1700–1701 Bray returned from Maryland, and in 1706 went to St. Bartolph-without-Aldgate. He was the author of numerous ecclesiastical works, and in 1726 appeared his *Primordia bibliothecaria*, containing several schemes of parochial libraries. Previous to this, however, an "Act for the better preservation of parochial libraries in that part of Great Britain called England" (7 Anne c. xiv), known as Dr. Bray's Act, had been passed in 1709.[1]

Bray desired to establish Marine libraries for chaplains of men-of-war, and left £25 in his will for that purpose. He founded about fifty libraries in America and elsewhere abroad, sixty-one parochial libraries in England and Wales, fifty-seven lending catechetical libraries in England and Wales, and sixteen in the Isle of Man. After his death the work was carried on by "The Associates of Dr. Bray"

[1] Reproduced in, Central Council for the Care of Churches. *The parochial libraries of Church of England*, [etc.], 1959, pp. 48–50.

who founded the following number of parochial libraries: 1757 (8); 1760 (1); 1761 (16); 1762 (1); 1764 (1); 1765 (16); 1766 (16); 1768 (8); 1807 (1); and thirty-six lending libraries between 1753 and 1807.

Thomas Bray died in London on February 15th, 1730, leaving a son and daughter. He bequeathed his library "for the use of the Rector of Sheldon, forever", and in 1867 it contained 378 items, including one incunabulum. It is now in the Birmingham Reference Library and consists of 371 volumes. The Annopolitan Library, the only provincial library actually collected and sent to America, numbered eleven hundred volumes, and was housed in Appopolis in King William's School. It later joined St. John's College Library when the school and college merged in 1784. Dr. Bray's Associates, a group formed to assist him in his work, still exists to provide libraries in theological colleges, of which there are 150 in Great Britain and 250 overseas. (Portrait, Plate 4.)

### REFERENCES

Fletcher, Charlotte. The Reverend Thomas Bray, M. Alexandre Vattemare, and library science. *Library Quarterly*, 27, 1957, pp. 95–99.

Houlette, William D. Parish libraries and the work of the Reverend Thomas Bray. *Library Quarterly*, 4, 1934, pp. 588–609.

Smith, George. Dr. Thomas Bray. *Library Association Record*, 12, 1910, pp. 242–260.

[Smith, Samuel]. *Publick spirit illustrated in the life and designs of the Reverend Thomas Bray, D.D., formerly Minister of St. Botolph Without Aldgate, London. To which are added the designs and proceedings of those who now form the Society which he instituted, and other illustrations.* The second edition, revised, 1808. First edition, 1746. In addition to his life and activities this contains the Act of Parliament (7 Anne, c. xiv) relating to Parochial libraries, lists of libraries founded by Bray, and by his Associates, a list of Associates, catalogues of his books and MSS. bequeathed to Sion College, *etc.*

Stych, F. S. The Thomas Bray Library from Sheldon in the Birmingham Reference Library. *Open Access*, 12, January 1964, pp. 1–3.

### BRAY ON PAROCHIAL LIBRARIES

He proposed "That Each Clergyman should subscribe some small matter proportionable to the value of his Living or Circumstances in the World; the Gentry, what in their Generosity they shall think fit."

"And the subscriptions of both to be taken and return'd to London; and the Libraries transmitted into the Country in the Method following.

"1. That one third of the Subscription-Money, viz. 10 £, be subscrib'd and paid at the next Easter-Visitation . . . and return'd up to the Treasurers of the Subscription, Mr. Francis Evans, Secretary to the Lord Bishop of Coventry and Litchfield, or Mr. Thomas Taylor at the Lord Almoner's Lodgings in Whate-Hall.

"2. That within a Month after, Books to the value of Thirty Pound, be sent down into the subscribing Deaneries, and that they be made.

up in such Boxes, or Book-Presses with Shelves in them, and Locks
and Doors to 'em, as will serve both to preserve 'em in the Carriage
down, and in the Place where they shall be deposited for the Publick
Benefit. And being kept in such moveable Repositories, they can at
any time be remov'd to any part of the Deanery, as by the vote of
the Clergy at a Visitation shall be judged most convenient to have
'em log'd in; and that without the Charge of building any Room
wherein to lay 'em up.

"3. That to make up the remaining Two Thirds for the Purchase of
the Books, each of the Clergy do in their respective Parishes, and
amongst the Gentry of their Acquaintance sollicit some small Subscription towards this Publick Design, by which such Subscribers, whether
Gentlemen or Ladies, will be entitled to the Priviledge of borrowing
at any time a Book of their own Reading; and that there may be proper
and acceptable Books for them, there are some of the most valuable
pieces of History, Geography, and Travels provided in the following
sett."

"That the Books shall be afforded to the Subscribers something
below the prices at which the Clergy or Gentry usually buy in by
Retail in the Booksellers' Shops," and

"That what *Gratis* Books will be obtain'd of the Bookseller in
consideration of so many bought of 'em towards these Lending
Libraries: that these be set apart towards making up Parochial
Libraries for the Foreign Plantations."

" . . . There is but one Objective I can forsee against this Method
of procuring these Lending Libraries, and that is the excessive scarcity
of Money."

"If it could be brought about by any means, that we might have
400 Lending Libraries fixt throughout the kingdom" each of which
would take one copy of every new edition of a father or ancient
writer such as St. Cyprian, Thucydides, or other book of value, then—
"whereas some Thousand Pounds worth of valuable Books, printed
in Foreign parts, have been Imported Yearly, we by reason of the
better Editions of the Ancient Writers, which our Learned Men are
able to give the World, might be able to employ our own Paper-
makers, Stationers, Printers, Book-binders, Book-sellers here at home,
to the maintaining many Thousand Persons amongst us, and might
export so much of our own, and Foreign Paper manufactured by our
Selves, as would turn the Balance of that part of Trade, considerably
to our own side."

He goes on, "As for our Younger Gentry, I cannot think but it
would tend extreamly to furnish their Minds also with that useful
Knowledge in History, Travels, Humanity, Agriculture, and all such

Noble Arts and Sciences, as will render 'em considerable both at home and abroad. And that it will very much keep 'em from idle Conversation, and the Debaucheries attending it, to have choice Collections of such Books dispers'd through all the Kingdom, and waiting upon 'em in their own parlors, as will ennoble their Minds with principles of Vertue and True Honour, and will file off that Roughness, Ferity and Barbarity, which are the never failing Fruits of Ignorance and Illiterature. Standing Libraries will signifie little in the Country, where Persons must ride some miles to look into a Book; such Journeys being too expensive of Time and Money: But Lending Libraries, which come home to 'em without Charge, may tolerably well supply the Vacancies in their own Studies, till such time as these Lending Libraries may be improv'd into Parochial Libraries."

From Smith, George. Dr. Thomas Bray. *Library Association Record*, 12, 1910, pp. 242–260.

## THE BRAY CLERICAL LIBRARIES

Dr. Bray believed most firmly in the necessity of the clergy keeping up their studies after ordination, if they were to be efficient ministers of Divine truth. His *Catechetical Lectures* (pub. 1696), the *Bibliotheca Parochialis*, with a catalogue of books (1697), and an *Essay towards Promoting all Necessary Useful Knowledge* (pub. 1697), together with his founding libraries at the seaports of Gravesend, Deal and Plymouth, before his voyage to Maryland, were succeeded on his return by the publication of a book on the Roman controversy, his *Directorium Missionarium*, *Primordia Bibliothecaria*, the *Ecclesiastes* of Erasmus, and the establishment of libraries in various rural deaneries. The Act "For the better preservation of parochial libraries," (7 Anne c. xiv. 1708), was passed at his instigation, and is still part of the statute law of the land, though not much acted upon, we fear. The Bray Libraries are under the control of a body known as the Associates of Dr. Bray; the Archbishop of Canterbury is the president, and the secretary is the Rev. H. W. Tucker, of the S.P.G. So far as we can learn, the work of control has been performed in a somewhat perfunctory way, the Associates doing little more than making grants from time to time, and at long intervals sending out inquiry forms, which in many cases are not answered. We know from personal observation that the condition of the Bray Libraries leaves a good deal to be desired, and from the last report received we find that no fewer than 160 of them, founded at various dates between 1750 and 1850, are "no longer existing," some of them being transferred to other places, but the majority we expect "lost," or, in plainer English, stolen. There are about 156 libraries existing in England and Wales, and over 150 in different colonies and foreign possessions; many of them seem to have been "augmented" in recent years, and are therefore, probably well used. The funds controlled by the Associates are, apparently, about £4,800 in amount, besides £64 a year or so received in subscriptions. The interest and the subscriptions amount to about £150 per annum. In the last report to hand, the grants of books cost £150, and the expenses of management came to £31.

From the figures quoted, it is clear that Dr. Bray's intentions have not been realized to any very great extent, and we suggest that before the S.P.G. Bicentenary has passed away a strenuous effort should be made to put the Association on a much better footing. Everybody knows by this time (booksellers especially) that the clergy are not able to buy books as they were able to do when the tithe was at par, whilst it is also true, though not so well known, that many of them are more diligent in reading than was the case some fifty years ago. Not to mention the modern institution of summer lectures, reading associations, book-clubs, etc., are probably more numerous to-day than at any time during the past century. Whether the reading is of the high character that was enterprised when fewer men read, we know not; probably it is in most cases lower. What needs encouragement is reading which involves research; and at a time when the laity, or many of them, are made familiar with the results of thought in other than clerical circles, by means of magazine articles and reviews, it is more than ever necessary that the clergy should bend themselves to studies which are really studies, and not mere *résumés* of what a few leading minds are thinking. Dr. Bray's mind would be, we feel sure, that his libraries should be stocked with works of the highest ability, works of reference, and books that from their cost are beyond the means of the average parish priest or his assistants. The Bray Associates ought, therefore, to have this before them as their proper function—the provision of books that otherwise would be beyond the reach of the clergy; and, as there are at least four or five hundred of such works that ought to be found within the library of every deanery, it is evident that the fund has a large task before it, and one incapable of fulfilment without considerable increment of invested money. But it is not an impossible task, for we have sufficient confidence in the desire of the laity that their clergy should be well-read men to believe that, if a general appeal were made in each deanery needing a library, or for the improvement of an existing library, the money would be forthcoming. Men of the learned professions, other than the clerical, do not hesitate to say that the clergy know less about the matters proper to their profession than the men of any other calling. The reproach ought not to continue to be deserved, nor will it if a strenuous effort be made in the direction we advocate.

By the admission of the Associates themselves, the oversight of the libraries needs reform; practically it is non-existent, for what can be the use of an inquiry form which is treated with contempt? One of two things is needed—either the appointment of an inspector, who should make a triennial visit to the whole of the Bray Libraries, and send his report to the bishop of the diocese as well as to the Associates, or that the bishops should require from their rural deans, or archdeacons —the former preferably—a yearly report as to the condition and use made of the several libraries. The scandalous neglect at present existing should at least be made a thing of the past.

In some deaneries the housing of the books is a difficulty, but it is not insuperable where men are really in earnest about sacred study, and it need not detain us further than to remark that the library, in deaneries where one room is always used for the chapter meetings, should be in that room. About the worst place for the library is in some vicarage, for we imagine a large percentage of the "lost" libraries must have disappeared at the death of clerics in whose houses libraries found repose. By the Act already referred to, the church-wardens are to lock up the books of such a library on the decease of an incumbent and their responsibility ceases only when they have handed the keys over to the new incumbent. Is this ever done? As in many other matters, we have the law clearly stated, if only men care to obey it.

Extract from *Library Association Record*, Vol. 3, 1901, pp. 29–31.

# CHAPTER 11

# Jean Baptiste Cotton Des Houssayes (1727-1783)

"The custodian of a literary deposit should especially guard himself against that unfortunate disposition which would render him like the dragon in the fable jealous of the treasures entrusted to his keeping, and lead him to conceal from the inspection of the public riches which had been brought together solely with the view of being placed at its disposition."

J. B. COTTON DES HOUSSAYES.

THE Abbé Cotton des Houssayes was born near Rouen on November 17th, 1727, and spent much of his life as a teacher in that town. About 1776 he went to reside in Paris, and became librarian of the Sorbonne. On December 23rd, 1780, he gave a discourse in Latin to the General Assembly on the qualifications and duties of a librarian, and M. Pierres, printer to the King, obtained permission to print a few copies. Brunet stated that not more than twenty-five copies of this edition were printed, and it was entitled *Oratorio habita in comitiis generalibus societatis sorbonicae die 23 decembris 1780 à DD. Joan. Bapt. Cotton des-Houssayes doct. th. pariensi, soc sorbonico, bibliothecae, sorb. praefecto, sct. Parisiis, proelio Philippi Dionysii Pierres regis typographi ordinarii, 1791.* Pierre Alexander Gratet Duplessis translated it into French, with the title *Discours sur les qualités et les devoirs du bibliothécaire,* [etc.] (*Bulletins de Bibliophile: Petite Revue d'Ancien Livres,* 3e série, No. 11, Janvier, 1839). This was reissued in 1857 by Aug. Aubry in the *Variétés Bibliographiques* (Numero 17e, 1er Septembre), and again in the same year as a pamphlet, limited to one hundred copies (Paris, 1857). English translations have appeared under various titles in *The Philobiblon* (New York, Vol. 2, March, 1863), *The Bibliographer* (Vol. 3, 1882), *Book-lore* (Vol. 2, 1885), and in Dana and Kent's *Literature of libraries in the seventeenth and eighteenth centuries* as *The duties & qualifications of a librarian: a discourse pronounced in the general assembly of the Sorbonne, December 23, 1780. By Jean-Baptiste Cotton des Houssayes,* Chicago, 1906.

Cotton des Houssayes planned a monumental bibliographical work with the title *Histoire litteraire universelle,* or *Bibliothèque raisonnée,* but he died in Paris on August 20th, 1783, before completing the project.

## REFERENCES

Bibliographical note to Dana and Kent's edition mentioned above.
What a librarian should be! *The Bibliographer,* 3, 1882–1883, pp. 10–13.

## ABBÉ COTTON DES HOUSSAYES ON THE DUTIES AND QUALIFICATIONS OF A LIBRARIAN

To receive a public testimony of esteem from an assembly by illustrious personages, whose merit places them above eulogium, has always appeared to me the highest and most glorious of distinctions. On learning that your suffrages had designated me as the guardian of your library, I experienced some difficulty, I must confess, in subduing a slight feeling of presumption; but reflection soon gave me to understand that what you desired by this circumstance to honour and reward in me was not successes, which my labours had not obtained, but some feeble efforts which you deigned to appreciate.

When I reflect, indeed, on the qualifications that should be united in your librarian, they present themselves to my mind in so great a number, and in such a character of perfection, that I distrust my ability not only to enumerate, but also to trace a true picture of them; for it cannot be denied, gentlemen, that the Society of the Sorbonne, so justly celebrated in all Europe, or more properly throughout the world, for the depth no less than for the extent of its erudition, ought not, as it has hitherto done, to present to the learned world, in the person of its librarian, one of those privileged men, capable of proving himself, upon occasion, instructed to the same degree in profane as in sacred learning – equally familiar with the researches of the highest erudition as with the productions of a more ephemeral and less elevated literature. Your librarian, gentlemen, is in some sort your official representative. To him is remitted the deposit of your glory. To him is intrusted, as a duty, the important mission of maintaining, and even of increasing, if that be possible, and as far as his ability will admit, – of increasing, I repeat, your brilliant reputation, whenever a stranger, illustrious by birth or his scientific merit, or doubly illustrious perhaps by both of these titles, comes to the Sorbonne with a curious, a learned, or even with a jealous eye, to examine the precious theological and literary treasures of your library, and to draw from it wherewith to increase his own riches.

Thus, therefore, your librarian should be, above all, a learned and profound theologian; but to this qualification, which I shall call fundamental, should be united vast literary acquisitions, an exact and precise knowledge of all the arts and sciences, great facility of expression, and lastly, that exquisite politeness which conciliates the affection of his visitors while his merit secures their esteem. A librarian truly worthy of the name should, if I may be permitted the expression, have explored in advance every region of the empire of letters, to enable him afterwards to serve as a faithful guide to all who may desire to survey it. And though it is by no means my intention to give the preference above all other sciences to the science of bibliography, which is nothing more than an exact and critical acquaintance with the productions of the intellect, it will nevertheless be permitted me to consider the science as the forerunner of all the others, as their guide, who is to light them with his torch,[1] nearly as a devoted and dutiful son precedes his father to secure and facilitate his progress by throwing light upon his path. Thus the superintendent of a library, whatever be its character, should be no stranger to any department of learning: sacred and profane literature, the fine arts, the exact sciences, all should be familiar to him. A diligent and indefatigable student, ardently devoted to letters, his sole and abiding aim should be to make sure their advancement. Especially should the superintendent of such a library as yours, – which is not, by right, designed for the public, – if he desired to increase the reputation of the illustrious society which he represents, if he also desires to give proofs of its devotion to learning, receive all its visitors, whether scholars or the simply curious, with an assiduous attention so polite and kindly, that his reception shall appear to each one the effect of a distinction purely personal. He will never seek to steal away from the notice of all into some solitary or unknown retreat. Neither cold not heat, nor his multiplied occupations, will ever be to him a pretext for evading the obligation he has contracted to be a friendly and intelligent guide to all the scholars who may visit him. Forgetting himself, on the contrary, and laying aside all occupations, he will lead them forward with a cheerful interest, taking pleasure in introducing them to his library: he will examine with them all its parts and divisions; everything precious or rare that it may contain he will himself put before them. Should a particular book appear to be an object of simple desire to one of his guests, he will quickly seize the occasion and obligingly place it at his service; he will even, moreover, have the delicate attention to lay open before him all the books relating to the same subject, in order to make his researches easier and more complete. When parting from the stranger whom he has just received, he will not fail to thank him for his visit and to assure him that the institution will always feel honoured by the presence of a man whose labours cannot but contribute to its renown. The custodian of a literary deposit should especially guard himself against that unfortunate disposition which would render him like the dragon in the fable jealous of the treasures entrusted to his keeping, and lead him to conceal from

---

[1] Notitia librorum est dimidium studiorum, et maxima eruditionis pars exactam librorum habere cognitionem: "An acquaintance with books abridges by one-half the path of knowledge; and he is already well advanced in learning who knows with exactness the works that contain it." (Gaspar Thurmann, quoted by the Abbé Rive, *Prospectus d'un ouvrage publie par souscription*, p. 59, notes.)

the inspection of the public riches which had been brought together solely with the view of being placed at its disposition. What, moreover, would be the object of these precious collections, gathered at so great expense by fortune or by science, if they were not consecrated, according to the intention of their generous founders, to the advancement, the glory, and the perfection of science and literature?

But that a library may fully attain the end of its foundation, – that it may be in reality useful, and useful with equal certainty and facility, – it should be administered by a librarian distinguished for soundness of judgment no less than for the readiness and accuracy of his memory. Men would love to find in him, not that vain and imperfect bibliographical knowledge that attaches itself merely to the surface, much less the narrow preferences inspired by the spirit of party, or those exclusive predilections that border upon mania; but an erudition at once ample and considerate, which has solely in view the advancement of knowledge, and which is ever able to distinguish, with equal taste and accuracy, original works that are worthy to be proposed as models, from those equivocal productions justly condemned to forgetfulness for their mediocrity. He will therefore not admit indiscriminately every book into his collection, but will select such only as are of genuine merit and of well approved utility; and his acquisitions, guided by the principles of an enlightened economy, will be rendered still more valuable by the substantial merits of an able classification. It is impossible, in fact, to attach too much importance to the advantages resulting from an intelligent and methodical order in the arrangement of a library. Of what utility would be the richest treasures if it were not possible to make use of them? Wherefore this complete arsenal of science, if the arms it keeps in reserve are not within reach of those who would wield them? And if, as is said, books are the medicine of the soul, what avail these intellectual pharmacopœias, if the remedies which they contain are not disposed in order and labelled with care?

In thus considering, gentlemen, all the various attainments that should characterize a librarian, will any one now wonder at the consideration which has ever been, and still is, accorded to men honoured with this title? Will he wonder to see at Rome, at the head of the Library of the Vatican, a learned Cardinal, equally distinguished for his immense erudition, and for superior merit in every department? Will he be surprised, in short, that in all ages, and even in our own times, the greater part of the scholars charged with the administration of libraries have shone with so much brilliancy in the empire of letters? And if I wished to give to my words the authority of example, I should have to name here only a few of those who have preceded me in the walk that has just been opened to me; I should content myself with citing the name of the venerable man whose place I supply, and whose retirement, caused by infirmities, inspires you with such poignant regrets. But for fear of exposing myself to the reproach of adulation, – though my praise would be but the expression of truth, – I shall endeavour to be silent. I shall not attempt further to lay open before you, as Naudé formerly did, the particular catalogue of librarians who rendered themselves distinguished; but you will at least permit me to recall to you the names of the illustrious Cardinals Quirini and Passionei;[1] that of Naudé,[2] who deserves particular mention; that of Muratori,[3] that admirable prodigy of learning whose writings in every department would of themselves alone form a library; and finally, the name of Franck,[4] whose *Catalogue of the Library of Bunau* has always seemed to me the first and most perfect of all the works devoted to bibliography. Thus, gentlemen, when the numerous duties of the librarian, and the consideration habitually attached to that title, present themselves to my mind, I have been surprised, as I still am, at having been the object of your suffrages; and my surprise is increased when I reflect that a single circumstance was the cause of the honourable preference which you have been pleased to accord me: I mean the assiduity with which I visited your library, during a spring and a summer, for the purpose of silently selecting from it the documents

[1] These two Cardinals were both librarians of the Vatican, and both foreign members of the French Academy of Inscriptions and Belles-lettres. Quirini, or rather Querini, was born at Venice, March 30th, 1680, and died January 6th, 1759. His eulogy, by Lebeau, may be found in vol. xxvii of *Mémoires de l'Académie des Inscriptions*. Passionei (Dominick) – born December 2nd, 1682, deceased July 5th, 1761 – succeeded Querini in the office of librarian of the Vatican. He was a man passionately devoted to letters, and somewhat vehement in character. At the conclave of 1758 he was on the point of being elected Pope: he had obtained eighteen votes; but the fears inspired by the inequality of his temper caused him to be set aside. His eulogy may be found in vol. xxxi of *Mémoires de l'Académie*.

[2] Naudé (Gabriel), a learned bibliographer, who may be regarded as in fact the creator of the Mazarine Library, was born at Paris, February 2nd, 1600, and died in the prime of his life, July 29th, 1653. Some particulars concerning him, equally curious and reliable, may be found in a work by M. Petit-Radel, entitled *Recherches sur les Bibliothèques Anciennes et Modernes*. . . . Paris, 1819: 8vo. Naudé was the dearest and most constant friend of the learned and caustic Guy-Patin; and, such an intimacy existing, it is difficult to explain how he could be the eulogist of the Saint Bartholomew. "Le sage dit, selon les gens," etc.

[3] Muratori (Louis-Antoine) was born October 21st, 1672, in the duchy of Modena, and died January 23rd, 1750. This indefatigable scholar left sixty-four works, which form a collection of thirty-six volumes quarto, published at Arezzo 1767-1780; or a selection of forty-eight volumes octavo, published at Venice, 1790-1810.

[4] Franck or Franke (Jean-Michel) was born in 1717 in Upper Saxony, and died June 19th, 1775. His *Catalogue de la Bibliothèque du Comte de Bunau* (Leipsic, 1750-1756), in seven volumes quarto, is a masterpiece of patience and bibliographical learning. Unfortunately for science, this work was not wholly completed. Franck merits in every respect the praise bestowed upon him by the author of the discourse; and it would be gratifying if all the editors of catalogues – though it would be too much to exact of them the power of this able bibliographer – would at least take him for a model before commencing their work.

needed to conduct to their conclusion some theological and literary labours, which I shall consider brought almost to perfection if they result in causing me to appear even in a moderate degree worthy of the honours which you have been pleased to confer upon me.

I therefore truly appreciate, gentlemen, all the honour of the glorious burden which you have just imposed upon me; but I feel, at the same time, how much it is beyond my strength, as well by its own nature as by the duties which circumstances may further add to it. But I venture to hope that your kindness will sustain my weakness; I shall have to support me your counsels, which I shall ever make it a duty to follow. Your spirit, your hands even, I am fain to believe, will aid me in arranging, in ornamenting, in maintaining, in enlarging your library; and what remains to me yet of vigour, what remains to me yet of a life which is advancing rapidly to its decline, I have firmly resolved shall be devoted to the task of proving myself in all respects worthy of your confidence and of the honours which you have been pleased to confer upon me.

Thus, gentlemen, all my cares, all my efforts, all my studies, will be devoted to the sole object of proving the deep gratitude with which your goodness has inspired me, of which I shall never lose the remembrance.

From 'What a librarian should be!' *The Bibliographer*, 3, 1882–1883, pp. 10–13.

# CHAPTER 12

# Samuel Brown (1779–1839)

"The scheme of itinerating libraries established in East Lothian in 1817 by Samuel Brown, Provost of Haddington, is interesting as a pioneer effort at forming a system of circulating libraries for a county area."

JOHN MINTO.

ONE hundred years before Brown was born, James Kirkwood had published his first pamphlet advocating the establishment of parochial libraries. Many had been founded, but the movement had died of stagnation, and Brown attempted to remedy the weakness in Kirkwood's scheme by interchanging the collections of books at regular intervals.

Samuel Brown was born at Haddington on April 30th, 1779, and in 1817, while Provost of Haddington, established a system of itinerating libraries in East Lothian. His ambition was to provide a library within one and a half miles of every person in the county, and with an initial stock of 200 volumes divided into four groups he established collections at Aberlady, Salton, Tyninghame and Garvald, each under an honorary librarian. Brown planned to interchange the books every two years and, after 1832, borrowers were charged one penny during the first year the books were at each centre. As a further method for the defrayment of expenses, new books were kept for two years at Haddington, North Berwick and Dunbar for the use of subscribers paying five shillings annually. During the two-year period 1817–1819 Brown's original two hundred volumes were issued 1,461 and 733 times respectively, and in 1819–1820 (after the first change), 1,313 and 928 issues were recorded.

By 1836 Brown had forty-seven libraries operating, the stock of 2,380 volumes having been obtained by means of donations, and books that had served for two years in the subscription libraries. The scheme was popular, and libraries were established in various parts of Great Britain, while Brown sent similar libraries to Canada, Jamaica, St. Petersburg and South Africa.

Finance was the chief obstacle to the growth of the movement, and Brown overworked, although he had never enjoyed good health. In fact his scheme of itinerating libraries had been planned during his recovery from protracted illness, which period he also spent visiting prisoners in a local jail, and lending them books. When Samuel Brown died on July 13th, 1839, his libraries contained 3,850 volumes. His brother, Dr. William Brown, who assisted him with the scheme, described it in a pamphlet entitled *Memoir relative to itinerating libraries*, which was translated into French and German, and extracts from which follow.

## REFERENCE

[Brown, Samuel]. *Some account of itinerating libraries and their founder*, Edinburgh, 1856. Portrait, which is reproduced as Plate 5.

### DR. WILLIAM BROWN ON ITINERATING LIBRARIES

I. The primary feature of these libraries is their itinerating character. ... It is well known that stationary libraries in country places very commonly cease, after a few years, to excite much interest, that the funds rapidly diminish, that the addition of new books which is made from time to time becomes, in consequence of this, too small to inspire any degree of curiosity, and that most of the volumes lie undisturbed on the shelves, unread and uncalled for. To persons acquainted with the issues from stationary libraries of a number of years standing, the following statement will appear almost incredible. The issues of new books at Haddington to subscribers, have on an average of the last two years, been nearly eight and a half times per annum for each volume: the gratuitous issues at Haddington, Gifford, Salton, Aberlady, North Berwick, Belhaven, and Spott have been seven times for each volume; and issues of the books of the whole establishment (now amounting to upwards of 2,000 volumes) have, so far as reported, been five times for each volume, or 10,000 issued of the whole. ... Such indeed has been the interest excited by the regular removal of the libraries, and the supply of new divisions, that in several places, during the winter season, the whole of the books have been issued at once, not a volume has been left in the library.

II. A second important feature of these libraries is their *cheapness*. When the object is to supply not a single town or village with a library, but a whole country or a whole kingdom, *cheapness* comes to be a primary *desideratum*. A single library of fifty volumes with bookcase, catalogue, labels, advertisements and issuing-books, may be procured for from £10 to £12; but the cost will of course depend in a considerable degree on the kind of books wanted, and whether they have been recently published. Very good divisions may be selected for from £8 to £10. Taking the medium of these rates, namely £10, the following number of libraries might be established for the sum stated:

| | | | | | |
|---|---|---|---|---|---|
| 1 for a village | . | . | . | . | £10 |
| 5 for a district of villages | | . | . | . | 50 |
| 50 for a county | . | . | . | . | 500 |

Supposing the books in these libraries to be read on an average annually, in the proportion which has just been stated, namely five times for each volume, this in twenty years, the period for which a library is found to last, will amount to 100 issues for every volume, or 5,000 issues for the whole of the books in each library: and 250,000 issues for the whole of the books in fifty libraries.

III. It is an important characteristic of these Libraries that there is in them a principle of *Self-production*. . . . Originally all the libraries were entirely gratuitous; a small box was merely attached to each library, to afford the readers an opportunity of giving any small donation they might think proper; but some years ago a plan was adopted of keeping *new* books at Haddington for the use of all persons who gave a small annual subscription, to the value of double the amount of their whole contributions, and the plan was extended to North Berwick and Dunbar. This arrangement has been extended with complete success. Previous to the adoption of this measure, the greatest number of annual subscribers did not exceed eight; now they amount to 162. . . .

In consequence of there being stations for *new* books in three different towns, it has been found practicable to furnish the subscribers with a much greater number of recent publications, by means of a mutual exchange between these places, than would have been practicable had the plan been limited to a single town. By the subscriptions too, the means are in part furnished for providing new books for the following year. In 1829, the subscriptions and donations from these three places, including an Agricultural branch, amounted to £39, 14s. 6d., and the donations from gratuitous readers to £7, 12s. 3d., making in all £47, 6s. 9d.

Hitherto the books have been issued gratuitously from the other libraries, but it is proposed in future, now that a spirit of reading has been excited in the county, to issue the books the first year that a division is in a place, at the rate of a penny a volume; but as a subscription, however small, might essentially impede the success of the scheme, and as it is of immense consequence to bring the books within the reach of the whole population, particularly of the young, whom it is of peculiar importance to form to habits of reading and reflection, they will still continue to be issued gratuitously, the second year. By such a system, combined with the plan of lending out the books when new to subscribers of 5s. – each division may, on an average, be expected to produce the sum of 25s. a-year, which, as the number of libraries increases, will prove the fruitful parent of new libraries.

If a British and Foreign Itinerating Library Society were established in London, and were able to raise £5000 a year for the formation of such libraries, they might, within a moderate period of time cover the whole of Europe with such Institutions, by getting up divisions of fifty volumes each, with book-cases, etc., granting them on loan for 25s. a year, which many individuals would willingly pay, as they might more than reimburse themselves by lending out the books; or by adopting the plan which has just been suggested, a sum equal to this would in most places be easily raised. . . .

If, however, it should be found impracticable to establish a society with an income of £5000 a year, the plan may be carried on, in consequence of this principle of self-production in a county or particular district, by a society of an individual who is able to raise, say £50 annually, for this purpose. By the regular application of such a sum yearly to this object, a whole county, or even a still larger district, would in the course of no long period, be completely covered with libraries.

Extracts from *Memoir relative to itinerating libraries* printed in Appendix of, [Brown, Samuel]. *Some account of itinerating libraries and their founder*, Edinburgh, 1856, pp. 105–109.

# CHAPTER 13

# Sir Anthony Panizzi (1797–1879)

> "He was conscious all the time that his achievements fell far short of his aims. What he might have done if he had an entirely free hand, one can onely guess. But one thing is certain. If the English nation now possesses a National Library of which it can be justly proud, it is Antonio Panizzi, more than any other man, to whom our thanks must go for this."
>
> C. B. OLDMAN.

THE name of Panizzi is always associated with that of the British Museum Library, and any mention of the latter recalls the energetic refugee from Italy who completely reorganized and revitalized that collection.

Antonio Genesio Maria Panizzi was born at Brescello, near Modena, on September 16th, 1797. In 1814 he entered Parma University, where he graduated LL.D., and after a brief legal career became inspector of public schools in Brescello in 1821. As the result of his political intrigues, Panizzi fled to England to escape certain death, and in 1828 became professor of Italian at University College, London. He resigned from the chair in 1837, but meanwhile he had been employed at the British Museum as assistant librarian since 1831, and he now became Keeper of Printed Books in that Library. Panizzi travelled extensively, visiting Continental libraries for the purpose of gaining experience, and observing methods of organization before he began reorganizing the British Museum Library. He first superintended the removal of the books to the new building on the north side of the Quadrangle, and then began re-cataloguing the collection. With a committee of colleagues, Panizzi drew up the ninety-one rules for cataloguing, and embarked upon his gigantic task. He strongly disapproved of the suggestion that the catalogue should be printed, but this was commenced, only to be abandoned at a very early stage.

Panizzi took every possible means to increase the stock and enhance the value of the Museum Library, and his methods frequently made him unpopular, often because of his foreign origin. He strictly enforced the Copyright Act, which former officers had neglected to do, and he thus made enemies among the booksellers. He was quick tempered, a strict disciplinarian, and sometimes unjust and unscrupulous. The name of Panizzi is particularly connected with the planning of the Reading Room, the circular plan of which has been copied to advantage elsewhere, and which effectively serves its purpose as the centre of the British Museum Library.

In 1856 Panizzi was appointed Principal Librarian, and retired ten years later, three years before his services to the Museum were rewarded with a knighthood. Sir Anthony's association with the British Museum will be remembered as a period of intense activity, and the results of his labours, those of a refugee in a strange land, remain as monuments to his industry and courage. He died on April 8th, 1879.

### REFERENCES

Brooks, Constance. *Antonio Panizzi, scholar and patriot*, Manchester, 1931. Almost entirely confined to his political activities.

Dowling, Basil. Sir Anthony Panizzi. *New Zealand Libraries*, 13, 1950, pp. 33–38.

Fagan, Louis. *The life of Sir Anthony Panizzi*, [etc.], 2 vols., 1880.

McCrimmon, Barbara. *Antonio Panizzi as administrator*. University of Illinois Library School, Occasional Papers, No. 68, 1963.

Oldman, C. B. Sir Anthony Panizzi and the British Museum today. *In*, Oldman, C. B., and others. *English libraries, 1800–1850. Three lectures delivered at University College, London*, 1958, pp. 5–32.

Predeek, Albert. Panizzi and the British Museum Catalogue, [etc.]. *Library Association Record*, 39, 1937, pp. 515–520, 579–582, 622–626.

## Panizzi's Letter to Professor S. P. Rigaud[1]

Sir,

A "Defence of the resolution for omitting Mr. Panizzi's bibliographical notes from the Catalogue of the Library of the Royal Society", which has lately been circulated, is so generally attributed to your pen that I am induced to address you as its author. My reason at first for doubting the fact was, that as you were not a party to the alterations which I was ordered to make in the Catalogue, you could have no motive for taking the field against one who is not concious of ever having given you the least cause of offence. In noticing your anonymous "defence", I give you the best proof of respect, since I depart from the rule of never noticing what comes from writers who shrink from the responsibility of avowing their opinions.

Allow me to assure you, that I neither felt hurt at the notes being omitted from the Catalogue, nor prided myself on having written them, although I felt deeply hurt at the conduct of the Committee. Permit me also to observe that, being more anxious for my character for candor and fairness than for my literary reputation, I did not "select those notes which made most for the strength of my case", as

---

[1] Panizzi was quick to reply to attacks upon himself and his work, and wrote several pamphlets in self-defence. This letter is typical of his style, and of his vigorous nature.

you accuse me of having done, in giving a specimen of the kind of notes which were to be erased by the Committee's order. I chose the first, as it was the identical one previously approved of by the Committee, of which you were a member: and the second, as giving an idea of the necessity under which I sometimes was of using the first person, which the Committee thought proper to forbid. The third and fourth were not selected, but follow in succession, as you must have seen on looking at the revises of *Astronomy*.

The only stricture which is not "unworthy of notice" in your "defence" is the first, respecting the "Eléments de Géométrie", by the Duc de Bourgogne. As this note was well considered by me when I printed the *specimen* of the Catalogue which I submitted to the Committee in 1833, I take it to be a fair subject of criticism. How far the opinions you have advanced are correct I shall now proceed to examine. You state that the allusion to the manuscript copy "certainly favours the title of the Duke to the authorship, and therefore might have suggested the propriety of further inquiry on this head"; and then quote Fontenelle's Eloge of Malezieu as if I had never seen it. I beg to inform you that I was induced to doubt the authorship of the Duke, notwithstanding Fontenelle's words, by what is said in the preface respecting the manuscript copy in the Duke's hand; and that it was after having given the best attention to the point that I stated that the work was "*generally supposed* to be by Malezieu".

In the preface to the book the editor says that he was the possessor of the manuscript of the work in the hand-writing of the Duke of Burgundy and *qu'on peut dire qu'il est de sa composition*. Consider well *on peut dire*, and then ask yourself if you should like your publisher to say of a work, undoubtedly your own, that he has the original manuscript in his possession and that one *may say* that the work is written by you. On reading these words, far from thinking as you do, that "the allusion to the manuscript copy certainly favours the title of the Duke to the authorship", I was induced to suspect that the authorship was more than doubtful, but that the editor durst not say more against the pretension of so great a personage, at a time when the Bastille was still in existence. I found that M. Michaud, jun. the author of the article concerning the *Duc de Bourgogne* in the *Biographie Universelle*, said not one word of this presumed work of his hero; and the silence of so staunch a Bourbonist is not a little remarkable. On the other hand, the article *Malezieu* written by Landrieux, assigns the work unconditionally to that *savant*, as you acknowledge. You say that this is not exact, because Fontenelle attributes the work to the Duke. M. Landrieux had undoubtedly read Fontenelle's éloge, and it might have occurred to you that he must have had some good reason for differing from him on this subject. The Son of the Duke of Burgundy was king of France when Fontenelle pronounced that éloge. Not one word is said in it of Malezieu's partizanship for the *Duc du Maine* against this very king, nor of his imprisonment in consequence of his honest and noble attachment to his disgraced patron. An historian who can thus conceal a truth unpleasant to his master will not hesitate in flattering the memory of that master's father.

Barbier in his *Dictionnaire des Ouvrages anonymes et pseudonymes* inserts this work, and adds a note by Bouillot (formerly Librarian at Versailles) who states that it is *communément attribué* to Malezieu. Quérard enters the work amongst others of Malezieu's, and transcribes the note by Bouillot, thereby concurring in his opinion. Saint-Aubin in his *Traité de l'Opinion* (edit. of 1735) attacks some positions of the Éléments de Géométrie in question, as if they were undoubtedly by Malezieu, and Claustre in his index to the *Journal des Savans*, writes as follows:—"M. de Malezieu est auteur des Éléments de Géométrie qui ont paru en 1715, sous le titre d'Éléments de Géométrie de M. le Duc de Bourgogne.

Not long after Malezieu's death, that is in 1732, Titon du Tillet printed his Parnasse Français, which he dedicated to the king. He had belonged to the household of the king's mother, the wife of the Duke of Burgundy. Even he, however, does not follow the courtly Fontenelle in giving the authorship of the *Éléments* to the Duke; yet not daring to say that they were Malezieu's, he recurs to the happy expedient of making them both share equally in the composition of that work. In Prudhomme's *Dictionnaire universal* no mention is made of the book in the biography of the Duke: but in the life of Malezieu the work is assigned to him with the title of "Éléments de Géométrie POUR M. le duc de Bourgogne". This title is the one translated by Chalmers and Watt in this country who both ascribe the work to Malezieu. Lastly, in the *proofs* of the Catalogue, drawn up in 1832 by the Committee of the Royal Society, of which you were a member, the work is not only "supposed to be by Malezieu", but entered as undoubtedly his, without even a cross reference to it either from *Louis* or *Bourgogne*. Was I or was I not justified in saying that "it is generally supposed to be by Malezieu?"

As you kindly suggest to me the propriety of further inquiry on the subject, allow me to observe, "without wishing to give unnecessary pain", that a little more research would have saved you from a few mistakes which you have committed (after having given the subject the best consideration, and deliberately sent forth to the world your "defence"), of a more serious nature than the errors pointed out by you in my unfinished work, still uncorrected and repeatedly declared imperfect by me. You call Fontenelle's statement respecting these *Éléments* "the *original* statement", which can only mean (I suppose) that you think Fontenelle's statement to be the first and most authentic on the subject. It so happens that the date which he gives of the first edition of the Duke's work, 1715, is erroneous: it ought to be 1705. It is, probably, an error of the press, which ought not to have escaped a gentleman so tender as you are about dates, deaths and dukes, had you observed that an edition with that date could not have been dedicated to the Duke of Burgundy, as Fontenelle says in the passage you have quoted. "For" as you very acutely observe, "the greater or less time which may elapse after the period of a man's decease, makes no difference in the objection to his having revived" to accept the dedication of a book: "and the fact is the Duke of Burgundy died" in 1712. The edition of 1705 was edited by Boissière, librarian to the Duc du Maine, Prince de Dombes, of which principality Malezieu was chancellor, and printed at Trevoux, the capital of Dombes. The famous journalists of Trevoux give an account of the work in their number for September, 1705, which is the "original statement". The *Mémoires de Trevoux* were collected by order of the Prince de Dombes, who was legitimated uncle to the Duke of Burgundy, whose countenance it was of the highest importance for him to secure. In giving an account of the book the journalists praise in the most fulsome language the nephew of their patron, its presumed author, who was then high in power, the favorite grandchild of the reigning king, Louis XIV., and heir apparent to his crown. I appeal to any man at all acquainted with French history to say whether under such circumstances either Malezieu, Boissière, the journalists, or any human being in France, would have dared to hint that the Duke was not the author of a work which he chose to adopt as his own.

Had these facts been "accidentally known" to you, (I am delighted when I can express myself with your own words,) you would have been "called upon to pause before you introduced" such remarks as you have done "into a *defence* which was to go forth to the world, under the sanction of the Royal Society". The world may think that "there is a doubt (and a very considerable one,) as to the value and accuracy of the remarks, which from your anxiety" of inflicting as deep an injury as you could on a man who never gave you offence, you have circulated anonymously, without even sending him a copy of the charges, and well knowing that not having access either to the manuscript titles or to the books, I should labour under incalculable disadvantage in my vindication.

That your remarks on the other three notes are, as you justly say, "minute criticisms unworthy of notice" is perfectly true; but surely I am not answerable for your having written them; and it is very singular, that knowing their worth, you should have printed them. In your "minute criticisms", you conceal from yourself and others, that the errors you point out are not to be found in a *Catalogue* (as you incorrectly say,) but in the *revises* of one, which was still in the press, and which I was to have read *twice* at least before it could be called a *Catalogue*, viz. a complete work. You moreover seem to forget that I have more than once declared, that I knew there were real errors in those *revises* which I meant to correct; one, amongst others, in the parts so minutely dissected by you, of which you are not in the least aware. In speaking of the notes, with which you now find so much fault, I had stated that they were given as specimens of the *kind* of notes ordered to be omitted by the Committee, and contended that the *rule* or *principle* of inserting them was unobjectionable; never presuming that I had been infallible in the application, or that the details did not want revision; but expressly saying the reverse.

With respect to my supposing the manuscript alterations in Charnière's Mémoire to be Bradley's, I hope you will be candid enough to admit, that had not your studies led you to enquire into Bradley's life, so as to have dates respecting him at your fingers' ends, you might yourself for a moment have committed the mistake I have done, as you in fact have, with respect to the death of the Duke of Burgundy. But you have not only discovered that Bradley was not the author of the additions and corrections, but that they were Bevis's, having done what you intimate I ought, namely, looked at the end of the volume. It was impossible for me to do so for the following reason.

At the time I hazarded it, with the guarded formula, "I suppose", the conjecture was to be subject to farther consideration when the work should come into my hands again to be compared with the *proofs* of the Catalogue. My intention has always been to collate every work with its title: that, and that alone, being the means of insuring as much correctness as can be expected in a compilation of this description. But this I was prevented from doing, as you will perceive from my letter to the Duke of Sussex, page 23. A gallery was ordered to be erected, which hindered my having access to the books. You will there see, that on the 18th of August, 1835, I protested against the erection of the gallery at that time, on the ground that I could not answer for the *correctness* of the Catalogue under such circumstances; and stated this, that no blame should be attached to me in consequence. On the 21st of the same month of August, I was obliged to send to press the class *Astronomy*, in the early part of which the last three notes are included. A proof of about the first half of that class was sent to me some time in September, certainly before the 21st, as on that day I received proofs of the remainder. At that time the books were all covered up, and the collection out of my reach, as you will find on enquiring from two friends of yours, Sir H. Ellis and the Rev. H. H. Baber, who came at my especial request to visit the Library, that they might bear evidence of the utter impossibility of *correcting* the work, as I intended doing, and of the unfairness of making me answerable for it under such circumstances. I was therefore obliged to alter my plan, to my great inconvenience, and defer to the second *revision*, that is the next but one after having read the proofs, the collation of each work with its title. Then it was that very circumstance connected with the actual state of the volumes would have been finally and carefully considered. The Catalogue, however, was taken out of my hands ere I could *read* the second revise. I hope I am not too presumptuous in thinking that, had I been able to peruse the volume, I should not have overlooked Bevis's name on the last leaf, and should have deprived you of the glory of this luminous discovery.

I can scarcely conceive how you can say, that "I set considerable value on my conjecture, for I return to it at the bottom of the 31st page". The reason why I return to this note is the very reverse of that of a man setting "considerable value on his conjecture", as it was to explain the necessity of using the first person, if I were *mistaken*; and I explicitly say so in the very place to which you refer. You, however, not only pass this *sub silentio*, but quote merely that part of my sentence that suits your purpose; and whilst I show that I was guided by a wish of not giving to my private opinion the *sanction* of the Royal Society, you make use of this very word, and charge me with introducing this note in a book which was "to go out to the world under the sanction of the Society". How candid! But anonymous writers claim privileges of a peculiar nature.

With respect to the "Liber novem judicum", I beg to say, that had I found but one discrepancy between Panzer's description and the volume before me, I should not have noticed it; but having a very high opinion of that great bibliographer's accuracy, and finding that not only the orthography of some words, but a whole word as well as the date did not agree with the volume in the library, I thought it my duty to mention the circumstance, that those who had the opportunity might inquire whether the discrepancy arose from Panzer's mistake (as I am inclined to think) or from variations in the title pages of the same edition, or from the existence of an edition of the book unknown to Panzer. The remark as to the difference in spelling the name *Mesehella* or *Meschella*, was expressly made in imitation of no less an authority than Lalande's who (Bibl. Astron. p. 31, No. 12,) names him *Messuhalah*, and thinks it right to note that d'Herbelot named him

*Maschahallah*; whilst (as I observed) Panzer, whether incorrectly or otherwise, calls him *Meschella*, as does also Lalande himself, speaking of the "Liber novem judicum".

As you do not disdain to take notice of an error in the first syllable of the name *Photolomeus*, in my letter to the Duke of Sussex (not in my note in the revise), instead of *Ptholomeus*, I beg to refer you to the title itself, in my revise, in which you must have seen the word spelt *Ptholomeus*. But, were it not even so, is it worthy of you to charge me with a transposed letter? You have written once *Charneires* instead of *Charnières*, in your "defence"; but shall I stoop to lay any stress on such a blunder, on the plea of your assumed accuracy? Again, you notice another mistake, and inform your readers, that Panzer "is more attentive to the etymology of Ptolemy's name than to introduce an *o* into the penultimate syllable of it", and also that "he prints it without a diphthong (Ptolomaeus)," and not as I have quoted it. You had the revises in your hands (as is evident from what you say three lines from the bottom of page 6 of your *defence*), and as it was with the accuracy in the orthography of the notes in those revises that you wanted to find fault, why did you not quote from them? But being aware that the name is spelt *Ptolomæus* not *Ptolomœus*, not only in this very note, but in fifty other places, you reconcile yourself to taking advantage of an erroneous quotation in my letter. To be sure Panzer prints it without a diphthong as you state: but you ought also to have stated that his printer *never* employs diphthongs, probably not having them. Thus printers who have not accented E, print Element, Eloge, Editeur, instead of Élément, Éloge, Éditeur, &c. as you may find in looking at your own extract from Fontenelle. And yet the well known correctness and richness of type of your printer might give fair ground for supposing that the fault does not rest with him. Be this as it may, however, no one will prefer the erroneous to the correct orthography, when he has the means. Whoever takes the trouble of critisicing such trifles in earnest (of course you did it in a joke, as is evident from calling these criticisms of yours "unworthy of notice",) must be born as well as have lived a pedant; and if he do not mend before coming of age, all is over with him, and he must die a pedant.

With respect to Dee's Monas, I copied the note without any comment or observation, because its extreme absurdity is apparent on the face of it, and I never expected to be accused of ignorance for not having lost my time in confuting a palpable and stupid falsehood of an anonymous writer. His note is another proof, if any were wanting of the truth of Gresset's line,

*Un écrit clandestin n'est pas d'un honnête homme.*

It is a pity you have condescended to expose him. Whenever I found two or more copies of the same book in the Library of the Royal Society, I entered but one in the Catalogue, adding at the end of the title the number of copies so found: for instance, "(*Two Copies.*)" One of the two copies of Dee's work having the manuscript note in question, and the other having no note whatever, they could not be considered *duplicates* in the strict sense of the word, and consequently I entered them both separately, transcribing the note, which I found in one of them, to show why I had made a second entry. In transcribing it, however, it seems that I forgot to put a stop and a stroke of the pen, "in a way which (as you say) cannot be imitated in common printing", before the date 1763. I dare say neither the stop nor the inimitable stroke of the pen would have escaped me, had I not been prevented from collating my entries with the book.

Your defence "has left me no choice but the admission" of culpable carelessness, inaccuracy, gross ignorance: in fact utter unfitness for the task I had undertaken, "or a justification" of my proceedings, "that the real state of the case should be properly explained: which alternative *most unfortunately* could not be realised but at your expence". In case you should again adventure as *a defender* of the Catalogue Committee, may I suggest to you a subject worthy of your talents? that would be a defence of such acts of the Committee of 1832, to which you were a party; for instance, of the union of *Pheumatics*, *Chemistry*, and *Meteorology*, and of certain entries which occur in the first sheet *Mathematics*, which was submitted to your special revision. It would require some skill, and the appellation of *defence* would be most appropriate to it, for you are responsible to the Royal Society for those acts. You might then take the opportunity of proving the close connexion of *Astronomy* with *inland navigation*, and of *stars with star-fish*, these being subjects peculiarly fit for your ingenuity and pursuits. *Macte animo*. I have the honour to be,

Sir, your very obedient Servant,

A. PANIZZI.

British Museum,
    Jan. 23, 1838.

# CHAPTER 14

# John Winter Jones (1805–1881)

"The man who proposes to himself to be a good librarian must be satisfied with knowing an infinite variety of things; he must be content with a general insight into the various faculties, but must not endeavour to be great in any."

JOHN WINTER JONES.

MOST born leaders in any profession need a right-hand man for encouragement in the face of difficulties raised by the inevitible opposition to most forms of progress. Problems must be discussed with kindred spirits before ideal solutions can be arrived at; details must be delegated if the master-mind is to be relieved of trivial worries; and even the greatest authority at times requires reassurance, stimulus and encouragement from a trusted colleague. John Winter Jones excelled as Panizzi's right-hand man at the British Museum, and later consolidated the work of his former chief. He was born at Lambeth on June 16th, 1805, and educated at St. Paul's School. In 1822 at the age of seventeen he published anonymously a small book entitled *Riddles, charades, and conundrums, [etc.]*, and on leaving school became a pupil of a Mr. Bythewood, of Lincoln's Inn. Jones published *A translation of all the Greek, Latin, Italian, and French quotations in Blackstone's commentaries, [etc.]* in 1823, and just before he should have been called to the Chancery Bar suffered a serious illness, being unable to follow any vocation for several years. He appears to have occupied his time in learning Spanish and Russian, and about 1835 was appointed secretary to the Charity Commissioners. In April, 1837, however, he became permanent assistant in the Printed Books Department of the British Museum, and was concerned with Panizzi in the preparation of the new cataloguing rules. Jones took a leading part in cataloguing and in reading proofs, became Assistant Keeper in 1850, Keeper of Printed Books six years later, to succeed Panizzi as Principal Librarian in July, 1866.

Jones was the first President of the Library Association in 1877, and that year delivered the inaugural address at the first International Conference of Librarians held in London. This was privately printed, and extracts are printed below.

In August, 1878, Jones resigned from the British Museum, and on September 7th, 1881, was found dead in bed. He appears to have excelled as the shadow of Panizzi, and to have carried on the latter's traditions. He was kind of heart, a tireless worker, and yet another example of a great librarian serving the British Museum as well as the profession as a whole. (Portrait, Plate 8A.)

### REFERENCES

Garnett, Richard. The late John Winter Jones, V.P.S.A., Principal Librarian of the British Museum, and first President of the Library Association of the United Kingdom. *In*, Garnett's *Essays in librarianship and bibliography*, 1899, pp. 304–324; also in *Transactions and Proceedings of the fourth and fifth annual meetings of the Library Association, . . . 1881, and . . . 1882*, 1884, pp. 59–67. Garnett also contributed the biography of Winter Jones to the *Dictionary of National Biography*, Vol. 30, 1892, pp. 145–146.

## WINTER JONES ON THE DEVELOPMENT OF LIBRARIES

We live in an age of congresses and conferences—which means that we live in an age when the advantages of the interchange of thoughts, ideas, and experiences are fully appreciated, and the benefits to be derived from unity of action in the affairs of life are recognised. The idea of holding a Conference of Librarians originated in America—in that country of energy and activity which has set the world so many good examples, and of which a Conference of Librarians is not the least valuable, looking to the practical results which may be anticipated from it. The present meeting differs somewhat from that held last year at Philadelphia. At Philadelphia there were few visitors from Europe, and the members were naturally and necessarily engaged in constructing plans, discussing questions, and arriving at conclusions with the object of perfecting their library system; but with little personal aid from the experience of other countries. The present Conference will have the advantage not only of the presence of several of the able and accomplished men who took a leading part in the Philadelphia Conference, but also of the representatives of many of the important libraries of the Continent, from whom we may also look for much assistance in our deliberations.

Prior to the year 1835 there had been little discussion, if any, about public libraries. In that and the following years a committee of the House of Commons held an inquiry into the condition of the British Museum, in the course of which much valuable information was collected bearing upon the questions which will form the subjects of our deliberations, and especially upon the nature and extent of libraries, home and foreign, and upon the degree in which they were made to promote study and learning. In the years 1848 and 1849 another inquiry by a Royal Commission took place into the constitution and

management of the British Museum, and of this inquiry the question
of catalogues and the principles upon which they should be compiled
formed a prominent feature. These inquiries, and the discussions to
which they gave rise, brought prominently forward the importance of
framing catalogues systematically, and, in fact, gave first impetus to
the study in this country of what the Germans call *Bibliothekswissenschaft*. The chief promoter of these questions in both inquiries, and
especially in the latter, was my predecessor, Sir Anthony Panizzi, who
fought his battle against difficulties which would have been discouraging
to many. But he was well supported by the sympathy of learned men,
not only in England but on the Continent and in America. There is
also another gentleman, whose early efforts for the extension of
libraries ought not to be passed over without acknowledgement. I
allude to Mr. Edward Edwards, whose works on libraries are well
known, and who exerted himself to bring together information
respecting the libraries of different countries under circumstances
necessarily of considerable difficulty.

[pp. 3–6].

.    .    .    .

Libraries for general readers are desirable in all localities, for,
however each particular community may be constituted, there must
always be many who desire general education, and many to be allured
from idleness and dissipation. But the formation of such libraries is a
serious charge, the weight of which increases in inverse proportion
with the extent of the population. A librarian ought to be much more
than an officer to take charge of a collection of books; he ought to be
an educator; he has to consider the characters of those for whom the
library is formed, and to make his selection of works accordingly.
Where the population is large, and the library to be formed large in
proportion, this is a comparatively easy task. But when the community
is small, the greatest care is required to insure the formation of such a
collection as shall be strictly adapted to its wants, and shall supply the
most nutritious pabulum for the mind.

Early in the present century efforts were made in several districts to
supply the means of self-culture by the formation of literary institutions,
of which a library was a prominent feature. These were followed by
mechanics' institutes; and for several years the movement was successful.
But some of these establishments, so far as London is concerned, have
not maintained their original vigour. Some are already dead—one at
least may be considered to be dying, for it has recently changed its
lecture room into a billiard and smoking room, which is certainly far
from a literary or intellectual purpose. The London Institution stands

out an honourable exception to these indications of decay. I do not here allude to the thirty or forty small associations established in the various suburban districts, or the Young Men's Christian Association with its 150 branches.

It may be asked, Why should there be this falling off amongst the older institutions of the necessity for the formation of libraries be so strongly felt? The reason may be looked for in the fact that mental inquiry has penetrated much deeper that it had when these institutions were first founded, and that the increase of knowledge has brought with it the natural subdivision of subjects, and the consequent concentration of thought upon the several distinct branches of investigation. Hence the multiplication of societies, each with its library devoted to the particular study which occupies the attention of its members.

[pp. 16–18].

.    .    .    .

It is questionable whether the selection of books for a library should be undertaken by a committee. The formation of a library should be carried out on one uniform plan, an arrangement which is hardly possible where several persons have the right to interfere, each of whom will in all probability have views of his own. There is danger of undue prominence being given to one faculty to the sacrifice of others; or of some class or classes being neglected or prohibited from a want of due appreciation of their value or utility. This risk is greater in small than in large libraries. The safest, and therefore the best, course is to be very careful in the choice of a librarian, and then to leave the selection of the books to him, subject, of course, to the control of the committee of management wherever the exercise of that control may be deemed to be advisable. However modest the library may be in extent and character, the librarian ought to be a man who has experience in his work. The necessity for this qualification of course increases with the extent and importance of the collection. A librarian cannot know too much, or be too catholic in his knowledge. Devotion to a particular branch of study is a rock which he ought to avoid; and this ought to be borne in mind by those who select him, for it is not given to many men to be able to resist the temptation to follow a favourite pursuit in order that they may devote themselves to the multifarious details of a librarian's office. The man who proposes to himself to be a good librarian must be satisfied with knowing an infinite variety of things; he must be content with a general insight into the various faculties, but must not endeavour to be great in any.

The learned author of the life of Isaac Casaubon, Mr. Mark Pattison, says "the librarian who reads is lost"; and this is to a great extent true. It was certainly true in the case of Casaubon, who, in his love for the contents of the books placed under his charge, forgot his duties as a librarian. The licence which a librarian may be allowed to take while in the discharge of his duties was well indicated by the amiable Cary, the translator of Dante, who used to describe himself and his colleagues, while engaged in their task of cataloguing the books of the British Museum Library, as sheep travelling along a road and stopping occasionally to nibble a little grass by the wayside.

A librarian who does not understand several languages besides his own, will find himself constantly at a loss. Many of the most important bibliographies and biographies will be sealed books to him, and it will be impossible for him either to select foreign books for his library, or to catalogue them properly if they come under his charge. He will be dependent on others, which is an unsatisfactory position for a librarian.

[pp. 26–29].

. . . .

There are other questions which are suggested for consideration by the Organizing Committee, such as—

1. The qualifications of librarians. I have already had the honour to express my opinion that the qualifications of librarians cannot be too high or too catholic, and that librarians ought to be good linguists. They ought also to be good administrators, to be prepared to exercise a strict and personal superintendence over the library staff, and to give their attention to details, however ordinary or minute. This attention to details (which was one of the secrets of the Duke of Wellington's success in his military operations) will amply repay all librarians who exercise it.

2. Distribution of functions. This point must be regulated to some extent by the size of the staff, but I would desire to express my opinion that no one operation ought to be entrusted exclusively to one person, unless of absolute necessity. There ought always to be two at least who can do the same thing, in order that the particular branch of work may never be impeded or suspended by absence on vacation or illness of the person employed upon it. I believe it to be the practice in some continental libraries to place particular classes of books under the exclusive charge of one librarian. By practice the librarian becomes so well acquainted with the books committed to his care that he is independent of press-marks, and deposits the book after use in any part of the division to which it belongs. The consequence is that no one but himself can find it again without great loss of time. It is not however, the principle which is here so much at fault as the application

of it. The Library of the British Museum is marked out into divisions for the purpose of supplying books to readers. In each division certain attendants are placed whose duty it is to receive readers' tickets, to enter the book wanted in a register, and then to hand the book to another attendant, who carries it to the Reading Room. By this division of labour a saving is effected of more than half the time which used to be occupied in procuring books for readers. The attendants become more ready by having their attention confined to a small section of the Library, but they are transferred from time to time to other divisions, in order that they may thus become familiarized with the contents of the entire Library.

3. As to the hours of duty and vacation, each library will form its own regulations. Care should, however, be taken that the hours of duty be not so long as to produce exhaustion of body or mind, and that the term of vacation should be sufficiently long to restore the tone of the tired energies.

4. The question of salary is a delicate one, upon which, it may be assumed, librarians can do little more than express an opinion. It is well, however, that it should be understood that the life of a librarian is a hard one; that his work never relaxes; and looking to the importance of his functions, and the special nature of his qualifications, he ought to be well paid. He ought to be so remunerated as to be placed above the necessity of supplementing his income by literary work. I have heard it said that the work of a librarian is so agreeable, that the constant association with books and learned men and students is so delightful, that he ought to take these charms of his occupation into account in estir..ting the value of the salary which may be awarded to him. The agreeableness and the delightfulness may be doubted; but, admitting them for the sake of argument, the hard fact remains that they cannot be employed in satisfying the charms of the butcher, the baker, and the schoolmaster, and, therefore, have little influence on the stern realities of life.

It is supposed to submit to this Conference a scheme for the formation of a Library Association of the United Kingdom. Such an association would appear to be a natural and, indeed, a necessary result of our labours, in order to reduce to a permanent form the various opinions which will be elicited in the course of our discussions, and to secure the maintenance of the resolutions at which the Conference may arrive.

The joint and continuous action which will be obtained by such an association will render practicable the accomplishment of many works which would otherwise be impossible. As an instance, I would beg to refer to the very numerous parochial libraries which are scattered over the kingdom. We possess incidental notices of a few of these, but by far the greater number are totally unknown. They are for the most part unguarded and uncared for; exposed to pillage and decay. It would be a work well worthy the attention of such an association as is proposed, to obtain lists of these books—catalogues would not be necessary—and to publish them from time to time in a journal, with a separate pagination and register. These lists could then be separated from the journal and bound by themselves, and would ultimately form a most important and instructive bibliographical work. Many rare and valuable books would be found amongst them. If the plan were extended, and made to include school libraries and cathedral and chapter libraries, the results would be still more remarkable and valuable. Mr. Beriah Botfield's work on Cathedral and Chapter Libraries contains much useful information, but it is very insufficient as a guide to those important collections.

[pp. 67–72].

From, Jones, John Winter. *Conference of librarians 2, 3, 4, 5, October 1877. London· Inaugural address*, for the author, 1877.

# Chapter 15

# Edward Edwards (1812–1886)

"Edward Edwards had in him the essentials of a strong mind, and an individuality which impressed itself upon everything he undertook; yet less could scarcely be known of anyone who had filled an important place in a great movement."

THOMAS GREENWOOD.

THOMAS GREENWOOD attempted a biography of Edward Edwards, collecting together a great deal of material, but only recently have we had available a fully-documented study of the "father of the public library movement". This was provided by W. A. Munford, who has thrown much new light on an amazing character. Edward Edwards made many enemies, and his own actions resulted in much of the poverty from which he suffered in later years, yet it was his initial labours which resulted in the legislation necessary to make public libraries possible.

Edward Edwards was born, probably in Whitechapel, on December 14th, 1812, the son of a builder. At the age of twelve he went with the family to reside at 12 Idol Lane, where a plaque commemorates his association with the house. On his fourteenth birthday, Edward was apprenticed for seven years to his father, a bricklayer, and was probably largely self-educated.

He daily frequented the British Museum, and was a constant contributor of letters and pamphlets on facilities at that institution and on the provision of libraries in general. On March 27th, 1835, it was ordered by Parliament that a Select Committee be appointed to enquire into the affairs of the British Museum, the report of this Committee running into 600 pages. Edwards commented on this report in a letter to Benjamin (afterwards Sir Benjamin) Hawes (1797–1862), dated December 14th, 1835. Hawes suggested that Edwards should give evidence should the Committee be revived, and Edwards then published anonymously his *Remarks on the "Minutes of Evidence" taken before the Select Committee on the British Museum*, dated February 15th, 1836, one of several pamphlets published by Edwards. On February 11th, 1836, Parliament ordered the formation of the second Select Committee, and on June 2nd Edwards was examined.

James Macarthur's *New South Wales: its present state and future prospects* was published in 1837 without a name on the title-page, and apparently it was "ghosted" by Edward Edwards, who occupied himself with a great deal of literary work. In February, 1839, Edwards was appointed supernumerary assistant in the British Museum Library, where he remained until 1850, his most important work being the cataloguing of the Thomason collection of pamphlets relating to the Civil War. After a disagreement with Panizzi, Edwards left the British Museum to become the first librarian of Manchester Public Library in 1850. Meanwhile he again gave evidence at the Select Committee of 1849, formed largely as the result of Ewart's interest in an article on "Public libraries in Europe", contributed by Edwards to the *Transactions of the Statistical Society of London*, 1848. William Ewart (1798–1869) and Joseph Brotherton (1783–1857) had been responsible for the Museums Act of 1845, and with the assistance of Edward Edwards they now successfully steered the 1850 Act through Parliament, largely as the result of the painstaking efforts of Edwards.

Manchester Free Library was opened on September 6th, 1852, and Edwards exerted himself to build it into a collection worthy of the city housing it. Unfortunately, he resented officialdom, and in 1858 he was dismissed. Edwards then worked spasmodically, cataloguing in some of the libraries of Oxford, and doing literary work to support himself. He wrote the article "Libraries" in the eighth edition of the *Encyclopaedia Britannica*, 1857, and in 1859 appeared his monumental *Memoirs of libraries*, in two volumes, (reprinted 1964), followed by *Libraries, and founders of libraries*, 1864, *Free town libraries* 1869, and *Lives of the founders of the British Museum*, 1870.

Edwards wrote numerous other books and articles, a chronological list of which is available in the life of Edwards written by Greenwood. Thomas Greenwood (see Chapter 31), a publisher, was keenly interested in the public library movement, and was an ardent admirer of Edwards, to whom he erected a memorial at Niton. In 1883 Edwards had been granted a civil pension of £80 per annum, upon which he could not hope to exist, and the struggles of the broken old gentleman against absolute poverty were pitiful. On February 10th, 1886 Edward Edwards died at Niton, Isle of Wight, and was buried there.

It has sometimes been suggested that Edward Edwards was ignored by the Library Association, and he was certainly disliked by Tedder and some other officers of the period. Edwards was elected an Honorary Member in 1882, but his own conduct had largely contributed to his unpopularity. W. A. Munford's *Edward Edwards, 1812–1886*, [etc.], 1963, based on extensive research, puts matters in their proper perspective, and we must appreciate that while Edwards must be acknowledged as the chief pioneer of the modern public library movement, and as author of some of the greatest studies of libraries and librarianship, he was very much a lone figure, mainly because he could not work amicably with others.

### REFERENCES

Greenwood, Thomas. *Edward Edwards, the chief pioneer of municipal public libraries*, 1902.
Metcalfe, John. *Edward Edwards: his association with "New South Wales, its present state and future prospects"*, Sydney, 1952.
Munford, W. A. *Edward Edwards, 1812–1886: portrait of a librarian*, 1963.
——. Edward Edwards in retrospect. *Library Review*, 146, 1963, pp. 90–93.
——. Edward Edwards reconsidered: (1) The man. [(2). The librarian and author.] *Library Review*, 133, 1960, pp. 310–313; 134, 1960, pp. 410–414.
Savage, Ernest A. Edward Edwards and the Library Association. *Library World*, 54, 1952–1953, pp. 132–136, 151–153.

[Edwards carefully revised his *Memoirs of libraries*, and some of the sheets of the second edition were printed in 1885. All the sheets revised and printed by him were bound together and issued for presentation by Thomas Greenwood in 1901, and the following preface by the author is of special interest.]

### EDWARDS' PREFACE TO THE SECOND EDITION OF HIS "MEMOIRS OF LIBRARIES"

The Work of which a new Edition is now submitted to the Public was published, in its original form, in January, 1859. It then consisted of *three* distinct sections, only one of which is, at present, reissued. It comprised (1,) A History of the Libraries of Greek and Roman Antiquity, together with—so far as is yet known to me—the *first* and *only* collection, textually complete, of those passages of the Greek and Latin writers in which the Ancient Libraries are described, referred to, or illustrated. That Section I do not propose (at least, for the time) to reprint. It comprised (2,) A History of Mediæval and Modern Libraries, complete, as far as the sources of knowledge available in 1858, admitted. Of this section, a first *instalment* is now before the Reader. Lapse of time has made the historical part of the "Memoirs of Libraries," of 1859, much in arrear. An enormous amount of new information concerning even the oldest Libraries of Europe, and concerning those, necessarily so recent, of America, is now available. And in addition, more that one hundred new Libraries have in our own country alone—Colonial as well as Metropolitan—been founded. Four-fifths at least of these (reckoning as well the "Free Libraries" of our Colonies as those of the Empire at home) are the results of those "Public Libraries Acts" of 1850, and subsequent years, down to the year of present publication (as it is hoped), which had their first inception, and origin in the labours, during the years 1847, 1848 and 1849, of the present Writer, and in his evidence before Parliamentary Committees— Acts procured, amidst difficulties and against opposition which, in 1885, seems scarcely credible, by the strenuous effort and perseverance of an eminent Member of Parliament whose name will ever be, most deservedly, linked with the "Free Libraries" of Her Gracious Majesty's whole Empire—Mr. William Ewart, the *parliamentary* author of the Library Legislation of 1850 and subsequent years—as will be shewn in due place hereinafter. It comprised (3,) an elaborate Treatise on the Legislation, the Economy, the Administration, and the Practical Working, of Public Libraries. This, also, is (at least for the present) *omitted* from the new Edition; though certain portions of those several topics must needs be adverted to either in the historical part of that "General Introduction" which is prefixed to the present volume, or in that review of public Legislation concerning or affecting Libraries which follows.

At the writer's advanced time of life, he could scarcely hope that— in addition to the final revision of this volume (and of its companion volumes, D.V.)—he might be able to give to the economical and administrative section of his former work of 1859 that patient and thorough correction, and improvement in details, which would alone justify him in offering a new edition of *it* to the learned and able Librarians, and to the Lovers of Books, of 1885, and of the years to come.

The "General Introduction" on the whole subject-matter of "Memoirs of Libraries, 1885," aims at tracing in the briefest possible form, consistent with clearness (1,) The foundation and growth of important Libraries both mediæval and modern, up to this date; (2,) the present *geographical* distribution, and the statistical place of the chief Libraries of the world; thus shewing, in this one particular, the relative position of the several States of which Christendom is composed.

The "Introduction" endeavours, finally, to trace in briefest outline the Public Legislation bearing (directly or indirectly) on the administration of Public Libraries, and on the State-distribution of Public Libraries, and on the State-distribution of Public Books—such books, namely, of every kind as are printed at the cost of the Nation, or produced, in other ways, for governmental purposes.

On the last-named subject the writer has bestowed special care and pains. It is a subject, the importance of which has greatly increased. Thirty years ago, a Select Committee of the House of Commons (presided over by the late Mr. Tufnell) reported its opinion that

Libraries freely accessible to the Public ought to receive Public Books (whether printed for Parliament, or for any of the various administrative Departments of State,) free of all cost. That recommendation remains yet to be carried out. The recent inquiries into the system pursued for the Promulgation of the Statutes have made it apparent that even as regards that most essential "promulgation," very great anomalies subsist. Substantially, the plan of distribution existing in 1884 was very nearly what it had been made in 1831. The claims of Public Libraries are still practically ignored; yet there are no books,—unless love of country is (under influence of "the modern spirit,") to be regarded as a thing only of the days that are no more,—the importance of bringing which under the eyes of all men, of what rank and condition in life soever, is greater or more urgent, than books of a governmental character. The Statutes, and the Papers of Parliament excepted, there is no class of books in the wide circulation of which the *Nation* has a deeper interest (especially under recent legislation,) than in that of the invaluable several series of publications printed for the Board of Admiralty;—for the Trustees of the British Museum;—for the Master of the Rolls;—for the Department of Education, Science and Art;—for the Commissioners of Patents;—and other like governmental bodies. A more liberal distribution of these, as well as of the "blue-books," proper, to our Public Libraries, would alike promote National Education (in the highest sense of the words), and would do honour to the Government that should wisely organise such a distribution.

It was the writer's strong desire to do somewhat more in the treatment of the subject-matter of the "General Introduction," by adding as an Appendix to it a corrected reproduction, in tabular form, of the "Statistical View of Public Libraries in Europe and in America" which he wrote in the year 1847 (it was, indeed, begun before the Christmas of 1846), and read to the Statistical Society of London in March, 1848, (at a meeting presided over by the late lamented Earl Fitzwilliam) with eventual results which without vanity or presumption he may say have, in their degree, made an epoch in the Annals of Libraries, not alone in Britain and on many parts of the Continent of Europe, but in most of the British Colonies throughout all parts of the world, and in many parts of the United States of America.

The substance of that "Statistical View" was again given, verbally, to a Select Committee of the House of Commons upon Public Libraries, during the writer's five or six several examinations before it in the Sessions of 1849 and 1850. That Committee was appointed in the first-named Session, on the motion (as I have already reminded the Reader, who may honour this Preface with a perusal,) of Mr. William Ewart, and at the solicitation of the present writer, who drew up in English, French, and German, those *"Questions on Public Libraries"* which, through the medium of the Foreign Office, were presented at every Court throughout the world, to which any British Envoy was accredited. The results were published in several "Appendices" to the various Reports of the Committee from 1849 to 1852 inclusive.

Finally, the "Statistical View" was itself reprinted in one of those Appendices; after it had been already reprinted, by the courtesy of Dr. Robert Naumann, in the Leipsic journal *"Serapeum"*—the greatest and most valuable repertory of information on Libraries and Public-Record Offices ever published in any country. That third and Parliamentary edition is hitherto the last. The paper is, I believe, worth reprinting once again, even after the able labours in the same field, of Messrs. Ernest C. Thomas and H. R. Tedder (to be mentioned hereinafter more specifically); but the needful additions and corrections, requisite in 1885, would so largely increase its bulk, that the prescribed limits of this book prelude the gratification of my desire. I the more regret that it is so, because the paper referred to led to a long and somewhat caustic literary and statistical controversy, in the columns of a journal known to literary readers throughout the world—*The* [London] *Athenæum*. The present writer gave a public pledge in its columns to reprint his much-controverted labours, and to establish their substantial and essential accuracy. He did more, for he pledged himself also to shew that such alleged errors as may have been substantiated against him, were errors of *under-statement*, and therefore, in respect of the argument for removing the reproach from Britain of having been, in the middle of the nineteenth century, less well-provided with freely accessible Libraries, than were many other States, greatly her inferiors, not only commercially, socially, and politically, but inferiors too in Literature and Science, and in the state, generally, of Public Education, strengthened, instead of weakening, that contention, which alone—in 1850—gave public importance even to the merely numerical Statistics of Libraries.

A writer who chooses his own topic has no right to allege for deficiencies in its treatment excuse that there was "a lion in the path." It is his business to struggle with difficulties, to overcome them if he may, and to avoid talking about them. To every rule, however, there is a possible exception. *"Res augusta domi"* should be kept to a man's self, usually. But a published pledge (however unimportant save to a narrow circle of readers) needs a public performance, or a public apology. Only circumstances of personal penury prevent the

Writer from publishing the "Statistical View of Libraries in Europe and in America" at his own cost, in redemption of his promise. In 1881 it was in his contemplation so to do, for in that year he was in enjoyment from the University of Oxford, as Calendarer of the State Papers and Political Correspondence known as the "Carte MSS.," contained in the University's Library, of payments which then averaged three hundred guineas a year. The lamented death of Mr. Henry Octavius Coxe led to a change of "Bodley's Librarian." The appointment then made was eminently justified by the high attainments of Mr. Coxe's successor, but the change was to the writer disastrous. The new "Bodley's Librarian" appointed in 1882 new employés in various offices and functions, and dismissed the Writer from his Calendarer-ship, at the beginning of 1883; giving instantly to a new employé the duty of collating and arranging in chronological order the Writer's Calendar-slips previously written—a task requiring more than the labour of a year.

That sudden dismissal utterly deprived the Writer of any assured income whatever. After six months of privation and debt he received from Her Gracious Majesty a Literary Pension upon the Civil List of *eighty pounds a year.*[1]

It was well known that he had been labouring for many years, at intervals, and for one year, 1876-77, wholly and exclusively, upon the book, a volume of which is now in the Reader's hands. And he had been asked as early as in the month of January, 1870, to apply to the then Prime Minister for a Civil List Pension, *i.e., thirteen years* earlier. He refused then, as he refused in 1883, to make any such application; deeming that both the solace and the grace of a grant of that sort rested wholly on its being conferred, by the Crown, without solicitation on his part.

The change of circumstances made it, for very many months, an extremely doubtful problem, whether the deeply-cherished ambition of a quarter-of-a-century—that of removing from the "Memoirs of Libraries," of 1859, some of their many blemishes and *seen* imperfections, and of leaving the labour of many toilsome years less unworthy of the social importance of its subject-matter,—must not (whatever the disappointment and regret of the writer) be finally given up.

It seems very possible that, at first impression, many Readers—glancing at my "Table of Contents,"—will incline to charge me with giving too much space to the Monastic Libraries of mediæval and of modern times. Indeed, upon occasion of the circulation of my first "Prospectus" of this new Edition, a well-known, and very able, provincial

---

[1] It dated from July, 1883. A copy of the List of the Pensions of the year, as presented to the House of Commons, is added, as an appendix to this Preface. [Omitted here. J.L.T].

Journalist made himself a little facetious, at my expense, about the Libraries of the "Solitaries of Nitria," in combination with the date "1884." But if that critic were some day, during his vacation, to introduce himself into the Department of MSS. at our National Museum, Mr. Maunde Thompson could shew him, in a quarter-of-an-hour, very cogent proofs of the importance—not historical alone, but presently *practical*—of those far-off Collections of the much-contemned Anchorites of the Nitrian desert. Nor would it be absolutely needful for him to go even so far as to the British Museum. Almost any considerable bookseller could place in his hands the deeply interesting and pregnant volume of the late regretted Lord Zouche, entitled "Visits to the Monasteries of the Levant." The evidence of that charming book would, in itself, suffice. And, were it even otherwise, I would not greatly sorrow to err, upon a theme like this, in company with Lord Zouche, and with my honoured friend of former days, Canon Cureton.

My own long-cherished conviction, indeed, of the illustrious part borne by Monks of mediæval and of modern times, as in many other noble and ardous tasks of Christian Civilisation, so also in the erection, the furnishing, and the maintenance of those great Arsenals of Civilisation and of Christianisation—the Public Libraries of the World, is somewhat out of harmony with certain prevalent ideas. But I am none the less confident in the substantial truth of my opinion that to Monks we are, in the matter of Libraries, primarily and permanently indebted. And that fact is no discovery of mine. I began to learn the lesson forty-six years ago at the feet (so to speak) of the noble Montalembert. I conned it over again, a long time afterwards, at the feet of Dr. Maitland, for so many years the honoured Librarian at Lambeth Palace; and I rejoice to see that a much more recent French author, not so fond or so proud of Monasticism as was Montalembert—the accomplished and erudite M. Alfred Franklin—has but recently shewn, from MSS. preserved in the National Library of France, that it was to French Monks that the World was indebted for the first really "Free Public Library" ever known to have been opened. When I originally published the book now re-edited, I assigned that credit to a great French statesman, though of Italian birth,—namely, to Cardinal Mazarin. To Mazarin, next after Richelieu, the France of other and of (in some respects) better days, owed the consolidation of its illustrious Monarchy, and it was, in 1859, my belief that to him, also, France, and Europe, owed the grand distinction of establishing the first of the now many hundreds of "Free Libraries." As an Ecclesiastic, no respect whatever is due to Mazarin; as a Statesman (his love of money excepted) very high respect is due. As a promoter of Learning and of Art, and as the free-handed disseminator of both, he stands out as prominently as he does in the long roll of the moulders of Modern Europe. And though the Mazarine Library cannot, after the recent researches of M. Alfred Franklin, take rank as first "Free Library" of the world, it still ranges as a very early one. The activities of its monastic predecessors were necessarily on a very humble scale. The monks had good will, but their means were small, and their "public" still smaller. The Mazarine Library, on the contrary, had a considerable sphere of activity at the very outset of its existence. It has now, in 1885, an enormous educational influence upon an important part of the youth of Paris. *Esto perpetua*! It is to the undying honour of our own Lancashire that to a Manchester merchant the distinction of founding the next, in order of time, of our subsisting Free Libraries is due.

The more the Reader does me the honour of studying those amongst the ensuing pages, and the authorities I employ for them, which relate to Monastic Libraries (the older as well as the more recent,—and on both classes I have spared neither research nor toil,) the more, I venture to think, he will be compelled to assent to Montalembert's saying:— "As to the 'Utility' of Monasticism—passing over, for the present, its Supreme Utility, supreme in the eyes of every Christian man, of Prayer; of the 'life hidden with God,'—let us come down to the lower 'utility' which alone is appreciated by those who habitually keep their eyes fixed on earth;—chained to the things that are transient, and to the things that bring lucre;—let us ask such men to point, in the long Annals of the World, to any body of men,—to any institution,— to any organisation whatever,—which, at any period, has rivalled, even approximately, those Monasteries that, for more than ten centuries, were the Schools, the Archives, the Libraries, [*some* of them, it might have been added, the Museums,]. . . . The Penitentiaries, the Hospitals, and the Public Gardens and Parks of Christian Society?".[1] I think that this true and fair statement will sufficiently justify the length—not in itself inordinate, or otherwise out of proportion (and for this assertion I have the express warrant of an "Edinburgh Reviewer,"[2] not likely to be overweeningly fond of the works and ways of Monks,)—at which I have ventured to treat of Mediæval Libraries, and of their Founders.

In dealing—at much greater length, of course,—with the modern Libraries and Museums of London and of Oxford, I have used my best endeavours to bring the information down to the latest dates; and have, as I believe, used the best authorities, in addition to the personal knowledge of nearly fifty years, taking the two cities together. My

---

[1] *Les Moines d'Occident*, Introd., cxxv (Edit. of 1860).
[2] *Edinburgh Review* (1874), Article 1.

intimate knowledge of the Museums, Libraries, and Archives of London began (I almost dread to remember it) in 1835; my acquaintance with those of Oxford in 1850—although, for too many years next thereafter, it was but a very slight and incidental acquaintance.

The "Library Returns" of 1849-52, referred to above, contain, as respects several countries of Europe,—contain, that is, in the year 1885,—the *latest official* and general accounts of the progress, and condition, of many Foreign Libraries, which have been any where *published* (in any language) or in any form whatsoever.

Still, in the year 1885—no "Book of Reference," as yet published— in any language—gives systematic and annual information on that subject, and on the condition and progress of Museums and Archives,— educationally, so important, and so pregnant with social results. Inquiries, and Publicists have to seek it by a multitude of indirect channels. Partially, indeed, the excellent *Library Chronicle*, so ably conducted by Mr. Ernest Thomas, and the *Centralblatt fur Bibliotheks- wesen*, not less ably managed by Dr. O. Hartwig and his staff of learned collaborators, contribute, from time to time, very important instalments of such information. The search for it is, nevertheless, still attended by much, and by quite needless, difficulty. When the searcher is, as in the writer's case, a very poor man, the difficulty is increased tenfold.

In relation to matters of mere "Trade," and occasionally to inventions, and discoveries bearing upon Trade, the Foreign Office it is well known, systematically confers inestimable benefit on the Nation, by instituting and by publishing periodical reports from our Secretaries of Legation. Is the present writer guilty of an unreasonable presumption, if he expresses the hope that, some day or other, a public boon which has widely diffused accurate knowledge, year by year, about Trade and Trading Establishments, may be so enlarged as also to communicate, annually and regularly, knowledge about the progress and present state, for the time being, of Foreign Museums, Foreign Libraries, and Foreign Public Archives?

Meanwhile, the able authors (Mr. Ernest C. Thomas and Mr. H. R. Tedder) of the Article "Libraries," in the ninth edition of the *Encyclopœdia Britannica* (now in course of publication), have done much towards the supply—so far as concerns Public Libraries, and up to the date of 1881,—of the deficiency of systematic *official* accounts, published annually. The statistical table printed at the end of that article is of eminent merit, and I avail myself thankfully of the new information it contains. More recently, the Library Association of the United Kingdom (which in so many ways has largely contributed to the increased efficiency of our Public Libraries, and has conspicuously promoted their interests,) has in a variety of forms, issued useful summaries of such Library Reports as have lately been printed, as well as much like information from other and original sources. To all of these I have likewise to acknowledge much indebtedness in the preparation of the volume now submitted, as well to future *purchasers*, as to my esteemed Subscribers, of 1883 and 1884.

For, although the announced intention of the writer that his new volumes should not become—in the ordinary sense of the phrase—a "Trade-book" is strictly adhered to, it came to be inevitable that the impression should extend to 500 copies, in order to cover the actual outlay, as well in preliminary expenses, as in paper and print. The Subscribers are still, in 1885, under 200 in number. The remainder of the impression will therefore be offered to purchasers, but only upon the Author's account and behalf.

It has also been found necessary, in order to keep within the limits announced in the Prospectus of this work, to deal with part of the wide subject,—more especially in the Mediæval Section above referred to—by way of typical and representative *examples* of the more eminent Libraries and Museums of each successive age, instead of attempting an exhaustive account of all that attained, at one time or other, to any conspicuous rank. This modification of the original plan, whilst somewhat abridging the text of the book, has necessarily increased, in a measure, the extent of the "General Introduction" prefixed thereto.

Of many and great obligations (other than those already noticed) which have been conferred on the writer, in the course of his labour, grateful acknowledgment will (D.V.) be made thereafter.

Edward Edwards.

*Sea-View, Niton,*
    *Queen's Accession-Day,* 1885.

From Edwards, Edward. *Memoirs of libraries, and of archives.* . . . *Second edition,* 1901, pp. vii–xxii.

# CHAPTER 16

# Sir Edward Augustus Bond (1815–1898)

"Would it not be practicable for certain of these wealthier libraries to agree on each making a particular branch of literature or science a special subject for attention – each assisting the others to make their specialities as complete as possible?"

SIR EDWARD AUGUSTUS BOND.

DURING the nineteenth century in particular the British Museum Library was the focal point for innovations in librarianship, some of which were later introduced into other systems. Large libraries are expected to be able to experiment, but the experiments are also expected to be successful, particularly if they entail the expenditure of public funds. The British Museum was fortunate in having men with ideas, and possibly suffered from having too many at the same time, which occasionally resulted in the clash of personalities. Reforms were, however, sometimes introduced with a minimum of opposition, and Bond appears to have served the Museum without making serious enemies.

Edward Augustus Bond was born at Hanwell on December 31st, 1815, and was educated at Merchant Taylors' School. At the age of seventeen he became an assistant in the Record Office, where he found material for the foundations of the study of palaeography. In 1837 he went to the British Museum, and in 1854 became assistant keeper of manuscripts, to be promoted to Keeper in 1867, succeeding Sir Frederic Madden. Bond completely reorganized the department, caught up with extensive arrears, and made a classified index of MSS. He founded the Palaeographical Society, and in 1875 succeeded Winter Jones as Principal Librarian. Bond continued his reforms, and initiated the introduction of electricity into the Museum, despite opposition. He induced the Treasury to finance the printing of the entire catalogue, introduced the sliding press into the Museum, and was awarded the C.B. in 1885. Upon his retirement in 1888 Bond was created K.C.B., Cambridge University having conferred upon him an honorary LL.D.

Sir Edward A. Bond died on January 2nd, 1898, just after his eighty-second birthday. He was mainly a palaeographer, contributing many papers to the *Transactions* of the Palaeographical Society, and wrote no separate book, but edited several texts for various societies. He was looked upon as cold and reserved, but was actually kind of heart and modest. Bond was President of the Library Association during the London meeting of 1886, and the following address reveals his interest in general librarianship. Some of his suggestions (e.g., public libraries to specialize in particular branches of knowledge) have a modern flavour, and many provide additional examples of ideas resurrected at intervals as new inspirations.

### REFERENCES

Garnett, Richard. The late Sir Edward A. Bond, K.C.B. *The Library*, 10, 1898, pp. 112–114, portrait. Also in Garnett, Richard, *Essays in librarianship and bibliography*, 1899, pp. 335–339, (without portrait). Garnett also contributed a biography of Bond to the *Dictionary of National Biography*, Supplement, Vol. 1, 1891, pp. 232–233.

## BOND ON PUBLIC LIBRARIES

It may justly be in a spirit of self-congratulation that the Members of the Library Association find themselves holding a ninth annual meeting this day. When the founders of the Association met their earliest supporters in the lecture-room of the London Institution in the year 1877, however confident they may have been in the practicability of their scheme, they must have had many doubts as to the methods of carrying it out, and they must have foreseen the difficulty of gaining an adequate number of subscribing members. The librarians, in whose interest the scheme was principally conceived, were few in number— they were used to having little intercourse with each other—and it was uncertain whether the habit of confining their attention to the actual duties of their particular charge might not have rendered them somewhat indifferent to the wider interests concerned in library administration—that many might hold aloof from a project, the very purpose of which was to enlarge their views, to better their position, and to facilitate the operation of their duties. The obstacles to success were not imaginary, but they have been overcome. The Association has maintained itself through these earlier years with recognised success and has achieved many of its objects. It has moreover pursued its aims by methods which must be universally approved—by personal discussion and by published proceedings.

But this has been done not without difficulty. Owing to the lowness of the annual subscription the want of sufficient funds has been severely felt. It has not been possible to have the support of a paid secretary— to purchase help in carrying on the organisation and the working of the society; and great, indeed, ought to be our gratitude to the two honorary secretaries who have so generously undergone the labours of directing and maintaining it. We want a more extended class of supporters. We ought to include in our list of members, not only managers and custodians of libraries, but more of those to whom libraries are indispensable for carrying on their literary and scientific researches, and who know how difficult it is to make them thoroughly efficient for this purpose—what a mere deception is a library casually brought together and ill-administered. To attract their attention we must make it clear by our proceedings that we are intent on perfecting systems of library formation and administration. We have done much in this direction, and if we persist in our efforts and enlarge our views our labours will be appreciated and will awaken more general interest.

It is most encouraging for the future prospects of the Association to look back on the valuable matter it has been able already, with its very limited means, to bring together in its *Transactions, Journal of Proceedings* and monthly *Chronicle*. But the subjects already discussed are by no means exhausted, and much remains to be done in bringing under view the earlier history of library formation—the efforts made at different times and in different countries for preserving for future generations the intellectual and historical records of each age as it passed. Much also remains to be done in collecting information of the growth and methods of administration of libraries abroad, of their comparative riches and deficiencies, of their systems of preservation and arrangement, what helps they give to students, what efforts of their influence can be traced in the character and condition of the people. The history of these libraries is of the greatest interest to us, and many good results will follow from the librarians of different countries being brought into intimate relations with each other through the agency of associations. I am happy to be able to state that a paper detailing the progress and particulars of administration of libraries in Germany may be expected for presentation to the present congress from Professor Dziatzko.

But, gentlemen, I do not propose to take up your time in reviewing what has already been done by the Association. In considering the attitude in which I might venture most reasonably to address you, it has seemed to me that, if I have any title to do so at all, it is that my experience of many years, principally in the work of the department of Manuscripts, and in some degree in connexion with that of Printed Books, in the British Museum, has necessarily suggested to me considerations in respect to the management of libraries which I might hope to be of value for practical application. And in presenting these to you I naturally have very much in mind the formation and management of Free Public Libraries, as now being established in our own country.

There is no need to dwell on the importance of the Free Library movement. The more we reflect on the many ways in which the introduction of libraries into districts hitherto without such resource is likely to act upon the inhabitants, the more our conviction deepens that the present movement will be the instrument of bringing into activity much dormant intellect and of sensibly affecting the national character. But how long we may have to wait for this result will greatly depend on the formation and management of the libraries— what shall be their contents, and how these shall be made both accessible and attractive. Obviously they cannot all be on the same scale. In the greater cities, they will from the first aim to be repositories of the best literature of all countries, but for the smaller towns humbler beginnings must be expected and more limited aims. As is already too apparent, they will need to economise their means with all possible strictness. Their funds will allow little margin for superfluity in purchases; and will provide little or no help to the librarian in carrying out his various duties of arranging his books, of cataloguing them, and of attending on readers.

It may well, therefore, be an early, if not immediate, work of the Association to take up and finally dispose of the suggestion already made by their honorary secretary, Mr. Thomas, and to prepare, with due deliberation and concert of members, a scheme of first selection of books suitable for the smaller library centres, and which may be accepted as a basis for the fuller library of future growth. The value of the scheme will be sensibly felt in its selection of works; but it will perhaps be even more effective in indicating the lines upon which the future extension of the library may best proceed. The selection of books being presented in the form of a printed catalogue, the librarian will be further assisted by having the list of his collection made to hand, convenient for the insertion of additional works as they are gradually acquired.

But when I think of the introduction of a Free Public Library into a populous town or district previously destitute of such an institution, picturing to myself the many ways in which it may be made to attract the interest and meet the wants of the surrounding inhabitants, and working out in my mind the course it ought to pursue to place itself in a position of the greatest utility, I cannot limit my view of such a library to its humble aim of supplying its ratepayers with the more general reading of the day. If the director of the library is in sympathy with the spirit of its foundation he will do his best to make it a very centre of intellectual activity. He will assuredly keep in view the object of providing for its growth on a broad basis—that it may eventually become a magazine of material for serious research. He will not be long in extending the first conception of the scope of its action and usefulness by taking opportunities for gathering into it not only local publications and local journals, but topographical records of every character. He will seek eagerly for all documents connected with the town and neighbouring landed estates—for charters and manorial rolls and accounts—for family correspondence and papers. A cry has already been raised for the need of public action in rescuing what remains of these invaluable records from destruction. The fittest agency for the purpose is the Public Library of the district. The endeavour to collect material for a county history has many a time worn out the strength and exhausted the means of the enthusiast who has undertaken it from his own resources. Let the Free Public Library be the recognised repository for the material, and the whole county will assist in collecting it.

And in advocating the interests of the local library in this respect I am not losing sight of the greater national library especially dear to me. The local librarian, in prosecuting his researches for books and documents illustrating the history of the neighbourhood, will frequently come upon material of more general interest, and while taking care of himself he may often do a good turn for the British Museum by making over to it offers of rare books too costly for his own funds, and historical collections and ancient manuscripts unsuitable for the local archives.

Further, in extension of the aims of the Free Library I would suggest that, as funds become available, it should endeavour to form a collection of engravings, giving chief consideration to native works in the first instance, and also should have in view the formation of a cabinet of coins and medals. In both these objects it may be expedient in starting the collections to take advantage of processes of casting and photographing from originals, in order at once to obtain sufficient materials for study; and I trust the electrotypes of ancient coins, and reproductions of prints and drawings, issued by the Trustees of the British Museum will be found serviceable for this purpose.

The prints, and the coins and medals, may be regarded as the adjuncts of the library; but the larger towns already establishing museums of natural history and antiquities, and the committees of management, it may be hoped, will see the advantage of placing these in immediate connexion with the library and thus forming an institution for general intellectual culture—the original scheme of the British Museum as conceived by its enlightened founders, but which unhappily has been foiled on the very eve of being realised, by the separation of the natural history portion of the collections and its removal to a distant locality. The progress of education, and the generally awakened interest in scientific and historical research, justify our regarding this development of the Free Public Library movement as something more than mere speculation. It is to the interest of the country that it should be carried out, and I would urge that our Association should make it their object to advocate this larger view of the movement, and use all opportunities to stimulate managing committees to adopt measures in harmony with it.

But a legitimate object of our Association is to encourage co-operation and mutual assistance in the administration of libraries, and general advantage may be gained by something of concert among the more richly endowed and supported of Free Libraries in making their acquisitions. Would it not be practicable for certain of these wealthier libraries to agree on each making a particular branch of literature or science a special subject for attention—each assisting the others to make their specialities as complete as possible? Every season, and perhaps more especially of late, we witness the dispersal of large and most precious collections of books and manuscripts by public auction. What becomes of them? Some few are secured by the great public libraries in the kingdom, but I fear our leading booksellers would tell us that the greater number of the rarer works are trans-ported to foreign countries and lost for ever to our own. The spirit of the collector of rare literature, so strong a hundred years ago, seems to have declined at the present time. What means can be found of securing for the country the treasures so providently brought together by enlightened book-collectors of a past generation? I see no hope but in the help of the Free Libraries; not, however, by their unconcerted efforts. It will be a vain aim for any but those of the few very large towns to endeavour to embrace universal literature, and to compete for its rarities. These will secure a portion of the dispersed collections, but let others combine and do by joint action in the manner suggested what is impossible to their single efforts. By com-bined action a network may be laid for securing what is of value in all classes, and making these acquisitions of common benefit. The securing the volume or manuscript would not be the only result. The spirit of co-operation might be further carried out by a system of interchange of books and manuscripts on loan for the convenience of students—so that in forming its specialty a library would be con-tributing to a great general collection for the use of all. Some help might be obtained from the British Museum. The Museum Library has a certain number of duplicate books, and in forming its collection must from time to time acquire others. Little good can be done by simply distributing these on no particular principle among other public libraries; but if the Trustees found that certain of the Free

Public Libraries were attending to special branches of literature, they would be encouraged to dispose of them and guided in doing so.

[pp. 1–4]

From Bond, E. A. Address to the Library Association. (Ninth Annual Meeting, London, 1886.) *Library Chronicle*, 4, 1887, pp. 1–10.

CHAPTER 17

# William Blades (1824–1890)

"An old book, whatever its subject or internal merits, is truly a portion of the national history; we may imitate it and print it in facsimile, but we can never exactly reproduce it, and as a historical document it should be carefully preserved."

WILLIAM BLADES.

WILLIAM BLADES is remembered more by bibliographers than by librarians, but the artificial fissure between the two is to be deplored. One cannot separate the scientific study of the physical make-up of books from their dispensation to readers, and the librarian who knows nothing of bibliography in the broadest sense of the word is unworthy of the name.

William Blades was born at Clapham on December 5th, 1824, and after attending Stockwell and Clapham Grammar Schools entered his father's printing office at the age of sixteen. Thus began his grounding in printing, which turned to interest in the history of the subject. In 1858 he wrote an introduction to a reprint of Caxton's *The governayle of helthe*, and initiated a lifelong study of William Caxton and his work. Blades personally inspected typographically 450 Caxtons in various libraries, and then wrote the monumental *Life and typography of William Caxton*, 2 vols., 1861–1863. While the first volume was in the press Blades met Henry Bradshaw, that kindred spirit in matters typographical, and made several other lifelong friends at home and abroad following the publication of this book. It was later published in one volume as *The biography and typography of William Caxton, England's first printer*, 1877, with a second edition in 1882.

Blades was constantly collecting fresh material, but maintained his printing business thoroughly up to date while studying the history of the craft. He took a prominent part in the Caxton Celebrations of 1877, writing a preface to the Caxton Catalogue, and became a member of the Library Association Council. He attended numerous annual conferences, and contributed several papers at these gatherings.

In 1881 appeared *The enemies of books*, a volume in lighter vein, where chapters are devoted to fire, water, gas and heat, dust and neglect, ignorance and bigotry, bookworms, other vermin, book-binders, collectors, and servants and children. The book was very popular, editions being published in 1881 (second edition), 1882 (third edition),

1887, 1888, 1896, with a French edition in 1883. Several of his books were privately printed, but his more popular writings include *The Pentateuch of printing*, [*etc.*], 1891, published posthumously, and prepared for the press by Talbot Baines Reed; *Books in chains*, 1892, a collection of Blades' bibliographical papers; and "An account of proposals made nearly two centuries ago to found public libraries" (*The Library*, 1st Ser., 1, 1889, pp. 9–12), which deals with James Kirkwood and Thomas Bray.

The centenary of the birth of William Blades was celebrated at the St. Bride Institute, where his library is housed. A *Catalogue of an exhibition in commemoration of the centenary of William Blades, held in the St. Bride Foundation*, 1924, was published to mark the event.

William Blades was gentle and kind, with a host of friends and a happy family life. His knowledge of typography was vast and his interests wide. He died on April 27th, 1890.

## REFERENCES

Moran, James. William Blades. *The Library*, 5th Ser., 16, 1961, pp. 251–266.

Obituary. *The Library*, 1st Ser., 2, 1890, pp. 191, 205–209.

Reed, Talbot Baines. Memoir of the late William Blades. *In*, Blades, William. *The Pentateuch of printing*, [*etc.*], 1891, pp. ix–xviii: (List of Blades' writings, pp. xix–xxiv.)

Tedder, H. R. Blades, William (1824–1890). *Dictionary of National Biography*, Supplement, Vol. 1, 1901, pp. 210–211.

W[heatley], Henry B. Introduction to, Blades, William. *Books in chains, and other bibliographical papers*, 1892, pp. ix–xxxviii. (The Book-Lover's Library.)

## BLADES ON ENEMIES OF BOOKS

Readers are you married? Have you offspring, boys especially I mean, say between six and twelve years of age? Have you also a literary workshop, supplied with choice tools, some for use, some for ornament, where you pass pleasant hours? And is—ah, there's the rub!—is there a special handmaid, whose special duty it is to keep your den daily dusted and in order? Plead you guilty of these indictments? Then am I sure of a sympathetic co-sufferer.

Dust! it is all a delusion. It is not the dust that makes women anxious to invade the inmost recesses of your sanctum; it is an ingrained curiosity. And this feminine weakness, which dates from Eve, is a common motive in the stories of our oldest literature and folklore. What made Fatima so anxious to know the contents of the room forbidden her by Bluebeard? It was positively nothing to her, and its contents caused not the slightest annoyance to anybody. That story had a bad moral, and it would, in many ways, have been more satisfactory had the heroine been left to take her place in the blood-stained chamber, side by side with her peccant predecessors.

Why need the women-folk (God forgive me!) bother themselves about the inside of a man's library, and whether it wants dusting or not? My boys' playroom, in which is a carpenter's bench, a lathe, and no end of litter, is never tidied—perhaps it can't be, or perhaps their youthful vigour won't stand it—but *my* workroom must needs be dusted daily, with the delusive promise that each book and paper shall be replaced exactly where it was. The damage done by such continued treatment is incalculable. At certain times these observances are kept more religiously than others; but especially should the book-lover, married or single, beware of the Ides of March. So soon as February is dead and gone, a feeling of unrest seizes the housewife's mind. This increases day by day, and becomes dominant towards the middle of the month, about which period sundry hints are thrown out as to whether you are likely to be absent for a day or two. Beware! the fever called "spring clean" is on, and unless you stand firm you will rue it. Go away, if the Fates so will, but take the key of your own domain with you.

Do not misunderstand. Not for a moment would I advocate dust and dirt; they are enemies, and should be routed; but let the necessary routing be done under your own eye. Explain where caution must be used, and in what cases tenderness is a virtue; and if one Eve in the family can be indoctrinated with book-reverence you are a happy man; her price is above that of rubies; she will prolong your life. Books *must* now and then be taken clean out of their shelves, but they should be tended lovingly and with judgment. If the dusting can be done just outside the room, so much the better. The books removed, the shelf should be lifted quite out of its bearings, cleansed and wiped, and then each volume should be taken separately, and gently rubbed on back and sides with a soft cloth. In returning the volumes to their places, notice should be taken of the binding, and especially when the books are in whole calf or morocco care should be taken not to let them rub together. The best bound books are soonest injured, and quickly deteriorate in bad company. Certain volumes, indeed, have evil tempers, and will scratch the faces of all their neighbours who are too familiar with them. Such are books with metal clasps and rivets on their edges; and such, again, are those abominable old rascals, chiefly born in the fifteenth century, who are proud of being dressed in *real* boards with brass corners, and pass their lives with fearful knobs and metal bosses, mostly five in number, firmly fixed on one of their sides. If the tendencies of such ruffians are not curbed, they will do as much mischief to their gentle neighbours as when a 'collie' worries the sheep. These evil results may always be minimized by placing a piece of millboard between the culprit and his victim. I have seen lovely bindings sadly marked by such uncanny neighbours.

When your books are being 'dusted', don't impute too much commonsense to your assistants; take their ignorance for granted, and tell them at once never to lift any book by one of its covers; that treatment is sure to strain the back, and ten to one the weight will be at the same time miscalculated, and the volume will fall. Your female 'help', too, dearly loves a good tall pile to work at, and, as a rule, her notions of the centre of gravity are not accurate, leading often to a general downfall, and the damage of many a corner. Again, if not supervised and instructed, she is very apt to rub the dust into instead of off the edges. Each volume should be held tightly, so as to prevent the leaves from gaping, and then wiped from the back to the fore-edge. A soft brush will be found useful if there is much dust. The whole exterior should also be rubbed with a soft cloth, and then the covers should be opened and the hinges of the binding examined; for mildew *will* assert itself both inside and outside certain books, and that most pertinaciously. It has unaccountable likes and dislikes. Some bindings seem positively to invite damp, and mildew will attack these when no other books on the same shelf show any signs of it. When discovered, carefully wipe it away, and then let the book remain a few days standing open in the driest and airiest spot you can select. Great care should be taken not to let grit, such as blows in at the open window from many a dusty road, be upon your duster, or you will probably find fine scratches, like an outline map of Europe, all over your smooth calf, by which your heart and eye, as well as your book, will be wounded.

'Helps' are very apt to fill the shelves too tightly, so that to extract a book you have to use force, often in the injury of the top-bands. Beware of this mistake. It frequently occurs through not noticing that one small book is purposely placed at each end of the shelf, beneath the movable shelf-supports, thus not only saving space, but preventing the injury which a book shelf-high would be sure to receive from uneven pressure.

After all, the best guide in these, as in many other matters, is 'common-sense', a quality which in olden times must have been much more 'common' than in these days, else the phrase would never have become rooted in our common tongue.

Children, with all their innocence, are often guilty of book-murder. I must confess to having once taken down Humphrey's "History of Writing", which contains many brightly-coloured plates, to amuse a sick daughter. The object was certainly gained, but the consequences of so bad a precedent were disastrous. That copy (which I am glad to say, was easily replaced), notwithstanding great care on my part, became soiled and torn, and at last was given up to nursery martyrdom. Can I regret it? Surely not, for, although bibliographically sinful, who can weigh the amount of real pleasure received, and the actual pain ignored, by the patient in the contemplation of those beautifully-blended colours?

A neighbour of mine some few years ago suffered severely from a propensity, apparently irresistible, in one of his daughters to tear his library books. She was six years old, and would go quietly to a shelf and take down a book or two, and, having torn a dozen leaves or so down the middle, would replace the volumes, fragments and all, in their places, the damage being undiscovered until the books were wanted for use. Reprimand, expostulation, and even punishment, were of no avail; but a single 'whipping' effected a cure.

Boys, however, are by far more destructive than girls, and have, naturally, no reverence for age, whether in man or books. Who does not fear a schoolboy with his first pocket-knife? As Wordsworth did not say:

> "You may trace him oft
> By scars which his activity has left
> Upon our shelves and volumes. . . .
> He who with pocket-knife will cut the edge
> Of luckless panel or of prominent book,
> Detaching with a stroke a label here, a back-band there."
>
> *Excursion*, III. 83.

Pleased, too, are they if, with mouths full of candy and sticky fingers, they can pull in and out the books on your bottom shelves, little knowing the damage and pain they will cause. One would fain cry out, calling on the Shade of Horace to pardon the false quantity:

> "Magna movet stomacho fastidia, si puer unctis
> Tractavit volumen manibus."
>
> *Sat. II. iv.*

What boys can do may be gathered from the following true story, sent me by a correspondent who was the immediate sufferer:

One summer day he met in town an acquaintance who for many years had been abroad, and, finding his appetite for old books as keen as ever, invited him home to have a mental feed upon 'fifteeners' and other bibliographical dainties, preliminary to the coarser pleasures enjoyed at the dinner-table. The 'home' was an old mansion in the outskirts of London, whose very architecture was suggestive of black-letter and sheepskin. The weather, alas! was rainy, and, as they approached the house, loud peals of laughter reached their ears. The children were keeping a birthday with a few young friends. The damp forbade all outdoor play, and, having been left too much to their own devices, they had invaded the library. It was just after the Battle of Balaclava, and the heroism of the combatants on that hard-fought field was in everybody's mouth. So the mischievous young imps divided themselves into two opposing camps—Britons and Russians. The Russian division was just inside the door, behind ramparts formed of old folios and quartos taken from the bottom shelves, and piled to the height of about four feet. It was a wall of old Fathers, fifteenth-century chronicles, county histories, Chaucer, Lydgate, and such-like. Some few yards off were the Britishers, provided with heaps of small books as missiles, with which they kept up a skirmishing cannonade against the foe. Imagine the tableau! Two elderly gentlemen enter hurriedly, paterfamilias receiving, quite unintentionally, the first edition of "Paradise Lost" in the pit of his stomach, his friend narrowly escaping a closer personal acquaintance with a quarto "Hamlet" than he had ever had before. Finale: Great outbursts of wrath, and rapid retreat of the combatants, many wounded (volumes) being left on the field.

[pp. 117–125.]

.    .    .    .

It is a great pity that there should be so many distinct enemies at work for the destruction of literature, and that they should so often be allowed to work out their sad end. Looked at rightly, the possession of any old book is a sacred trust, which a conscientious owner or guardian would as soon think of ignoring as a parent would of neglecting his child. An old book, whatever its subject or internal merits, is truly a portion of the national history; we may imitate it and print it in facsimile, but we can never exactly reproduce it, and as a historical document it should be carefully preserved.

I do not envy any man that absence of sentiment which makes some people careless of the memorials of their ancestors, and whose blood can be warmed up only by talking of horses or the price of hops. To them solitude means *ennui*, and anybody's company is preferable to their own. What an immense amount of calm enjoyment and mental renovation do such men miss! Even a millionaire will ease his toils, lengthen his life, and add a hundred per cent. to his daily pleasures, if he becomes a bibliophile; while to the man of business with a taste for books, who through the day has struggled in the battle of life, with all its irritating rebuffs and anxieties, what a blessed season of pleasurable repose opens upon him as he enters his sanctum, where every article wafts to him a welcome, and every book is a personal friend!

[pp. 137–138.]

From Blades, William. *The enemies of books*, [etc.], 1896.

# CHAPTER 18

# Henry Bradshaw (1831–1886)

"The first duty of a librarian is to save the time of others."
HENRY BRADSHAW.

THE father of Henry Bradshaw was Joseph Hoare Bradshaw, who made a remarkable collection of Irish books, and it was probably his close association with these volumes that inspired Henry in his love for bibliography, manuscripts, Irish history and early printing.

Henry Bradshaw was born at Finsbury Square, London, on February 2nd, 1831, but shortly afterwards the family removed to Hornsey, and there Henry spent the first eight years of his life. At the age of twelve he went to Eton, spending much of his spare time in the library. When he went to King's College, Cambridge seven years later he possessed a personal library of 500 volumes. In 1853 Henry Bradshaw was elected a Fellow of King's, and the following year took a second class in the classical tripos. He then went as assistant master at St. Columba's College, near Dublin, remaining there for two years.

Bradshaw studied Irish antiquities, and became keenly interested in bibliography. He was not cut out to be a schoolmaster, and in November, 1856 was appointed principal assistant in the University Library at Cambridge. This position he resigned after two years, but was employed in cataloguing the MSS. During the next seven years he made numerous important discoveries among this material, including the Waldensian MSS. in 1862. The following year he was engaged in a controversy regarding the authenticity of the Codex Sinaiticus, which had been discovered by Tischendorf in 1859. Simonides, a notorious forger, in an attempt to discredit Tischendorf, claimed to have forged the Codex, but Bradshaw's evidence assisted in disproving this assertion.

In 1867 Henry Bradshaw was appointed University Librarian at Cambridge. He presented his entire Irish collection to the Library, and continued to devote his wide knowledge to the benefit of readers. He had a thorough knowledge of the contents of libraries in this country and on the Continent, but despite the fact that Bradshaw possessed a remarkable memory he was unable to concentrate upon a subject for any length of time, and left many projects half completed. It has been said of him that "much of his labour took shape in the production of others", and "never was there such a helpful man as he", for he gave freely of his advice based on deep scholarship to all who consulted him.

As an administrator Henry Bradshaw was not a great success, and there was some criticism of the Library during his librarianship. Yet he admirably filled the office of President to the Library Association, presiding over the fifth annual meeting held at Cambridge in September, 1882. His Presidential Address is reproduced below, and represents one of his few contributions to library literature as distinct from bibliography.

Henry Bradshaw had a thorough knowledge of early printing and typography, and his major contributions to the subject are contained in his *Collected papers*, published in 1889. He died suddenly of heart disease on the night of February 10th/11th, 1886, and a portrait of him by J. Herkomer, R.A., hangs in the hall of King's College, Cambridge. In 1890 the Henry Bradshaw Society was founded for the editing of liturgical tracts, but outside Cambridge and a limited circle of bibliographers few appreciate the qualities of this great scholar and librarian. (Portrait, Plate 6.)

## REFERENCES

Crone, John S. *Henry Bradshaw, his life and work*, Dublin, *Printed at the sign of the Three Candles*, 1931.

Grant, C. E. In memoriam, Henry Bradshaw. *Library Chronicle*, 3, 1886, pp. 25–36.

Newcombe, C. F. Some aspects of the work of Henry Bradshaw. *Library Association Record*, 7, 1905, pp. 392–403; discussion, pp. 145–147.

Prothero, Sir George Walter. *A memoir of Henry Bradshaw, Fellow of King's College, Cambridge, and University Librarian*, London, 1888. (Prothero also contributed the biography of Bradshaw to the *Dictionary of National Biography*, Supplement, Vol. 1, 1891, pp. 251–254.

## BRADSHAW'S PRESIDENTIAL ADDRESS TO THE LIBRARY ASSOCIATION, 1882

... There are three definitions which I must in the first place ask you to accept, seeing that much of what I shall have to say depends upon a clear understanding of these points. What is a *Library*? What is a *Librarian*? What is the *Library Association* to which we all belong? My definitions are these:

(1) A *Library* is a collection of books brought together for the use of those who wish to read them; these readers falling for the most part into the two very distinct classes of readers of books and writers of books.

(2) A *Librarian* is one who earns his living by attending to the wants of those for whose use the library under his charge exists; his primary

duty being, in the widest possible sense of the phrase, to save the time of those who seek his services.

(3) The *Library Association* is an organised collection of librarians and others interested in the administration of libraries, who come together at intervals for the purpose of comparing notes and interchanging experience, with the view of effecting a general improvement in the machinery by which the work of a library is carried on.

We are, beyond a doubt, a purely professional body. So far as our profession is concerned, we are neither the producers nor the consumers of books, neither writers nor readers; we are the middlemen, to whom all who read to any purpose, and all who write, are bound sooner or later to come for help. If any one not personally concerned with the administration of a library joins our Association, we attribute the fact to the known charm which books and their belongings never fail to exercise over certain minds; we welcome him gladly, and we express a charitable hope that in the thick of professional discussion he may find something to repay him for his venture.

Of the *Library*, and of the *Librarian* I am bound to say something, although my chief anxiety is to draw your attention to certain details of library work, in which Cambridge ought to afford to many of you points of comparison which are well worth studying. I say this without any hesitation, without any fear of being thought to exaggerate the importance of what is done here; because I am convinced that in every library, however insignificant in extent, good ideas will be started and practical suggestions worked out, which the most experienced librarian will do well to take note of, and perhaps to adopt. No library is too small to afford scope for such ideas; no librarian is so great that he can afford to neglect such suggestions.

But something has to be said about the *Library*. In what I have said already as to the two distinct classes of people who use a library, readers of books and writers of books, it will be understood that all are readers, though all are not (happily for us) writers of books.

Libraries may be said to go through several successive stages, though the higher stages are frequently never reached or even contemplated. The most elementary kind exists only for readers. It is represented by the lower class of circulating library, and by the simplest form of branch, in places where central free libraries exist. It must not be thought that I am depreciating the value of the elementary institution. It corresponds to the boys' library of our schools and (though you will perhaps be surprised to hear me say so) to the whole of our University and College libraries here, as they existed in the fourteenth and fifteenth centuries. Their object was exclusively practical; they were collections of books brought together simply for the use of those who wanted to read, and had not the means to buy books for themselves. Education makes people want to read, and the libraries exist to supply this want.

A higher stage is reached when the funds at the disposal of a library come to be in part devoted to the acquisition of books which form the necessary working materials of those who are engaged in writing books, but cannot afford to buy all the books which they need for their work. What is useful in this to one person will almost certainly be useful to another, and thus it becomes worth while to incur some outlay with this object and so to make the libraries available for study as well as simply for reading what are called readable books. The character, the higher stamp, thus given to a library, soon produces results. We know that "to every one that hath shall be given, and he shall have abundance". When even small resources are well husbanded and made useful for a higher class of work by good management, donations flow in; and men who have spent half a life-time and half a fortune upon the formation of a library will leave or even give their books to a place where they feel confidence that good use will be made of them. This is the process by which all our great libraries have been formed. I have no reason to fear contradiction if I say that in every library of note in the kingdom down to the last fifty or sixty years the bought books formed but a very minute portion of the whole collection in comparison with those which were given or bequeathed.

Every library formed by one man and left to the more or less public library of an institution, must needs contain many books for which no immediate use can be found among the habitual frequenters of the place. It is at this point, therefore, that the antiquarian element first appears, an element which I may safely say was as heartily despised by our forefathers before the Reformation as it is despised, not to say detested, by many excellent people in the present day. Any one who has examined the inventories of early libraries before the Reformation will be familiar with the note of "old and useless books" (*libri vetusti et inutiles*) applied to early copies of the Gospels, early volumes of Anglo-Saxon literature, and other such, which from their purely practical point of view were treated as so much rubbish, fit only for the waste-paper basket, while to us, unless animated by the spirit of a recent writer in the *Quarterly Review*, the same volumes are justly looked upon as priceless and unique remnants of a literature which would otherwise be wholly lost to us. This antiquarian element may fairly be said to have come into existence after the Reformation. We all remember the interesting paper which our excellent Treasurer gave us last year on the necessity of ridding our libraries of obsolete books, and from his point of view and that of the library which he represents, I think he was undoubtedly right. Every library must be governed according to its particular constitution, or, as I should say, the treatment which each library requires must depend upon the stage of development which it has reached. It was precisely this line which the advocates of the Reforming movement followed in the reign of Edward the Sixth, when they made an almost clean sweep of all the monuments of the old learning which they found, or sometimes mistakenly thought they found, in our University and College libraries. We must not suppose that they hated books, that they hated learning; but they did not and could not see that any good result was likely to arise from having the shelves of their libraries filled with what they considered certainly poisonous, and (as they hoped) henceforth obsolete, books. Even with Archbishop Parker, who outlives this movement nearly thirty years, and may truly be looked upon as the first of the long line of modern book-collectors, we often find an apologetic tone, which sounds strangely in our ears, when he puts a note into a volume, explaining to posterity that it is desirable to preserve specimens of such and such books, however undesirable or useless they may be considered from the customary point of view. But I must return to my point. When the antiquarian element becomes developed in a library, a higher stage still is reached. By this I mean, what I must be allowed to consider a higher stage in the character and in the usefulness of a library. To any one engaged in historical research upon any subject it soon becomes manifest that this destruction of obsolete books which our forefathers encouraged, led to the result, which we their successors now find so extremely inconvenient, that many books which alone contain certain pieces of much desired information, have come down to us in single copies, or at best in copies preserved in some half-dozen widely scattered libraries, where for want of a printed catalogue they are for the present as good as lost. Hence arises a new demand. The library which, in the lower stages which I have noticed already, contained nothing but common books to serve the purpose of its habitual frequenters, becomes gradually more and more, as its contents are better known, an object of pilgrimage to students living at a distance sometimes, as we know, of many thousand miles, solely for the purpose of examining these books, of which the library in question is the only known repository. Thus it is that by the existence of this antiquarian element in its composition, whether of old printed books or manuscripts, the library acquires a prestige which in its earlier stages it could never have possessed; and the appreciation of this prestige is apt to make its importance more keenly felt among those on the spot, who had never before been awakened to a sense of the treasures of which they were the guardians.

This leads me to the last stage in the development of a library of which I need take any account. The very existence of treasures which it is seen can never be replaced, leads naturally to the formation of a reserved portion of the library, where the most precious things are brought together as into a museum; and it is eventually found that they are deserving of a study of quite a different kind. They become, like specimens in any other museum, the object of more or less scientific investigation, while they are none the less available for the purely literary purpose for which they may need to be consulted. If their home be the central library of any town or district, this museum will rapidly absorb all local antiquities in the way of books and other specimens of printing, and these again will demand their own special study. But as I shall have to say something on this head in connexion with Mr. Wright's paper on Local Bibliography, there is no need for me to enlarge upon the subject here, and I am content to pass on.

About the Librarian I need not say much, as you will to-morrow have the benefit of hearing from Mr. Tedder his views, and I hope his experience, on librarianship as a profession. When I define a librarian as "one who earns his living by attending to the wants of those for whose use the library under his charge exists", you will perhaps be inclined to ask in what respect my librarian or his assistant differs from a bookseller or bookseller's assistant. The only substantial difference which I see consists in this: that the bookseller caters for the reader or writer of books, in order to make what living he can; while the librarian caters for the same people, in order to make such living as the trustees of his library assign to him. In saying this I do not consider that I either degrade the one occupation or exalt the other. Everything depends, and must depend, upon the individual man. If you have been able to follow my sketch of the various stages in the development of a library, you will easily follow my meaning here when I say that the librarian follows precisely the same stages. By the bookseller I mean not the publisher proper, whose dealings with his author must always be more or less purely commercial, but the bookseller who collects and sells books new and old, who knows the books themselves and not merely their value in the market, who caters for the real student rather than for the rich collector, the class of which old William Pickering, C. J. Stewart, and others whom I could mention are such splendid types. In the lowest grade of library, neither bookseller nor librarian will have much to raise them to any high state of culture. But for both men, when brought into contact with writers of good books or even with students who are content not to write, the very fact that they are helping these men to find the books they want, compels them if they are in any way worth their salt, to enter into their wants and gain some acquaintance with the varied subjects which they are studying. It is this constant intercourse between the genuine student and the man who supplies his wants, which forms such a humanising training to the librarian and the bookseller alike, when it is not primarily the market value of the book which is wanted (however necessary this knowledge may be), but the intrinsic value and quality and contents of the book. The librarian under these circumstances is one whose life is wholly devoted to the service of his fellowmen, and the more it is so, the more, most assuredly, will he find himself appreciated. When I say that his primary duty is to save the time of those who frequent his library, I of course use these words in their very broadest sense. It will consist in procuring the right books, in procuring them and making them ready for use with as little delay as possible, in having them well and rationally catalogued, and easily to be found in their places. Our friends in Cambridge have had so much experience of our shortcomings in many of these points, while we see how important the minutes are, which a stranger has to waste while his wants are being supplied, that I have been forced into the adoption of this formula as best expressing the primary duties of any one entrusted with the direction of a library. But I must leave these suggestions, and hasten to give you that slight guide to what you may expect to find here, which I promised at the beginning.

As I have assumed that the object of these meetings of the Library Association is to enable our members to visit different libraries and to compare notes and interchange experience with their fellow-librarians, I am bound to tell you (1) something of what Cambridge libraries are, and (2) to direct your attention to certain points which you will, in my opinion, find worth your consideration.

It will perhaps be a matter of surprise to some to learn that, putting aside all such more or less private institutions as the Union Society and other similar bodies which possess some of them very useful collections of books, there are twenty-nine libraries in Cambridge which deserve more or less consideration. Of these the Town claims two and the University twenty-seven.

About the Central Free Library at the Guildhall, and the Barnwell Branch Library, you will have no difficulty in gaining on the spot information better and more direct than I can give. Though of comparatively recent date, like all the Free Libraries, it has already reached what I have called both the antiquarian and the museum stage of development, and everything points to continued advance under the direction of my friend Mr. Pink, who has watched over it throughout its infancy and subsequent growth. As, next to this place where we are at this moment, the Free Library may be said to form the headquarters of the Association in Cambridge, it would be waste of your time for me to do more than give it the place of honour in my list.

In dealing with the University I must make a distinction between the University properly so called and the Colleges. I hope that a very brief sketch will serve in some measure to enable those who are unacquainted with Cambridge to form something like an accurate notion of what must be to every stranger a most complicated system. The English Universities come to the surface of history in the early part of the thirteenth century. Just as the Chancellor in most cathedral churches had the privilege of unlimited control over all the schools of his district, so the Chancellor of the University had exclusive rights of jurisdiction over the scholars who frequented the schools of the University, and the power of protecting them in all matters concerning their lodging in the town. Before the end of the thirteenth century we find the first college established, a College being strictly speaking an endowed lodging-house for University students, which saved those who were fortunate enough to obtain house-room within its walls, from any extortion on the part of the lodginghouse-keepers in the town. Six more of these Colleges were established by the middle of the fourteenth century, six more in the course of the fifteenth, and others since, mostly on the ruins of older decayed foundations. These Colleges are places where students have always carried on their studies during their University course, each having its own chapel and hall, its own library, &c., while the University has of course independently its own schools, museums, libraries, &c., which the occupants of the Colleges use and frequent as members of the University. I will take the seven associated libraries first, and then say something of those of the several Colleges.

The greatest library of all, that long known as the Public Library of the University, though now more generally called the University Library, ranks as third of the most prominent libraries in the kingdom, though of all the more public collections it is, I believe, far the most ancient. The University buildings go back to the close of the fourteenth century, and we still possess books which have formed part of our library since the first quarter of the fifteenth century. We are always assumed by the world to be somewhat slow in our steps at Cambridge, and many of us can recollect the vivid language in which we were told here a few weeks ago by Mr. Matthew Arnold that Oxford had always been the home of great movements, while Cambridge had to content itself with being the home of great men. It is quite possible that the characteristic energy of the movement in Oxford against the old learning, and the comparative sluggishness of our own university, may be in part the cause of the fact that, while we still have a number of links to witness the continuity of our own library, the destruction at Oxford was so thoroughgoing that no vestige has been preserved, and Sir Thomas Bodley must be looked upon as the actual creator rather than the restorer of the library which bears his name. Drastic remedies were, we know, applied even to our own library in the reign of Edward the Sixth; but by a sort of nemesis the very man who as Proctor declared the vote of the Senate by which our library was doomed to pillage was the very man who in after years became the leading spirit in the restoration of the library to more than its previous magnificence. It is to this Dr. Andrew Perne, Master of Peterhouse, the friend of Archbishop Parker and other leading men of Queen Elizabeth's time, that we really owe not only the complete restoration of our library but also the first permanent endowment of a librarian. I need not trouble you with details of the noble libraries of Holdsworth, Lucas, Hacket and Moore, which came to us during the sixty years succeeding the Restoration of the monarchy, nor with more than the mention of what was more fruitful than all these, the national gift of the Copyright Act during the same period, an Act which has provided us, at an infinitesimal cost, with a perpetual supply of what may truly be called the very bread of our life, the staple food of our own national literature. Details of our principal endowments you can easily find in the commonest guide-books, and I have no intention of giving orally information which you will do better to read at leisure for yourselves.

Some of my friends, even in Cambridge, will be surprised to hear me speak of seven associated libraries in connexion with the University. But when I speculate upon the probable contents of Mr. Bowker's paper on the work of the librarians of our own century in preparation for our successors of the Twentieth, I find a pleasure in drawing out lines which my successors will I hope one day fill up in a way really worthy of the University. There are several departments of University study which are at present provided with special collections, in each of which it pleases me to see the nucleus of a special branch library for the freest possible use of those who are studying these several subjects. One of the most admirable features of the Bodleian Library, to my mind, is the way in which the private library of a specialist like Gough or Malone, has become, when bequeathed to Oxford, the germ of a still more precious collection in which the University has constituted itself the man's heir and continued his collection. So with us, I look upon the small library attached by gift to the Divinity School and now preserved there, the old library of the Modern History School and the more recent Political Economy collections of Professor Pryme, together with the equally special libraries of the Antiquarian and Philological Societies, all four now temporarily housed in the New Museums, as capable, one and all, of a wide development for the use of special students, after the model of the recently organised Philosophical Library. This last, owing to the liberality of the Philosophical Society and the untiring zeal of Mr. J. W. Clark, has now been thrown open as a scientific library free to all who are engaged in those branches of study which display to the utmost the vitality of Cambridge work. Only let the others be worked on the same principle and in the same spirit, with the University Library as a centre and feeder of the rest.

I have omitted only one belonging to the University which cannot be included in the same category as those just mentioned, though it may perfectly be worked in the same spirit; I mean the Fitzwilliam Museum. Here the library of necessity falls into a subordinate position, being overshadowed by the more precious collection of pictures and engravings. Lord Fitzwilliam's is a good specimen of a nobleman's library of the beginning of the present century. Much is here of course to illustrate his own special collections, though this is far from being the exclusive character of the library; and constant additions are being made to render it useful, especially to the student of art and archaeology. The more recent addition of Colonel Leake's library is an instance of that special development which I have alluded to before as such a hopeful course of action.

I have left but little space for the College libraries, and the pressure of the day's coming work urges me to be brief. I will just enumerate the seventeen Colleges, that you may form some idea of what remains to be done.

Peterhouse, our only thirteenth-century College, is one of the few which preserved its books nearly intact through the storm of the sixteenth century.

Of the fourteenth-century Colleges, Clare, Trinity, Pembroke, Gonville and Caius, Trinity Hall, and Corpus Christi, much might be said, but I cannot say it. Clare has some priceless books but is as yet little explored. For Trinity College you will have an exhaustive paper from our Vice-President, Mr. Sinker, so I will not attempt to anticipate his remarks. Pembroke has lately built a new library, and has taken a fresh start; a collection which embodies the whole library of Bishop Andrewes cannot well be devoid of interest. Gonville and Caius College, as you will see under Mr. Bensly's guidance, contains many most precious things, and like Peterhouse preserved itself from destruction in the sixteenth century. Trinity Hall library is a great curiosity in itself, as containing a rare example of the manner in which libraries were arranged more than three hundred years ago. I hope much that Mr. Clark will be able to give you some interesting details about it when you visit it. Corpus Christi College, as you know, is famous for the library of Archbishop Parker. Mr. Lewis will spare no pains to introduce you to the principal treasures of the collection, which is quite unrivalled in England.

Of the fifteenth-century colleges, Magdalene, King's, Christ's, Queens', St. Catherine's, and Jesus College, all offer various attractions, though almost exclusively from an antiquarian point of view. Magdalene, the immediate successor of Buckingham College, which was founded for the Benedictines in 1428, has an interesting old library of its own, though the Pepysian of course throws the older collection into the shade. The library of Samuel Pepys is housed in a small room containing his own little carved book-cases, all the three thousand volumes to which he limited himself being kept in precisely the order in which he left them. The small size of the room renders it impossible for many people to be there at one time; but thanks to the kindness of the Master and of Prof. Newton, you will have as good an opportunity of seeing it and its contents as can be managed. King's College library, having a small endowment of its own, has never been allowed to fall either into decay or disuse; its most precious portion is the library of Jacob Bryant, the well-known scholar of the latter half of the eighteenth century. For those who love to look at samples of early Italian printing in choice Harleian bindings, the Bryant collection offers a rare feast. The remaining four Colleges I have mentioned are all interesting in their way, Jesus College, especially, offering an example of an old library with its stalls, of which the original contents are indicated by the subjects in stained glass placed by the founder in the several windows.

Coming down to the colleges of the sixteenth century, St. John's affords an excellent specimen of the library of its date (1624), and Prof. Mayor will gladly show you both the room and its principal treasures. It is literally full of interesting matter. As St. John's occupies the ground of the old Hospital of St. John the Evangelist and Jesus College that of the decayed nunnery of St. Rhadegund, so Emmanuel and Sidney stand on the site of the Dominican and Franciscan Convents. Emmanual library is very rich in old books, and bears a distinctive character of its own, from having inherited the whole of Archbishop Sancroft's printed library. Dr. Pearson will kindly show you many of the treasures there under his charge. Sidney-Sussex College, besides having an old library of great value, has a special and more modern collection, the Taylor library, instituted for the use of students of mathematics and natural science, one of those special libraries which are so warmly appreciated by the students of the present day. Downing, the most modern of our recognised Colleges, has also its library, but it is the only one of which I can say nothing from personal experience of its contents.

You must look upon all these as, for the most part, repositories of old and precious books, which when they come to be better known, will assuredly yield rich fruit to the enquirer. Being made up chiefly of gifts, they have all long since reached what I have called the antiquarian stage of development, while in the greater number almost all provision for the supply of new books has been allowed to fall into abeyance. Many however are beginning to show signs of renewed life, and are being made useful for present studies. [etc.]

From, *Collected papers of Henry Bradshaw, late University Librarian, [etc.]*, 1889, pp. 372–384.

# CHAPTER 19

# *Richard Garnett (1835–1906)*

"We cannot have the ideal classification without the ideal library."
RICHARD GARNETT.

THE above was the elder son of Richard Garnett (1789–1850), Assistant Keeper of Printed Books at the British Museum, and was born at Lichfield on February 27th, 1835. Largely self-educated, and with a remarkable memory, he was a brilliant linguist and student of foreign literature, so that he was eminently qualified for his career at the British Museum, which he entered in 1851. Garnett was keenly concerned with cataloguing, and when the printing of the general catalogue was begun in 1881, he retired from his position as Assistant Keeper of Printed Books and Superintendent of the Reading Room to devote his time entirely to seeing the catalogue through the press. In 1890 he was appointed Keeper of Printed Books, retiring nine years later, after which Garnett turned to literature, to which subject he made many notable contributions.

His reputation as Superintendent of the Reading Room survives as a legend, for his services to readers were phenomenal. He remembered not only the backs of books, but much of their contents, and his knowledge was made freely available. He was a poet, contributed numerous biographical studies to the *Dictionary of National Biography*, and was also the author of lives of Thomas Carlyle (1887), Ralph Waldo Emerson (1888); John Milton (1890); William Blake (1895), and others.

In 1883 the University of Edinburgh conferred the honorary degree of LL.D. upon Garnett, and he was created C.B. in 1895. Garnett was an original member of the Library Association, serving on the Council for several years until 1893, when he was elected President. His contributions to library literature are numerous, many of them referring to the activities of the British Museum, and he was responsible for the idea of the sliding press, which greatly eased the storage situation in that institution. Some of his papers were collected together in *Essays in librarianship and bibliography*, 1899, and *Essays of an ex-librarian*, 1901. Garnett died on April 13th, 1906, and his wide scholarship and keen interest in librarianship were sorely missed in the profession he had graced with such distinction.

REFERENCES

Fortescue, G. K. Obituary notice. *Library Association Record*, 8, 1906, pp. 201–203.
Heilbrun, Carolyn G. *The Garnett family*, 1961. Richard Garnett (1835–1906) is dealt
with in Chapter 2, pp. 37–64, and a list of his literary works is given on pp. 202–205.

## GARNETT ON THE SYSTEM OF CLASSIFICATION OF BOOKS
### AT THE BRITISH MUSEUM

The classification of a great library is equivalent to a classification of human knowledge, and may, if men please, become the standard or symbol of conflicting schools of thought. It might, for example, be plausibly maintained that knowledge, and therefore the library, should begin with the definition of man's relation to the unseen powers around him—that is, with Natural Theology. Or with man himself as the unit of all things human—that is, with Anthropology. Or, on Nature's own pattern, with the most rudimentary forms of existence. Hence, as we heard yesterday from the distinguished gentleman who here represents the fifth part of the world, the reading-room library at Melbourne begins with works on the subject of Sponges. Fortunately for the neutral bibliographer, there exists a book which not only holds in civilized countries a place unique among books, but which has further established its claim to precedence by the practical test of being the first to get itself printed. The Museum classification accordingly begins with the Bible, and I venture to express the opinion that every sound classification will do the same.

When the next question emerges, how to arrange the Bible itself, we alight at once upon a few simple principles, which, with the necessary modifications, will prove applicable throughout. It is obvious that entire Bibles should precede parts of Bibles; that originals should precede translations; the more ancient originals the more recent; and Bibles in both the original tongues those in one only. We thus obtain the following arrangement at starting: Polyglots, Hebrew Bibles, Greek Bibles. It is equally apparent that Greek cannot be fitly succeeded by any tongue but Latin; that Latin is most naturally followed by its modern derivatives; that these draw after them the other European languages in due order; the Slavonic forming a link with the Oriental, which in their turn usher in the African, American, and Polynesian.

Concordances, consisting of the words of the Bible detached from their context, form a convenient link with Commentaries. The latter fall into two principal sections, according as they relate to Scripture in its entirety or to some particular part. In arranging the former, the erudite labours of scholars are, as far as possible, kept apart from the popular illustrative literature of modern days. The order of commentaries on separate books must, of course, correspond with that of the books themselves in the canon of the Bible. . . .

Divine Law is evidently most fitly succeeded by Human Law, or Jurisprudence. The fulness with which the preceding section has been treated will enable me to pass very cursorily over this and its successors. I may be pardoned, however, one remark suggested by the introduction of a new division—that in the classification of a library it should be considered whether the scope of the collection is special or general. In arranging a mere collection of Law Books it would be proper to commence with works treating of the general principles of Jurisprudence. In arranging a great library, regard must be had to the harmonious connexion of the parts, and accordingly the Museum arrangement commences with Ecclesiastical Law as the natural sequel of Theology. Bulls, Councils, Canon-Law and Modern Church-Law introduce the great section of Roman Law. Oriental Law follows, the Laws of the Continental Nations succeed in the order previously explained, and thus room is only found for General Jurisprudence at a comparatively late period, at the beginning of the numeral series 6000. It brings after it such minor subjects as Prison-Discipline and Forensic Medicine. The remaining space of the section is occupied by the Law of the English-speaking nations, which requires most minute sub-division.

Next to Divinity and Law, the third rank among the pursuits of the human mind was anciently assigned to Medicine. We have learned to recognise that Medicine, however practically important, ranks scientifically only as a department of Biology. The next section, accordingly, commences with general Natural History, continuing through the natural kingdoms of Botany, Geology and Zoology, including Veterinary Surgery, with their appropriate sub-divisions, and then embracing Medicine—first in its general aspect, as medical principle and practice; then in its great leading divisions of Physiology, Pathology, Therapeutics, etc.; again, as Special Pathology; finally, in such comparative minutiæ as professional controversies and bills of mortality. The divisions of Art—the next class—are simple and obvious. They may be enumerated as Archæology, Costumes, Numismatics, Architecture, Painting, Sculpture, first as treated collectively, and then as treated separately; and, finally, Music. Fine Art is succeeded by Useful Art, and the interval bridged over by Field-Sports, Games of Chance, and Games of Skill. No sub-division of the Useful Arts has been attempted beyond the separation of Cookery and Domestic Economy from the rest, and the addition of two special sections, one for the catalogues of industrial exhibitions, the other for the voluminous and important publications of the South Kensington Museum.

The extensive and miscellaneous division which succeeds may, perhaps, best be defined under the head of Philosophy, alike in its scientific principles and in its application to human life. Commencing with Political Philosophy, or the Science of Government, it runs rapidly through the politics of the various nations, in the geographical order previously detailed, passes into Political Economy, with the allied subjects of Finance, Commerce, and Social Science; thence into Education, and, by the minor morals so intimately allied with the latter subject, into Ethics, including works on the condition of Woman, Peace, Temperance and similar topics. Speculative Philosophy succeeds, introducing Mathematics, on which hangs the great department of Applied Mathematics, including all physical sciences except the biological. The various branches are carefully discriminated, and room is found among them for the so-called Occult Sciences, and for Military and Naval matters, the series appropriately concluding with Chemistry, or the science which aims at the resolution of all matters into its original elements. The remaining sections, though most important and extensive, are very simple in arrangement, and may be dismissed very briefly. They are: History; Geography, with Voyages and Topography; Biography; Poetry and the Drama; Belles Lettres, including Fiction; and Philology. The arrangement is invariably the same: collected works on each subject being placed first, and a geographical order being adopted for the rest when the conditions of the case allow. Genealogy is regarded as an appendix to History; Letters to Biography; Elocution with Literary Criticism and Bibliography, to Poetry and the Dramatic Art. The class of Belles Lettres is headed by Libraries and Cyclopædias. . . .

Such is, in its main features, the system of book-press arrangements which I have undertaken to describe. I have no fear but that it will be pronounced in essentials logical and philosophical. It has undoubtedly proved eminently convenient in practice. That it should be open to revision on some points is inevitable from the nature of things, and from two circumstances more especially—its gradual development as subject after subject was added to the library, and the degree in which it represents the idiosyncrasy of a single mind. Some minor oversights must be admitted. Geology, for example, should unquestionably have preceded Botany. I venture more extensive criticisms with hesitation, yet I cannot help remarking that I perceive no valid reason for the severance of so manifest a branch of History as Biography from the parent stem by the intrusion of the entire department of Geography; while it appears to me that the Useful Arts would have formed, through Domestic Economy, a more natural sequel to Medicine than Fine Art, and in arranging the latter department I should have assigned the last instead of the first place to Archæology and its allied subjects. Forensic Medicine might also have been conveniently placed at the *end* of Law, to connect that subject with Natural Science. I should further feel much inclined to form a class for Encyclopædias immediately after Philology; both because dictionaries of general knowledge seem legitimate successors to dictionaries of languages, and that the end of the classification might be answerable in dignity to the beginning. I am aware how much room for diversity of opinion may exist on these and similar points. On a more serious defect there can be no difference of opinion, but it is a defect inherent in all finite things. In an ideal classification by book-press one separate press, at least, would be provided for each subject, however minute. But an ideal library would also have room for each sub-division. We cannot have the ideal classification without the ideal library, and although I hazard nothing in saying that, thanks to the genius of the designer, Sir Anthony Panizzi, economy of space in the new buildings of the Museum has been carried to the utmost extent conceivable, space is still insufficient to provide a distinct niche for every well-marked division of a subject. Upwards of five hundred such sub-divisions are provided for; nevertheless this large number is not exhaustive. Without such an exhaustive distribution, the actual classification on the shelves, which is all I have undertaken to describe here, can never be conterminous with the ideal classification of the study.

From, Garnett, Richard. On the system of classifying books on the shelves followed at the British Museum. *Transactions and Proceedings of the Conference of Librarians held in London; October, 1877,* [etc.], 1878, pp. 108–114.

PLATE 5

SAMUEL BROWN

(1779 – 1839)

PLATE 6

HENRY BRADSHAW
(1831 – 1886)

(From the posthumous bust executed by Hamo Thornycroft, R.A., in 1888,
in Cambridge University Library, by kind permission of the Librarian)

# CHAPTER 20

# Charles Ammi Cutter (1837–1903)

"Cataloguing is an art, not a science. No rules can take the place of
experience and good judgement, but some of the results of experience
may be best indicated by rules."

C. A. CUTTER.

IT can truthfully be said of Charles Ammi Cutter that he was a born
librarian. Although originally intended for the ministry, but never
ordained, his intense love of books and his remarkable organizing
ability drew him during his early student days towards the career of
which he made such a success.

Cutter was born on March 14th, 1837, at Boston, and was educated
at Harvard. The Divinity School of the University acquired the library
of Professor Lücke in 1856, and Cutter and Charles Noyes catalogued
the collection, an early experience that profited Cutter in a subject
which he made particularly his own. In 1860 he became assistant to
Dr. Ezra Abbot, the head cataloguer, and the two compiled author and
classified catalogues on cards, probably the first public card catalogue
in America. At the same time Cutter was special assistant at Boston
Public Library, and became Librarian of the Boston Athenæum in 1869,
which position he held until 1893.

Cutter's *Rules for a dictionary catalog* first appeared in 1876 as Part II
of the United States report on *Public Libraries in the United States*, and
it has been said that the modern dictionary catalogue is a monument
to Charles Ammi Cutter. His *Rules* were the result of wide experience
gained chiefly during his preparation of the printed catalogue of the
Boston Athenæum published between 1874 and 1882 in five volumes.
Classification had also received his attention and in 1877 he had begun
the rearrangement of the Boston Athenæum by his Expansive Classification. The first six sections of this were published between 1891 and
1893,[1] but the seventh was left unfinished at his death. The scheme is
known as 'expansive' because the sections are intended for libraries of
successive sizes, and it is still of great interest. Cutter also compiled the
author tables, which with Miss Kate Sanborn he developed into the
Cutter-Sanborn Table.

In 1894 Cutter went to the Forbes Library, Northampton, Mass., a
new foundation, where he was given a free hand to create a library.

[1] First published in outline in *Library Journal*, 4, 1879, pp. 234–243.

He visited Europe collecting books, pictures and music, and succeeded in amassing a collection that was widely used by students, pupils and children, and loaned books to "anyone of good repute anywhere." Cutter accomplished valuable work for the American Library Association, especially for the Cataloguing Section, as a member of the Publication Committee, and as Chairman of the Co-operative Committee. He was President of the Association in 1888 and 1889, representing the Association at the International Conferences held in London in 1877 and 1897. Cutter was first President of the Massachusetts Library Club, and also of the Western Massachusetts Library Club, which he founded.

Most of Cutter's time appears to have been devoted to cataloguing, a subject in which he excelled on account of his thoroughness and accuracy, and it is for his work in connection with cataloguing and classification that his name will endure among librarians.

REFERENCE

Cutter, William Parker. *Charles Ammi Cutter*, Chicago, 1931. (American Library Pioneers, III.)

CUTTER'S PREFACE TO THE FOURTH EDITION OF HIS RULES
FOR A DICTIONARY CATALOG[1]

On seeing the great success of the Library of Congress cataloging, I doubted whether it was worth while to prepare and issue this fourth edition of my Rules; but I reflected that it would be a considerable time before all libraries would use the cards of that library, and a long time before the Library of Congress could furnish cards for all books, long enough for the libraries to absorb another edition and use it up in that part of their cataloging which they must do themselves. Still I cannot help thinking that the golden age of cataloging is over, and that the difficulties and discussions which have furnished an innocent pleasure to so many will interest them no more. Another lost art. But it will be all the better for the pockets of the public, or rather it will be better for other parts of the service—the children's room and the information desk, perhaps.

In the last two years a great change has come upon the status of cataloging in the United States. The Library of Congress has begun furnishing its printed catalog cards on such liberal terms that any new library would be very foolish not to make its catalog mainly of them, and the older libraries find them a valuable assistance in the cataloging of their accessions, not so much because they are cheaper as because in

[1] This edition also includes the preface to the first edition, 1876. [J.L.T.]

the case of most libraries they are better than the library is likely to make for itself.

The difference between these rules and those adopted by the Library of Congress are of two classes. The first class of differences is in the trifles of punctuation, capitalization, the place of certain items on the cards, and the like. If one already has a catalog with a large number of cards, and merely inserts in it as many of the Library of Congress cards as possible, I see no reason for altering one's own style, either on the past accumulations or on the new cards that one is to write. The two kinds of cards can stand together in the drawers and the public will never notice the difference. But if one is commencing a new catalog to be composed mainly of Library of Congress cards, I advise following the Library of Congress rules closely. It will save much trouble.

In the second class of differences those relating to place of entry of the card in the catalog, or of choice of heading, we must note that it is very easy to alter the entry of a Library of Congress card, as there is room enough above the heading on the printed card to write in the one preferred. A librarian who already has a large catalog will therefore find no difficulty in continuing his present heading and need change only if he thinks the Library of Congress practice better. Nevertheless, as it is some trouble to look for differences of practice, and there is always a chance of overlooking one and so getting different entries for similar books, it would be well to adopt the Library of Congress rules unless there is some decided reason against them. The librarian who is just commencing his catalog has still more reason for this course. In the matter of capitalization, on which the advisory committee give no advice, the course I recommend was decidedly favoured by the votes of the Catalog Section, at the meeting of the American Library Association at Magnolia in 1902. This course does not agree with the present practice at the Library of Congress.

The convenience of the public is always to be set before the ease of the cataloger. In most cases they coincide. A plain rule without exceptions is not only easy for us to carry out, but easy for the public to understand and work by. But strict consistency in a rule and uniformity in its application sometimes lead to practices which clash with the public's habitual way of looking at things. When these habits are general and deeply rooted, it is unwise for the cataloger to ignore them, even if they demand a sacrifice of system and simplicity.

The rules issued by the advisory committee of the American Library Association are according to the preface of the printed edition of these rules, expressly designed to be made for the use of a learned library. The old catalogs were not made for children, but the modern ones have to be, especially in a circulating library, for the children are the library's best clients. That the committee has always understood the public's views, estimated correctly its power of changing them, and drawn the line in the right place between a conservative regard for custom and a wish to lead the public towards a desirable simplicity and consistency is too much to assume, but I have at least always looked for the reasons on both sides.

The increase in the number of rules is due chiefly not to making new rules, but to taking out from the long notes many recommendations that were in effect rules, and are more easily referred to and found in their present place. The changes are largely for the sake of greater clearness and of better classification.

Cataloging is an art, not a science. No rules can take the place of experience and good judgement, but some of the results of experience may be best indicated by rules.

Preface to *U.S. Bureau of Education. Special Report on public libraries. Part II. Rules for a dictionary catalog. By C. A. Cutter. Fourth edition, rewritten*, Washington, 1904.

# CHAPTER 21

# Samuel Swett Green (1837–1918)

"He wrote . . . an excellent account of the public library movement in America."

DURING the latter half of the nineteenth century the United States of America could boast several prominent librarians who actively furthered the comparatively new public library movement. Justin Winsor, C. A. Cutter, Melvil Dewey, James L. Witney, Fred B. Perkins, together with Samuel Swett Green, all closely connected with the early years of the American Library Association, did much to encourage the development of librarianship in America, and their influence remains impressed on the annals of their profession.

Samuel Swett Green was born on February 20th, 1837, at Worcester, Mass., his family having been long associated with that locality. He was educated at Cambridge and Harvard, but suffered from poor health in his early life, and did not graduate until 1864. Six years later Harvard conferred its Mastership of Arts on him. Although he had studied for the Ministry, Green at the age of 27 became book-keeper in the Mechanics' National Bank of Worcester, shortly to become teller there, but in 1867 he was elected one of the twelve trustees of the Worcester Public Library, these having been provided by the will of his uncle, Dr. Green. After four years as trustee, Samuel Swett Green became Librarian of the Library, which had been founded in 1859 by the gift of 7,500 volumes from Dr. Green, and the offer of the Worcester Lyceum and Library Association to donate 4,350 volumes to begin a circulation department.

Green believed in personal contact between librarian and reader. He attended the annual conferences of the American Library Association, actively supported national and international librarianship, visiting Europe in 1877, 1902, 1903, 1904 and 1906. Green wrote numerous articles for the *Library Journal*, published several catalogues of his Library, and greatly extended co-operation between school and library.

In 1891 Samuel Swett Green was elected President of the American Library Association, and on April 1st of that year a new library building for the Worcester Public Library was opened. He introduced the Dewey Decimal Classification for the Reference and Green

Library, later organizing branch libraries, and in 1900 the Children's Department was opened. In 1872 Green had first opened the Library to the public on Sundays. He resigned in 1909 after thirty-eight years' service, and four years later published *The public library movement in the United States, 1853-1893. From 1876, reminiscences of the writer,* Boston, 1913, which is invaluable for reminiscences and anecdotes of personalities closely connected with librarianship. Selected passages from this book are printed below. Green died on December 8th, 1918, but his influence on librarianship and his work at Worcester will long be remembered not only in the United States but also abroad.

## REFERENCE

Shaw, Robert Kendall. *Samuel Swett Green*, Chicago, 1926. Two portraits; bibliography of his writings, pp. 83–86.

## GREEN ON THE PUBLIC LIBRARY MOVEMENT IN THE UNITED STATES, 1853–1893

The years 1880 and 1881 were memorable in the annals of the libraries of Great Britain as well as those of other countries because of the start then made in printing the great author catalogue of the British Museum. Work of this kind has long been urged in the interests of students and, owing to the existing and growing bulk of the manuscript catalogue, at that time filling more than 2,000 volumes, was earnestly called for to supply a much needed convenience, if not a practical necessity, in the administration of the library. The Museum began printing lists of its accessions, English and foreign, with the commencement of the year 1880. By the middle of the year 1881 the government had made an annual appropriation of sixteen hundred pounds with which to enable it to begin the publication of the great catalogue of books already bought and belonging to the printed books department. At that rate of expenditure it was calculated that four volumes could be issued yearly and that forty years would be required for printing the whole work. Circumstances favoured an earlier date of publication, the work was completed several years ago and a supplement has been begun.

It was in the years 1881 and 1882 that the introduction of the use of electric lighting in libraries came to be seriously considered. Richard Garnett of the British Museum is quoted in the *Library Journal* of June of the former year as saying: "Our electric light is a great success." This statement, of course, created great interest, especially in London, on account of the safety incident to the use of electricity and the absence of the heat which makes gas so disagreeable to men and so injurious to the binding of books.

An editorial in the number of the *Journal* for March, 1882, states emphatically that the time has come to consider carefully the desirability of the substitution of electricity for other means of lighting in libraries. In the *Journal* for June of the same year it is stated that the Bibliothèque Royale of Brussels is to be lighted by electricity.

[pp. 99–100]

.    .    .

In 1881, Mr. Carnegie began his great work of founding and aiding libraries by announcing in the spring of that year his purpose of establishing a free library at Braddock for the benefit of his workmen. That declaration was soon followed by his first gift for a library to the city of Pittsburgh, $250,000.

Early in 1882 Mr. Enoch Pratt, also, established and endowed a free circulating library for the people of Baltimore, putting up a fireproof building and inducing the city government to agree to pay $50,000 a year for support of the library and its branches in consideration of the gift to the municipality of a sum of money which at 6 per cent, would yield that amount. The whole of Mr. Pratt's gift was more than $1,000,000.

Mr. Poole, speaking for the editors of the *Index of Periodicals*, expressed the hope at the conference in 1881 at Washington, as stated before, that the work would be published in the early part of 1883. At the conference in Cincinnati, May 24, 1882, such progress had been made that he was able to say: "I have the pleasure of stating that the manuscript is finished; that the printing is begun; and that bound copies of the completed work will be in the hands of the collaborators and the public before the close of the present year."

The second volume of the index catalogue of the library of the Surgeon-General's office was issued in 1881.

The printed catalogue of the Boston Athenæum was finished in 1882.

[pp. 102–103]

.    .    .

The most important event in the library life of this country in 1883 was the announcement at the meeting of the American Library Association in Buffalo that the trustees of Columbia College had under consideration the question of the establishment in that institution of a school of library economy for giving instruction in practical bibliography and the use of books and for training by means of teachers, lecturers and practice work, persons desirous of fitting themselves to become assistants in libraries (including cataloguers), assistant librarians or even librarians, and to aid persons already working in libraries to obtain increased knowledge of the principles underlying the labors required in their occupation and to learn the best methods in vogue for making libraries as serviceable as possible.

The importance of the establishment of such a school had been brought to the attention of the trustees by Mr. Melvil Dewey who had recently been chosen librarian of the College, and by whom also a rough outline was presented to them of the general aims which should be kept in mind in the conduct of the proposed school.

After explaining the project to the members of the Association as well as could be done at its present early state, Mr. Dewey said that it seemed to him desirable that a committee should be appointed to present a resolution expressing the interest of the Association in the proposed experiment. A few librarians thought that the passage of such a resolution would be premature. More than one member expressed his confidence in the superiority of the training obtained by persons actually engaging in library work in good institutions. Some members thought that as there were doubts as to the subjects which could be taught by lectures, and uncertainty as to the procurement of suitable teachers and the demand for instruction by students, no action should be taken then but that the Association should await the development of the plan.

Still, the great body of members of the conference judged that however excellent present methods were of educating librarians, they did not meet the demand for library officers and that they might be improved; so they were very glad to learn that a distinguished institution like Columbia College was willing to give consideration to the new project. A committee was appointed "to consider what resolution, if any, could be presented for action." The next day it reported the resolution "that the Association desires to express its gratification that the trustees of Columbia College are considering the prioriety of giving instruction in library work, and hope that the experiment may be tried."

[pp. 108–109]

.        .        .

A remarkable interest was manifested in New York City early in 1886 in having measures adopted to increase its free library facilities. January 27, three acts were introduced into the Assembly of the New York legislative: one for the erection, payment and maintenance of a

building for a free public library in the City of New York, another
to establish and incorporate a body corporate and politic by the name
of the New York Public Library, and a third providing for the removal
of the reservoir on Fifth Avenue to furnish a site for a new building.
It was intended, it will be seen, by the persons engaged in the movement,
to place the library building on the same lot of land afterwards selected
for the occupancy of the present building of the New York Public
Library.

The passage of these acts was opposed by the friends of the then
existing New York Free Circulating Library, they contending that
the wiser course to pursue was to start the library movement by
establishing small libraries in different sections of the city. Persons
holding those views advocated the passage of "an act" to encourage
the growth of free public libraries and free circulating libraries in the
cities of the state of New York. Such an act passed the legislature and
was approved by the governor.

Later in the year, however, it was announced that the late Samuel
J. Tilden had made most liberal provision for the establishment of a
free library and reading-rooms in the City of New York and it was
believed that the legacy practically solved "the long-mooted question
of a free public library of adequate proportions for New York."
Protracted litigation followed, however, and, as is well known, only
a portion of the bequest was secured for public purposes.

That, however, joined with the funds of the Astor and Lenox
Libraries, which were united with the Tilden Trust, serves the giver's
purpose in helping to support the great New York Public Library for
which the City of New York has erected an immense building and
with which the New York Free Circulating Library has been joined,
its buildings having been supplemented and very largely increased
in numbers by numerous other branch library buildings put up with
money given by Mr. Carnegie.

[pp. 131–132]

.  .  .  .  .

In the latter portion of 1890 and 1891, several state library associations
were formed. As stated before, societies of this kind have now (1913)
become quite general. A tabulation of reports from existing
organizations made by Miss H. E. Green for the conference in October,
1891, showed that only nine state associations existed at the date of
that meeting. The establishment of the first, that of New York,
July 11, 1890, has already been noticed. This was followed by organizations in Iowa, New Hampshire, Massachusetts and New Jersey in
1890, and in Wisconsin, Connecticut and Maine early in 1891. An

association in Michigan was founded on September 1 of the latter year. September 26, a meeting was held at Topeka to consider the question of the formation of a society for the State of Kansas.

In Massachusetts, circulars were sent out October 22, 1890, to 480 libraries of 1,000 volumes or more. The organization was effected November 13.

[p. 216]

.    .    .    .

Early in 1892, earnest criticism was publicly made of the "excessive cost and questionable plans" of the building for the Public Library going up in Copley Square, Boston, and of the failure for a long period of the trustees of the library to appoint a librarian and the incompetence shown in the administration of the library. Specific statements of shortcomings were made in a series of carefully prepared letters from Charles C. Soule, published in the Boston *Herald*.

The building was generally recognized as sure to be architecturally very beautiful both without and within. The criticism of the plans had to do with the adaptability of the building for the practical uses for which it was being erected.

The Boston Public Library was the leader in the accelerated library movement which began in 1876, but had lost its position of leadership. . .

The Public Library did not regain prominence among the libraries of the country until Mr. Herbert Putnam was chosen librarian early in 1895. Mr. Putman was appointed executive head of the institution February 5 of that year, and on March 15 the new building was opened for the delivery of books and carrying on the regular business routine of the library. Extensive and costly changes were soon made in the arrangement of the interior of the building to adapt it so far as might be to the convenience and efficiency of administration of the affairs of the library and Mr. Putnam began at once with good sense and fine executive ability to make changes in methods and introduce new kinds of work which had been found advantageous in the best managed libraries; in fact bringing administration up to date and carrying if forward so successfully as to bring the institution again into deserved prominence and make it worthy of study by persons interested in library advancement.

[pp. 252–253]

From, Green, Samuel Swett. *The public library movement in the United States, 1853–1893. From 1876, reminiscences of the writer*, Boston. Boston Book Co., 1913.

CHAPTER 22

# John Shaw Billings (1838–1913)

"There are a great number of men in all professions, and in all parts of the world, of whom it may be said, that if they knew more, they would say less."

J. S. BILLINGS.

PROBABLY the most eminent medical librarian of all times was John Shaw Billings, yet he was distinguished for so many other things that it is sometimes forgotten that his greatest achievement was the virtual creation of the Library of the Surgeon-General's Office at Washington, now the National Library of Medicine, Bethesda, Maryland. This rôle has been emphasized by the publication by the Medical Library Association of a volume to celebrate the one hundreth anniversary of Billings' appointment to the Surgeon-General Office Library. Entitled *Selected papers of John Shaw Billings. Compiled with a life of Billings, by Frank Bradway Rogers,* 1965 this contains interesting biographical material, a bibliography of his writings, and a selection of his more significant papers.

John Shaw Billings was born April 12, 1838, at Cotton township, Switzerland County, Indiana, graduating from Miami University in 1857. Three years later he took a medical degree at the Medical College of Ohio, and at the outbreak of the Civil War became an assistant surgeon in the United States Army. After a brilliant career in that capacity, on December 31st, 1864, Billings was assigned to the Surgeon-General's Office at Washington, where he remained for thirty-one years. He took charge of the 2,253 books forming the Library there, which in 1868 had grown to 6,066 volumes. Three years later an author and subject catalogue of 13,000 volumes was prepared, followed by another of 25,000 volumes and 15,000 pamphlets in 1873.

Billings planned, accumulated, catalogued and arranged, until he had acquired the nucleus of the largest medical library in the world, now known as the National Library of Medicine. He planned and organized the monumental dictionary catalogue of the collection, issuing a specimen *fasciculus* in 1876 before the first series of the *Index-Catalogue* began publication in 1880. The first series of sixteen volumes was completed in 1895, and since that date it has continued publication as a model catalogue, and an invaluable tool for medical bibliographers.

With Dr. Robert Fletcher, Billings inaugurated the *Index Medicus* in 1879 as a monthly bibliography of current medical literature. In 1927 this was merged with the *Quarterly Cumulative Index* to become the *Quarterly Cumulative Index Medicus*.

In 1881 Billings addressed the International Medical Congress in London on "Our Medical Literature". Among the many honours conferred upon him were the degrees of LL.D. at Edinburgh (1884), D.C.L. at Oxford (1889), and M.D. at Dublin (1892).

In 1895 Billings retired from the Surgeon-General's Office Library to accept the Chair of Hygiene and Bacteriology at the University of Pennsylvania, but in 1896 he became Director of the New York Public Library. He succeeded in welding together the existing facilities into one organized body for the supply of books to the public. He planned branch libraries, secured financial support for the upkeep of the system and left it expanding into the efficient public library system that it is today.

Billings was President at the American Library Association in 1902, and died on March 11th, 1913. He was an expert in sanitation, hygiene, hospital planning and vital statistics, but his greatest memorial is the National Library of Medicine and its Catalogue.

## REFERENCES

Billings, John Shaw. *An autobiographical fragment, 1905. A facsimile copy of the original manuscript*, Bethesda, Md., 1965.

Garrison, Fielding H. Billings: a maker of American medicine. In, *Lectures on the history of medicine; a series of lectures at the Mayo Foundation*, [etc.], (1933), pp. 187–200.

Garrison, Fielding H. *John Shaw Billings: a memoir*, [etc.], New York, London, 1915. Portraits and other illustrations; genealogy and bibliography of 171 items.

Lydenberg, Harry Miller. *John Shaw Billings, creator of the National Medical Library, and its catalogue; first Director of the New York Public Library*, Chicago, 1924. (American Library Pioneers, 1.) Portrait and list of his books; the portrait is reproduced as Plate 7 by kind permission of the American Library Association.

Rogers, Frank Bradway. John Shaw Billings: 1838–1913. *Library Journal*, 88, 1963, pp. 2622–2624.

*Selected papers of John Shaw Billings. Compiled with a life of Billings*, by Frank Bradway Rogers, Medical Library Association, 1965. Life of John Shaw Billings, pp. 1–13; Bibliography of the writings of John Shaw Billings, pp. 285–300; Portrait of Billings, frontispiece.

## BILLINGS ON THE ORIGIN OF THE INDEX CATALOGUE

This has happened in this wise: In the thesis just referred to[1] it was desirable to give statistics of the results obtained from certain surgical operations as applied to the treatment of epilepsy. To find these data in their original and authentic form required the consulting of many books, and to get at these books I not only ransacked all the

[1] His graduation dissertation. (J.L.T.)

libraries, public and private, to which I could get access in Cincinnati, but for those volumes not found here (and these were the greater portion), search was made in Philadelphia, New York and elsewhere, to ascertain if they were in any accessible libraries in this country.

After about six months of this sort of work and correspondence, I became convinced of three things. The first was, that it involves a vast amount of time and labour to search through a thousand volumes of medical books and journals for items on a particular subject, and that the indexes of such books and journals cannot always be relied on as a guide to their contents. The second was, that there are, in existence somewhere over 100,000 volumes of such medical books and journals, not counting pamphlets and reprints. And the third was, that while there was nowhere, in the world, a library which contained all medical literature, there was not in the United States any fairly good library, one in which a student might hope to find a large part of the literature relating to any medical subject, and that if one wished to do good bibliographical work to verify the references given by European medical writers, or to make reasonably sure that one had before him all that had been seen or done by previous observers or experimenters on a given subject, he must go to Europe and visit not merely one but several of the great capital cities in order to accomplish his desire.

It was this experience which led me when a favourable opportunity offered at the close of the war to try to establish, for the use of American physicians, a fairly complete medical library, and in connection with this to prepare a comprehensive catalogue and index which should spare medical teachers and writers the drudgery of consulting ten thousand or more different indexes, or of turning over the leaves of as many volumes to find the dozen or so references of which they might be in search.

*Cincinnati Lancet Clinic*, N.S.20, 1888, p. 297. Extract from, Garrison, Fielding H. *John Shaw Billings; a memoir,* [etc.], 1915, pp. 15–16.

## BILLINGS ON MEDICAL LIBRARIES IN THE UNITED STATES

Comparatively few persons have any idea of the amount of medical literature in existence, or of its proper use and true value, and the result is that the same ground is traversed over and over again. Cases are reported as unique and inexplicable which, when compared with accounts of others buried in obscure periodicals or collections of observations, fall into their proper place and both receive and give explanation. Old theories and hypotheses, evolved from the depths of the inner consciousness of men too zealous or too indolent to undergo the labour of examining the works of their predecessors, reappear, and are re-exploded with the regular periodicity of organic life; and even when literary research is attempted, it is often either for controversial purposes, to serve the ends of prejudiced criticism, or to support a charge of plagiarism, or else for the purpose of obtaining a goodly array of footnotes, which shall imply that the subject is exhausted, and give flavour of erudition to the work. This state of things is by no means peculiar to medicine, but its literature is certainly an excellent illustration of the maxim "The thing which has been is that which shall be, and there is no new thing under the sun."

The record of the researches, experiences and speculations relating to medical science during the last four hundred years is contained in between two and three hundred thousand volumes and pamphlets; and while the immense majority of these have little or nothing of what we call "practical value", yet there is no one of them which would not be called for by some inquirer if he knew of its existence.

Hence, it is desirable, in this branch of literature, as in others, that in each country there should be at least one collection embracing everything that is too costly, too ephemeral, or of too little interest to be obtained and preserved in private libraries.

When the great work of Mr. Caxton, the History of Human Error, is written, the medical section will be among the most instructive and important, and also that for which it will be most difficult to obtain the data.

There is a number of valuable private medical libraries in this country of from four to ten thousand volumes each. Having been collected for the most part with reference to some special subject or department, they are the more valuable on that account. The majority of the medical schools also have libraries of greater or less value to the student.

The collections relating to medicine and the cognate sciences, which are available to the public and are of sufficient interest to require notice in this connection, are those of Boston, Philadelphia, New York, Cincinnati, and Washington. No one of these indeed approaches completeness, but each supplements the other to such an extent that it seldom happens that bibliographical inquiries cannot be answered by referring to them in succession.

[pp. 171–172]

.    .    .    .

The important part of a medical library, that which will give it character and value and for deficiency in which nothing can compensate, is its file of medical journals and translations. The difficulty of obtaining and preserving these is in proportion to the importance of the matter. The majority of them are essentially ephemeral in character; small editions are published; they are rarely preserved with care, and even when attempts are made to preserve them by binding, it is often, and indeed usually, without sufficient attention to the collation, so that in examining files of old journals it will be found that at least one-half lack a leaf, a signature, or a number. This fact causes much trouble and disappointment to the librarian, and must always be kept in view in the collection of this class of literature. In the attempt to make a complete collection of American medical journals for the library, it has been repeatedly found that what purported to be the volume or number wanting to complete a file was defective. It is probable that there is not a complete collection in existence at any one point, although there are two public and at least three private collections in this country which are very full, those of the library of the Surgeon-General's Office; of the College of Physicians of Philadelphia; of Dr. Toner, of Washington; of Dr. Hays, of Philadelphia and of Dr. Purple, of New York.

The rarest American medical journals are probably some of those printed in the West and South; for instance, the Ohio Medical Repository (1826–'27) and the Confederate States Medical and Surgical Journal (1864–'65).

Another class of medical literature which is important to the librarian, and the value of which is usually underestimated, consists of medical theses and inaugural dissertations. To obtain complete series of these is even more difficult than to get journals, for the reason that they are more ephemeral, and because it is scarcely possible to ascertain what have been published, or when the series may be considered complete. For a few schools, lists have been published of theses presented by their graduates, such as Paris and Edinburgh, but even for Edinburgh, the only catalogue of the theses which the writer has been able to obtain, does not show when the regular printing of all theses ceased. Callisen has been led into error in this way in his otherwise very complete Bibliographical Lexicon, in which he gives the titles of many theses which were never printed, notably of the Universities of Pennsylvania and Transylvania. The value of these is fourfold. As material for the history of medicine they may be taken to represent the theories and teaching of the school; they often contain reports of cases, or accounts of investigations made by the student under the direction of a professor, which are of much value, and they are necessary to medical biography, the more so as in most of the German universities a sketch of the life of the candidate is appended to the thesis. In addition to this, prior to the era of medical journalism, it was the custom for the president or one of the professors to add an introduction of ten or twelve pages to the dissertation, treating on some subject usually having no direct relation to the thesis, and forming the sort of paper which would now be sent to a medical journal. The number of these theses in existence is very great; there are in the Library of the Surgeon-General's Office about 40,000.

[pp. 178–179]

From, Billings, J. S. Medical libraries in the United States. *U.S. Department of the Interior, Bureau of Education; Public Libraries in the United States of America; their history, condition, and management. Special report*, Washington, 1876, Chapter VI, pp. 171–182.

PLATE 7

JOHN SHAW BILLINGS

(1838 – 1913)

(By kind permission of the American Library Association)

PLATE 8

HENRY RICHARD TEDDER
(1850 – 1924)

C

B

EDWARD WILLIAMS BYRON
NICHOLSON
(1849 – 1912)

A

JOHN WINTER JONES
(1805 – 1881)

# Chapter 23

# Henry Benjamin Wheatley (1838 - 1917)

"The good cataloguer will try to put himself into the place of the intelligent consulter – that is, the person who brings ordinary intelligence to bear upon the catalogue, but has not, necessarily, any technical knowledge."

H. B. Wheatley.

Henry Benjamin Wheatley was born on May 2nd, 1838 as the posthumous son of Benjamin Wheatley, a book auctioneer of Piccadilly. He was brought up by a half-sister and his half-brother, Benjamin Robert Wheatley, who became Secretary of the Royal Medico-Chirurgical Society. Henry was privately educated, and became Clerk to the Royal Society (1861–1869) also acting as librarian, and Assistant Secretary to the Royal Society of Arts (1879–1908). The brothers Henry and Benjamin catalogued the Athenaeum Library, and Henry catalogued the collection at the Oxford and Cambridge Club. Among numerous other appointments he was President of the Sette of Odde Volumes (1909) and of the Bibliographical Society from 1911 to 1916.

His publications include an excellent edition of Pepys' *Diary*, and of Evelyn's *Diary*, Pepys in particular being his special study, for he was President of the Samuel Pepys Club from 1903–1916. He was also keenly interested in Shakespeare, and was Chairman of the Council of the Shakespeare Association from 1914 to 1916. He founded the Index Society, the London Topographical Society and the Samuel Pepys Club (1903). He was preparing a life of Pepys at the time of his death, and the material eventually passed to Arthur Bryant. H. B. Wheatley was Honorary Secretary and Treasurer of the Early English Text Society, editor of *The Bibliographer*, and was associated with several other literary organizations. Numerous writings on various topics came from his pen, and these are recorded by L. M. Harrod (see References). Wheatley contributed several volumes to the *Handbooks of Practical Art* series, and edited the attractive little *Book-Lover's Library*, contributing several volumes, all of which remain of great interest to-day. His chief contributions to the literature of librarianship include *What is an index?*, 1878 with a second edition in 1879; *How to form a library*, 1886; *How to catalogue a library*, 1889; *How to make an index*, 1902; *Remarkable bindings in the British Museum*,

1889, and *Prices of books*, 1898. The University of Durham awarded him an honorary D.C.L. Wheatley died on April 30th, 1917, but his interesting books remain to remind us of a remarkable character who contributed usefully to the literature of librarianship, and who has come to be regarded as a pioneer of modern indexing. The Library Association awards annually the Wheatley Medal for an outstanding index published during the previous year, the initiation of which has led to an increased interest in adequate indexes. (Portrait, Plate 9.)

## REFERENCES

Green, Evelyn K. [Grand-daughter of H.B.W.]. Henry Benjamin Wheatley, D.C.L., F.S.A. (Born May 2nd, 1838, died April 30th, 1917). *The Indexer*, 4, 1964–1965, pp. 115–116.

Harrod, L. M. Bibliography of works by H. B. Wheatley. *The Indexer*, 4, 1964–1965, pp. 116–117; 5, 1965–1966, pp. 35–37.

Henry Benjamin Wheatley, D.C.L., F.S.A. *Occasional Papers Published for the Members of the Samuel Pepys Club*, 2, 1917–23, 1925, pp. 207–210.

## WHEATLEY ON HOW TO FORM A LIBRARY

It is greatly to the credit of the rich and busy man to spend his time and riches in the collection of a fine library, but still greater honour is due to the poor man who does not allow himself to be pulled down by his sordid surroundings. The once famous small-coalman, Thomas Britton, furnishes a most remarkable instance of true greatness in a humble station, and one, moreover, which was fully recognized in his own day. He lived next door to St. John's Gate, Clerkenwell, and although he gained his living by selling coals from door to door, many persons of the highest station were in the habit of attending the musical meetings held at his house. He was an excellent chemist as well as a good musician, and Thomas Hearne tells us that he left behind him "a valuable collection of musick mostly pricked by himself, which was sold upon his death for near an hundred pounds," "a considerable collection of musical instruments which was sold for fourscore pounds," "not to mention the excellent collection of printed books that he also left behind him, both of chemistry and musick. Besides these books that he left, he had some years before his death (1714) sold by auction a noble collection of books, most of them in the Rosicrucian faculty (of which he was a great admirer), whereof there is a printed catalogue extant, as there is of those that were sold after his death, which catalogue I have by me (by the gift of my very good friend Mr. Bagford), and have often looked over with no small surprize and wonder, and particularly for the great number of MSS. in the before-mentioned faculties that are specified in it."[1]

Dr. Johnson, although a great reader, was not a collector of books. He was forced to possess many volumes while he was compiling his Dictionary, but when that great labour was completed, he no longer felt the want of them. Goldsmith, on the other hand, died possessed of a considerable number of books which he required, or had at some time required, for his studies.

[pp. 38–40]

.     .     .     .

Gibbon was a true collector, who loved his books, and he must have needed them greatly, working as he did at Lausanne away from public libraries. After his death the library was purchased by "Vathek" Beckford, but he kept it buried, and it was of no use to any one. Eventually it was sold by auction, a portion being bought for the Canton, and another portion going to America.[2] There was little in the man Gibbon to be enthusiastic about, but it is impossible for any true book lover not to delight in the thoroughness of the author of one of the noblest books ever written. The fine old house where the *Decline and Fall* was written and the noble library was stored still stands, and the traveller may stroll in the garden so beautifully described by Gibbon when he walked to the historical *berceau* and felt that his herculean labour was completed. His heart must be preternaturally dull which does not beat quicker as he walks on that ground. The thought of a visit some years ago forms one of the most vivid of the author's pleasures of memory.

[pp. 41–42]

.     .     .

Libraries may broadly be divided into Public and Private, and as private libraries will vary according to the special idiosyncrasies of their owners, so still more will public libraries vary in character according to the public they are intended for. The answer therefore to the question—How to form a Public Library?—must depend upon the character of the library which it is proposed to form. Up to the period when free town libraries were first formed, collections of books were usually intended for students; but when the Public Libraries' Acts were passed, a great change took place, and libraries being formed for general readers, and largely with the object of fostering

---

[1] *Reliquiæ Hearnianæ*, by Bliss, 2nd edition, 1869, vol. ii, p. 14.
[2] For fuller details of Gibbon's library see *The library of Edward Gibbon; a catalogue of his books. With an introduction by Geoffrey Keynes*, 1940. [J.L.T.]

the habit of reading, an entirely new idea of libraries came into existence. The old idea of a library was that of a place where books that were wanted could be found, but the new idea is that of an educational establishment, where persons who know little or nothing of books can go to learn what to read. The new idea has naturally caused a number of points to de discussed which were never thought of before.

But even in Town Libraries there will be great differences. Thus in such places as Birmingham, Liverpool, and Manchester, the Free Libraries should be smaller British Museums, and in this spirit their founders have worked; but in smaller and less important towns a more modest object has to be kept in view, and the wants of readers, more than those of consulters of books, have to be considered.

[pp. 73–74]

. . . . .

The idea of a Child's Library is to a great extent modern, and it is not altogether clear that it is a good one, except in the case of those children who have no books of their own. It is far better that each child should have his own good books, which he can read over and over again, thus thoroughly mastering their contents.

It is a rather wide-spread notion that there is some sort of virtue in reading for reading's sake, although really a reading boy may be an idle boy. When a book is read, it should be well thought over before another is begun, for reading without thought generates no ideas.

One advantage of a Child's Library should be that the reader is necessarily forced to be careful, so as to return the books uninjured. This is a very important point, for children should be taught from their earliest years to treat books well, and not to destroy them as they often do. We might go farther than this and say that children should be taught at school how to handle a book. It is really astonishing to see how few persons (not necessarily children) among those who have not grown up among books know how to handle them. It is positive torture to a man who loves books to see the way they are ordinarily treated. Of course it is not necessary to mention the crimes of wetting the fingers to turn over the leaves, or turning down pages to mark the place; but those who ought to know better will turn a book over on its face at the place where they have left off reading, or will turn over pages so carelessly that they give a crease to each which will never come out.

For a healthy education it is probably best that a child should have the run of a library for adults (always provided that dangerous books are carefully excluded). A boy is much more likely to enjoy and find benefit from the books he selects himself than from those selected for him.

The circumstances of the child should be considered in the selection of books; thus it is scarcely fair when children are working hard at school all day that they should be made to read so-called instructive books in the evening. They have earned the right to relaxation and should be allowed good novels. To some boys books of Travels and History are more acceptable than novels, but all children require some Fiction, and save in a few exceptional cases, their imaginations require to be cultivated.

[pp. 217–219]

From, *How to form a library.* By H. B. Wheatley. *Third edition,* 1887. (The Book-Lover's Library.)

. . . . .

## WHEATLEY ON HOW TO CATALOGUE A LIBRARY

It was formerly very much the fashion for those who knew little of the subject to speak as if nothing was easier than to make a catalogue. All you had to do was to have a sheet of paper and the book to be catalogued before you, and then transfer the title to the paper. No previous knowledge was necessary. But those who were better acquainted with the difficulties that beset even the cataloguer, realized that Sheridan's joke about "easy writing being damned hard reading" was applicable to the work produced under these circumstances. Since the discussion on the British Museum Catalogue, and the consequent attention to the first principles of bibliography, these ignorant views are not so generally held, but still many erroneous opinions are abroad. One of these is that the clerical portion of the work of cataloguing or indexing is derogatory to a superior person, and therefore that he should have an inferior person to help him. The superior person dictates, and the inferior person copies down; and the result in practice is that endless blunders are produced, which might have been saved if one person had done the work.

Another vulgar error is that cataloguers form a guild, with secrets which they wish to keep from the public. This is a grievous mistake. The main object of the good cataloguer should be to make the consultation of his work easy. He knows the difficulties, and knows that rules must be made to overcome these difficulties; but he does not care to multiply these rules more than is absolutely necessary. The good cataloguer will try to put himself into the place of the intelligent consulter—-that is, the person who brings ordinary intelligence to bear

Some persons seem to think that everything is to be brought down to the comprehension of the fool; but if by doing this we make it more difficult for the intelligent person, the action is surely not politic. The consulter of a catalogue might at least take the trouble to understand the plan upon which it is compiled before using it.

[pp. 2-4]

.           .           .           .

The uses of a catalogue are something quite different. This is in the same house as the books it describes, and is merely a help to the finding of those books. It would be absurd to copy out long titles in a catalogue and be at the cost of printing them when the title itself in the book can be in our hands in a couple of minutes. Sufficient information only is required to help us to find the right book and the right edition. How far this should be given will be discussed in a later chapter. It is necessary for us, however, to remember that when the catalogue is printed and away from the library it becomes to some extent a bibliography, and therefore when a library contains rare or unique books it is usual, for love of the cause, to describe these fully, as if the catalogue was a bibliography. This is the more necessary because we are so deficient in good bibliographies. The ideal state, from which we are still far off, would be a complete and full bibliography of all literature, and then cataloguers could be less full in their descriptions, and reference might be made to the bibliography for further particulars. It is a standing disgrace to this country that we have no complete bibliography of English authors, much less of English literature generally.

[pp. 5-6]

From, Wheatley, Henry B. *How to catalogue a library*, 1889. (The Book-Lover's Library.)

## WHEATLEY ON INDEXING

What, then, are the chief characteristics that are required to form a good indexer? I think they may be stated under five headings:

1. Common sense.
2. Insight into the meaning of the author.
3. Power of analysis.
4. Common feeling with the consulter and insight into his mind, so that the indexer may put the references he has drawn from the book under headings where they are most likely to be sought.
5. General knowledge, with the power of overcoming difficulties.

The ignorant man cannot make a good index. The indexer will

find that his miscellaneous knowledge is sure to come in useful, and that which he might doubt would ever be used by him will be found to be helpful when least expected. It may seem absurd to make out that the good indexer should be a sort of Admirable Crichton. There can be no doubt, however, that he requires a certain amount of knowledge; and the good cataloguer and indexer, without knowing everything, will be found to possess a keen sense of knowledge.

[pp. 115–116]

.     .     .     .

Scientific books are the most difficult to index; but here there is a difference between the science of fact and the science of thought, the latter being the most difficult to deal with. The indexing of books of logic and ethics will call forth all the powers if the indexer and show his capabilities; but what we call the science of fact contains opinions as well as facts, and some branches of political economy are subjects by no means easy to index.

Some authors indicate their line of reasoning by the compilation of headings. This is a great help to the indexer; but if the author does not present such headings, the indexer has to make them himself, and he therefore needs the abilities of the *précis*-writer.

There are indexes of Books, of Transactions, Periodicals, etc., and indexes of Catalogues. Each of these classes demands a different method. A book must be thoroughly indexed; but the index of Journals and Transactions may be confined to the titles of the papers and articles. It is, however, better to index the contents of the essays as well as their titles.

Before the indexer commences his work he must consider whether his index is to be full or short. Sometimes it is not necessary to adopt the full index – frequently it is too expensive a luxury for publisher or author; but the short index can be done well if necessary.

Whatever plan is followed, the indexer must use his judgment. This ought to be the marked characteristic of the good indexer. The bad indexer is entirely without this great gift.

While trying to be complete, the indexer must reject the trivial; and this is not always easy. He must not follow in the steps of the lady who confessed that she only indexed those points which specially interested her.

[pp. 120–122]

.     .     .     .

Before commencing his work, the indexer must think out the plan and the kind of index he is to produce; he will consider how he is to draw out the references.

Whatever system is adopted, it is well to bear in mind that the indexer should obtain some knowledge of the book he is about to index before he sets to work. . . .

During his work the indexer must constantly ask himself what it is for which the consulter is likely to seek. The author frequently uses periphrases to escape from the repetition of the same fact in the same form, but these periphrases will give little information when inserted as headings in an index; and it is in this point of selecting the best catchword that the good indexer will show his superiority over the commonplace worker.

This paramount characteristic of the good indexer is by no means an easy one to acquire. When the indexer is absorbed in the work upon which he is working, he takes for granted much with which the consulter coming fresh to the subject is not familiar. The want of this characteristic is most marked in the case of the bad indexer.

[pp. 177–179]

From, Wheatley, Henry B. *How to make an index*, 1902. (The Book-Lover's Library.)

# CHAPTER 24

# Francis Thornton Barrett (1838–1919)

"In Scotland, Barrett was a leader: he made a library national before the nation had one. . . . In the Association he offered candid criticism with such gentleness and courtesy that the faulty enjoyed having their faults pointed out."

E. A. SAVAGE.

FRANCIS THORNTON BARRETT was born at Liverpool in 1838 and was engaged in the bookselling and printing trades before 1866, when at the age of twenty-eight he joined the staff of Birmingham Public Libraries. He was sub-librarian of the Reference Library when in January, 1877 he was appointed first librarian of the Mitchell Library, Glasgow. This was founded by Stephen Mitchell, and was opened on November 1st, 1877, by which date Barrett had collected about 15,000 volumes. By 1889 these had increased to 89,000. Larger premises were acquired, and opened on October 7th, 1891. Once more the collection outgrew its premises, and the new Mitchell Library in North Street was opened in 1911. But in 1899 Glasgow established a public library under a special Act, and Barrett became its first City Librarian.

Barrett was an original member of the Library Association, serving as President in 1907. He was a member of several societies, and as a promoter of the Scottish Library Association became its first President, serving the Glasgow Bibliographical Society in a similar capacity. In 1913 Glasgow conferred the honorary degree of LL.D. on Barrett for his public services, and the following year, at the age of seventy-five, he retired from librarianship, having numbered among other distinguished men on his staff Thomas Mason and James Duff Brown. He devoted his life mainly to library service in Glasgow, but fostered the progress of libraries in general. Many articles from his pen appeared in periodical literature, and he contributed to the proceedings of the Library Association conferences, as evidenced by the *Transactions*.

Francis T. Barrett died in January 21st, 1919, having earned the regard of the City he had served for so many years, and the respect of his fellow librarians, one of whom described Barrett in an obituary as a "quiet, courteous, and kindly gentleman whose gracious manner and simple dignity won for him a revered place in the hearts of all". There is a medallion plaque of him in the Mitchell Library.

REFERENCES

Obituary; signed S. A. P[itt]. *Library Association Record*, 21, 1919, pp. 70–71; portrait, p. 41.

Personalities of the Past. 1. Dr. Francis T. Barrett. *Librarian & Book World*, 30, 1940–1941, p. 89.

## BARRETT ON THE MITCHELL LIBRARY, GLASGOW

The Mitchell Library had its origin in a trust disposition and settlement by the late Stephen Mitchell, tobacco manufacturer, formerly of Linlithgow, but for many years in St. Andrew's Square, Glasgow, where the firm still carries on business. By this deed, which bears date 5th January, 1866, with codicil dated 4th May, 1870, Mr. Mitchell bequeathed the residue of his estate to the city of Glasgow, to "form the nucleus of a fund for the establishment and endowment of a large public library in Glasgow, with all the modern accessories connected therewith", and he provided that the residue "should be allowed to accumulate until, by its own natural increase, or by contributions from others, the fund should amount to £70,000, or even a larger sum should that be considered necessary by the Lord Provost, Magistrates, and Councillors for the time being, before the formation of the library is begun." ...

Mr. Mitchell, who had for some time been resident at Moffat, died on 21st April, 1874. His agents intimated the bequest, with its probable amount, to the Town Council on 6th May, and the Council on 16th July accepted the trust.

[pp. 101–102]

.    .    .    .    .

The net sum paid over to the Town Council by the founder's representatives was £66,998 10s. 6d. In accordance with the directions of the will this remained at interest until 1876, when it had increased to £70,000. Before proceeding to the history of the library —up to this point we have been dealing only with the fund—the few changes in the committee which took place between 1874 and the opening of the library in 1877 may be noted. In November, 1875, Bailie Morrison and Councillor James Moir joined the committee, and Councillor Mackenzie left it. Dean of Guild Playfair was succeeded by Dean of Guild James King, and Deacon-Convenor Smith by Deacon-Convenor Archibald Gilchrist. In November, 1876, Councillor William Brown took the place of Bailie Morrison. In 1876, the sum named by Mr. Mitchell having been reached, the Council determined on putting the testator's intentions into operation, and as a first step,

Dr. Marwich, the Town Clerk, was desired to draw up a report on the subject.

[p. 104]

.    .    .    .    .

As there was no suitable public building available, The Town Council resolved to commence in temporary premises. A very liberal offer was received from Councillor (now Bailie) Neil to give for the purposes of the library the free use for five years of the second floor of a large building recently erected by him in Ingram Street for business purposes. The Council cordially accepted this offer. It was soon found that the space would be insufficient, and an arrangement was made with Mr. Neil to take for a similar period the floor below in addition, at a rent fixed by the official assessor. These two floors, each about 100 feet by 40, form the premises in which the library has up to the present time remained. The period of five years first arranged for expired 31st May, 1882; but Bailie Neil very generously intimated that he does not wish to alter the terms of occupancy for the present; and the library thus continues to enjoy the free use of the upper floor.

The question of premises thus temporarily settled, the next step was the appointment of a librarian. Advertisements were issued towards the end of 1876, and a large number of offers of service were received. After a patient examination of the credentials of the applicants, and visits to a number of them in their respective libraries, in different towns, by a sub-committee, the committee recommended the appointment of Mr. Francis Thornton Barrett, and the recommendation was approved by the Town Council in February, 1877. Mr Barrett's claim on the consideration of the Committee consisted of his ten years' service as sub-librarian in the Free Libraries of Birmingham, which, it is well known, are among the most successful in the kingdom. In addition to testimonials from the Committee at Birmingham, and from Mr. J. D. Mullins, the chief librarian, he had recommendations from the late Mr. George Dawson, Rev. R. W. Dale, D.D., the Right Hon. Joseph Chamberlain, and others. Later in the year Mr. John Ingram, librarian of the Select Subscription Library at Edinburgh, was appointed sub-librarian, and Mr. Thomas Mason, who had had some previous experience in library work, was appointed senior assistant. Mr. Ingram still remains on the staff; but Mr. Mason left in 1881 to take the post of librarian to Stirling's and Glasgow Public Library, his place being filled by the promotion of Messrs. J. D. Brown and Robert Adams, who had been engaged as assistants for some years.

On the appointment of the librarian the work was proceeded with.

The books already acquired were registered and catalogued, and the principles of selection for further purchases were defined with greater fulness. The views quoted by Dr. Marwich in the preceding report, from Lord Provost Blackie's report in 1864, were strongly approved, and particularly the great importance of catholicity and comprehensiveness was recognized. The following rules, which had been observed in the formation of the great Reference Library at Birmingham, and which, as will be seen, are quite consistent with the previous decisions for the Mitchell Library, were noted with approval:

I.   That the library should, as far as practicable, represent every phase of human thought and every variety of human opinion.

II.   That books of permanent value and of standard interest should form the principal portion of the library, and that modern books of value and importance should be added from time to time, as they are published.

III.   That it should contain those rare and costly works which are generally out of the reach of individual students, and which are not usually found in provincial or private libraries.

It was remarked that in such a city as Glasgow, with so great a population, with such variety of circumstances and interests, with students of every branch of knowledge, with professors of every shade of opinion in politics, in philosophy, and in religion, the demands upon the library would be of the most various kinds, and that if it was to fulfil its founder's intentions, these demands should as far as possible be met. It was decided also that special attention should be given to securing books on Scottish subjects, and particularly those relating to the city.

With these objects in view, lists of representative standard works were prepared, and distributed to most of the leading dealers in books in the kingdom, with a request that they would report such of the works as they had in stock. Nearly fifty sets of the lists were sent out, and a large proportion of them returned with offers. By this means the Committee were enabled to select a large number of books on very advantageous terms.

In the meantime, the temporary rooms in Mr. Neil's building were furnished for the service of the library. The arrangement adopted was to devote the western portion of each of the rooms to readers, and the eastern portion of each was fitted with book-cases, the service-counter, the catalogues, and the staff being in the centre. The accommodation for readers consisted of chairs fitted with hat-rails, and tables furnished with umbrella rails. A hoist was provided to communicate between the two floors. The books were removed from the City Chambers to the library rooms in July.

[pp. 112–115]

The books were next placed upon the shelves, an attempt being made to combine the advantages of an arrangement by subjects with those of arrangement by size. As far as possible, all the books on a given subject were placed in the same press, while those of the same size on the same shelf. For example, in the department of Foreign History and Topography, the works on Asia and Asiatic countries were placed together in one press—the larger books on the lower, and the smaller on the upper shelves. On each shelf the books were arranged in geographical order, commencing with the western and ending with the eastern countries of Asia, the result being that all the works relating to Palestine, Syria, etc., were at the left hand or first end of the shelves, while books on China, Japan, and the east coast, were at the right hand or last end, with the central parts of Asia between. The adjacency of books on the same subject was thus secured, but made vertical instead of, as is more usual, horizontal; and the waste and unsightliness of varying sizes of books on the same shelf avoided. A similar plan of arrangement was attempted in other classes, though all subjects do not lend themselves to this treatment so readily as does topography.

The alphabetical form of catalogue was adopted, from a strong conviction of its great superiority in libraries frequented by the general public. In this kind of catalogue each work is entered under the name of its author, when known, under its subject or subjects, and under its title, for example:—Gilfillan's "Bards of the Bible" is under Gilfillan, Bible, and Bards; Conder's "Tent-work in Palestine," under Conder, Tent-work and Palestine; Davy's "Salmonia or Fly-fishing," under Davy, Salmonia, and Angling.

The result of this arrangement is that a reader, wishing to see a work by any given author, refers to his name, and sees at once if it is in the library; while a reader who desires to see what the library possesses on a given subject, finds under the name of that subject what books may be seen. . . .

Slips were printed as books were added, and mounted in order, in large guard books, which are laid on the counters for the use of readers. A catalogue of a more comprehensive description, in which the same general principles are to be carried out with more thoroughness, is in preparation.

The library was formally opened on 1st November by the Hon. James Bain (now Sir James Bain), Lord Provost. Amongst those who supported his lordship were, in addition to the members of the committee, Professor W. P. Dickson, Professor Grant, Sir James Watson, Dr. Marshall Lang, Mr. Michael Connal, Sheriff Lees, Mr. J. Wyllie Guild, Mr. Wm. Mitchell, and others. Addresses appropriate to the occasion were delivered, and earnest wishes expressed that the library might prove to be a popular and useful institution in the city.

The issue of books was commenced on Monday, 5th November, 1877. The first book asked for was "Liber Officialis Sancti Andree . . . Sententiarum in Causis Consistorialibus que extant", edited by Cosmo Innes. The number of volumes issued during the day was 186, and a commencement was made in what has since become one of the marked characteristics in the use of the library, namely, the making of extracts for future reference, and the copying designs for artistic purposes. It is not known what the first quotation extracted was; but pencil sketches were made from Collins's picture, "Rustic Hospitality", and from a number of the illustrations in Lavater's "Physiognomy".

[pp. 116–119]

.    .    .    .    .

With respect to the financial position of the library it may be stated that all that has yet been done,—the acquisition of a library of 57,100 volumes and the issue to readers of more than two and a half millions, together with the extensive use made of the current periodicals,—has practically been accomplished by the interest of the fund, the capital sum now being only some £1,500 less than when handed over by Mr. Mitchell's agents. The full realization of the objects pointed to in Lord Provost Blackie's report would require longer time and larger resources than have been at the disposal of the committee. After, payment of rent, lighting and warming, salaries and wages, insurance annuities under the founder's will, and incidental expenses, the amount available for the purchase of books and periodicals and for binding has in recent years averaged about £800. Considerable as this appears, when it is compared with corresponding expenditures at Liverpool, Manchester, and Birmingham (not to speak of cities in the United States), it will be seen how far it is from enabling the committee to secure for public use the greater and rarer works of our own and other times and countries, and otherwise giving full effect to the liberal policy they have adopted.

The principal inconveniences to which readers have been subjected arise entirely from the fact that the business of the library has long outgrown the premises in which it is placed. The overcrowding has been very great, so much so as to deter many from taking advantage of the books provided. Literary men and students particularly, who require quiet and space for their work, have been at a great disadvantage. The ventilation, originally defective, has with greater numbers present become much worse, and offers another serious hindrance to the use of the library.

Notwithstanding all these disadvantages, however, it has to be recorded that the library has so far had a remarkable and unlooked-for measure of success, and has become one of the most popular of the city institutions. As a recent observer has remarked, it has already "established a claim to be called a great library—great in progress, great in usefulness, greater still in promise".

[pp. 174–175]

From, Mason, Thomas. *Public and private libraries of Glasgow*, Glasgow, 1885. Chapters by F. T. Barrett on The Mitchell Library, pp. 101–175. Also privately printed as separate booklet.

# CHAPTER 25

# William Henry Kearley Wright (1844–1915)

"A librarian should endeavour to identify himself with his work, so as to become in course of time an authority upon matters relating to his particular locality."

W. H. K. WRIGHT.

AMONG the early members of the Library Association who rendered invaluable services to the young institution, the name of W. H. K. Wright remains prominent. His long, useful association with librarianship contributed to the development of the subject to a remarkable degree, for he presented numerous papers, and was ever ready to discuss those of his fellow librarians.

William Henry Kearley Wright was born in Plymouth on September 14th, 1844, serving as Librarian of his native city from 1876 until his death on April 27th, 1915. He was an original member of the Library Association, attending the first International Conference of Librarians in 1877, and reading the first paper. Wright served on the Council for a number of years, and was Vice-President on several occasions, attending the annual meeting for thirty-six consecutive years, in addition to the two International Conferences held in London.

Wright was the founder of the Ex-Libris Society, and was keenly interested in historical research, particularly in connection with his native Plymouth. His early contributions to gatherings of librarians many of which are available in the *Transactions*, etc., and his continued interest in the development of the library movement ensure that his name will endure among the builders of modern librarianship as one who assisted at the laying of its foundations.

REFERENCE

Obituary [Signed J.P.B.]. *Library Association Record*, 17, 1915, p. 304.

## WRIGHT ON THE BEST MEANS OF PROMOTING THE FREE LIBRARY MOVEMENT IN SMALL TOWNS AND VILLAGES

During the short time I have held the office of public librarian, I have felt it my duty to make myself acquainted with certain questions closely concerning those institutions with which I have become connected. I have realized to a considerable degree the importance of the work in which we are all engaged; and by personal visits to some of our principal libraries have obtained an insight into the working of those great higher-educational centres, as well as some idea of the main causes that have contributed to their prosperity.

Seeing, therefore, the extraordinary success which has attended the establishment and working of these institutions in the larger towns, has led me to look at the question in its relation to our small towns, which up to the present time have been in a measure shut out from a participation in the benefits of special legislation in this direction.

From a careful consideration of the subject, I could see no reason why the studious youth, the aspiring artisan, or the more advanced thinker of our small communities, should not possess an equal chance with the dwellers in large towns of obtaining literary food suited to their several capacities and requirements. . . .

Now comes *the* question: Is the Free Library movement *the* best means that can be adopted to supply the *need*, and, if so, in what way can it best be placed within the reach of all?

It may be fairly assumed that the Free Library has up to the present time fulfilled the purpose of its projectors, and the secret of its success lies in the fact that the movement was not started so much in the interests of any particular class or section of the community, as by and for the whole community. It is open and free to all—knowing no caste, acknowledging no precedence of rank, birth, wealth or station; making no stipulation as to a man's political or religious convictions.

We will assume therefore that the *need* which the Mechanics' Institure and Working Men's Club failed to supply, the Free Library has to a certain extent already provided.

Our large towns have the power in their own hands to establish and support these institutions—a power, moreover, conferred upon them by legislative enactments; and the Free Library, once established, is thenceforward recognized as a municipal and as a national institution.

Even in towns where the revenue is large, however, the amount realized under the provisions of the Act is insufficient to meet the growing demand, and to keep these institutions in a thorough state of efficiency. If therefore this difficulty of revenue be felt in the larger towns, how much more must it affect those towns of which I speak, where the means is altogether lacking.

Supposing the work to have commenced by securing the adoption of the Act, the rates are found to be so low that the sum realized annually would be quite inadequate to pay for the services of a librarian, to provide premises, furniture, books and periodicals. Unless, therefore, the promoters can see their way to realize a proper income to carry on their labours, and could by dint of great exertions raise enough money to start the scheme, what is the use of beginning? . . .

*First.*    By the union of small towns around a central one for mutual help. Thus, in a district in which a large city or town has within a radius of twenty miles a number of small towns or villages, not one of which is wealthy enough to start and support an institution by itself, a central depot might be established, with branches in the outlaying districts, from which supplies could be drawn; a continued exchange and interchange of the best books might thus be obtainable, while Branch Reading Rooms might be supplied in a similar manner. . . .

My *second* proposition refers to the utilization of Board Schools as branch or general libraries. That this plan is practicable may be attested by the experience of my friend, Mr. James Yates, of the Leeds Libraries. where the Board Schools have been thus used for some time. I trust that gentleman will furnish the Conference with fuller information upon this very interesting point than can be gathered from the Annual Reports of the Leeds Libraries, interesting as those reports undoubtedly are.

My *third* and last proposition is by far the most important, and perhaps the most difficult of execution.

It is, that an effort should be made to secure *State aid* in the formation and for the support of free libraries and museums, and I trust that the action recently taken by the authorities at Birmingham, in concert with other towns, may be closely followed up and enlarged upon, until success is assured.

The State provides elementary schools, nay rather, it compels the ratepayers to establish schools. It uses compulsion towards the children themselves, but it also aids such schools from imperial funds according to the results of the teaching in those schools.

Now, seeing that the State does all this, might it not go a step farther, extending its aid to our libraries, which are, after all, but higher-class schools?

Would it be an extraordinary stretch of liberality if the State, after training the children for a few years in these elementary schools, were to supplement that training by assisting the progress of these higher educational establishments, when, by the force of circumstances, the children are compelled to leave those schools?

The taste for reading has been instilled into the young mind, and ought to be encouraged and developed; but what chance is there of such development, unless material is provided for it to feed upon?

I do not say that the State should entirely provide these institutions, but that it should aid the community in sustaining them by government grants, as in the case of our schools. . . .

Thus, if a penny rate were collected, the State might supplement with a similar sum, or at least one-half, the existing Act being duly altered to meet the requirements of each case.

I have within my recollection several towns where the movement languishes for lack of just such support, where a few earnest men are willing to spend their time and money to bring about the desired result; and I also know of others in which the adoption of the Act has been opposed on the ground that the promoters could not give a clear idea as to *ways and means*. . . .

In conclusion, I would fain indulge the hope that this, the first Conference of Librarians held in this country, will give an impetus to the work; being firmly persuaded that, ere another generation shall have passed away, the Free Library movement will have spread like a great tidal-wave over the whole country—every town, village, and hamlet participating in its advantages.

A few days since I witnessed several thousands of children from our Board Schools assembled to receive prizes for regular and punctual attendance. The prizes selected were *books*.

Here, thought I, were the evidences of what must be in the future. The seed was being sown; pure literature was being disseminated, and the taste for it must spread: the rising generation, the generation now being educated in our Board Schools, bids fair to be a more reading generation than any which has preceded it: there is, therefore, all the more necessity for the present generation of workers to establish unfailing storehouses from which to draw.

The present is the time to prepare the way. There is much to be done for the future. The School Board system, which has struggled against ignorance and prejudice up to this moment, is prevailing at last, and will continue to prevail, and is laying a foundation upon which the Free Library must build.

It is well, therefore, that the materials should be made ready, in order that the grand superstructure of national education in its external appliances, at least, may be complete.

From, Wright, William H. K. On the best means of promoting the free library movement in small towns and villages. *Transactions and Proceedings of the Conference of Librarians held in London, October, 1877, [etc.],* 1878, pp. 22–28.

## WRIGHT ON SPECIAL COLLECTIONS OF LOCAL BOOKS IN PROVINCIAL LIBRARIES

The design of the present paper is to advocate the special collection of books in provincial libraries—not according to subject, but according to locality. With due deference to the larger experience of those whom I address, I would endeavour to awaken in the minds of my brother provincial librarians a special interest in the collection of works relating to their several localities, urging them to encourage as much as lies in their power the formation of representative local libraries in connexion with the institutions over which they preside. My plea is that every provincial library which is designed to be the central or public one of its district, should, in addition to its recognized reference department, be the repository for works connected with the city, town, county, or district of which it is the centre, and that efforts should be made to collect therein all useful books, pamphlets, or manuscripts having any connexion with the district, whether descriptive of, relating to, published in, or written by natives of, or sometime residents within the limits of such district. By this means, in course of time, a large and valuable collection of books would be made, and an interest awakened in local as well as general literature. In this way, too, local authors and publishers would be encouraged, a new impulse given to literary workers, and an additional inducement offered to the general public to frequent and use our public libraries for purposes of study and research.

Permit me, however, to observe, that I have no intention to take credit to myself for any originality in this matter. The idea is not a novel one, as I shall endeavour hereafter to show. The only originality I can lay claim to is in the introduction of the matter to your notice on this occasion, in order, if possible, to induce those who have not yet devoted themselves to this special work to take it in hand at once, believing that they will find it amply remunerative, both in its general interest and practical results. Those who have already commenced the work will, I trust, pardon me if I urge them to renewed exertion, not only in the work itself, but in the equally useful and interesting task of letting their co-workers know what they are about. It would be well if we as members of this Association would be apprised of the particular direction in which our fellow labourers are engaged—provided that their work is of general utility, and likely to further the great aims of our organization. I feel assured that such knowledge would be welcomed by one and all, and that each librarian would appreciate the efforts being put forth by his brother workers, striving to aid in the accomplishment of the several objects engaged in. Some earnest workers there are doubtless among us, who are ready to say that they are quite satisfied still to pursue the even tenour of their way, and do their work. even such work as that now proposed, without talk or publicity. This may be so, but those who work for the public must be willing to forego their inclinations for the general good, and must not shrink from that necessary publicity which appears inseparable from their prominent positions. They must be content, in a word, to let others know what they have done, or what they are striving to accomplish. Hereafter I purpose to refer to some instances of special collections in provincial libraries which have come under my own observation, but I cannot refrain from remarking at this point that instances of special cataloguing of local books are few and incomplete. If a library is of any real value, it is worthy of a catalogue, and surely the best means of making the existence of such special libraries known, is by having them duly and specifically catalogued, and wherever practicable their peculiarities and eccentricities set forth in detail.

Next to the necessity of a good catalogue is the desirability of the librarian having some special knowledge of the works under his charge, which may have been to a great extent collected by him. A librarian should endeavour to identify himself with his work, so as to become in course of time an authority upon matters relating to his particular locality. He should have a large acquaintance with the literature of his town or district—information not very difficult to acquire. As the curator of a museum is generally a man who has devoted himself to some particular scientific pursuit, and is considered to be an authority upon matters connected with his subject, so a librarian should acquire a knowledge of local books which would stand in him in good stead, and enable him to be of great help to his readers by directing their search for information in the proper channels. For my own part, I have found a little superficial knowledge of this kind of considerable service; how much more then would be the result of systematic application and research? Further, I have found the task of collecting special local books an exceedingly interesting one, and one which I hope to follow with increased satisfaction to myself and service to the public. . . .

In regard to the indiscriminate collection of books, we ought surely to follow the British Museum authorities, when they tell us that everything is collected that is issued from the English press, down to the most insignificant work on embroidery, juvenile tale, country magazine, or almanack of some obscure hamlet. Everything that is collected finds a place in the catalogue also, as well as in the library; the principle being that nothing is so insignificant but that it may one day be valuable to someone for reference, and by this means in one place a copy of everything so published will be secured to future generations. The same principle might guide us in making our local collections without fear of becoming burdened with a very large mass of superfluous rubbish. Reference to the British Museum reminds me of another point in which we should do well to follow its leading if by any means practicable. It is well known that the British Museum and some other national institutions have long enjoyed, under the provisions of the Copyright Act, peculiar advantages over town libraries for obtaining copies of all works issued from the press of the United Kingdom. Although we in the provinces lack such a privilege, we might seek to do by moral suasion what the law is hardly likely to aid us in effecting—we might seek to interest local authors and publishers in the special work in which we are engaged to the extent of presenting to us for our shelves copies of their written or published works. Possibly such a course might prove serviceable to authors and publishers themselves by promoting the circulation of their volumes, especially were they included in the published catalogues of our special local departments. This, however, is a matter upon which I can touch but lightly, trusting that the passing hint may not be altogether lost sight of. If we in our provincial libraries could follow to some extent the course adopted and advocated by the authorities of the national libraries—seeking to gather within our building all the literature relating to the district we each represent—in course of time collections of great value and immense importance would be formed, an ever-increasing source of interest and field for research for the enterprising bibliographical student: remembering the maxim of the British Museum and "accepting everything, disdaining nothing."

From, Wright, William H. K. Special collections of local books in provincial libraries *Transactions and Proceedings of the First Annual Meeting of the Library Association of the United Kingdom, held at Oxford, October 1, 2, 3, 1878, [etc.],* 1879, pp. 44–50.

## WRIGHT ON THE PUBLIC FREE LIBRARY AND THE BOARD SCHOOL

At our meeting in London, I urged the expediency of bringing into closer relationship the free library and the board school as a means whereby the library system might be extended at comparatively little cost. Since that time the question has frequently occupied my thoughts, and as it appears to demand further consideration from our Association, I have ventured to bring it again before you. The occasion of our meeting in this important city—which may be called the birthplace and nursery of the free library movement, and where it has been so eminently successful—added to the fact that free town libraries and their administration form a prominent and special feature of our programme, leads me to hope that this subject may have your best and most patient attention, and that the librarians of our great communities may be willing to offer a word of advice to their brethren who in the less wealthy towns have difficulties to overcome of which they—more highly favoured—know comparatively nothing. In such a centre of wealth as Manchester, there can be but little, if any, difficulty in extending the working of its library system in every direction. That such is the case, the number of establishments in active work and their flourishing condition afford abundant testimony. But it is different in many other towns where, nevertheless, the free library is acknowledged to be a popular public institution. . . .

Our board schools have now become so much a part of our municipal system, they are so spread over every portion of our towns in the very districts in which it would be desirable to establish branch libraries and reading-rooms, that it appears to me as if the means for this work is ready to our hands. Provided a satisfactory arrangement could be made between the school board and the library committee— the one agreeing to provide the room and gas; the other, books, periodicals and attendance—much of the difficulty would be removed, or, at any rate, would be greatly diminished. Board schools and free libraries have much in common; they are both established in accordance with special legislation, they are both supported by local rates, and they are certainly engaged in the same important work— the education and social welfare of the people. In this case, however, the funds are supplemented by Governmental grants; in the other, the work has to be carried on without any such additional aid. There is also this great difference between the two organizations, that the income of the library is fixed, and cannot be materially increased, while that of the school board is virtually unlimited.

Now it appears to me not at all unreasonable to ask that the school board should be willing to co-operate with the library committee for such a desirable object—not by any special outlay of funds, but simply by utilizing the property already provided at the cost of the ratepayers, by permitting a more extended use of the school premises.

My suggestion is simply this,—that in populous but poor towns, and in fact wherever it is desired, and where the Public Libraries Acts have come into operation, and where there exists a well-arranged system of board schools, advantage should be taken of those establishments to provide, by the united action of the two governing bodies, a room in each district school to be used as an evening reading-room, with, if possible, a small lending library attached.

In this way would the work of the one institution follow that of the other: there would be mutual help, and I believe mutual advantage, resulting from the amalgamation. I have already proposed such a plan in my own town, and I trust ere long to see it carried out. The experience of those who have seen the working of such a project will be of value to their colleagues.

But this matter has still another aspect to which I shall briefly refer. The first I may call the business aspect of the scheme; the second, the moral or social aspect.

It is that some mutual understanding or relationship between librarians and public school teachers should be brought about, with a view to exercising a reasonable amount of supervision over the reading of the children connected with both establishments. . . .

Reducing my ideas into something of a practical character, my proposition is as follows:—That in connexion with each district library, such as that I have proposed, there should be a small collection of books approved by both library and school authorities for the use of the children attending that school; and that those children should not be allowed the run of the central or general library, except at the special request of parents or teachers. This arrangement might be supplemented in various ways to suit the particular circumstances of each case.

A pre-arranged plan such as this would tend to remove much of the difficulty now experienced by librarians on the question "what the children should, or should not read"; and further, it would prevent that oft-repeated charge brought against our fraternity of disseminating worthless rubbish amongst our borrowers, and thereby doing much moral damage.

Under some particularly favourable circumstances a librarian has it in his power to direct the taste of those who come to him for books; but in large libraries having an extensive circulation this is impossible, the demands upon his time and that of his assistants rendering such a course impracticable. I have myself endeavoured to meet the difficulty by establishing a juvenile section in my lending library; but I find that it is one thing to say—"*There are the books, read them,*" and another to get borrowers, no matter how young, to take exactly what we might wish them to read. They prefer, as do most of us, to wander at will "to fresh woods and pastures new"—in fact to select for themselves, with or without judgment.

From, Wright, William H. K. The Public Free Library and the Board School. *Transactions and Proceedings of the Second Annual Meeting of the Library Association of the United Kingdom, held at Manchester, September 23, 24 and 25, 1879, [etc.],* 1880, pp. 38–41.

CHAPTER 26

# William Edward Armytage Axon (1846–1913)

"Bibliography is sometimes called a science, but even at the lowest estimate it may claim to be the handmaid of all the others."

W. E. A. AXON.

AXON represents yet another librarian who, while forsaking our profession for another, retained sincere affection for his first love during the remainder of his life. At the age of fifteen he was appointed assistant in Manchester Public Library, where he rose to become sub-librarian, but left librarianship after serving for seven years in that capacity. Axon then entered commerce, and later served on the literary staff of the *Manchester Guardian*, where he remained until 1905.

Little was known of the early life of Axon until the publication of a paper by Robert Walmsley, who acquired the Axon Papers from the executors of E. A. Axon. These contain a wealth of information, including letters, manuscripts and copies of the numerous pamphlets written by W. E. A. Axon. He was born at Chorlton-on-Medlock on January 13th, 1846, the natural son of a widower, Edward Armytage, and Lydia Whitehead. He was brought up by a family named Axon, and acquired their surname. Axon never attended a day-school, but was largely self-educated, being particularly keen on reading, and on foreign languages. He first worked in an auctioneer's office, but in 1861 became an assistant in the lending department of the Manchester Free Library at Campfield. Axon was the author of a very useful *Handbook of the public libraries of Manchester and Salford*, 1877, edited *Book Lore* from 1884 to 1886, and contributed to the *Dictionary of National Biography*, *Encyclopaedia Britannica* and *Notes and Queries*.

W. E. A. Axon was a member of numerous literary and scientific societies, and served on the Salford School Board, the Salford Museum and Libraries Committee, the Southport Libraries Committee and Moss Side Urban District Council. He was the author of several hundred articles, some of which were later published in volume form, and also wrote biographies and poetry. He made a classified catalogue of the Thomas Greenwood Library for Librarians at Manchester.

In 1899 the Wilberforce University, Ohio, awarded Axon an honorary LL.D., and two months before his death, which occurred on December 27th, 1913, he received an honorary M.A. from Manchester University.

Axon wrote several bibliographical articles for inclusion in the *Papers of the Manchester Literary Club* (of which he was honorary secretary and later vice-president), and contributed many items to other professional journals. He wrote "An appreciation of the 'Bibliotheca Lindesiana' " (*Library Association Record*, 14, 1912, pp. 4–13), and presented many papers at Library Association conferences, including "The British Museum in its relation to provincial culture" (*Transactions ... 1877*, 1878, pp. 29–32); "Is a printed catalogue of the British Museum practicable?" (*Transactions ... 1878*, 1879, pp. 65–67); "The libraries of Lancashire and Cheshire" (*Transactions ... 1879*, 1880, pp. 47–53); "Legislation for free public libraries" (*Transactions ... 1881, ... 1882*, 1884, pp. 31–33); and the interesting typical paper devoted to "Professors of Bibliography", which is reproduced below.

As an original member of the Library Association Council William Edward Armytage Axon was prominently associated with the early development of public libraries. His writings remain of deep interest, for they represent carefully thought-out contributions to librarianship, and his break with library work was a great loss to the profession.

## REFERENCES

Obituary. *Library Association Record*, 16, 1914, pp. 134–136.
Walmsley, Robert. Dr. Axon – Manchester bookman. *Manchester Review*, 10, 1964, pp. 138–154.

## Axon on Professorships of Bibliography

A century ago he who had suffused his mind with the thought of Greece and Rome, had all that was necessary for either a lover of literature or a professional man of letters. If to this he added some acquaintance with the authors of Spain and Italy, he stood above the level of his peers. Since then we have witnessed a revived interest, not only in classical literature, but in the productions of those languages which have supplanted Greek and Latin as the vehicles of the highest thought. We have witnessed the vigorous development of German literature, essentially informed by the spirit of the present time. We are gradually becoming familiarized with the genius of the Scandinavian peoples, and the novelists and satirists of the Sclavonic races. In the East, too, there has been a corresponding advance. *Ex oriente lux* is still true in a sense, though we are repaying the debt; and the pundits of India may look to Oxford and Berlin for the interpretation of the venerable documents they have kept through centuries of storm and change. The ancient civilizations of Babylon and Assyria have shaken off the dust of centuries, and risen from their desert graves. With all these new conquests it has also been found requisite to re-study much of the old. In our own language what a flood of light has been thrown upon the condition of mediæval England by the publications of the Early English Text Society alone. These have not merely helped us to a better understanding of the past, but have given back to us forgotten poets, not unworthy to take their place in the society of Chaucer and of Spenser.

The continual widening of the boundaries of human knowledge and the consequent extension of the sphere of intellectual interest and activity give fresh importance to bibliography and render acquaintance with its methods indispensable. Centuries ago it was said by the authors of Ecclesiastes, that "of making many books there is no end". If the literary activity of that age was sufficient to daunt the spirit, what shall we say of the present time, with its myriad newspapers, journals, reviews, and magazines—of an age when the printing presses of our own country alone produce above a hundred volumes for each day in the year? The literary problem of the present is that of selection.

The weighty words of Emerson may fittingly be quoted:— "Meantime the colleges, whilst they provide us with libraries, furnish no professor of books; and I think no chair is so much wanted. In a library we are surrounded by many hundreds of dear friends, but they are imprisoned by an enchanter in these paper and leathern boxes; and though they know us, and have been waiting two, ten, or twenty centuries for us—some of them—and are eager to give us a sign, and unbosom themselves, it is the law of their limbo that they must not speak until spoken to; and as the enchanter has dressed them, like battalions of infantry, in coat and jacket of one cut, by the thousand and ten thousand, your chance of hitting on the right one is to be computed by the arithmetical rule of permutation and combination, not a choice out of three caskets, but out of half a million caskets all alike. But it happens in our experience, that in this lottery there are at least fifty or a hundred blanks to a prize. It seems then as if some charitable soul, after losing a great deal of time among the false books, and alighting upon a few true ones which made him happy and wise, would do a right act in naming those which have been bridges or ships to carry him safely over dark morasses and barren oceans into the hearts of sacred cities, into palaces and temples."[1]

There is a suggestive passage in Carlyle's noble address on the "Choice of Books":—"It remains, however, a very curious truth, what has been said by observant people, that the main use of the Universities in the present age is that after you have done with all your classes, the next thing is a collection of books, a great library of good

[1] See the chapter on Books in Emerson's *Society and Solitude*, London, 1870, 12mo, p. 160.

books, which you proceed to study and read. What the Universities have mainly done—what I have found the University did for me, was that it taught me to read in various languages and various sciences, so that I could go into the books that treated of these things, and try anything that I wanted to make myself master of gradually, as I found it suit me. Whatever you may think of all that, the clearest and most imperative duty lies on every one of you to be assidious in your reading; and learn to be good readers, which is, perhaps, a more difficult thing than you imagine."[1]

The difficulty of learning to read well is the justification of the plea for the appointment of professors whose special duty it should be to explain theoretically and experimentally the methods of literary investigation. Books should be used for the acquisition of facts, for the strengthening of the intellect, and for help in the right conduct of life, since, as Bacon phrases it, all knowledge should be "bounded by religion and referred to use and wont". By communion with the lofty souls of the past we may hope to imbibe some of their spirit, and even to see a wider horizon than theirs, as a dwarf mounted upon a giant's shoulder will have the further view. These master minds are few in number, coming not always once in every century. Even in profiting by the rich legacies left by these greatest intellects, a certain caution and discretion are necessary in order to discriminate between eternal truths and temporary illusions or expediences. Gold has its alloy, and no man can entirely resist the superstitions and the prejudices of his own day. In most cases we need to know something of the personality and environment before we can select the good and avoid the errors in the teachings of even the wisest of the sons of men.

If there is a difficulty in rightly using and making the most of even those who have been confessedly the epoch-makers in what De Quincey has called the literature of power, how much greater is the bewilderment of the inexperienced student in the vaster field of the literature of facts. The extent of printed matter upon even minutely small sections of the domain of knowledge is simply astounding. How is the student to thread his way through the tangled mazes of ancient and modern literature? Bibliography is sometimes called a science, but even at the lowest estimation it may claim to be the handmaid of all the others. Like other useful arts it has to be learned. Bibliography has a commercial as well as an educational aspect, but it is with the latter only that we are now concerned. Its object is to preserve a record of all efforts of intellectual activity, and to facilitate their communication to

[1] *On the Choice of Books*, by Thomas Carlyle, 4th edition, with a new Life of the Author (by R. H. Shepherd), London: Chatto and Windus, 1875, p. 136. London, 1870, 12mo, p. 160.

other minds. For the individual, the unknown in literature is the non-existent. Bibliography is the grammar, so to speak, of literary investigation. Some have the faculty of pursuing their subject from book to book without any special acquaintance with bibliography. Some speak correctly and even elegantly without a formal knowledge of the rules of grammar. If it is useful to teach the one art to all the children of the nation, it is equally useful to teach the other to those who in after life will have to freely employ books as their weapons in the warfare of civilization. One thing is quite clear, that those who have to engage in the work of literature and of science, will find their way greatly impeded by the lack of this knowledge. Even great men from this ignorance have wasted their time in "discovering" that which was already known. In a lower range we see the Testaments of the Twelve Patriarchs republished as a canonical book, and D'Holbach's "System of Nature", gravely ascribed to Mirabeau. Even where gross error is avoided, how frequent is the occurrence of literary work which is thin and poor, because the writer has not known how to gain access to the best that had been previously written upon the subject. A professor of bibliography would find a distinct place and have a mission of his own. It would be his province to show the history of literature in its concrete form, tracing it from the fabled pillars of Seth, through the monkish *scriptorium* to the chapel of Gutenberg, and the studio of Senefelder. This would include not only a good deal of palæography, but also information respecting paper, typography, bookbinding, and all the other arts employed to give visible form and expression to literature. The systems for the classification of knowledge, and all the more essential features of library-science might also be explained. It would be his task to indicate the methods for the strengthening of the powers of the memory, so that it might be

"Wax to receive, and marble to retain."

It would be his to indicate, however broadly, the clues that have already been devised by the patient skill of Querard, Brunet, Watt, Lowndes, and a thousand others, to wide and important fields of literature. He would point to such master-pieces as Dr. Billing's Bibliography of Cholera, and Professor Abbot's monograph on the Literature of the Doctrine of a Future Life. It would be his to show how courses of reading may be at once systematic and varied; how the poet, the humorist, the satirist, not less than the historian, may help us to understand the past. It would be his to prove that even reading for entertainment may be made to serve a higher purpose. He would point out that "Romola" is not less charming a story because it contains a life-like portrait of Savonarola, and that "Barnaby Rudge" loses none of its dramatic power because it gives a picturesque painting of London during the Gordon riots. An active-minded man in such a position would find a thousand possibilities of useful action. He could do much to stimulate and direct an intelligent curiosity, and would be able in countless ways to help those who were seeking the prophecy of the future in the records of the past.

Axon, William E. A. Professorships of bibliography. *Transactions and Proceedings of the first annual meeting of the Library Association . . . 1878*, 1879, pp. 104–107.

# CHAPTER 27

# John Potter Briscoe (1848-1926)

"His was a completely genial and lovable nature, and it is good for us and for the city he so faithfully served that he lived – more and better cannot be said of any of us, when we, too, come to close the volume of our doing."

L. S. JAST.

SEVERAL prominent librarians have been connected with particular libraries throughout their entire careers, spending their lives building up systems that have become monuments to their memories. One such person was John Potter Briscoe, who served as Chief Librarian of Nottingham Public Library.

He was born at Lever Bridge, near Bolton, on July 20th, 1848, and after spending some years as a teacher in Bolton, served as assistant librarian in the Public Library there from 1866 to 1869. In the latter year he was appointed to Nottingham, serving the City as librarian and historian for the remainder of his life. J. P. Briscoe was an original member of the Library Association, served on the Council from 1881 to 1890, and was vice-president from 1891 to 1920. He was a founder of the North Midland Library Association, serving as its first President in 1890, and he actively supported Library Association conferences. He contributed numerous papers to the *Transactions*, one of the earliest of which is reproduced below.

John Potter Briscoe wrote extensively on Nottinghamshire history, including *Bypaths of Nottinghamshire history*, *Concise history of Nottingham Castle*, *Old Nottinghamshire*, 2 vols., and was editor of the *Bibelots Series*, 29 vols., *The Sportsman's Classics*, 3 vols., and *Nottinghamshire and Derbyshire Notes and Queries*, 6 vols.

Briscoe inaugurated a series of talks in the library on books and writers, and was a pioneer in several branches of librarianship. As early as 1885 he read a paper to the Plymouth Conference of the Library Association entitled "Libraries for the young" (*Library Chronicle*, 3, 1886, pp. 45–48), and he established a separate building for the children's library at Nottingham. When he died on January 7th, 1926 he was mourned by the profession at large, but particularly by the City he had faithfully served as librarian and historian for fifty-seven years.

REFERENCES

Obituary. [By L. S. Jast.] *Library Association Record*, N.S. 4, 1926, pp. 5–6.
Personalities of the Past: V. John Potter Briscoe. *Librarian & Book World*, 30, 1940–1941, pp. 164–165.

## BRISCOE ON SUBSCRIPTION LIBRARIES IN CONNEXION WITH FREE PUBLIC LIBRARIES

The question as to whether it is advisable that subscription libraries should or should not exist in connexion with libraries established under the Public Libraries Acts, is one which is worthy of the best consideration of librarians and others interested in library work, and is, I believe, eminently suitable for discussion at a meeting of the Library Association. My connexion with the first library in the country where there was a combination of a subscription with a free public library—I refer to Bolton—gave me an opportunity of studying the working of the system there, and of arriving at some conclusions which I shall refer to in this paper.

When the Public Libraries Act was first introduced into the large centres of industry and population, there was a strong inclination on the part of a certain section of the community, to introduce a system of payment in one form or another. Whether this feeling arose from the too frequent use of the word "free" in connexion with the library movement, or whether it sprang from a desire on the part of a narrow-minded class of people to be thought superior to the ordinary ratepayer and inhabitant, it is not for me to say; but from whatever motive this feeling arose, a great evil was introduced at Bolton by creating classes in an institution where all grades of society ought to meet on an equal footing. This was brought about by making "first-class" members by means of the combination of a Subscription Library with a Free Public Library. This combination partakes undeniably of the essential nature of an evasion of the spirit of the Public Libraries Acts, and "is a union of things which conflict as well as differ". Such is my opinion, in which I am supported by Mr. Edward Edwards. "This union," says that authority, in his work on "Free Town Libraries" (1869, p. 59), "of the subscription principle with the rating principle as far as regards the Town Library of Bolton, was so framed at the outset as to increase its objectionable character. The worst conceivable classification of men (under any circumstances whatever) in relation to mental culture or to any appliance or appendage of that, is certainly the breeches-pocket classification. Yet the framers of the subscription arrangement at Bolton," continues Mr. Edwards, "were not content with divaricating the readers at the Free Library—so far as concerns the circulating

branch of it—into a 'first class', consisting of subscription-paying
borrowers, and a 'second class', consisting of non-subscribers; but they
must have three classes, graduated entirely by the breeches-pocket
scale; namely, (1), borrowers of books who could afford to pay a
guinea a year; (2), borrowers of books who could afford to pay only
ten shillings a year; (3), borrowers of books who could afford to pay—
directly and indirectly—only their share of the library-rate. The
borrowing privileges of each class were made more or less ample in
proportion, exactly on the principle which gives a first-class railway
traveller very soft cushions; to the second-class traveller very hard
cushions; and to the third-class traveller no cushions at all." The
regulation as to the subscribing members stated that the subscription of
the "first-class" members should "be expended in the purchase of
books and periodical literature, which shall circulate among the subscribers only, for twelve months next after purchase, and shall then be
transferred to, and become the property of, the Town Council, and
be added to the Public Library, provided that each subscriber shall be
allowed the privilege of taking out, for perusal at home [note this],
one volume from the books of that portion of the library known as
the Reference Library, which the Library Committee of the Town
Council for the time being shall authorize to be put into circulation".
At the same library the subscriptions of the "second-class", of half-
sovereign members, were directed to be expended in the purchase of
new publications in the arts and sciences, to be selected by the Town
Council Committee, and the right of reading them was confined to the
members of this class for a period of six months from the time of
purchase, after which the books merged into the Free Public Library.
In consideration of these transfers, the cost entailed in circulating these
books was, as it is now, defrayed out of the library-rate. This cost
includes a proportion of the rent of the building, or warming, of
lighting, and of the librarian's salary, together with the payment of the
salary of a clerk, whose whole time is, at Bolton, devoted to the work
of entering the books, issued to subscribers. The "second-class" member
at Bolton has ceased to exist, there being at the present time only
"first" and "third" class members.

There is no doubt that the combination of the Subscription Library
with the Public Library has tended to cramp the proper development
of the Act under which the Bolton Library was established in 1853.
In the first place, only one-half of the sum allowed to be levied for
library purposes was obtained for many years, because it was expected
that the library would be supplied with nearly all the books it would
require from the Subscription Library, the result being that the funds
at the disposal of the Committee were inadequate to provide such

salaries as would secure the services of an efficient staff, or if they did secure such a staff (when the income was less than it is at the present time), they were for the same reason unable to keep them. This system of false economy places beyond the reach of the committee those standard books of reference of an expensive character which every efficient reference library ought to possess, and consequently, works of this class are withheld from students of limited means, and thus one of the great objects of the library is not attained. It ought, perhaps, to have been stated earlier that the management of the Subscription Department at Bolton is vested in a committee of gentlemen (selected from the subscribers and from the Public Library Committee), who have the selection of books for the subscribers. This committee consists of two-thirds of the Free Public Library Committee, and one-third of the subscribers not on the General Committee, so that theoretically the selection of books rests with the Public Library Committee; but (as librarians well know who have mixed committees) practically the selection rests with a majority of the outside members of the library committee, and consequently the interests of the subscribers are more likely to be consulted than those of the general public. I find, from an examination of the catalogues of the Subscription Library in connexion with the Free Public Library at Bolton, for the half-year ending June of this year, that about 60 per cent. of the purchases for that period were works of fiction and miscellaneous literature; while there were only 10 per cent. of works of biography, 10 per cent. of voyages, travels, and topography, 7 per cent. of history and antiquities, 4 per cent. of science and the fine and useful arts, the same proportion of theology and mental and moral philosophy, and 3 per cent. of political economy, commerce, and education. At the Rochdale Subscription Library in connexion with the Public Library, at least 90 per cent. of the volumes noted in a recent catalogue consist of fiction and miscellaneous works, 6 per cent. of history, voyages, travels, and topography, not 1 per cent. of poetry and the drama, and ½ per cent. of works on the fine and industrial arts and sciences, whilst theology, philosophy, politics and commerce are unrepresented. As the Bolton librarian's classification of the reading of the subscribers shows that more than four-fifths of the reading of these "first-class" members consists of novels, periodicals, and miscellaneous literature, of course that class of reading is catered for, and consequently a great quantity of this literature finds its way, in the shape of three-volume novels, into the Reference Library as well as the Lending Library, with only a small proportion of literature of a healthy and substantial character. Subscribers, as a rule, do not care to have any connexion whatever with ordinary members (for they are "first-class" members, and subscribe at Bolton a fraction more than fourpence three-farthings a week for their extra privileges, although some of them are not even ratepayers), and consequently a great quantity of literature which ought not to exist in a reference library finds its way there. The annual report fails to state in what proportion this literature is drafted into the Reference and Lending Libraries, but from personal knowledge I can say that the literature which is most likely to be wanted by subscribers is placed in the Reference Library. Here the ordinary inhabitants may occasionally meet with books which have been transferred from the Subscription Department, but the probability is that for several months they will be "out" in the hands of the subscribers, who, as I have stated, are permitted to take "reference" works home for consultation (or rather reading), with very few exceptions, and even these by special permission, which is readily granted.

Where the combination of a Subscription with a Free Public Library exists, there is a natural inclination on the part of the Public Library Committee to spend as little of their income in books as possible, because works which they might deem advisable to obtain for the Public Library may ultimately be transferred to them from the Subscription Library. A plan which has been resorted to in a public library in one of the northern counties, in order to obtain certain works, was to get the books proposed in the Subscription Library Proposal Book, and thus new books proposed by ratepayers were very seldom added to the library for at least twelve months. In the cases where the Subscription Committee did not purchase the works from the publisher, but obtained them as "remainders" or second-hand books, the volumes recommended would not find their way into the Public Library for a year and a half or thereabouts. And the proposer might find that the book he suggested to purchase for the Lending Library had even then been transferred to the Reference Library, where he might not be able to meet with it for weeks, and perhaps for months, if it was a popular book, for it would be pretty certain to be in the hands of one subscriber or another. As a result the general public (for whose benefit the library was formed, and who have to pay rates for its maintenance) are unable to keep themselves posted up in the literature of the day, and the working man who is desirous of studying what has been published which will benefit him in his trade, has to wait a long time before he is enabled to consult the literature which his fellow-workman in neighbouring towns is enabled to do in those free public libraries which do not depend upon extraneous aid for the supply of technical works. Consequently the public library of the one town fails in a great measure to perform the work which the originators of the public libraries scheme had in view when the movement was commenced. Where the subscription library system has grown to a great extent, the time and attention of the librarian is greatly occupied in discharging the duties attached to this portion of his office. The subscribers feel that they have a claim to the attention of the librarian in preference to that of the general public, and thus the librarian is unable to render to the general public that assistance in their researches which they have a right to expect, and which a librarian who fully comprehends his mission is always ready to render. It is a difficult matter to serve two masters; and it is equally difficult to serve two committees with perfect satisfaction to each. One committee may imagine that the librarian devotes too much time in furthering the objects of the other committee, and does not give the necessary attention to their work. When such is the case, as it must sometimes be, the position of librarian to two committees, representing two classes of people, is not an enviable one.

The system in operation at Bolton and Rochdale, by which the books are transferred to the Public Library after being set aside for subscribers for a year, may appear to be one worthy of more general adoption on the ground that a large quantity of literature is thus added to the Public Library at little cost to the Library Committee, but the advantages are not so great when the system is examined. I have shown what class of literature is as a rule most in request, and consequently is most extensively purchased by Subscription Library Committees, and the comparative worthlessness of the majority of this literature. When such a mass of ephemeral literature, especially in the three-volume form, is transferred to the town, a great proportion (particularly when obtained second-hand) has to be re-bound at the cost of the ratepayers, very few of whom, except subscribing rate-payers, care to peruse those transferred to the Reference Library. Thus a three-volume novel frequently costs the town at the outset nearly, if not quite, as much as if the work had been obtained second-hand some months before it came into their possession through the Subscription Library, and when there might be a passing interest in the work; or a new one-volume edition might be obtained for even less than the amount spent in binding the old three volumes. By adopting the latter system the cost of subsequently binding is lessened by two-thirds. Less shelf-room is required also by throwing out, or rather not accepting, three-volume editions. It will be seen that very little saving is effected by the union of Subscription with Free Public Libraries as far as the novels are concerned. The question next comes: —is it worth while to adopt the Subscription Library system for obtaining books other than novels? My answer is not favourable to the adoption. Take the proportion of rent, of warming, of lighting, and of the librarian's salary, the payment of a clerk for the Subscription Library, and it will be seen that the saving by the adoption of the system is not so great as it appears on the surface.

As a matter of principle or of expediency, the introduction of the two classes in a public institution intended for all classes alike is one to be deprecated. Where subscribers are permitted to take books from the Reference Library, a great evil has been introduced which cannot fail to act detrimentally to the interests of the institution, as the public lose confidence in that library, because the works they want to consult may be in the hands of the subscribers; and the librarian is not so accessible to the general public who want some assistance, his time being very likely monopolized by the Subscription Library. Another objection to the introduction of the system is, that works not of a reference character find their way (at Bolton certainly) into the Reference Library, instead of into the Lending Library, and thus a quantity of literature adapted for home reading is rendered comparatively inaccessible to the general public. The librarian has to serve two distinct committees. The ratepayers have to provide superior shelving in the Reference Library for books placed there for the convenience of subscribers; and have to defray the cost of superior bindings for novels and other works for the benefit of subscribers; whereas, if the books were placed in the Lending Library, ordinary shelving and ordinary binding would suffice, and thus not only would a saving be effected, but the books would be of greater service to larger numbers. The rate-paying members feel that they are only occupying a secondary position at their own library where this system is in operation, or else the subscribing members show by their manner that they regard themselves as far superior in the social scale to those who do not subscribe.

From, Briscoe, John Potter. Subscription libraries in connexion with free public libraries. *Transactions and Proceedings of the first Annual Meeting of the Library Association of the United Kingdom held at Oxford, October 1, 2, 3, 1878,* 1879, pp. 19–23.

# CHAPTER 28

# Edward Williams Byron Nicholson (1849–1912)

> "He was impatient of opposition, but even those who were most opposed to him recognised his unselfish aims, his thorough zeal for his duty, his restless energy, and his untiring efforts on behalf of the institution over which he presided."
>
> JOHN MINTO.

EDWARD W. B. NICHOLSON has been acclaimed as virtual founder of the Library Association, and that together with the fact that he was also Bodley's Librarian would render him worthy of remembrance by librarians, but he was also a devoted friend of librarianship in all its aspects throughout his career.

Nicholson was born at St. Helier, Jersey, on March 16th, 1849, being educated at Llanrwst Grammar School, Liverpool College and Tonbridge School before entering Trinity College, Oxford in 1867. There he obtained his B.A. in 1872, two years later M.A., and became Librarian of the London Institution in 1873, after a brief period as a teacher. He completely reorganized the collection at the Institution, and organized the Metropolitan Free Libraries Association.

In January, 1877 Nicholson wrote a report on the Philadelphia Conference of Librarians held in October, 1876 suggesting that one should be held in London. *The Times* of February 16th, 1877 also contained a note by him in the same strain, and he became secretary of a committee to organize the Conference, which was held at the London Institution from October 2nd to 5th, 1877. At this Conference it was decided to found the Library Association of the United Kingdom.

In 1882 Nicholson was appointed Bodley's Librarian, succeeding Henry Octavius Coxe. He was continuously involved in conflicts with the Curators, and became a "solitary, frustrated, and a very unhappy man." Nicholson was a strict disciplinarian with his staff, but was grossly overworked because of his inability to delegate responsibility.

Nicholson was a prominent member of the Library Association until his appointment to the Bodleian, and his activities in those early days of the Association were invaluable. At the Bodleian he carried out drastic reorganization, and his *Staff Calendar* is a monument of meticulous precision and ingenuity. He contributed few articles to our professional literature, two dealing with buckram, but his influence was wide, and his death on March 17th, 1912 occurred while he was still actively interested in the work he had so keenly supported. Nicholson was interested in music, the composition of limericks, and was the author of several commentaries on the Gospels. He wrote *The Christ-child*, 1877, a book of verse with phonetic spelling; *The rights of an animal*, 1879, expressing his views as a life-long anti-vivisectionist; *Golspie: contributions to its folklore*, 1897; *The man with two souls*, 1898; *Bodleian staff kalendar*, 1902, to which was later added the *Staff manual*; and *Keltic researches*, 1904. Following his appointment to the Bodleian Nicholson appears to have devoted his entire time to that Library, and to have taken little further interest in the Library Association and in librarianship in general. (Portrait, Plate 8B.)

### REFERENCES

Gibson, Strickland. E. W. B. Nicholson (1849-1912): some impressions. *Library Association Record*, 51, 1949, pp. 137-143.

Munford, W. A. Nicholson of the Bodleian. *Library Review*, 143, 1962, pp. 507-512.

Tedder, Henry R. E. W. B. Nicholson (Bodley's Librarian, 1882-1912): in memoriam. *Library Association Record*, 16, 1914, pp. 95-108; discussion of this paper by Falconer Madan, C. Madeley, T. W. Lister and others, Vol. 15, 1913, pp. 630-633.

## NICHOLSON'S LETTER TO "THE TIMES"

### A CONFERENCE OF LIBRARIANS

### To The Editor of "The Times"

Sir,—Reviewing in a recent number of the "Academy" the proceedings of the Philadelphia Conference of Librarians, I suggested a similar meeting in England for the interchange of ideas upon all points of library management. As you reproduced most of the review in question, I trust you consider the subject important enough to allow my appealing in your columns for co-operation in realizing the suggestion.

I have written to the Principal Librarian of the British Museum, Mr. J. Winter Jones, asking whether, on receipt of a reasonable number of requisitions, he would consent to preside over such a Conference. In his reply he says:—

"Strenuous efforts are now being made, and made successfully, for the establishment of public libraries in large centres, and I think that such a Conference as you suggest might produce good practical results. Whether my presidency would be beneficial is a question upon which I cannot presume to offer an opinion; but should others think that my services in such a position might be useful, I shall be prepared to give them to the best of my ability."

I have also written to the Librarians of the Bodleian Library, Oxford, the Cambridge University Library, the Advocates' Library, Edinburgh —the largest in Scotland—and the Library of Trinity College, Dublin— the largest in Ireland—asking whether they would be willing to act as Vice-presidents. I give extracts from their answers.

The Rev. H. O. Coxe, of the Bodleian, writes: "I am in your hands to use me as you like in forwarding the Conference you suggest. Only good can come of it."

Mr. Bradshaw of Cambridge writes: "I shall be very glad to take part in your Conference, and do what I can, and learn what I can; but I had very much rather not be a Vice-President or anything of the kind."

Mr. Clark of Edinburgh writes: "I say at once that I concur very heartily with your suggestion as to a Conference of English Librarians— a subject that I have thought and spoken strongly about for some time past. I believe we have already lost a good deal from the want of united work. Use my name in any way you think best."

The Rev. Dr. Malet of Dublin writes: "I am sure the proposed Conference will prove to be a matter of great importance. I shall have much pleasure in co-operating in any way I can."

I now ask the rest of our profession whether they will join in promoting a Conference to be held under the auspices of these gentlemen. I would willingly call on all librarians in London and write to those of the largest provincial libraries, but official duties would prevent my doing this very quickly. If a sufficient number will do me the favour of writing to acquaint me with their assent, I propose to ask the London librarians to meet and elect a committee, which, corresponding with the provincial librarians and the officers-designate, should arrange all the details.

I hope the Conference might be held in London, where members would have the opportunity of inspecting, not only the largest library in the kingdom, but many others of very considerable size. Were such meetings to be of at all frequent occurrence, they might be held at other towns in turn.

The time should not be so near as to prevent the perfect organization of the Conference. Many of its members would, moreover, wish to master beforehand such works as Edwards' Memoirs of Libraries, and the great "Library Report", just published by the Government of the United States. Some would have papers to prepare for the Conference. The summer or early autumn would interfere with out holidays. Altogether, the end of autumn or beginning of winter seems the most fitting time. But these are points to be settled by the future committee. I only offer the above remarks to elicit the views of others.

I shall not occupy your space with the reasons why such a Conference would be most useful until I know that a single librarian disputes its utility. I fail to see how there can be two opinions on this head among those of us who have had any experience. Those who have not will, I trust, grant some weight to the judgement of men in the position of Mr. Winter Jones, Mr. Coxe, Mr. Bradshaw, Mr. Clark, and Dr. Malet.

I remain, Sir, faithfully yours,

EDWARD B. NICHOLSON.

London Institution, Feb. 14.

## NICHOLSON ON THE CONSOLIDATION AND AMENDMENT OF THE PUBLIC LIBRARIES ACTS FOR ENGLAND

As secretary of the late Metropolitan Free Libraries Committee and of the present Metropolitan Free Libraries Association, I have seen and heard so much of the difficulties which the existing conditions of these Acts throws in the way of their adoption—difficulties many of which are, I believe, unknown either to legislators or to librarians—that I have thought a statement of them with suggestions for their easy removal would be of interest, and might some day be of use.

Before remarking on the contents of the Acts, let me call attention to their number. There are no fewer than four of them,—the Act of 1855, and the Amendment Acts of 1866, 1871 and 1877. They are all to be found in Mr. Mullin's very admirable and cheap little book: "Free Libraries and News-rooms: their formation and management"; but, though this should be in the hands of every public librarian and his committee, we cannot reasonably expect that it should be known in places where the Acts have not been adopted. Now it is of the utmost importance that Acts of which the adoption depends entirely on local initiative and a local vote should be in a form readily obtainable and understandable by the ordinary local man. The ordinary local man, however, has to procure four separate Acts with a very fair chance of missing one of the four; or, if he does not miss an Act itself, of at least overlooking its provisions. The "Municipal Directory," for example, has an abstract of the Acts, drawn by a well-known barrister, who, although he has mentioned the existence of an Act of 1866, has nevertheless overlooked its provisions. The result is that he has stated the legal majority needed for the adoption of the Acts as upwards of two-thirds instead of upwards of one-half, a mistake which may have prevented many an alderman or town-councillor from moving their adoption. Nor is the alteration of the majority the only vitally important change which has been made in the Act of 1855. In the Act of 1866 leave is also given to the parishes adjoining a borough to combine with it for the purpose of adopting the Acts, while the very short Act of 1877 sets up a new mode of taking the votes, on the adoption of which the adoption of the Acts themselves is in many cases certain to depend. . . .

### AMENDMENTS OF PRINCIPLE

*Number of requisitionists.*—The number of ratepayers' signatures needed for a requisition is only ten. This is far too low. If the adoption of the Acts is to remain dependent upon a popular vote, it is grossly unfair that any ten ratepayers should be able to put their fellow-ratepayers to fresh trouble and expense once a year in cases where there is no probability of the Acts being adopted. I do not know that a small minority in favour of the adoption of the Acts ever have employed such tactics, but, as I have said before, Acts of Parliament ought to be framed so as to meet possibilities. And, if at least fifty ratepayers' signatures cannot be got, one of two things is certain—either there is no chance whatever of the Acts being adopted on a poll, or else the number of ratepayers is so small that a 1d. rate would not maintain a library in common decency.

*Power of disestablishment.*—I am equally in favour of giving the ratepayers a power to disestablish their library. One of the arguments most vigorously used against the adoption of the Acts is that, however great a failure the library might turn out, the ratepayers would be saddled with it for ever. I would certainly give them power to disestablish their library by a vote of three-fourths at intervals of five years. Such a provision would greatly assist the adoption of the Acts, and would do no kind of harm to libraries. In all libraries which do succeed the success is patent to every one, and they become an object of local pride even to those who do not use them. As a Liverpool man once said to me, "Liverpool would as soon think of tearing up its pavements and pulling down its gas-lamps as of doing away with its Free Library."

I believe that, on the contrary, such a provision would have the best possible effect on some libraries. However little reason any one of us may have for finding fault with his committee (and no one has less than myself), we know that library-committees are not always in intelligent sympathy with the needs of the people; and, however hardworking and enthusiastic we may be (I think I may say we are) as a body, we know that librarianship, like every other profession and employment, has its spiritless idlers. I cannot but think that on such committees and such librarians the knowledge that the very existence of their libraries depended upon their efforts would exercise a most healthy influence. . . .

*Corrupt practices.*—A clause against corrupt practices should be added. I am not aware of any cases of bribery, but in June 1878, Hackney voters are said to have been treated in public-houses and brought to the poll in vans, while in some cases intimidation of the grossest kind was practised. A landlord, whose name I can give, avowed in the presence of some of the leading supporters of the Acts that he had threatened to raise his tenants' rent sixpence a week unless they voted against the Acts; and the compound-householders, who in that parish form a very decided majority of voters, are said to have polled an almost unanimous No.

It is, however, even more necessary to make penal the corrupt mis-representation of the amount of the library-rate. It is to such mis-representation that the Hackney vote was due. It was not enough to state that Mr. Mundella had at that time a Bill before Parliament to increase the rate; it was not enough to name the day on which he brought in this imaginary Bill; it was not enough to placard the streets with prophecies that the library-rate, like the School-Board rate, would rise to sixpence. No; even after a letter of denial from Mr. Mundella had been widely published, tens of thousands of handbills were printed and distributed up to the last minute of the poll, broadly telling the ignorant voter that the question on which he had to vote was whether or not he would pay another three-pence in the pound.

*The Act of 1877 should be enforced at the requisitionists' option.*—The Act of 1877, which allowed the votes of the rate-payers to be taken by voting papers left at and collected from each house, instead of by public meeting and subsequent poll, would, if it were put in force more often, be of the greatest service to the Free Libraries movement. The friends of that movement desire nothing more than to have the question argued out in public, but, unhappily, they cannot always satisfy their desire. Each of the three meetings last year—at Hackney, Kensington, and Whitechapel—was attended by a mob of rowdies who refused to allow any speeches to be heard in favour of the adoption of the Acts. Whatever a man's position in his parish, however great and universally recognized his services to it, he was howled down if he advocated the adoption of the Acts. The results of such organized disturbance is, of course, to make it appear that the movement is hopelessly unpopular, to decide wavering voters against it, and to prevent lukewarm or timid voters from supporting it. Thus at Hackney a committee of 150 leading men of all politics and creeds polled only some four times their own number of votes, while at Whitechapel perhaps not more than one-fourth of the votes actually promised were given.

I urge, therefore, that the requisitionists themselves should be allowed to claim that the votes be taken under the Act of 1877; and I will add that, as far as one can judge from the single instance in which to my knowledge this mode of taking them has been adopted—namely, at Richmond—it secures a far more general expression of opinion; for, while at Hackney and Whitechapel only one-fifth of the rate-payers polled, nearly three-fifths of the Richmond ratepayers filled in their voting papers.

I fully grant that the voting paper system is capable of being misused, but the chief danger of such misuse comes from a certain class of opponents of the Acts, namely, the landlords of compound-house-holders. We have hitherto feared that many hostile landlords would go round to their tenants and see that they wrote "No" on their voting-paper. But, if we choose to face this risk, we ought to be allowed to claim that the decision of the ratepayers be taken in a way which will elicit the opinion of three out of five ratepayers, rather than a way which will elicit that of only one. . . .

*Power to adopt the Acts to be given to Town Councils, Vestries and Boards of Guardians.*—I maintain, however, that any new Act ought to go much further, and extend the power of adopting the Acts to Town Councils, Vestries and Boards of Guardians. It has long been in the power of these bodies to adopt the Baths and Washhouses Acts and to tax the ratepayers in respect of them, not merely to the amount of a penny in the pound, but to an amount altogether unlimited. Is Parliament not yet prepared to allow that a well-kept mind is as important both to the individual and to society as a well-kept skin? Surely Parliament, in passing the Elementary Education Act, has already allowed it? Or are we to consider that all the book-knowledge which is worth putting into us can be put in before the age of fourteen?

I do not, indeed, blame the framers of the original Act for making its adoption dependent on a popular vote. The working of the Act had yet to be tested; and in any case the opposition in the House was strong enough to make this concession prudent. But I do say that, after the Acts have been in force a quarter of a century, with a success which goes on increasing every year, the continuance of such a limitation is as great a slur on the reasonableness of our laws as it is an hindrance to the object for which those laws were enacted. . . .

*Inspection of libraries.*—Lastly: at least two inspectors of public libraries should be appointed, who should report yearly to Parliament on the administration and use of all libraries established under the Acts, and to all other libraries to which free admission is given, and which did not object to the inspection. It is obvious that such inspection is as much to be desired as the inspection of schools, whether by the ratepayer, the student or the librarian; and I am happy to think that we of the last class are so little influenced by any other feeling than a desire to serve the public good that, if such a proposal were not under the consideration of Government, from no body of men would it receive more enthusiastic support than from the Library Association of the United Kingdom.

From, Nicholson, Edward B. The consolidation and amendment of the Public Libraries Acts for England. *Transactions and Proceedings of the Second Annual Meeting of the Library Association of the United Kingdom, held at Manchester, September 23, 24 and 25, 1879, [etc.],* 1880, pp. 21–27.

# Chapter 29

# Sir William Osler (1849–1919)

"I should like to see added to the schools of at least one University in each division of the Kingdom a *School of the Book*, in all its relations, historical, technical, and commercial – every aspect of bibliography, every detail of typography, every possible side of bibliopoly."

Sir William Osler.

At regular intervals in the history of librarianship there have appeared personalities from other professions who have left their mark upon our calling. As collectors of large libraries, legislators, social workers, educationists, booksellers, or perhaps merely as book-lovers, they have contributed to the enhancement of book collecting and library administration as professional subjects. Several members of the medical profession have so honoured us, a few of them being mentioned in this volume, but probably the foremost friend of librarianship among medical men was Sir William Osler. As author, bibliographer, book collector, and particularly by his donations of books, he rendered invaluable service to libraries on both sides of the Atlantic. First and foremost Sir William was an ardent booklover who believed that every bibliographical item had a natural home, and it was his delight to purchase books solely for the purpose of presenting them to carefully selected libraries. He periodically ransacked the bookshops of Europe, and, particularly in his early years, his acquisitions frequently caused him to have "cobwebs in his pockets."

William Osler was born in 1849 at Bond Head, Canada, and after periods of study in Toronto and Montreal graduated at McGill University in 1872. For two years he pursued his medical studies in Europe, to return as Lecturer, and then Professor of Medicine at McGill, before occupying a similar position at the University of Pennsylvania in 1884. Five years later Osler went to the Johns Hopkins Medical School, but in 1905 he left America to become Regius Professor of Medicine at Oxford. Honorary degrees and other honours were bestowed upon him, and in 1911 William Osler was created a baronet. His clinical writings and teaching, his deep classical knowledge, and his charming bedside manner caused him to be described by Garrison as "the greatest physician of our time", but he also found time to assemble a remarkable collection of first editions and early classics of medicine and allied subjects. At his death this was bequeathed to McGill University "for the use of students of the history of science and of medicine, without any other qualifications." A catalogue of the collection was published ten years after Osler's death, being carefully edited by W. W. Francis, R. H. Hill and A. Malloch. Entitled *Bibliotheca Osleriana; a catalogue of books illustrating the history of medicine and science collected, arranged, and annotated by Sir William Osler, Bt., and bequeathed to McGill University*, Oxford, 1929, it is probably the most readable catalogue ever published, and lists about 7,600 bound volumes. Osler carefully classified the entries under the following eight headings, Bibliotheca Prima (to contain fundamental contributions), Bibliotheca Secunda (for those of less importance), Bibliotheca Litteraria, Bibliotheca Historica, Bibliotheca Biographica, Bibliotheca Bibliographica, Incunabula, and Manuscripts. The introduction to the catalogue consists of an outline of Osler's book-collecting career, while the value of the entries is greatly enhanced by characteristic annotations in typical Oslerian style.

In 1913 Osler became President of the Bibliographical Society, his Presidential Address being published in *Incunabula medica* in 1923. He was also first President of the British Medical Library Association, founded in 1909, but which unfortunately did not long survive.

During the Great War Sir William did not spare himself in the cause of his country, but the death of his only son on active service in 1917 struck him a blow from which he never quite recovered. On December 29th, 1919, he departed this life, and his ashes were deposited in McGill University among the books he had loved.

Osler was the author of a large number of writings, a bibliography of which has been compiled by Maude E. Abbott. They include several devoted to bibliography and librarianship, such as "Some aspects of American bibliography", 1902; "On the library of a medical school", 1907; "Remarks on the medical library in post-graduate work", 1909; and "The library school in the college", 1917. A selection of his papers was reprinted in *Selected writings of Sir William Osler, [etc.]*, 1951, published by the Osler Club, and reprinted as *A way of life, [etc.]*, 1958. Osler was a great friend to librarians, and inspired several medical men, including Harvey Cushing and John Fulton, to collect books. Medical librarians will remain indebted to him for his enthusiasm as a book-collector, which resulted in numerous valuable gifts to other libraries in addition to McGill; for his *Bibliotheca Osleriana*, which, on account of Osler's fascinating annotations, must surely be the most readable catalogue ever compiled; and for his general interest in libraries and their custodians. (Portrait, Plate 10.)

REFERENCES

The following are selected from a wealth of material relating to Sir William Osler:

Abbott, Maude E., ed. *Classified and annotated bibliography of Sir William Osler's publications. . . . Second edition, revised and indexed*, Montreal, 1939.

Ardagh, Philip. Sir William Osler as bibliophile and bibliographer. *Librarian*, 46, 1957, pp. 35–36.

Cushing, Harvey. *The life of Sir William Osler*, 2 vols., 1925. (One-volume edition, 1940.)

Keys, Thomas E. Sir William Osler and the medical library. Part I[–II]. *Bulletin of the Medical Library Association*, 49, 1961, pp. 24–39, 127–148.

MacNalty, Sir Arthur Salusbury. Osler, the medical historian. *Proceedings of the Royal Society of Medicine*, 56, 1963, Supplement, pp. 3–9.

## OSLER ON BOOKS AND MEN

But when one considers the unending making of books, who does not sigh for the happy days of that thrice happy Sir William Browne whose pocket library sufficed for his life's needs; drawing from a Greek testament his divinity, from the aphorisms of Hippocrates his medicine, and from an Elzevir Horace his good sense and vivacity. There should be in connection with every library a corps of instructors in the art of reading, who would, as a labour of love, teach the young idea how to read. An old writer says that there are four sorts of readers: "Sponges which attract all without distinguishing; Howre-glasses which receive and powre out as fast; Bagges which only retain the dregges of the spices and let the wine escape, and Sives which retaine the best onely." A man wastes a great many years before he reaches the "sive" stage.

[pp. 210–211]

. . .

There is a third class of men in the profession to whom books are dearer than to teachers and practitioners—a small, a silent band, but in reality the leaven of the whole lump. The profane call them bibliomaniacs, and in truth they are at times irresponsible and do not always know the difference between *meum* and *tuum*. . . . Loving books partly for their contents, partly for the sake of the authors, they not alone keep alive the sentiment of historical continuity in the profession, but they are the men who make possible such gatherings as the one we are enjoying this evening.[1] We need more men of their class, particularly in this country, where every one carries in his pocket the tape-measure of utility. Along two lines their work is valuable. By the historical method alone can many problems in medicine be approached profitably. For example, the student who dates his knowledge of tuberculosis

[1] Taken from an address delivered at the Boston Medical Library, 1901. [J.L.T.]

from Koch may have a very correct, but he has a very incomplete, appreciation of the subject. Within a quarter of a century our libraries will have certain alcoves devoted to the historical consideration of the great diseases, which will give to the student that mental perspective which is so valuable an equipment in life. The past is a good nurse, as Lowell remarks, particularly for the weanlings of the fold.

> 'Tis man's worst deed
> To let the things that have been, run to waste
> And in the unmeaning Present sink the Past.

But in a more excellent way these *laudatores temporis acti* render a royal service. For each one of us to-day, as in Plato's time, there is a higher as well as a lower education. The very marrow and fatness of books may not suffice to save a man from becoming a poor, mean-spirited devil, without a spark of fine professional feeling, and without thought above the sordid issues of the day. The men I speak of keep alive in us an interest in the great men of the past and not alone in their works, which they cherish, but in their lives, which they emulate. They would remind us continually that in the records of no other profession is there to be found so large a number of men who have combined intellectual pre-eminence with nobility of character. This higher education so much needed today is not given in the school, is not to be bought in the market place, but it has to be wrought out in each one of us for himself; it is the silent influence of character on character and in no way more potently than in the contemplation of the lives of the great and good of the past, in no way more than in "the touch divine of noble natures gone."

[pp. 212–213]

## OSLER'S BED-SIDE LIBRARY FOR MEDICAL STUDENTS[1]

A liberal education may be had at a very slight cost of time and money. Well filled though the day be with appointed tasks, to make the best possible use of your one or your ten talents, rest not satisfied with this professional training, but try to get the education, if not of a scholar, at least of a gentleman. Before going to sleep read for half an hour, and in the morning have a book open on your dressing table. You will be surprised to find how much can be accomplished in the course of a year. I have put down a list of ten books which you may make close friends. There are many others; studied carefully in your student days these will help in the inner education of which I speak.

---

[1] Suitable for all students, as shown. [J.L.T.]

I. Old and New Testament. II. Shakespeare. III. Montaigne. IV. Pultarch's *Lives*. V. Marcus Aurelius. VI. Epictetus. VII. *Religio Medici*[1]. VIII. Don Quixote. IX. Emerson. X. Oliver Wendell Holmes—Breakfast-Table Series.

[p. 453]

[1] By Sir Thomas Browne (1605–1682). [J.L.T.]

From, Osler, Sir William. *Aequanimitas; with other addresses to medical students, nurses and practitioners of medicine. . . . Reprinted from the third edition. Biographical note by Sir Walter Langdon-Brown. With a portrait,* 1939.

# CHAPTER 30

# Henry Richard Tedder (1850–1924)

"It is impossible to train librarians except in connexion with a large library. No amount of professional lecturing or intimate acquaintance with mere book-lore is, without practical experience, of much value in preparing for the administration of a library."

H. R. TEDDER.

HENRY RICHARD TEDDER was born on June 25th, 1850 at South Kensington, and after a private education was appointed Librarian to Lord Acton in 1873. The following year he became Assistant Librarian to the Athenaeum Club, London, and later occupied the positions of Librarian and Secretary to the Club, holding the joint offices until his retirement in 1922.

Tedder was a founder of the Library Association, having been one of the organizers of the first International Conference of Librarians held in 1877, and acting as Joint Secretary and Editor of the *Transactions* with E. W. B. Nicholson. When the Library Association was formed, he and E. C. Thomas edited the *Transactions* of the first two annual meetings, and Tedder was also Honorary Treasurer of the Association from 1889 until his death on August 1st, 1924, with the exception of the years 1897–1898, when he held the office of President. He was Treasurer and Secretary to the Metropolitan Free Libraries Committee, which later became the Metropolitan Libraries Association, and held office in numerous other organizations.

In 1882 Tedder read a paper on "Librarianship as a profession" at the Cambridge meeting, and was deeply interested in the training of library assistants. This paper is reproduced below. Tedder was Chairman of the Education Committee from 1902 to 1924, and contributed numerous papers to the *Transactions* and to other librarianship periodicals.

With James Duff Brown he was author of the remarkable article on "Libraries" in the eleventh edition of *Encyclopaedia Britannica*, which has not been approached for clarity and usefulness in later editions. Tedder also contributed to the *Dictionary of National Biography* and Palgrave's *Dictionary of Political Economy*.

Tedder was active in founding the University of London School of Librarianship, which represented an important step in his plans for the improvement of the training of library assistants. He spent much of his time serving the Library Association, acting as Chairman of the Cataloguing Rules Committee, of the Conference on New Books, 1907, and in fact monopolizing the major official positions. E. A. Savage has stated: "Tedder was our pet goblin. He hated change and loved petty power." He was Treasurer for thirty-four years, presided over Council for thirty years, and chaired the Education Committee for twenty-two years. This made him a virtual dictator, which was resented by many members who considered him to be adverse to development in certain branches of librarianship. This caused dissension, but although Tedder was not regarded with united favour by his contemporaries, he certainly made his mark on the history of the Library Association, and of librarianship in general. (Portrait, Plate 8C.)

## REFERENCES

Henry Richard Tedder, F.S.A. – Obituary notice and list of his published works. (Signed J.B.). *Library Association Record*, 2nd Ser., 2, 1924, pp. 141–145; portrait, *ibid.*, 18, 1916, p. 93.

Personalities of the Past. IX. Henry Richard Tedder. *Librarian & Book World*, 31, 1941, p. 7.

## TEDDER ON LIBRARIANSHIP AS A PROFESSION

The thoughts which this subject suggest may be grouped under the following heads:—1. Professional Qualifications; 2. Training, including library-assistants and examinations; 3. Duties; 4. Remuneration; and 5. The question of opening librarianship as a calling for women.

The time has come when a librarian may, without assumption, speak of his occupation as a profession. One happy result of the establishment of this Association has been to foster and consolidate something like a professional spirit; and the creation of a high standard of librarianship, and the promotion of a fellow-feeling of mutual helpfulness are among the most valuable objects to be sought by us. While possessing, I hope, a full share of the learning of his predecessors, the librarian of the future must look forward to occupy a very different position towards both his library and the public. He must be a thorough and systematic worker, one eager to avail himself of every new professional improvement, either in appliances or methods, but above all one whose principal aim shall be that readers may derive the utmost possible benefit from a collection it is his pride to maintain in the highest state of efficiency.

With the new and increasing duties cast upon him, the social status of the librarian will surely improve. Librarianship is gradually assuming exact and scientific proportions, and when librarians make the educational value of their profession more apparent, they will certainly attain in public estimation the high position deserved by the importance of their functions.

Librarians are naturally prone to regard library-economy from the standpoint of their own requirements. A college librarian would seem to think that no libraries exist save those for learned readers, the custodian of a special collection sometimes takes a specialist's view of all other classes of literature, and the free public librarian is apt to look at his own popular library as the typical one upon which discussion should be based. But certain general and fundamental principles really govern all libraries, and it is those principles that I have endeavoured to hold in view in the course of this paper.

## I. QUALIFICATIONS

F. A. Ebert in his *Bildung des Bibliothekars* (Leipzig, 1820), has given a formidable list of the requirements wanted in a good librarian. Such universitality as he asked for may be desirable, but it is very rarely to be obtained in one individual. Without going into particulars, however, one may expect the ordinary librarian to me a man of refinement, of liberal education, and especially endowed with sympathy with books and reading. But a general taste for literature is not all that is required, and a finished scholar or accomplished specialist may often turn out a very incompetent person to have charge of a library. In an institution for the use of learned readers wide general culture and extensive knowledge of ancient and modern literatures are absolutely essential in the librarian, an acquaintance with bibliography, including palæography and diplomatics, being also necessary, as well as the theory and practice of library management. To be thoroughly qualified a librarian should have had the practical experience of library wotk which it is impossible to obtain from any amount of book-reading, and if without practical experience he must possess the faculty of teaching himself. He should be a man of business habits and a good administrator; above all, he must be willing to devote his whole life to the study of his profession, for a librarian should never consider that he has finished his education. These requirements imply qualifications of a somewhat higher character than may perhaps be needed in all libraries, but some knowledge of languages and literatures, of bibliography, bibliology, and general library management, must be possessed by any person holding the chief position in the administration of a library, however small this may be.

Knowledge of local literature is now becoming a necessity, and the history of libraries should not be overlooked by a man who desires to form accurate views of librarianship based upon general principles. Very closely connected with the history of libraries is the history of bookselling, both as regards its past stages and its actual condition.

The different varieties of libraries being so numerous, it must seem at the first glance impossible to specify at once the qualifications expected in the principal librarian of the British Museum and those which benefit the librarian of a small circulating library. But apart from scholarly acquirements, which must vary in each case, there are certain essential requisites in every librarian. In the first place, he must possess some idea of library technicalities, he must be filled with a sincere love of books, he must be of a methodical and organizing mind, he must have business habits, and he must be of a courteous demeanour.

Since Mr. Winter Jones ("London Conference", 1878) quoted the Rector of Lincoln's epigram in the Life of Casaubon, "The librarian who reads is lost", the quotation has been so frequently misapplied and misunderstood that the author must rather wince to hear it again. No amount of reading can harm a librarian if he only refrains from reading in working hours. "The librarian who *writes* is lost" is much more to the point, and if librarians would make good catalogues instead of indifferent books, the world would be much better served by them. In my opinion a librarian cannot know too much nor be too catholic in his range, but he should be content with wide rather than deep knowledge. He should possess an indexing mind, and cultivate the art of reading with his fingers, so as to know where to find information without storing the information in his memory. He should be technical without being mechanical. Besides his general cultivation and professional acquirements in bibliography and bibliology, he ought to keep himself thoroughly acquainted with the progress made throughout the world in every department of library organization. There is of course the danger of resorting overmuch to mechanical aids; for instance, with regard to the proposal to introduce co-operative cataloguing, it has been urged that if so much of his work were done for him outside, the good librarian would soon become an extinct creature. In his technical equipment, practical knowledge of the work in a printing office and in a bookbinder's shop should not be omitted. I may add that perhaps few places offer a better field for a wide and varied acquaintance with books than a bookseller's shop, and it was to such a training that the late David Laing owed his marvellous bibliographical knowledge.

A man should try to be a librarian and nothing else, or, if he attempts other occupations as well, he should subordinate them to his profession. He should be a librarian first, and a man of letters or a specialist afterwards. There is quite enough in librarianship (even in the management of the most humble library) to occupy an energetic man all the years he is likely to care to enjoy in this world.

But besides these intellectual gifts there are certain diplomatic qualifications desirable in men connected with public bodies. First, as to dealing with undesirable gifts; secondly, in the treatment of bores; thirdly, and chiefly, in his relations with the library committee or governing body. A little treatise on the last subject would, I am sure, meet with a ready sale, but I think the only difficulty which may exist lies in the constitution of most committees. They are not a permanent, but a constantly changing body without traditions or policy. If the librarian would educate his committee instead of trying to "manage', them, things would always work smoothly and consistently. Before leaving this portion of my subject I ought to remark that even the most expert officials must not fancy that his readers have nothing to teach him in library management. He should always be ready to listen to hints and suggestions from the users of his books.

## 2. TRAINING

Since the need of a proper organization of libraries, and of a more systematic study of library science, is now recognized, it may be hoped that the time is not distant when librarians shall be properly trained like the members of the other liberal professions.

The professorship of books and reading so frequently advocated by Emerson, and which we had hoped to see carried into active working at Harvard, would at once have laid the foundation of the "School for Librarians" ("London Conference", p. 146), which the late Bodleian librarian held to be a point of such importance. Mr. C. H. Robarts, in his paper on "University Libraries as National Institutions" ("London", p. 35), said that "Assistants qualified in that special knowledge which has been termed *Bibliothekswissenschaft* are more and more essential to a great University library, and amongst the advantages of the development of University libraries we may hope for the rise of a school of highly-trained students in bibliographical knowledge." Mr. Robarts sketched out a University library system for Oxford, based upon an association of the Bodleian and All Souls';—a suggestion supported by Mr. Coxe and many leading Oxonians as a step in the right direction.

At our Oxford meeting the subject came before us again in Mr. Axon's paper on "Professorships of Bibliography"[1] ("Oxford Meeting", p. 104), which, although without showing how such a thing could be carried out, and although dealing chiefly with books,

[1] See pp. 186–190 [J.L.T.].

suggested that "the systems for the classification of knowledge, and all the more essential features of library science might also be explained" (p. 189). One thing is certain. It is impossible to train librarians except in connexion with a large library. No amount of professional lecturing or intimate acquaintance with mere book-lore is, without practical experience, of much value in preparing for the administration of a library. Every large library is a training-school in an informal manner. Birmingham has been a nursery of librarians, and such has been the London Library. In America the Boston Athenæum and Public Library have turned out many excellent officials. But some system of professional education and practical training is very much wanted in order to furnish a criterion of librarianship for beginners. Youths ought not to have to depend upon their own exertions, or upon the tolerance of their superiors, to acquire the general principles of their profession. At any rate, whether library assistants are trained before or after they enter the service, they should certainly receive technical instruction some time or other, and not be suffered to do their duties in a rule of thumb style without being well grounded in general principles. Not unfrequently is a librarian to be at once placed in office without any previous training whatever, and has to educate himself as he can. In such a case the example of the energetic American librarian (*Library Journal*, iv., 24) who made himself conversant in turn with every duty connected with the institution, from opening the doors in the morning to the selection, purchase, and cataloguing of the books,—might well be followed. Thanks to the existence of a ministry of public instruction in France and Italy, there is some prospect of seeing the foundation of a system of technical training in those countries. By an order of M. Ferry in 1879, candidates for librarianships in the French Universities must have two years' probation, and pass successfully a professional examination which requires a dissertation upon a given subject of bibliography, and also the classification of fifteen works treating of different matters, and belonging to several periods of the history of printing (*Library Journal*, iv., 460).

These requirements are not very formidable, but they show that the French are fully alive to the importance of technical education in libraries. In Italy a system of examination and training was drawn up for the public libraries by Signor Bonghi in 1876,[1] and Dr. Rullmann in his pamphlet (*Die Bibliothekseinrichtungskunde*, 1874)[2] has elaborated a plan suitable more especially for German libraries.

[1] On the Regulations of Italian Public Libraries, by Count Ugo Balzani. *Library Journal*, 1879, iv., p. 183, etc.
[2] See *Report on United States Libraries*, p. xxiv.

*Library Assistants and Examination*

There is no question of deeper importance to us in the future than the training of a body of assistants fit to fill subordinate positions, but who may eventually look forward to occupy higher posts. Mr. Mullins ("Edinburgh Meeting", see p. 72) lamented the dearth of juniors. "As a rule the librarian has to educate his own assistants; in other professions it is possible to obtain trained help, but the rapid growth of the library movement has so quickly promoted juniors into principals, that the librarian of to-day has to be to a certain degree the trainer for to-morrow." At the Manchester Free Public Library the same difficulty of procuring and keeping intelligent youths has led to the introduction of female labour. The candidates for the position of assistants in the British Museum have to undergo a preliminary examination of a literary and Civil Service character. The subject seemed to me so thoroughly within the scope of the Association that at the Edinburgh meeting the following motion was moved in my name:—"That it is desirable that the Council of this Association should consider how library assistants may best be aided in their training in the general principles of their profession." This was cordially supported by most of our leading members, and carried unanimously. I had always thought it would be advisable to make some arrangements for imposing a preliminary examination upon librarians, and for the granting of certificates of proficiency; and by what body could this be better carried out than by the Library Association? This view of the duties of the Association was taken by the Committee appointed by the Council in pursuance of the motion. At the ensuing meeting held at Gray's Inn in September last (*Monthly Notes*, ii, 63), their Report, with a scheme of examination was, for some reasons which have never transpired, "received", but not "adopted". The Committee were strongly of opinion that the question might be made an extremely useful feature of the practical work of the Association, and after due deliberation had concluded that the end would best be served by providing for the examination of candidates and the granting of certificates of proficiency. This course would naturally involve some direction as regards special studies and the choice of books to be read, with perhaps arrangements for lectures on matters connected with librarianship. It was suggested that for the present the Council should also undertake to examine candidates who have not been actually engaged as library assistants. The practical performance of the examination and the appointment of examiners would of course devolve upon the Council. It was also recommended that library assistants should be admitted to some of the advantages of membership at a nominal or greatly reduced subscription. Other points would have doubtless occurred to the Council, such as that of prizes for the best essays on topics of library management. At one of the monthly meetings (*Library Journal*, iv, 14) Mr. Scarse made an excellent suggestion as to the exchange among librarians of the right of borrowing books from each other's stores. It would be highly desirable if assistants could be transferred from one library to another from time to time as a means of affording them broader views of books and library management than could be obtained in one institution. The examination proposal excited warm approval in America, and some observations by a very competent judge (Mr. Cutter, in *Library Journal*, vi, 289) may be read with profit.

In the course of the interesting discussion at Edinburgh upon the proposal, several members spoke in praise of the apprenticeship of young librarians, and this system is said to work well at Liverpool, Plymouth, Worcester, Newcastle, and other places. At Bolton youths are bound over for two years, while at Liverpool and Plymouth the term extends to five years. I am willing to believe that the system works well in all these cases, but I think it is one so contrary to all the teachings of social economy, and, I must say, so contrary to the best interests of our profession, that I feel bound to lift up my voice against it. It may be retorted that the *word* "apprentice" is the chief stumbling-block, and if the term "articled pupil" were adopted, as is the case with lawyers' clerks, young surveyors, and teachers, to the *thing* no objection would have arisen. But "articled pupil" is but a genteel name for apprentice. The anomalies of the law do not need discussion; as regards surveyors and teachers, they will soon come under a recognized examination system. The only solid argument in favour of apprenticeship is that in public libraries youths are not paid sufficient to tempt them to devote themselves to library work; they would get better pay as clerks or shopmen. In plain language, a boy is forced to follow a calling he may not like, at wages less than his market value. It is possible to make the service sufficiently attractive without resorting to any such devices.

"Apprenticeship, or industrial slavery of youths," as it is aptly called by our late distinguished member, Dr. Stanley Jevons, in his last work, *The State in relation to Labour*, is a relic of the middle ages, whose "origin is to be sought on the mediæval gilds from the twelfth century onwards, the purpose being obviously to combine instruction with that limitation of numbers entering a trade, which was always a prime point of gild policy." After relating the history of the different statutes relating to apprentices, Dr. Stanley Jevons continues: "It is now simply a survival, an obsolete relic of a former state of things. There is, however, little need to argue about the matter, because the greatest authorities have denounced the custom" (pp. 75–79).

Mr. Nicholson recommended ("Oxford Meeting", p. 137) librarians to try as assistants boys with a fairly good education, who should be taken at a teachable age. Much could be done by the chief librarians and library committees taking a direct personal interest in the technical training of assistants. We know of the excellent library society established by Mr. Cowell among the members of his own staff. (*Monthly Notes*, iii, 36.)

One eminent authority is reported to be of the opinion that gentlemen's servants make the best librarians. Although an efficient officer may have begun life in that or any similar capacity, his efficiency is not due to, but it in spite of, his previous occupation.

The fundamental difference between a liberal profession and a handicraft union is that in the former some kind of preparatory examination is obligatory. To quote Dr. Stanley Jevons again: "Examinations have become the sole mode of entry, not only in the medical profession, the lower branch of the law, the civil service, the army and navy, and even the church, but many other bodies of professional men have taken steps in the like direction" (p. 123). The Institute of Actuaries, the Bankers' Institute, the Society of Chartered Accountants, and the Teachers in secondary schools, are examples. There is no analogy between these bodies and trade unions. No trade society in modern times has ever made any pretence of demanding a test of proficiency.

We ought to set our faces against any unconscious tendency towards making a trades union of our Association. The limitation of the number of non-professional members is a line of policy which I hope may be altered. The system of apprenticeship I trust may be radically reformed. I have no abstract love of examinations and examiners, indeed personally I nourish a profound dislike to examiners, but I am firmly of the opinion that nothing better can be contrived, which will maintain a high standard among librarians, than a well-considered system of examination.

### 3. DUTIES

I will not tire you with the oft-told tale of a librarian's duties, but one or two points of general policy deserve attention. Besides furnishing the materials for study, it is now recognized that the librarian has also the function of indicating lines of reading and research. A librarian should not consider his work ended with the actual management of his institution. He has a higher duty to perform. He should bear in mind that he stands as it were in the position of host to the reader; that it is his duty to make the collection under his care of the greatest possible use to those who have the privilege of using it, and he should not only cheerfully assist when asked for help, but readily volunteer help to any reader who might be unwilling to request it. The practical value of public libraries should be made so manifest, that the public would as soon think of dispensing with them as with the rail-road or the post office. At Worcester (Mass.) intimate relations have been organized between the library and the public schools, and in many college libraries, especially in America, the librarian has become a valuable coadjutor to the professional staff. Direct personal relations between librarians and readers are always highly desirable. The librarian should endeavour to make himself as accessible as possible, even at the risk of having his time occupied with idle gossip. For this reason he should be thoroughly familiar with the contents of his library, since the best subject-catalogue to which a reader can refer is a competent librarian. To do this, it is desirable that he should share in the compilation of the catalogue, at any sacrifice of time and trouble, for by no other means can he obtain so exact acquaintance with his books.

After having fully recognized that the librarian should be literally the servant as well as the guide, of the reader, a mild protest against the unreasonable character of the exigencies of some readers may be permitted. Many highly cultivated persons seem to be ignorant of the most rudimentary matters in library management. Two injunctions from the late Dr. Maitland's amusing skit issued during the British Museum agitation of 1848, are examples of what one is sometimes asked.

"*Thes been the Lawes for the Keper of the Bokys*" taken from an ancient MS.

vii. "Item, he shall make the same kalendars and inventories lyke as everyche man wold haue them to be.

viii. "Item, whan anie man comith and wotteth not what he wold haue, then he shall tell hym, and doe hym to understonde hys besynesse."

(See "London Conference", p. 208.)


## 4. REMUNERATION

Librarianship, like every other calling, is dependent upon the great economic law of supply and demand, and doubtless the plain reason of the want of competent librarians and the difficulty of getting and keeping good assistants, is really owing to the low rate of remuneration with which it is thought necessary to reward their labour. That this remuneration is generally inadequate has frequently been the subject of discussion at our meetings. In his Inaugural Address, the Principal Librarian of the British Museum, Mr. Winter Jones, said, "It is well that it should be understood that the life of a librarian is a hard one; that his work never relaxes; and, looking to the importance of his functions, and the special nature of his qualifications, he ought to be well paid. He ought to be so remunerated as to be placed above the necessity of supplementing his income by literary work."[1] ("London Conference", p. 20.) Some people think a librarian's work is so easy and agreeable, and the constant association with books and scholars so delightful, that these charms ought to be taken into account in estimating his rate of pay.

I have never heard of a librarian boasting of the extent of his professional earnings; an eloquent silence is generally preserved on this head; and, except in the great public institutions (where apart, perhaps, from the pay of the subordinate officials, there is not much to complain of) and the free public libraries (where, on the other hand, there is much to complain of), we know little of the general rate of pay, but we may confidently assume that it is not on a very exalted scale. A glance at the "Statistical Report on the Free Public Libraries of the United Kingdom", by Mr. C. W. Sutton and G. L. Campbell, appended to the Manchester volume, will show that the salaries paid, with very few exceptions, are creditable neither to the liberality nor to the intelligence of English provincial towns. The circumstance doubtless arises in some instances from the insufficiency of the penny rate. Although this may be unavoidable, it is not the less to be deprecated. Said Mr. Nicholson at the London Conference (p. 177), "seeing that the energy and ingenuity required for the efficient working of a free public library would make a man's fortune in business in a few years, his wonder was that such towns ever got or kept a good librarian." The "Salaries of Librarians" was the title of a paper read at Oxford, in which our Treasurer, with his natural financial bent, entered into elaborate calculations, showing that such officials were paid at a less rate than shoeblacks. In his opinion "exceptional acquirements and great responsibilities may justly entitle the accomplished librarian to a higher remuneration, but £250 should be the lowest stipend to a duly qualified person" ("Oxford Meeting", p. 94).[2] We find that in college and cathedral libraries things are much worse.[3] Here the position of librarian is usually regarded as merely ornamental, and rewarded accordingly.

[1] See pp. 98-103. [J.L.T.]
[2] A proposal was made for a "Librarians' and Curators' Fund", about which I am sorry to say nothing more has since been heard.
[3] "The Libraries of Oxford", by E. C. Thomas ("Oxford Meeting", p. 27); and "Our Cathedral Libraries", by Rev. H. E. Reynolds (*ibid.*, p. 41).

The question of the remuneration of French librarians was touched upon at the same meeting by the Baron de Watteville, a competent authority, who remarked that, as in this country, the pay was not equal to the importance of the functions (see "Oxford", p. 137). It must be acknowledged, however, that in continental libraries salaries are generally upon a much lower scale than is the case with us. This may be the cause of the Dean of Chichester's well-known distinction between English and foreign libraries (see "Oxford Meeting", p. 141), which consisted in the fact that you never needed to *tip* anyone in this country. In the United States salaries range higher, chiefly because librarianship is there recognized as a calling requiring technical education and experience, and not a refuge for the failures in other professions.

In America, libraries are something better than museums of old books; their custodians have a business-like view of their duties, and are better paid in consequence. But in speaking thus of insufficient salaries, it must not be thought that all librarians are fully competent and underpaid officials. Some are doubtless not underpaid, but over-paid. I ought to add that personally I have nothing to complain of, but I see no reason to be squeamish on the salary question. Nothing touches us more intimately, and the subject is closely connected with the dignity and prosperity of our calling. It has been very pointedly observed ("Oxford Meeting", p. 90), "There can be very little doubt that you greatly help to raise a man's status when you raise his salary."

As the office of librarian demands very special qualifications and education, why is it that he earns so much less than other professional men? It is not that the market is overstocked. There is really a great want of qualified candidates. The fact is, that librarianship has too long been regarded as an easy and amateur existence; one of lettered idleness, and not of enterprise and activity. A position which it is thought any educated (or, indeed, uneducated) man can hold is not likely to be well paid: but, as the necessity of looking out for technically trained librarians becomes more obvious, prospects will become brighter. The expert has a right to command a sum which the amateur would not dream of demanding.

### 5. WOMEN AS LIBRARIANS

I am glad to say that women are gradually making their way in libraries, and happily it is no longer necessary to give reasons why they should not be so employed. It is easy to find young women fully qualified, both by education and natural aptness, and they are generally more refined and more teachable than the young men of their own class. Of course there are many objections to placing women in any public office. They are said to be wanting in intelligence or physical strength; they are reported to distract the attention of male readers; and the duties of a library are considered inappropriate to their sex. Some people object to the presence of young women as assistants in a library on the ground that such a proceeding savours of novelty, and therefore ought to be opposed. Now I don't mind anyone holding erroneous opinions or nursing prejudice. The latter, in particular, is a very natural and pleasant exercise of the mind. I only ask objectors to state their reasons, good or bad, as I am sure they will change them before long. The success of the employment of women in libraries is a recognized fact, and if the system, having once been adopted anywhere, has had to be dropped, I believe it is owing to the way in which it was worked, and not to the system itself. In the United States most of the librarians are women, and we know how strongly in their favour were Mr. J. Winsor, Mr. W. F. Poole, and Mr. L. P. Smith "London Conference", see p. 177). In the Boston Public Library two-thirds of the staff are ladies, and for £100 to £160 a year the pick of Vassar and Wellesley can be readily obtained. Some of the most accomplished cataloguers in America are women, and they find constant employment in this special work, at wages far above those of the chiefs in many English libraries. In a recent letter Mr. Cutter told me that his way out of the difficulty of procuring efficient assistants in the Boston Athenæum has been the employment of female labour, chiefly selected from the "Brahmin class". The same difficulty in securing and keeping capable youths has led to the adoption of a similar course at Manchester, which is believed to be the first place in England where young women were employed as library assistants. The practice has been greatly extended and followed with marked success.[1]

At several other places in this country they are employed as assistants, and at Notting Hill, Blackpool, and other places, the chief charge of the library is maintained in a very efficient manner by a lady. Ladies also find employment in Swedish libraries, but I am not aware of any other European country which follows so good an example.

Mr. Walford has told us (Library Journal, v, 14) that he found lady librarians in America suffering both as regards health and personal appearance. The deteriorating influence cannot exist in this country, for at Manchester I believe the complaint is that young ladies no sooner become competent than they secure husbands, and enter another sphere of usefulness. But I hope it may not be understood that the sole

---

[1] See Mr. Alderman Baker, "On the Employment of Young Women, &c." ("Manchester Meeting", p. 33).

reason for advocating librarianship as a field for the employment of women is that they fill subordinate positions for less money than men. Here at Cambridge, Newnham College will be able to supply highly educated young ladies, fit, after proper technical training, to occupy much more important offices, and I sincerely trust that at no distant time we may welcome a Cambridge girl-graduate as one of our most distinguished members.

In the course of my remarks I have tried to avoid rhetorical flourishes as to the elevated character of a librarian's duties and the sacred nature of a librarian's rights and personal position, but have limited my considerations to the following practical points:—

*Firstly.* In speaking of professional qualifications, I have merely indicated the direction in which they should lie.

*Secondly.* I have endeavoured to show that it is impossible to maintain a proper professional spirit without some sort of organized training, supported by a recognized system of preliminary examination.

*Thirdly.* I have touched upon some views of the higher duties of librarians towards readers.

*Fourthly.* The frequently inadequate nature of the emoluments of librarians is discussed, and,

*Finally.* The further employment of lady librarians is warmly supported.

Complaints are frequently heard that well-educated youths cannot find employment in consequence of the overcrowding of all the liberal professions. There is a large field open in librarianship, if those young men would only add to their previous acquirements a certain amount of technical knowledge. There is a want of competent librarians, as anyone must confess on looking through the lists of candidates for vacant appointments.

The profession of librarian has a great future. No man can form any idea of what will be the extent of printed literature as time goes on, and while books increase, and the difficulties of dealing with them grow in a like degree, so must the librarian become a more important factor in the work of intellectual development and the advancement of civilization.

From, Tedder, H. R. Librarianship as a profession. *Transactions and Proceedings of the . . . Fifth Annual Meeting of the Library Association, . . . 1882*, 1884, pp. 163–172.

PLATE 9

HENRY BENJAMIN WHEATLEY

(1838 – 1917)

PLATE 10

SIR WILLIAM OSLER

(1849 – 1919)

(By kind permission of Messrs. Elliott & Fry Ltd.)

# CHAPTER 31

# Thomas Greenwood (1851–1908)

"The State has not done everything for the people that it is called upon to do when it has provided a gaol, a workhouse, a lunatic asylum, a policeman, and a share in the common hangman."

THOMAS GREENWOOD.

ALTHOUGH librarians may have heard of Greenwood's *Yearbook*, or have encountered his biography of Edward Edwards and other writings, few appreciated the details of his career until the publication in 1949 of *Spade work*, a biography of Greenwood, by Grace Carlton. That volume sets down the life story of a man who devoted much of his time to the development of the library movement, although he himself had only served as a librarian for a very limited period.

Thomas Greenwood was born on May 9th, 1851, at Mount Pleasant, near Stockport, and at the death of his father his mother worked in a mill to support her children. Following intermittent schooling, Greenwood took a job at W. H. Smith & Son's railway bookstall at Stockport, and later went to London Road Station, Manchester, where he was engaged in checking telegrams. In 1870 he became traveller to a Sheffield hardware firm, and was on the road for three years. He then entered Sheffield Public Library as assistant librarian, and became librarian at the Upperthorne branch. Greenwood married in 1874, when earning £75 per annum, and was soon forced to resume travelling. He became business manager of *The Ironmonger*, and moved to London. He founded several other technical periodicals, and set up with a partner to publish technical books and journals. Success followed, and in April, 1882 Greenwood visited America, on his return writing *The tour of the United States and Canada*, which was followed by *Eminent naturalists; Grace Montrose: an unfashionable novel*, which is largely autobiographical; and *Free public libraries*, all published in 1886. This latter was written to stimulate interest in public libraries, and the second edition, published the following year with the edition of two new chapters, was priced at one shilling. A third edition appeared in 1887, and a fourth in 1894, the title having changed to *Public libraries: a history of the movement, and a manual for the organization and management of rate-supported libraries*.

Thomas Greenwood was interested in the provision of village and

Sunday-school libraries, museums and art galleries. He made a thorough study of the subject, and had a voluminous correspondence with librarians. In 1897 he brought out his *Library Year Book*, the second edition of which was entitled *The British Library Year Book*, 1900. The third edition, 1910, was edited by Alex. J. Philip, and this reference book continued to appear at intervals under various editors, and with differing titles.

Greenwood was a close friend of James Duff Brown, who aided him with his library publications, and Greenwood's firm published the first edition of Brown's *Manual of library economy*.

In April, 1897 the death of the sister of Edward Edwards led Greenwood to investigate the life of the latter, and he had bound the sheets of the unfinished second edition of Edwards' *Memoirs of libraries*, distributing the copies to libraries and interested persons. Greenwood also acquired Edwards' library and other relics, and suggested that the Library Association might house his Edward Edwards material, but this offer was not accepted, and it went to Manchester. Greenwood caused a memorial to be erected over the unmarked grave of Edwards at Niton, and his biography appeared in 1902 as *Edward Edwards, the chief pioneer of municipal public libraries*. It is dedicated "To the Forgotten Benefactors of Humanity", and up to the end of July, 1903, only 338 copies had been sold. It tends to ignore the short-comings of its subject, and although a fascinating study, it should be read in conjunction with the more recent scholarly study by W. A. Munford entitled *Edward Edwards, 1812–1886: portrait of a librarian*, 1963.

Greenwood formed a remarkable "Library for Librarians" containing 12,000 items, including rare books, early printings, and examples of fine bindings, which he presented to Manchester. He left £5,000 in his will for the endowment of the Thomas Greenwood Library for Librarians, which now houses about 26,000 volumes and is maintained for the use of librarians upon application.

Thomas Greenwood was a philanthropist who spent not only money, but precious time, for the benefit of his fellow men. He carefully investigated the history and development of librarianship, and considerably furthered its objectives, which he did not consider to include the erection of elaborate buildings that would prove to be "white elephants". Thomas Greenwood, the "apostle of the library movement" died on November 9th, 1908. (Portrait, Plate 12A.)

## REFERENCES

Carlton, Grace. *Spade work: the story of Thomas Greenwood*, [1949].

Horrocks, Sidney. Thomas Greenwood and his Library *Manchester Review*, 8, Spring, 1959, pp. 269–277.

Sparke, Archibald. Thomas Greenwood. *Library Association Record*, 52, 1950, p. 383.
Obituary. By James Duff Brown. *Library Association Record*, 10, 1908, pp. 633–636.
Obituary. By W. E. A. Axon. *Library Association Record*, 10, 1908, pp. 683–685.

## Greenwood on the Place of Public Libraries in our National Life

There is no more marked characteristic of our national life than the growing self-dependence of the people, which has been the outcome of municipal corporations. Where these corporations are the strongest and most vigorous, there must we look for the highest sense of the duties of citizenship and the most self-reliant populations. It is again in these municipalities, such as Birmingham, Manchester, Liverpool, Leeds, and Nottingham, that the most has been done for the education of the people, in the way of Board Schools, Public Libraries, Museums, and Technical Schools. The same municipalities have the best street lighting and street cleansing arrangements, and the police force are under the most perfect control. Surely this fact should dispel the fear that the energies of the poor in the way of self-help may be relaxed, and the rich become apathetic to their higher duties, by the spread of Public Libraries and kindred institutions, supported out of the same funds as are the local police, the street lighting and cleansing.

It may be asked, What is a corporation? There are various kinds, but we are here concerned with the corporation as a body politic elected by the people, and responsible to them. The word is used as equivalent to incorporated joint-stock companies, where the whole of the citizens are shareholders, and are banded together for a common purpose, that purpose being the common weal of the entire local community.

The one vital principle which surrounds corporations is that they are gifted with perpetual life. They may well have been in some laws designated immortal, although in some cases their privileges have run only for a definite number of years, but during the period, when well organized, they cannot die, notwithstanding all the original members are withdrawn, for they are continued by succession. A corporation has, in fact, been compared to a stream which maintains its identity throughout all the continuous changes of its parts. Men come and go, Acts of Parliament are passed and become often a dead letter, to swell the number of much similarly cumbrous stuff already on the statute book, but the corporation lives on. In many of the municipal corporations all the men who were elected representatives when the charter was first granted have gone over to the majority, but the tide of corporate life is not stayed; yea, rather, time has consolidated and added strength. This is the main reason why no private enterprise can possibly do for Public Libraries and education what the corporation can do, and it is on this rests the plea for municipal Public Libraries, Museums, and Technical Schools, which shall be the property of the citizens, administered by their own elected representatives, and forming an integral part of the local life. Lord Salisbury, when speaking a few months ago at a Mansion House banquet, said that while the Executive Government of the country recognizes the importance of municipal institutions, so long will this country of ours maintain its prestige, but if the day should ever come when the Government of the country fails to appreciate the value and importance of municipalities then, indeed, our progress would be downward and not upward.

The term "ratepayer" is a designation altogether cramped and unsuitable: the general use of the name citizen or burgess would be an infinitely better and more appropriate one. There can scarcely be a more pressing matter of importance at the present time than that of infusing into the minds of the people a high sense of the duties and privileges of citizenship.

It is a happy and healthy characteristic of public life in this country that in the midst of controversies which go down to the roots of our national existence, our statesmen of all parties are regarded by their countrymen as men of light and leading, whose views on subjects of general and non-political interest are entitled at all times to respectful hearing and attention. This same characteristic is evident in municipal life, and men of opposite politics meet and discuss matters for the general good. Around what institutions could local life better gather than Museums and Public Libraries? There is too much sentimental patriotism, too much lip patter about love of country, and far too little of the real thing itself. National patriotism is an excellent thing, but so also is local patriotism, and no institutions are more likely to cultivate the latter quality than these. The State has not done everything for the people that it is called upon to do when it has provided a gaol, a workhouse, a lunatic asylum, a policeman, and a share in the common hangman.

Why, again, should our pauper life be so heavy a tax on the thrifty and rich? Why is it not made more self-supporting either in farm labour or other ways? Not that its being brought into competition with the labour out of its doors is advocated, but surely in the raising of food, and in the making of their own clothing, there is ample scope for such productive labour. Oh ye great British people, with all your wealth and boasted common sense, how long is this national waste of money and force to go on, and the country idly look on, content with an occasional futile protest? The more vigorous grumbling seems to be when educational matters are under discussion, and with the majority the huge leaks in our national expenditure are forgotten or hidden from view.

The higher life of the citizen has received too little attention, and the lower and baser life seems to have absorbed all the sympathy and care of the authorities. But we have touched the fringe of better days, and soon no municipality or local governing body will be considered complete unless it has under its administration a library and a museum, as well as a workhouse, a prison, and the preservers of law and order. It is for the provision for this higher national life that this plea is made, and upon municipalities is earnestly urged the need of giving the fullest and best attention to this question. The fact should be emphasized that the municipality can do for the people in the way of libraries and museums what cannot possibly be done by private enterprise. It may be unhesitatatingly asserted that in fullest usefulness, economical management, and best value for money invested, the existing rate-supported libraries are far in advance of the private institutions of this nature.

It is some forty years since Carlyle asked the question, "Why is there not a Majesty's library in every town? there is a Majesty's gaol and gallows in every one"; and it is as long since the Public Libraries Act was passed, and yet the lack of libraries is still one of the most startling deficiencies in these islands. We have given the people ever greater and greater political power, but they displayed no marked inclination to benefit themselves by means of books or other means of culture. "We must now educate our masters," said Mr. Lowe when the Reform Bill of 1867 was passed. He was quite right, for the said masters were by no means quick to educate themselves, and the number of Public Libraries which they consented to establish for three years after 1867 was about ten. Then came Mr. Foster's Education Act: that was not permissive, and great things were expected of it. Now that everybody was to be taught his letters, everybody would surely want books to read also. What, indeed, would be the good of teaching people to read at all unless they were also to have a supply of good books? You might as well teach a man the use of his knife and fork and then not give him any meat. Public Libraries would be the natural and legitimate outcome of compulsory education. So it was confidently expected, but the exceptions have only been partially fulfilled, as a perusal of the present volume shows.

The effect of education upon crime has been a subject much discussed by social reformers. It may be assumed that there is a relation between the two things, although it is not possible to ascertain the precise ration in which crime diminishes with the spread of education. It may, however, be maintained that the increase of mental power raises the mind of the people above the temptations which lead to crime, and that, as a rule, mental and moral strength are likely to advance together. The case is stronger when we regard education not merely as a process by which knowledge is imparted, but as a system of careful training in which the subject is surrounded by guiding, restraining, and uplifting influences, when the environment of the individual is of a character to bring out its best characteristics, and to check the growth of selfishness and passion. The effect of such a course of what in the best sense must be called education may be expected to be greatest when it is employed towards the children of that class of parents who do not or cannot perform the primary parental duties. It is well known that there exists a degraded residuum from which the criminal class is constantly recruited. The result is seen in the records of the police-courts, where conviction after conviction is recorded against the same person. It is therefore a problem of the greatest social importance to ascertain how far the higher and better influences of education can be brought to bear upon these children, and if it is possible to cut off the entail of misery, to bar the gates of crime, and as Dickens says, "throw but ajar the portals to a decent life". Such a question as this has long formed an interesting subject for speculative discussion amongst moral and social philosophers. On the one side we are told that the influence of heredity is too great to be overcome, that the criminal is born, and not made, and that, however well intended, such efforts at moral reform are doomed to disappointment. On the other side, the more hopeful spirits maintain that, whatever may be the tendencies derived from parentage, there is sufficient elasticity and adaptability in the moral nature of humanity to enable us to act upon it effectually if care is taken that all the surroundings of the individual are properly and judiciously selected.

In another fifteen or twenty years, when some millions more children have passed through the Board Schools, and Public Libraries and other similar institutions have been established all over the kingdom, then we shall become a cultivated people. In these or similar words, half hopeful, half regretful, the grown-up generation summarize their estimate of popular culture. The Board School is the star to steer by; the Board School boy and girl are the hope of civilization. There is humility in the confession. But while Young England is, doubtless, a fine promising fellow, something may surely be also said for his seniors. If the question is considered closely, it is found that what the adult generation of working men—using this last word in its ordinary acceptation—have accomplished in self-instruction for themselves is as promising a feature of modern society as the progress which the young are making, more or less under compulsion. The increased access to the great stores of literature, brought about by the establishment of Public Libraries, is, therefore one of the indications which help to show us the tendency of the educational movement of the present day. That tendency is strongly towards the equality which means the placing of the same opportunities of knowledge within the reach of all. The University Extension movement, with its gatherings of students at the great shrines of knowledge, is a striking illustration of the tendency. But that extension has rested largely upon voluntary work, and the devotion of the students themselves to the branches of knowledge taught by the university lectures. The Public Library movement, however, represents the determination of the community to offer special facilities for the cultivation of the mind at the expense of the community itself. The readiness of the people to second and support that determination shows how great has been the growth of the feeling, not only among individuals, but among the public at large. The educational welfare of the multitude has at length become a matter of importance to us all. There has been a revolution in public opinion as to the true functions of Public Libraries. For a time they may be said to have had only a slight relation to the life of the community, but the authorities are now ready to acknowledge that success or failure is to be measured by the extent to which they come in contact with and shape for good the mental life of the nation.

·    ·    ·    ·

The one great need of the age, and it is one which cannot be too strongly emphasized, is the appointment, without delay, of a Minister of Public Instruction. After many contradictions of various natures, the country has seen the appointment of a Minister of Agriculture. And so there is room for large hope that the next new public official, with or without a seat in the Cabinet, will be a Minister whose department shall have under its control the entire system of our national education, Public Libraries, Museums, and technical schools. The same official would of course, be responsible for our national institutions, comprising the British Museum, South Kensington, and their offshoots in Edinburgh, Dublin, and elsewhere. This is a subject vital to the educational interests in our national life, and if the press and those who aid in forming public opinion will only take up the matter vigorously, we may soon be within measurable distance of seeing a Minister of Public Instruction appointed. In this respect our own Government are behind other Governments. The value of the governmental reports upon the libraries of the United States is fully recognized by all who take an interest in the work of libraries. When the little which has been done in this country is compared with what has been in this respect done by the United States and German Governments, the comparison is greatly against us. There is before us at the present moment the whole of the Blue Books and parliamentary returns referring to Public Libraries which have been presented to the British House of Commons. It will be interesting to name them in the order in which they have been issued. First and foremost are the reports from the select committee on Public Libraries issued in 1849 and 1850. Each of these is a volume of between 300 and 400 pages of elaborate statistics, and the evidence before the select committee appointed in 1849 on the best means of extending the establishment of libraries freely to the public. Judging from the cost of other select committees and commissions, the net cost to the country of this committee must have been some thousands of pounds. These two Blue Books constitute our one national ewe lamb in publications of real value dealing with Public Libraries. Then follow the other returns, which can be dismissed in a sentence. In 1852 there was a return of Public Libraries, some of which had adopted the Ewart Act of 1850. This return consists of nine pages. Then, in 1856, there was a further return, and as matters were growing a little this reached a total of fifteen pages. In 1857 the House of Commons added a further instalment of six pages, the extent of an utterly useless return. Our legislators kindly took a rest after so laborious a task, and for twelve years there was no official document issued respecting these institutions. They then gave us a return of libraries and museums actually reaching twenty-nine pages. There was then a further leap to 1875, when we have a further instalment of thirty-one pages. Those in charge of this return must have been napping, for all through it there is the term "Free Libraries Acts"—a designation which had not appeared in the Acts themselves, and the use of such a phrase ought never to have been allowed to creep into this parliamentary document. In 1876 there appeared the bulkiest of these returns. This is a Blue Book of statistics totalling up to ninety-one pages. So exhausted did Parliament become after so extraordinary an effort that nothing appeared between a short return of 1877 and one of 1885, to be purchased for a penny. In the spring of 1890 a return of Public Libraries under the Acts was called for by a Scotch member. This is supposed to give all the places where the Acts had been adopted prior to the 25th March, 1890, and some statistics of the number of books and issues. As a specimen of slovenly return making, it would be difficult to surpass it, and it is about as disgraceful a production of its kind as could be named. Places are given where the Acts have not yet been adopted, and places where the Acts had been adopted at the time the return was made are omitted.

The return represents little else but a gross waste of public money.

It has thus been left to private individuals, out of a pure desire to serve the commonwealth, to supply the deficiency, and to do what should have been done by Government long ago. It is perhaps too bad to expose the nakedness of the land to this extent, but it is only a reiteration of a few simple and pertinent facts which wakes up John Bull to the flood of utterly useless talk at St. Stephen's, and how small a portion of what is done there touches the vitals of our national life. It is not further statistical returns for which it is necessary to plead. That has now been done. But in the making of a department in the State where Public Libraries and Museums will find a centre and a head. Further, the most pressing educational need which can be advanced is that of State aid for the formation and maintenance of Public Libraries in villages—a question which is more fully discussed in a succeeding chapter.

The most ready reply which is given to these requests for State aid to national institutions is, Where is the money to come from for the purpose? That, surely, with the resources which lie at hand should not be an insurmountable difficulty. If it were a question of a few additional pensions, or a new torpedo—the "Brennan" cost us £100,000 in 1891—the matter would doubtless be solved in a prompt way. As a commentary on the cry of an empty exchequer, there may be quoted the following two or three salient facts. A Government clerk recently died at Ventnor, in the Isle of Wight, who was a contemporary in official harness of Charles Lamb and John Stuart Mill. This in itself is not a remarkable event to chronicle. The special point in his case is, that he retired from the public service under medical certificate of unfitness in 1835, and that during fifty-four years he drew a pension. In the Chancery Court, a side clerk was retired at the age of thirty-one on a pension of £1,381; and a sworn clerk, whose emoluments had averaged £6,580 a year, was pensioned off with £4,953 a year; another side clerk was granted £1,540 a year at the age of twenty-nine. The Accountant-General took £4,200 a year, and a humble door-keeper got £366 a year. In the Office of Works we find the surveyor retiring in 1875, after seven-and-a-half years' service, with a pension of £800; and the Clerk of the Furniture went off to draw £306 a year from the revenues of the country. The most outrageous example, however, of "re-organization" is afforded by the case of the Rev. Thomas Thurlow, a nephew of Lord Chancellor Thurlow, who was "Patentee of Bankrupts," and "Keeper and Clerk of the Hanaper." These sinecures were abolished when he was forty-three, and he was given pensions (as compensation) amounting in the aggregate to £11,715 a year, which pensions he continued to draw for forty years.

Records of this character are not scarce in the English service. How long Englishmen will tolerate with indifference this waste of national money it is difficult to say. It would be too much to expect the Government, whichever party is in power, to attack these abuses. They perpetually, with their ideas of economy, carp and grumble at the moneys already expended in the interest of science, literature, and art, and are too disposed to cut down the scanty grant to the British Museum, the South Kensington Museum, and other national institutions. It can hardly be expected that the State will establish a Departmental Register of English literature, such as the Keeper of the Public Records has under his control; yet the advantages of such, or a similar permanent record and means of intercommunication between widely scattered libraries and librarians need only be mentioned to be appreciated. Nor is it wise in this connection to forget that Public Libraries abroad frequently possess unique treasures which are not in any of our collections—Wittenberg, Berne, Basle, and Vienna containing, especially, rarities of considerable literary importance.

China is waking up in the matter of Public Libraries. A Public Library was established recently in Canton city. Speaking officially of the inauguration of this institution, the Viceroy of the province declared "how important it is to the good government of the country that educational projects should be promoted, so that the people may gain the benefits of good learning". With the Public Library is connected a large printing establishment for the production of "good and useful books, whereby the present and the past may be compared, help obtained in the path of rectitude, and morals and manners strengthened". The Viceroy himself, with certain benevolent associations and trade guilds subscribed a sum equivalent to £11,000 for the maintenance of this institution, and the interest of this, and annual subscriptions promised, yield an annual income of £2,000.

The Japanese are going beyond this. The Government of that progressive country sent over Mr. J. Tanaka as a special commissioner to spend two years in this country, the United States, and some parts of the Continent, to study the Public Library system. This accomplished gentleman left England on his return to Japan in December, 1889, and in several conferences which the present writer had with him prior to his departure, he gave an outline of the plan he has suggested to his Government for establishing Public Libraries throughout Japan. As chief librarian of the national library at Tokio, his experience is not by any means slight. The permissive feature, which forms so essential a part of our library work in England, is to be entirely absent in Japan, and municipalities and other governing bodies are to have the power of establishing Public Libraries, and the cost of maintenance, without any restrictions as to the amount, is to come out of the general local taxation. It will thus be seen from this and other facts that as a nation we must indeed be up and doing.

The place of Public Libraries in our national life is of so great importance that it cannot be over-estimated. The growing popularity of these institutions proves this unmistakably. One of many examples which could be named is that at one of the London Public Libraries recently established under the Acts, a most unusual and encouraging scene was witnessed. The building had been closed for a week for the ordinary purpose of cleaning and arranging, so that readers had been deprived of their privileges for that short period. When the day of reopening arrived the doors were surrounded by an eager crowd. This happened in Lambeth, and at West Norwood the road was blocked by an expectant throng of three or four hundred people long before the library was opened. All day long the people came pouring in to borrow books, and at nightfall no fewer that 1,148 volumes had been taken out—about one-fifth of the whole stock the lending library possesses. At the other Public Library, almost at the opposite end of the parish, similar scenes were witnessed, and the number of books distributed there in the day was 1,009. These facts are as good a testimonial in favour of Public Libraries as could well be conceived. Give a man the run of a large library, and free him from the anxious reflection that the money it costs him, be it ever so little, might be more profitably spent elsewhere, and he is open on all sides to refining influences, many of them not due to literature itself. Should he want it, he will acquire the civility of silence in a public reading-room, and he will emulate the courtesy which oils the wheels of every organization. Too much, perhaps, is made of the Puritanical argument that a taste for literature keeps a man away from the pot-house. The bane of luxury lies not in moderate indulgence, but in excess. Time, and health, and mental energy may be wrongfully frittered away in reading as well as in tippling. But a temperate gratification of one pleasure is the strongest of all checks to excessive indulgence in another. The natural faculties of the mind are exercised in wholesome recreation in the Public Library. They ripen in the active work of life, in intercourse with active minds; but in solitude and in idle company they rot. And from a literary playground, where they may gain health and vigour for these faculties, many of the poorer classes, who may in no disrespectful sense be called children in intellect, are debarred by lack of means. Thus, to view the matter from a point whence only its narrow aspect of mere entertainment is visible, much may be said for the institution of Public Libraries throughout the entire country.

The Chancellor of the Exchequer promised us in his 1891 Budget a considerable share of the surplus towards assisted education, and many people who are protesting loudly against what is not quite accurately called "free education" in elementary schools, seem to overlook the fact that, under the Public Libraries Acts, something very much like free education is being provided not only for children of the poorer classes, but for the sons and daughters of the middle classes, and all classes, so far as they choose to read or borrow the thousands of educational works placed at their disposal. The Public Library is the university of the working man. But a university is not for every man. Its true value is only appreciated by those whose previous training fits them to profit by its advantages. Books are only valuable to those who know how to read them, and libraries are only valuable to those who know how to use them. Nevertheless, the growth of the Public Library system is at least a proof of the gradual development of more active intellectual interests throughout the industry community. This is an advantage in every way. It is indisputable that the industrial competition throughout the world is daily becoming more and more a competition of intelligence. It is certain that if we cannot hold our own in this competition, we must make up our minds to witness the beginnings of national decline. Knowledge is power, and in the long run it is the power that prevails. But it is as well not to forget, in the recognition of the power, that dwells in knowledge, that knowledge is a good in itself, and contains attractions within itself. Intellectual pursuits, even such as men immersed in daily industry can compass, often carry within themselves their own best fruits to the pursuer. In the present condition of the world we can none of us afford to neglect the material profit that resides in knowledge and in the cultivation of the intelligence; but knowledge, like virtue, is its own true reward, and the pleasures of a cultivated intelligence are so pure and so unalloyed that even if no profit ensued from them they are worthy of pursuit for their own sake alone. It is clear that as a nation we are on the right road to educational excellence, and have become, if we may put any trust in arithmetic and appearances, a nation of learned and learning people. From the swaddling clothes of Celtic Druidism, the youthful habiliments of Saxon Paganism, and the corduroys of mediaeval barbarism and ignorance, we have come to the full, well-made garments (mentally) of science, art, and general useful knowledge. Epictetus said that you will "do the greatest service to the State if you should raise not the roofs of the house, but the souls of the citizens; for it is better that great souls dwell in small houses rather than for mean slaves to burrow in great palaces." Sir John Herschel uttered a similar truth when he said that "there is a want too much lost sight of in our estimation of the privations of the humbler classes, though it is one of the most incessantly craving of all our wants, and is actually the impelling power which, in the vast majority of cases, urges men into vice and crime—it is the want of amusement." Like the indulgence of all other appetites, it only requires to be kept within due bounds, and turned upon innocent or beneficial objects, to become a spring of happiness; but gratified to a certain moderate extent it must be, in the case of every man, if we desire him to be either a useful, active, or contented member of society. It is therefore a matter of very great consequence, that those who are at their ease in this world should look about for means of harmless gratification to the industrious and well-disposed classes, who are prepared to prize highly every accession of true enjoyment. Of all the amusements which can possibly be imagined for a hard-working man after his daily toil, or in its intervals, there is nothing like reading an entertaining book. It calls for no bodily exertion, of which he has had enough or too much. It relieves his home of its dulness and sameness, which, in nine cases out of ten, is what drives him to the ale-house, to his own ruin and to that of his family. Supposing him to have been fortunate in the choice of his book, and to have alighted upon one really good, what a source of domestic enjoyment is laid open! He may read it aloud or get his wife to read it, or his eldest boy or girl, or pass it round from hand to hand. A feeling of common interest and pleasure is excited. Nothing unites people like companionship in intellectual enjoyment. It does more, it gives them self-respect, that corner-stone of all virtue. If we would generate a taste for reading, we must begin by pleasing. Give a man this taste, and the means of gratifying it, and you can hardly fail of making him a happy man. He is at once placed in contact with the best society in every period of history, with the wisest, the wittiest, with the tenderest, the bravest, and the purest characters who have adorned humanity. It is hardly possible but the character should take a higher and better tone. There is a gentle, but perfectly irresistible coercion in the habit of reading, well directed over the whole tenor of man's character, which is not the less effectual because it works insensibly.

The one truth which it appears necessary to bring home again and again to the heart of the people is the sense of the duties and responsibilities of citizenship, and it may be maintained that Public Libraries and Museums, with their concomitants of reading-rooms, lectures, and all the other departments which are now being added are *the* institutions, *par excellence*, which are best calculated to bring home the privileges of citizenship. And so in the immediate future the place of Public Libraries in our national life will be more and more firmly established. These progressive instincts in our national life find an echo in the language of Lowell:—

> "New occasions teach new duties!
>     Time makes ancient good uncouth;
> They must upward still, and onward,
>     Who would keep abreast of Truth."

From, Greenwood, Thomas. *Public libraries: a history of the movement and a manual for the organization and management of rate-supported libraries. . . . Fourth edition,* [etc.], 1894, pp. 7–20.

# CHAPTER 32

# Melvil Dewey (1851–1931)

"He inspired his pupils and staffs, and led librarianship when he himself was only in his twenties."

THE name of "Dewey" is known to most users of public libraries, to whom it implies all too frequently the incomprehensible arrangement of the books on the shelves. That there existed a man bearing that name rarely occurs to them, and many librarians also are ignorant of the details of the life of the man whose name is a household word.

Melvil Dewey was born on December 10th, 1851, at Adams Center, New York, and was then named Melville Louis Kossuth Dewey, although he appears to have drastically curtailed this at the earliest possible opportunity. At the age of 17 he became a teacher, and while studying at Amherst, which he entered in 1870, he continued to assist his father in his business. Dewey was assistant librarian at Amherst from 1874 to 1876, and as early as 1873 had completed his Decimal Classification Scheme, which was applied to the Library, and published in 1876 as *A classification and subject index for cataloguing and arranging the books and pamphlets of a library.* It was then a slight booklet of 42 pages, with 1,000 placings in the schedules of the scheme. It was first applied to a large collection at Columbia College, where Dewey was appointed Chief Librarian on May 7th, 1883. Here he established the School of Library Service four years later, but after disagreements with the trustees over the admission of women to the courses, Dewey transferred himself and the School to Albany, where he became State Librarian and Secretary to the Regent of the University of the State of New York. He resigned from these appointments in 1905, but it was by no means a retirement, and Dewey was active in the advancement of librarianship until his death.

Melvil Dewey was prominent among American librarians in the early days of public libraries. In 1876 he became head of the firm of Library Bureau, managing editor of the *American Library Journal* (founded in that year), and also founded the Metric Bureau and the Spelling Reform Association. He published his *Rules for author and classed catalogs as used in Columbia College Library* in 1888, and his *Library school card catalog rules* a year later.

In 1904 Dewey proposed that the American Library Association and the Library Association should collaborate in the preparation of an Anglo-American Cataloguing Code, which was published in 1908. He held several prominent positions, being elected first President of the Association of State Libraries in 1889, and the following year he founded the New York State Library Association. He planned and organized the Lake Placid Club, which has published successive editions of his Classification.

Melvil Dewey probably influenced the development of librarianship more than any other single person. He did not spare himself in actively supporting the numerous organisations with which he was associated, and his death on December 26th, 1931 occurred while he was still active on their behalf. His scheme of classification is now used in libraries throughout the world, and although subject to much criticism has not been superseded for practical purposes in general libraries. It is continuously revised in successive editions, and although certain sections remain unsuitable for very specialized collections, "Dewey" is still employed in libraries where it is outmoded. Many libraries retain it because of the difficulties involved in re-classifying. It was created by Melvil Dewey to serve an urgent need, and it prospered because it then had no competitors. Adaptations, translations and modifications of the scheme abound, and although it fails to keep abreast of modern advances in science, for example, and the arrangement of the scheme itself has invoked much criticism, it remains the basic scheme for most public libraries, and for many specialist collections.

### REFERENCES

Dawe, Grosvenor. *Melvil Dewey; seer, inspirer, doer, 1851–1931,* [etc.], Lake Placid Club, New York, 1932. Bibliography, list of editions of his Classification, etc. Unfortunately it is written in Dewey's revised spelling.

Dewey, Godfrey. Dewey, 1851–1951. *Library Journal,* 76, 1951, pp. 1964–1965.

Macleod, R. D. Melvil Dewey and his famous school. *Library Review,* 135, 1960, pp. 479–484.

Melvil Dewey on change in D.C. Foreword by Verner W. Clapp. *Library Journal,* 81, 1956, pp. 1363–1365.

Rider, Fremont. *Melvil Dewey,* Chicago, 1944. (American Library Pioneers, VI.)

Sayers, W. C. Berwick. The centenary of Melvil Dewey. *British Book News,* 136, December, 1951, pp. 749–753.

### Preface to the First Edition of Dewey's Classification

The plan of the following Classification and index was developed early in 1873. It was the result of several months' study of library economy as found in some hundreds of books and pamphlets, and in over fifty personal visits to various American libraries. In this study, the author became convinced that the usefulness of these libraries

PLATE II

SIR JOHN YOUNG WALKER MacALISTER

(1856 – 1925)

PLATE 12

C

JAMES DOUGLAS STEWART

(1880 – 1965)

ARUNDELL JAMES KENNEDY
ESDAILE

(1880 – 1956)

A

THOMAS GREENWOOD

(1851 – 1908)

might be greatly increased without additional expenditure. Three years practical use of the system here explained, leads him to believe that it will accomplish this result; for with its aid, the catalogues, shelf lists, indexes, and cross-references essential to this increased usefulness, can be made more economically than by any other method which he has been able to find. The system was devised for cataloguing and indexing purposes, but it was found on trial to be equally valuable for numbering and arranging books and pamphlets on the shelves. . . .

    ·     ·     ·     ·

In arranging books in the classification, as in filling out the scheme, practical usefulness has been esteemed the most important thing. The effort has been made to put each book under the subject to the student of which it would be most useful. The content or the real subject of which the book treats, and not the form or the accidental wording of the title, determines its place. Following this rule, a Philosophy of Art is put with Art, not with Philosophy; a History of Mathematics, with Mathematics, not with History, for the philosophy and history are simply the *form* which these books have taken. The true content or subject is Art, and Mathematics, and to the student of these subjects they are most useful. The predominant tendency or obvious purpose of the book, usually decides its class number at once; still many books treat of two or more different subjects, and in such cases it is assigned to the place where it will be most useful, and underneath the class number are written the numbers of any other subjects on which it also treats. These *Cross References* are given both on the plate and the subject card as well as on the cross reference card. If a book treats of a majority of the sections of any division, it is given the Division number instead of the most important Section number with cross references. . . .

    ·     ·     ·     ·

Thus all the books on any given subject are found standing together, and no additions or changes ever separate them. Not only are all the books on the subject sought, found together, but the most nearly allied subjects precede and follow, they in turn being preceded and followed by other allied subjects as far as practicable. Readers not having access to the shelves find the short titles arranged in the same order in the Shelf Catalogue, and the full titles, imprints, cross references, notes, etc., in the Subject Catalogue. The uncatalogued pamphlets treating of any subject bear the same class number and are arranged on the shelves immediately after the books of each section. . . .

    ·     ·     ·     ·

The plan was adopted in the Amherst College Library in 1873, and the work of transferring the entire library to the new catalogue at once commenced. It was found entirely practicable to make the change gradually, as means allowed, without interfering in any appreciable degree with the circulation of the books. The three years' trial to which it has been there subjected has more than justified the claims of its friends, and it is now printed with the more confidence on this account. It has been kept in manuscript up to this time, in order that the many minor details might be subjected to actual trial and modified where improvement was possible. The labor involved in preparing the Classification and Index has been wholly beyond the appreciation of any who have never attempted a similar task. Much valuable aid has been rendered by specialists in many departments, and nearly every member of the Faculty has given advice from time to time. . . .

.    .    .    .

In his varied reading, correspondence and conversation on the subject, the author doubtless received suggestions and gained ideas which it is now impossible for him to acknowledge. Perhaps the most fruitful source of ideas was the *Nuovo Sistema di Catalogo Bibliografico Generale* of Natale Battezzati, of Milan. Certainly he is indebted to this system adopted by the Italian publishers in 1871, though he has copied nothing from it. The plan of the St. Louis Public School Library, and that of the Apprentices' Library of New York, which in some respects resembles his own, were not seen till all the essential features were decided upon, though not given to the public. In filling the nine classes of the scheme the inverted Baconian arrangement of the St. Louis Library has been followed. The author has no desire to claim original invention for any part of his system where another has been before him, and would most gladly make specific acknowledgement of every aid and suggestion were it in his power to do so. With these general explanations and acknowledgements he submits the scheme, hoping it may prove as useful to others as it has to himself.

AMHERST COLLEGE LIBRARY,
    June 10th, 1876.

Paragraphs from Preface (pp. 1–10), of *A classification and subject index for cataloguing and arranging the books and pamphlets of a library.* By Melvil Dewey. Amherst, Mass., 1876. Printed with the permission of the Lake Placid Club Education Foundation, the copyright owner.

CHAPTER 33

# Minnie Stewart Rhodes James (died 1903)

"To be a librarian one cannot form too high an ideal of the work required, . . . one cannot have too much patience or tact, and above all the more one knows, the more one must of necessity realise how much there is yet to learn."

MINNIE STEWART RHODES JAMES.

ALTHOUGH women have played an important part in the development of librarianship during this century, and have taken major roles in certain aspects of the subject, very few have emerged as initiators of projects of historical importance, or have attained the most significant posts of distinction. This has been partially remedied in recent years, and one of the most important "break-throughs" was the appointment of Miss Lorna V. Paulin as the first woman President of the Library Association for 1966. A great honour for a worthy representative of women librarians, who has done so much for the Association and for librarianship in general, and a fitting recognition of the work of women in librarianship. First recruited as cheap labour, cultivated because of their contributions both as attractions and their ability to do the work, they were eventually encouraged to educate themselves for librarianship, and gradually given positions of authority, although often at a cheaper rate than that offered to men. Today, librarianship is becoming a profession mainly for women, and they should look back to their predecessors who initiated this development and particularly to those who ensured the success of the venture. One such was Minnie Stewart Rhodes James.

In 1887 Miss James was appointed Librarian of the People's Palace, London, a library not supported by the rates, and of which Sir Walter Besant was Chairman of the Committee. In 1889 Miss James joined the Library Association, and took a prominent part at its meetings. She contributed numerous papers, and keenly supported the employment of women in librarianship, stressing the necessity for the adequate education and training of library assistants. Her articles in the professional press include: "People's Palace Library" (*The Library*, 2, 1890, pp. 341–351); "Women librarians" (*Ibid*, 4, 1892, pp. 217–224), which is reprinted below; "Plan for providing technical instruction for library students and assistants" (*Ibid.*, 4, 1892, pp. 313–318); "American women as librarians" (*Ibid.*, 5, 1893, pp. 270–274);

and "Women librarians and their future prospects" (*Library Association Record*, 2, i, 1900, pp. 291–304), which was a paper read at the International Congress of Women held in London, June, 1899.

In 1894 Miss James resigned and took employment at Boston, Mass., with Library Bureau, but after six months returned to England to organise a London branch. She returned to Boston in 1879, dying there on June 5th, 1903.

Miss James impressed her acquaintances by her personal charm, by the sincerity of her action and the thoroughness displayed in her work and writings. She proved a fitting advocate for the employment of women librarians, set an example that few have equalled, and championed a cause that has proved most successful in execution.

### REFERENCES

Minto, John. *A history of the public library movement in Great Britain and Ireland*, 1932. Minnie Stewart Rhodes James, pp. 321–323.
    Obituary. *Public Libraries*, 8, 1903, pp. 314–315, 330.

### Miss James on Women Librarians

Owing to existing economic conditions a large number of women have now to enter the lists as workers; whether or no this is a matter for regret is an open question, the ethics of which we will pass over for the present. Certain it is that if women come forward as candidates for posts hitherto associated only with men, they must be prepared to stand on the same footing, and not imagine that they can do the pleasant work and leave that which is distasteful to others.

There is a tendency to generalise about "women's work" which has led and is leading to most erroneous ideas as to careers open to women; this cannot be too greatly deplored as much disappointment is necessarily caused by incautious statements.

One or two articles have already been written on the subject of this paper, treating of the matter as a "new career for women", whereas it is not a new career in reality, but a fresh aspect of an old one; for women were employed in libraries long before the era of the People's Palace, therefore the credit of the idea cannot be said to belong entirely to Mr. Walter Besant, who is generally supposed to have originated it by appointing women as managing librarians at the People's Palace Library, which was opened in 1887.

There can be no doubt that women are in every way as well fitted for such posts as men, although they have hitherto laboured under the great disadvantage of having no regular business training, which is essential to the adequate fulfilment of the duties required.

There are one hundred and one little business details of which most women are kept lamentably ignorant, until chance necessitates their entering into office life or taking up some branch work; and even then the knowledge acquired is but one-sided, and attained by sad experience: not that business details are difficult to master, but simply because they are so mechanically easy that no one takes the trouble to explain technicalities which present no difficulty to the majority.

If every woman were given at least the elements of a business training there would be fewer cases of financial extravagance, and better management would result.

The advantage of a knowledge of business for women has been perceived by our French neighbours, for nearly every woman whose husband is in business is a partner in the concern, and is consulted on various matters relating to the firm with the most satisfactory results, whereas in England our sisters are kept totally ignorant of any business matters, and very often do not in the least realise the nature of the occupation followed daily by their husbands and brothers; in consequence very few women in England are capable of managing or carrying on a business entirely alone as is done with such éclat by many French widows.

It is useless for any woman to imagine that she can take up the work of a librarian without some previous training, added to a knowledge of literature of all kinds and a fondness for books.

The day of a librarian as caretaker is happily becoming extinct, and it is expected of every librarian nowadays, and rightly so, that he or she should at least know something of the books they issue, and the best ways of classifying and cataloguing them; in fact library economy is about to become an exact science and no one who wishes to take up the duties of a librarian must imagine for one moment that all they have to do will be to give out books and sit and read them all day long, though even now one hears the remark "it must be so nice to be a librarian; you must have such a lot of time for reading".

If you want to be of any use the *greater* part of your reading must have been done before you enter into the duties of such a post, and also remember that you must not rest your oars here, for knowledge, like a brass knocker, is apt to become tarnished unless constantly polished up, and albeit it is sometimes a hard struggle to find time for this necessary reading, the literature of the day must not be forgotten.

To be a librarian one cannot form too high an ideal of the work required, one cannot (though there is a saying "the librarian who reads is lost") read too much to keep abreast of the times, and become the walking encyclopædia (popular edition) that one is expected to be, one cannot have too much patience or tact, and above all the more one knows, the more one must of necessity realise how much there is yet to learn.

Perhaps it would be as well to state a few of the duties of a librarian. One of the first is to draw up a list of books required in different departments of literature, to be submitted to the committee, and the best way to act about this is to consult catalogues of the leading London and Provincial Libraries taking into special consideration the probable needs of your particular district as to technical and scientific works, etc., and not only this, but the list must be made in proportion to the income or sum to be spent in stocking the library so that this work needs a degree of nicety.

These lists are constantly being drawn up to include the most recently published books on various subjects, and it must be remembered that for a Public Library nothing but the best works and standard fiction should be purchased.

Works of ephemeral interest should have no place in a library whose income is naturally limited, for it is impossible to cater for all à la Mudie, and nothing that has not been tested should be placed on the shelves, any more than one would purchase a sword that had not been tested and found reliable.

Next, these books must be bought in the best and cheapest market, and here the value of a business training comes in; also, one of the drawbacks to the employment of women, for men can at present attend sales and auctions with greater success, because with greater experience, than women.

After this, the books have to be unpacked, checked, cut, stamped and entered in the stock-book, and last and most important, the catalogue has to be compiled.

This must be arranged in the best way for the needs of the readers; nearly every library has a different method, though the principle that underlies them is the same. It must be cheap and good, and, if possible, part of the cost should be defrayed by judicious advertisement; the expense of printing is considerably lessened by typewriting the slips, only one proof, as a rule, being necessary where this is done.

Here again comes in a drawback to the employment of women. How many, I wonder, know anything of the wily ways of the advertisement contractor, or of the many and varied founts of type from which they shall make selection, though, perhaps, most would know how to correct a proof sheet? Rare books will not often come into the hands of the public librarian, but the keeper of the books should be able to distinguish an Aldine, a Pickering or an Elzevir when seen, and also to be able to size books correctly. It is to be hoped that the long looked for Standard Size Notation will soon be adopted, and also a system of exchanging duplicates.

Perhaps it will be found desirable to have a Card Catalogue, as well as a printed one, and to understand the construction of these, visits should be made to libraries where they are in use; indeed, I cannot too forcibly insist on the value of periodical visits to other libraries, no matter in what district, or place, not only to obtain knowledge of the doings therein, but also to encourage and keep up the feeling of brotherhood which ought to exist between the members of such a profession, especially if they also belong to the Library Association.

Personally, whenever I have a holiday, I always visit the library of the place I go to; this may seem rather a shoppy statement, but no opportunity should be lost of forming ideas from the work of others; and one is never too old to learn, thanks to a merciful, though somewhat painful, dispensation of Providence.

There are certain works which every aspiring librarian ought to possess, and these are, Greenwood's *Public Libraries*, 4th edition, Cutter's *Cataloguing Rules*, Dewey's *System of Classification*, the *L.A.U.K. Yearbook* and *Series of Handbooks*, as well as other books bearing on the subject.

The *Yearbook* contains information concerning the excellent examination held by the L.A.U.K., to enter for which is a capital training, from an elementary point of view; although, of course, technical knowledge can only be obtained by practical work as an assistant, under some able librarian. It also contains the Cataloguing Rules and other useful information.

Amongst other duties are those of keeping the library accounts, making up reports, answering letters, and numerous other secretarial functions.

The librarian should always be accessible; and should realise that her position, to be prosaic, much resembles that of the sign post at the four cross country roads; the great thing in all guidance is to be clear, direct, and comprehensive, and the librarian's relation to her readers should be that of the proverbial "friend in need".

Besides all this, a librarian must know something of the art of binding and repairing books, attending to small repairs in the library, which work should be peculiarly suited to women's fingers. Many libraries have their binding done by contract; and I think it is a mistake to suppose much saving is effected by binding on the premises. Added to this, a librarian must possess a knowledge of periodical literature and newspapers, as to who edits and publishes them, at what prices they are sold, and what days they are issued.

The time-table and discipline of the staff must also be considered; and no one should expect duties to be performed by others that she could not, if necessary, perform herself, and here comes in the great advantage of gradual promotion from assistant-ship to the post of head librarian, by which time every detail of the work should have been mastered.

The matter of training is of great moment; unfortunately we have no Library School, such as our American cousins have established; and the poor salaries offered to assistants, combined with the long hours required, naturally deter many well educated persons from entering as candidates. This is especially so in the case of women, who are, as a rule, employed in discharging the most mechanical duties connected with the Lending Department, and who, in consequence, get but little insight into the higher branches of the work.

Perhaps later on, some means can be devised by which women can be trained efficiently by correspondence, or coaching in special subjects, in various libraries. This, however, is a matter for mature consideration, as, at present, there are too many applicants for the posts. Until such time as a system of training be worked out, one of the best ways to prepare for a possible berth, is to read up all matter connected with libraries, and to enter for the L.A.U.K. Examinations, reading the course advised by that body; also, the organs of the L.A.U.K. and A.L.A., as well as the important articles in the *Encyclopædia Britannica* on Typography, Printing, Libraries, and Bibliography.

As before said, a great deal of useful and technical knowledge may be picked up by visiting public libraries, examining application forms, rules, catalogues and other details, all of which can be done without troubling the librarian; and, if a question be necessary, it will generally be found that an assistant can answer it quite satisfactorily.

The librarian has gorgeous opportunities, and her work can never be really finished. I say this thus emphatically, as I fear some of the articles written on the subject would lead readers to suppose that library work is a pleasant sort of way of obtaining an occupation combined with a certain amount of pocket or "dress" money, and there are too many women already in the ranks who work for "filthy lucre" only, so that they might increase their allowance or income, regardless of the honour and dignity of work as work.

Members of this class abound and for the most part live at home, so that they are able to accept salaries on which other women having to support themselves entirely would simply starve, and this is one of the deep-seated causes of the miserable pay offered to women. Salaries are of course an interesting question as the labourer should be worthy of his or her hire. I do not think that any woman ever received more that £100 per annum, this being probably the maximum, and I should say that from £40 to £80 would be much nearer the mark. Greenwood says from 12s. to 22s. per week; indeed some men receive less though perhaps where this is the case the librarian lives rent free on the premises.

It has been said that the work of a library is light, but let no one run off with this idea. It is interesting, delightful, absorbing, but it cannot be called light if performed with any degree of thoroughness, and it must be remembered that the work is what the worker makes it to a certain extent. We must not forget that it yet remains for us to prove ourselves capable of fulfilling such responsible posts in the eyes of our brother librarians, who at present I fear look upon us with some degree of suspicion. In America they manage these things differently and there are quite as many women as men employed as librarians, and, at the meetings of the A.L.A., there are often more women present than men. So I was told by an American lady librarian, only last year, whereas ladies at the Annual meeting of the L.A.U.K. are at present in a hopeless minority.

It is expedient to take into consideration opinions of the Press and of various librarians as to the employment of women in libraries.

*The Pall Mall Gazette* says, of the engaging of women as assistants at Battersea in 1890, "Few even of the most determined opponents of the employment of women in public institutions can object to this new departure" which it goes on to say it believes to be the first of the kind in London! And here are a few statements made by librarians at St. Helens, March 1890, when a paper was read by Miss Richardson.

Mr. Lancaster (St. Helens) said "he had considerable experience of male and female assistants, and found girls very attentive and obliging".

Mr. Sutton (Manchester) said "he thought that ladies were an acquisition in any library and did their work well".

Mr. Hand (Oldham) thought "that female labour had a tendency to keep down wages, but he thought that women did the work as well as men and ought to receive the same pay".

Alderman Thomas Baker said "he believed the plan was first tried in Manchester and was found successful".

Mr. Greenwood says "there is no doubt that ladies (how much better it would be if we used the good old word 'women', which is infinitely more dignified) make very efficient assistants and their services are being more generally sought".

Mr. Inkster (Battersea) says "his assistants show an aptitude and liking for the work which augur well for their future as librarians". (Note this, Mr. Inkster is the only librarian who realises the possibility of a future for women in this so-called new field.)

Mr. Brown, of Clerkenwell, employs women and continues to do so, a fact which speaks for itself.

A correspondent writing to the *Spectator*, May 1890, advocates the cause of women, urging that they can hold their own with men as regards the necessary attainments.

Objections have been made as to physical unfitness of women for the work, and I have heard it said that women expect to be waited on too much and think they must not be asked to do anything they consider menial work; but I am quite sure that women really in earnest would no more think of giving themselves airs than they would of flying.

As to keeping order, personally I think that a word or look from a woman has more effect on a miscreant, than the forcible ejection or emphatic language a man might use under the same circumstances, and having had several years in an East End district I consider I am entitled to speak on this matter. Coercion is always to be avoided, as a confession of weakness; but, if force is really necessary, there is usually a man at hand to attend to such work, the necessity for which is rare.

Of course most librarians employ women merely as assistants and there are not many women in the position of Head, partly because so few posts are to be had, partly because women are not yet prepared to take them, and *chiefly* because the best educated women will not accept the salary and social position in such a capacity.

Miss Stamp of Notting Hill was the first lady appointed in London, Miss Abbott of Hampstead, I think came next, then Miss Low and Miss Black of the People's Palace, and Miss Easty and Miss Jervois of the Goldsmiths' Institute, New Cross; but in the provinces there are one or two women in leading positions, employing other women as assistants.

Richard le Gallienne, one of the msrst graceful writers of the present day, treats of the subject in a poetically dilletante way, he says "books of all things should be tended by reverent hands (what would he say to the thumb mark of Lord Rosebery's artisan?) they should be given out as a priest dispenses the sacrament and the next step to this ideal ministry is to have them issued by women".

So we see that although there is no very great cordiality extended to women wishing to become librarians, yet there are no insurmountable objections to their employment as such.

Mr. MacAlister has proposed a Library Bureau, which would be a kind of Librarian's Elysium, and Mr. Brown of Clerkenwell is even now forming the nucleus of a Library Museum which ought to be of immense help to the library student.

The exhibition of library appliances and catalogues at Nottingham last year was of great use to those who had the privilege of seeing it.

We ought to make public any little library "dodges" we may

have, for the old days of keeping inventions to oneself are over:
"Nous avons changé tout cela."

To conclude, had I to begin all over again I should certainly do
everything I have suggested in this paper. Everyone knows that the
best art students are those who have gone through the whole course
from its most elementary stages, and it is of no use taking up any work
unless you can throw yourself into it; as Shakespeare says

> "No profit grows where is no pleasure ta'en
> In brief Sir, study what you most affect."

From, J[ames], M. S. R. Women librarians. *The Library*, 4, 1892, pp. 217–224.

# CHAPTER 34

# Sir John Young Walker MacAlister (1856–1925)

"He understood the dignity of history, the necessity of tracing and holding our roots in the past. It is not meet that he be forgotten."

E. A. SAVAGE.

SIR JOHN YOUNG WALKER MACALISTER has been described by Ernest A. Savage as "the best friend the Library Association has had so far," and his work in connection with librarianship was but one of his numerous activities. Endowed with remarkable foresight and resolution he not only originated brilliant ideas, but courageously saw them put into execution, frequently at no small personal cost and inconvenience. It is only possible to record his activities as a brief list, from which it may be difficult to appreciate the true value of his services, but medicine, the Library Association and librarianship in general will remain for ever grateful that such an amazing personality took so great an interest in their development.

John Y. W. MacAlister was born at Perth on May 10th, 1856, and was educated at the High School, Liverpool. For three years he studied medicine at Edinburgh University, but ill-health compelled him to give up medicine as a profession, although he later became closely connected with it as a medical librarian. In 1878 MacAlister became Sub-Librarian of the Liverpool Library, and two years later Librarian of the Leeds Library. There he catalogued and classified the collection, using his own scheme of classification. In 1887 he became librarian of the newly founded Gladstone Library at the National Liberal Club, but on April 9th of the same year was elected Resident Librarian of the Royal Medical and Chirurgical Society, then at 53 Berners Street, London. At that time numerous medical societies existed in London in poor financial circumstances, and MacAlister worked for several years in an endeavour to amalgamate them into one strong body. In June, 1907 this was effected, and a large number of medical societies joined the Royal Medical and Chirurgical Society to become the Royal Society of Medicine, which at its headquarters in Wimpole Street now houses the largest medical library in Great Britian.

In 1889 MacAlister founded *The Library*, which after being the official organ of the Library Association, became that of the Bibliographical Society. From 1887 to 1897 he was Secretary of the

Library Association, and it was largely due to his efforts that the 1892 Public Libraries Act was passed. In 1898 he was instrumental in obtaining the Royal Charter of Incorporation for the Library Association, and was President of the Association during the difficult period 1914–1919. He suggested the official Manual of Librarianship, several sections of which were published, and also assisted in founding the School of Librarianship at University College, London.

MacAlister was knighted in 1919 and he also received the Order of the British Empire. Unfortunately, six years later, on December 1st, 1925, he died after a long period of ill-health. (Portrait, Plate II.)

### REFERENCE

*Sir John Young Walker MacAlister; a memorial for his family and friends,* 1926. Five portraits; a collection of obituary notices, appreciations, *etc.*

## MacAlister on the Osler Library

The other day I was "assisting" at the unveiling of a fine cast of the famous "Hope Asklepios," which now provides a noble decoration for the principal reading room in the library of the Royal Society of Medicine. Making the necessary arrangements and the time occupied by the ceremony made such a hole in official hours that I had to take home with me a larger batch of proof than usual, and, as frequently happens, the interest of the work made me forget time and space, and it was only in rising to rekindle a cold pipe that I discovered it was nearly 2 a.m., so I put aside my proofs, relit my pipe, and sat down for a little quiet thinking before going to bed.

A sudden ring of the telephone brought back memories of raids and night calls, but on going to the instrument I heard a voice that I thought familiar but could not identify. "You are wanted at once at the Osler Library. The committee has adjourned until you can come, and we are sending up one of the staff cars for you." I murmured something about the lateness of the hour, and said I should be ready. In a few minutes a haughty-looking chauffeur drove up, helped me in, put a magnificent fur rug over my knees, for the night was cold, and drove off in the direction of the Regent's Park. He stopped at a lodge gate which gave entrance to a large enclosure, and pulled up at the portico of a magnificent building which seemed strangely familiar, and yet I could not recall where or when I had seen it.

It was built in the form of a quadrangle, with a great open courtyard in the centre, in which was a noble marble statue. At first I thought I recognised it as the "Hope Asklepios," but going closer I was startled to observe that while in every other respect apparently a copy of the

Asklepios, the face was that of our revered friend and teacher William Osler. Everything was so strange I did not at the time even think it odd that on gazing at his face, his characteristic smile, which we all love, was a *living* smile, and I could have sworn that one of those wonderful eyes solemnly winked at me.

I suddenly found by my side an elderly gentleman who introduced himself as the Bibliothecarius-in-chief, and with grave dignity welcomed me on my first visit to the great institution of which he was proud to be the head, and proudest of all because it realised the ideals of that great benefactor Osler.

"And yet," he added, "the realisation of the scheme is in some respects entirely due to yourself, and I have been deputed by the committee to take you over the entire building and invite any criticisms you may have to make before the ceremonial opening."

It all seemed curiously puzzling, and yet somehow "all right," and I told him how delighted I was, but that if Osler were pleased, it was not likely I would be able to suggest any improvements.

He began by asking me to observe the stately Greek architecture, cleverly adapted in the matter of windows, lighting and ventilation to meet modern demands. He then led the way inside to a great circular entrance hall, lighted from the top of a lofty dome which reminded me of the Pantheon at Rome. There was only one light, at the top, which at first seemed too small for such a vast hall, and yet illuminated the whole space perfectly. I guessed the opening was covered in by glass as a concession to English weather, but it was so cleverly done that it seemed to be open, and my guide explained to me that at night the light was equally good, provided from outside by a powerful searchlight.

In the spaces between the corridors opening out of the central hall there were numerous marble statues, which my guide informed me had been provided by the greatest artists of all the civilised nations that had contributed in any way to the advancement of Medicine, and pointed out with particular pride the latest gift, which had been received from the King of Hedjaz, a noble image of Avicenna, the work of a young Arab sculptor, who, he assured me, would very soon be recognised as one of the greatest artists the world had ever known. To my surprise and delight I recognised effigies not only of the past, but of some of the present masters of Medicine. Of course Æsculapius, Hippocrates, Galen and Celsus were there; down the ages with Harvey and the Hunters to Lister, Pasteur and, as my guide explained, by the special request of Osler, living men who had done most for the history of Medicine, such as Norman Moore, who was figured as presenting his monumental "History of St. Bartholomew's,"

D'Arcy Power, Raymond Crawfurd, Cumston, and the indefatigable Singer.

My guide, taking out his watch, remarked that we should just be in time for breakfast with the staff, and led the way to the refectory, which I found to be a noble room with a southern aspect, set out with long tables where many of the staff were already seated, and in spite of the tempting meal set before them, were already engaged either in earnest conversation or disputation, and my guide explained to me that the rule of the house was that the members of the staff, with himself, took their meals together, as in this way they could discuss questions and difficulties without trenching on the time devoted to their official duties. "An excellent plan," I said, "and I suppose you preside?" "No," he replied, "I just take my place here or there among the members of my staff, and I find it does not in any way interfere with discipline to be on the friendliest terms with even the humblest, and encourage them to bring all their difficulties before me. I often find that I get valuable suggestions from even the youngest. Now sit down," said he, "and 'partake' of a good breakfast." In spite of the shock I suffered at hearing him use the vile verb, I accepted his invitation. "For," said he, "you will want all your strength before the day is out if you are to see everything." (Later I discovered an explanation, if not an excuse, for my learned friend's language, for in the course of our talk I found he was a regular and diligent reader of the *Daily Mail*.) So I "partook" of a very excellent breakfast, and announced myself ready to follow him to the bitter end.

Leaving the refectory he led me downstairs to what he called the upper basement, the lower basement being reserved for machinery. "Machinery!" I said; "what do you want with machinery in a library?" "We have our engines for various purposes, for working printing presses, lifts, and anything else requiring power," and with that he led me into the compositors' room, which, though in the basement, was a large, well-lighted and well-ventilated apartment, where I found compositors busy filling up forms from written copies of catalogue slips.

"We find it much cheaper to print our catalogue cards, and an economy of time for our readers and searchers. In the usual card catalogues there is one principal entry, which contains the full description of a book, while the numerous cross-references are limited to 'See so and so'. We print as many copies of the principal entry as we think necessary, and then write a short heading on each of the cards to be distributed through the rest of the alphabet for cross-references, so that the searcher, on finding any cross-reference, gets all necessary details. Had these cards to be sent out to a printer much time would be lost, whereas by the 'Osler' method an hour after a book is received cards with full descriptions can be placed in our catalogue. When the cards for the day are printed off, *clichés* of them are made and stored away until the time comes when they can be used for printing a great General Catalogue."

In the next apartment were the printing machines, and I asked whether their noise did not disturb the readers upstairs. "No," said my guide; "we have safeguarded against that, for the architects have interposed double floors packed so that not the slightest sound is heard but occasionally a slight vibration."

From there he led me to the bindery. "No book ever leaves the house except to go to a reader. 'A stitch in time saves nine' is nowhere so true as in a library, where a loose leaf or cover neglected often means the destruction of the book, so whenever a book shows the slightest signs of disrepair, it is sent down here at once and dealt with by skilled workmen, who know how to repair a book without spoiling it. In the next room the actual binding work is done by men specially trained in binding books *for library use*—a very different art from that of the ordinary trade binder. I should allow no one to pass as a qualified librarian who had not a practical knowledge of binding. I don't mean to say he should be skilled enough to do the work himself, but he should know how instantly to detect bad workmanship. There is no reason why a man should not be a scholar and yet have a practical knowledge of the arts connected with his work. He may be a student of Lamb and know him by heart, and yet should know better than to bind books in sheepskin and—while properly despising 'rogues in buckram'—should know how excellent a covering is buckram for what we call 'upper shelf books,' i.e., books which we must have but are rarely referred to.

"By doing all this work inside we practically enrich our library, for is it not an impoverishment to have books away at the binder's for sometimes three months? And here in the case of a single copy of a book which may be in the bindery, if it is important for our reader to see it at once, he is allowed to look through the book, which as a rule serves his turn. If he must have it for a longer time, the binder's slip is marked 'urgent,' and rarely has he to wait for it more than three days.'

I noticed an extraordinary number of tubes attached to the upper part of the walls and almost covering the ceiling of the basement, some of them were about 2 or 3 inches in diameter others much larger, which my guide explained were pneumatic tubes for all kinds of purposes. The smallest ones were for the passage of messages from one department to another. These messages were enclosed in a small leathern cylinder, literally flashed from one end of the building to the other, and so contrived that they were released almost at the desk of the official they were intended for. The larger ones were used for books up to a limited size. By this means instead of waiting for an hour or more for a book, a reader could be sitting down before his book within five minutes of entering the building.

Beyond the bindery, and next the engine room, there was an electric plant. "We believe in having two strings to our bow in every important essential, and cannot risk a breakdown of the municipal supply, so we produce our own current, and find it economical, while we have an alternative connection with the city plant, to be turned on only if our own breaks down. Here we have the power required for every other purpose, including warming, for we decided not to run the risk, however remote, of our galleries and shelves being flooded by bursting water or steam pipes, and the radiators are heated by electricity, while in the staff offices the cheerier electric stove is installed. Current for everything requiring power is provides here."

I expressed admiration but ventured a criticism. "You appear to have taken every precaution against fire, and yet some of the worst fires have taken place in so-called fireproof buildings, for even if there are no open fires in the building, an accidental spark from the electric plant, or a short circuit, encouraged by such excellent fuel as furniture, wooden shelves etc., soon provides a bonfire."

My guide smiled and said: "I am glad you mentioned that; otherwise I might have forgotten to mention that our furniture and carpets are fireproof—a very simple and inexpensive process—and you will see why we do not dread fire."

As we turned towards the upper regions I observed a large trolley full of books emerging from one of the lift doors, and I remarked, "I suppose these are going to the bindery." "Oh, dear me, no! They don't need binding, they are going to the dusting room." Dusting room!" I exclaimed; "what do you mean?" "I will show you. In discussing the plans for our building with our great Chief, he said, 'Can you not contrive some way of getting rid of that infernal nuisance, the annual closing down of the library for cleaning?' It practically means that in most libraries it is useless for sometimes two months of the year, and to me it has always seemed that the 'cleaning' would be honestly defined as 'shifting the dirt from one place to another.'

"Well, we took the matter 'into avizandum,' as our friends in the north say, and this is the result. We don't intend ever to close the library for cleaning. The cleaning goes on day by day and every day, in regular rotation. The books are lifted gently (so as not to disturb the dust) from the shelves and placed on one of these noiseless rubber-wheeled trolleys, conveyed to a lift and brought down here by the cleaning staff, while others during their absence wipe down the shelves with a preparation which holds the dust and leaves the shelf perfectly clean. Come into the dusting room."

We followed the trolley and I found myself walking nearly ankle-deep in moist sawdust. The expert cleaners seized the books one at a time, and holding the fore edges tightly, sprinkled the tops with clean damp sawdust, which immediately licked up the dust and was thrown on the ground, when the book was then carefully dusted clean cloths containing the same preparation, which not only cleaned them, but I was assured acted as preservative to the binding. When all were clean they were restored to their place on the trolley and carried back to the shelves.

We accompanied the trolley on the lift and were carried to the main library room, a magnificent, well-lighted apartment shelved all round the walls and with projecting cases in the old-fashioned style, forming little bays to give nervous readers an opportunity of doing their work in modified isolation. The shelving seemed of oak, but my guide asked me to examine it more closely, and I found that both shelves and uprights were formed of steel, so artistically enamelled that unless actually handled they appeared to be of fine-grained oak.

My guide went to one of the bays, and, putting his hands under one of the shelves, lifted it and the books together and laid it on the reading table, and then showed me how, by a cunning invention, the shelves, while quite safely fixed in position, could, by touching a couple of springs at the ends, be instantly released and thus enabled space to be economised to the minutest degree. The tables were of the same material as the shelves, and the oaken chairs, designed for comfort but yet artistically, were, as he explained to me, absolutely fireproof.

My guide explained that this room, called the general, or main library, was the largest, and for the general reader, the favourite room. The other rooms, to which he proposed to lead me presently, were for special study, for the use of readers who were engaged on research, or themselves writing books, and for whom it was desirable to have a certain amount of seclusion, and their books kept together.

The general lighting was by reflected light thrown by powerful electric lamps against the white ceiling, by which a delightfully equal light diffused through every corner of the room, while on each reading table I saw there was a separate shaded electric lamp provided with current through a cunning attachment to the pedestal.

"How do you classify your books?" I asked. "We don't classify them. You can't classify a medical library without doing more harm than good. If all medical books were monographs, it could be done, and probably would be useful; but when you remember under how many subjects medical books might be looked for, you will recognize that to classify them under one subject would be hiding them in all the others. Therefore, we find that for practical purposes, both as regards economy of space and quickness of service, it is better to shelve the books chronologically and according to size. This means that our library begins with the earliest books, which are in the remoter parts of the library, and so we march down through the ages, and the books published during the last ten years are the most accessible, and the book last received is the last one on the shelves. We depend for our classification on the catalogue in which a reference should be found to any particular book, under every subject with which it deals," I noticed on the larger tables bulky volumes that looked like atlases, and on turning them over found they were filled with original drawings of all kinds—pathological, anatomical, surgical, and bacteriological. "Ah," said my guide, "that is a feature we are proud of. Beautiful and valuable drawings are constantly being made for authors, to illustrate their books and papers published in Transactions, etc., and for the most part, these were destroyed, or at least wasted. Some authors might keep them for a while, but sooner or later they find their way to the dust bin. Now, we have a clerk who, as soon as any particularly good drawing is published, writes to the author and begs him to let us have the original for preservation and display. They are then mounted in these albums with a reference to the paper or book for which they were prepared, and are duly entered in our index. No reproduction of a good drawing can ever equal the original, if only for the reason that, as a rule, they have necessarily to be reduced; and we find our collection immensely appreciated and in constant use. You will see that there is some attempt at classification in these albums. One album will be devoted to drawings of the surgery or anatomy of the thorax, another to the bacteriology of a particular disease, and so on. Sometimes the author will not part with his drawings, and in that case we get the loan of them and make full-size permanent photographs of them to mount in our albums. When our photographer is not busy with such work, he fills in his time by photographing from perfect copies illustrations and sometimes title pages to enable us to make good imperfect copies of our rarer treasures; and we have even been able in this way to produce wonderfully good complete copies of unique books and manuscripts, which can only be found in older libraries."

"What are those type-written folios I see displaced on that desk?"

"Let us look at them," said the Chief, "as that, too, is a feature we are rather proud of. In a library like this, men are constantly looking up references in connection with their own work, compiling bibliographies, so essential an adjunct to any good medical book. Formerly, this work done, we saw the last of it when their sheets were taken away for the printer; and so we offered all such workers to present them with a fair typed copy of their work on condition that they allowed us to keep a duplicate, and in this way we have secured many hundreds of valuable bibliographies, which are preserved here for the use of others."

We walked on to the adjoining room, equally lofty and equally handsome but smaller, but this I found to be a reference library, from which, my guide explained, no book was ever allowed to be removed except to the bindery. "Not under any circumstances," he said; "for we regard it as essential that there should be a copy of every important book *always available*. In the practice of medicine and surgery, 'next week' or even 'to-morrow' should never be heard in a library. Where life or human suffering is the price to be paid for delay, there must be none, and therefore a sudden demand for any book likely to be required must be instantly answered.

"Without our reference library another of our departments would be handicapped if not impossible. One of the items in Osler's prescription ran: 'Make the library as useful to the worker in Timbuctoo and Tierra del Fuego as to the man who lives round the corner.' I wrote him, 'Excellent idea, but how?' He wired back, 'Oh, *you* know—quite simple—I'm busy.'

"So we had to work it out. We invite our readers abroad and at a distance to keep us informed as to their lines of work or research. Their names are registered and classified—and every month we send them a 'Bulletin' containing references and abstracts of all that has been published on their subject during the previous month. If they want more, they write to the head of our Abstracting Department, and copies and abstracts of articles in books or journals (translated when necessary) are despatched without delay. One of our correspondents lately wrote, in the preface of an epoch-marking book which he had written on the slopes of the Andes, that our help had made it easier for him than if he had been living in London, for he had been saved the time he would have had to spend in making his own researches in the library!"

"But," I said, "all this must cost a fabulous amount. The running expenses alone must equal those of a township. You must have an enormous number of members who pay a high subscription."

"Members," he answered, almost indignantly, "our members, as you call them, include every qualified man and woman throughout the civilised world. Once on a Register a man or a woman is entitled to the best we can do for them without any subscription." "Ah, you are a State Department?" "No, we are absolutely untrammelled. I thought you knew the origin of the scheme. You remember that twenty years ago Osler celebrated his seventieth birthday and now, although by the calendar, ninety, he seems determined to prove that a man is not too old at a hundred. The whole civilised world, on the approach of his seventieth birthday, wanted to celebrate it in a way really worthy of their hero, and many meetings and long discussions were held on the best way of doing it. Carnefeller got to hear of it and summoned the testimonial committee to meet him; brushed all their suggestions on one side and said, 'The only sane way of celebrating Osler's biological palinode is by erecting a library which will realise all his ideals, and if you will carry it out I will provide the dollars,' and here he handed a cheque to the chairman and left us. On examining it we found the cheque was signed in blank, and in the course of a few minutes it was filled up with such a sum as would cover the most ambitious scheme, with a sufficient margin for a liberal endowment and, just in case of accidents, promptly banked."

"The *body* is wonderful," I said, "and your mechanical part seems to be as perfect as could be devised. But what about the *soul*—the *intellect*, of this wonderful *body*?" "I was hoping you would come to that," said my guide. "I am the Chief, but I don't pretend to be either the soul or the intellect of such an institution as this. The Chief should be before all things an administrator and a business man, or the whole institution will suffer. We have in all, at present twelve librarians, each of whom is supreme in his own department, and I verily believe each is the greatest living authority on the subject he deals with." "But how can you get men of such attainments to accept such positions? For while I am sure that the matter of salaries is dealt with as liberally as everything else in this wonderful institution, men of such attainments would probably be earning princely incomes by the practice of their profession." "No, you are quite wrong. You will find in every profession men who are by temperament students rather than practitioners, and who would rather work for a modest competence in extending their knowledge than in the practice of their profession, and this is notably so in that of Medicine. And so we have here, for example, a man who has, perhaps, a better knowledge of anatomy than all the professors put together, but he is happier here adding to and administering our anatomical collection, than he would be if he held the most important professorship. He has no faculty for teaching, and knows it; but raise any abstruse point in anatomy with him, and he will at once, without consulting any index or catalogue, place before you the answer to your question. It is the same with our surgical librarian. When he inadvertently removed the second kidney, leaving an overlooked forceps in its place, he decided that the practice of surgery was not his forte, and his love for and wide knowledge of the literature of the subject brought him to us. And so it is with each of the others. They have not exactly a free hand in their departments, for some of them would spend all our available income on their own department; but they come to me with their lists of desiderata and I decide, having in view the necessity of a fair balance between one department and another. We are in constant communication, in addition to the practice of taking our meals together in the refectory. And each has his own room, connected by telephone with mine. We make great use of the telephone." At this moment, I saw one of the assistants on a high ladder perilously balancing some heavy volumes, and before I realised the danger, boy, books, and ladder fell with a crash towards me.—When I came to myself, I heard the telephone ringing, started up, and found I was in my own chair by my own fireside, and rushed to the telephone. "Hello! Is that Mayfair 3271?" "No, wrong number!"

From, *Contributions to medical and biological research dedicated to Sir William Osler, Bart.,
M.D., F.R.S., in honour of his seventieth birthday, July 12, 1919, by his pupils and co-workers,*
Vol. 1, New York, 1919, pp. 111-121.

# CHAPTER 35

# John Cotton Dana (1856–1929)

"A collection of books gathered at public expense does not justify itself by the simple fact that it is. If a library be not a live educational institution it were better never established. It is ours to justify to the world the literary warehouse. A library is good only as the librarian makes it so."

JOHN COTTON DANA.

JOHN COTTON DANA was born on August 19th, 1856, at Woodstock, Vermont, U.S.A., and in 1874 entered Dartmouth College, where he graduated four years later. Dana returned to his native Woodstock and commenced the study of law, but was interrupted by ill health, and compelled to lead an outdoor life for two years. In 1880 he was admitted to the Colorado bar, continued law studies in New York City, and in 1883 was admitted to the New York bar. Dana practised law, edited a periodical, and undertook surveying work to be in the open air, before marrying in 1888, when he settled on a ranch in Colorado. He wrote letters and articles for periodicals, but in 1889 was appointed librarian of the new Denver Public Library. By 1893 Dana had increased the stock from 2,000 to 23,000 volumes. He commenced a monthly journal entitled *Books*, organized classes for training assistants, threw the shelves open to readers and borrowers, opened the first special room for children, and encouraged schools to use the library.

Dana was President of the Colorado Library Association in 1895, and in November, 1897 was appointed librarian of the Springfield, Massachusetts, City Library Association, where he introduced extensive reforms. Dana wrote a series of articles which was published in the first six numbers of *Public Libraries*, 1896, and appeared in book form as *A library primer*, 1899, 1909 and 1920.

After four years at Springfield, Dana became librarian of Newark Public Library on January 15th, 1902. He stressed the value of encouraging children to read, persuaded business men to use the library, and opened a separate branch for the latter. From 1909 he was director of the Newark Museum, for which new premises were erected.

Dana wrote several books on library work, and with Henry W. Kent edited *Literature and libraries in the seventeenth and eighteenth centuries*, of which six volumes were published, including Dana's

263

translation of Lipsius' *De bibliothecis syntagma*. His articles were collected together and published in 1916 as *Libraries: addresses and essays*. He refused several honorary degrees, but was proud of the title "The First Citizen of Newark".

John Cotton Dana attended several American Library Association conferences, and was elected President at that held at Denver in 1895, delivering his presidential address at Cleveland in 1896. In 1904 he represented the A.L.A. at the Library Association Conference, was President of the New Jersey Library Association, 1904–1906 and 1910–1911, and was first President of the Special Libraries Association, 1910–1900.

Dana died on July 21st, 1929. He was a stern, but constructive critic of the American Library Association, which was concerned chiefly with public libraries, and he stressed the use of books rather than their acquisition as collections. His favourite maxim was "The worth of a book is in its use", and his achievements at Newark, and on behalf of librarianship in general, place him among the most prominent American librarians. (Portrait, Plate 13.)

## REFERENCES

Hadley, Chalmers. *John Cotton Dana: a sketch*, Chicago, 1943. (American Library Pioneers.)

Kingdon, F. *John Cotton Dana: a life*, Newark, New Jersey, 1940.

Lansberg, William R. John Cotton Dana, 1856–1929. [etc.], *Bulletin of the Free Public Library Commission and of the State Library Vermont*, 52, June, 1956, pp. 2–6.

[Winser, Beatrice.] *John Cotton Dana, 1856–1929*, Newark, New Jersey, 1930.

Winser, Marian Manley. John Cotton Dana and the Special Libraries Association. *Special Libraries*, 50, 1959, pp. 208–211.

## DANA LOOKS AT LIBRARIANS

"Failures confessed are guide-posts to success; weaknesses discovered are no longer weaknesses."

I sometimes fear my enthusiasm for the free public library is born more of contagion than of conviction. Consider the thing in some of its more evident aspects.

Here is a building, perhaps erected to perpetuate a good man's memory, a monument and of use only as a monument; or constructed in accordance with the views of an architect whose ideas of beauty are crude and whose thought of utility is naught; ill-adapted to the purpose for which it is intended; poorly lighted, badly ventilated. In it are stored a few thousand volumes, including, of course, the best books of all times—which no one reads—and a generous percentage of fiction of the cheaper sort. To this place come in good proportion the idle and the lazy; also the people who cannot endure the burden of a thought, and who fancy they are improving their minds, while in fact they are simply letting cool waters from fountains of knowledge trickle through the sieves of an idle curiosity. The more persistent visitors are often men who either have failed in a career, or never had a career, or do not wish a career. Libraries all have their indolents, idlers and "boarders".

There is little that is inspiring, *per se*, in the sight of the men who gather in the newspaper reading room of any free public library. There is not much that is encouraging in a careful look at many of those who are the more constant visitors to the shelves of the reference department. Who wear out our dictionaries, the students of language or the competitors in a word building contest? Of those who come to the delivery desk 60 to 80 per cent rarely concern themselves, as far as the library knows them, with anything but fiction, and in that field concern themselves generally only with the latest novel, which they wish because it is the latest. And of this 60 to 80 per cent, a large proportion—probably at least half—prefer to get, and generally do get, a novel of the poorer kind.

I am stating the case plainly. I share the librarian's enthusiasm; but that enthusiasm is sometimes to me, and I believe to many others, a cause for surprise. Has it not often come sharply home to every librarian—the hopelessness of the task we assume to set ourselves? The triviality of the great mass of the free public library's educational work? The discouraging nature of the field? The pettiness, the awful pettiness, of results?

Nor is this all. That we strive for great things and accomplish so little; that our output seems commensurate with the size of the plant and the cost of its maintenance, this is by no means the only fact which may rightly sober our enthusiasms.

Fathers and mothers love their children and look after their happiness. The more they do this, the more they concern themselves that the human beings they have brought into the world be self-reliant, self-supporting people, knowing how to live in harmony with their fellows, and wishing so to live, the more civilized are they. Parental responsibility is something the sense of which has never been too acute. That I may rightly scorn and despise my neighbor if his children be not decent, attractive, civilized; that my neighbor may rightly consider himself disgraced if his offspring grow not up in the fear and admonition of the good citizen; these things are not yet commonly received. The native manners and the education of the American child are looked upon, not so much as the result of parentage and home training, as the good gift of God and the public school.

A strong sense of parental responsibility, this is a prime essential to the growth of knowledge and to the increase of social efficiency. And this feeling of obligation to train properly the souls of one's own creation; this sense that the parent can win public approval as a parent only when the result is an additional factor in the public's happiness and comfort; this rule of living would surely result, if rightly applied, in careful consideration of the child's education. But what have we done? We have turned the whole subject of education over to the community. We have made it depend very largely on the result of an annual election. We have let it slip gradually into the hands of those veritable and inevitable children of government—the politicians. The American parent is indifferent to the character of the education of his children. The interposition of the community in what should be his affairs has not only made him indifferent to those affairs, it has made others indifferent that he is so. He pays his taxes. If the schools are poor the fault is at the school-board's door, not his.

The free public library not only relieves the idle and incompetent and indifferent from the necessity—would he have books—of going to work to earn them; it not only checks the growth of the tendency of the private individual to collect a library of his own, adapted to his own needs, and suiting his own tastes and those of his children; it also tends to lead parents to become indifferent to the general reading of their children, just as the free public school may lead them to be indifferent to their formal education. Certainly, fathers and mothers whose children use public libraries seem to care very little what and how much their children read. They conceal their solicitude from librarian and assistants, if it exists. Yet, if a collection of books in a community is a good thing for the community—and we seem to think it is; and if it is a good thing particularly for the children of the community—and we seem to think it is, then it is a good thing, not in itself simply, not as an object of worship, not as an adequate excuse for the erection of a pleasing mortuary monument on the public street, but for its effect on young folks' manners and on young folks' brains. But to produce a maximum effect herein, to produce even a modest effect, the right books must be put into the right hand at the right time. Can public servants do this rightly unless the parents cooperate with them? But the public library is not an institution which the mother helps to support because she has come to believe in it; because it is her pleasure; because she can and does keep a watchful eye on its growth and its methods. It is part of the machinery of the state. She confides her children to its tender mercies in the same spirit with which her forbears confided in their king!

Furthermore, the essence of government is force. This essence remains whether the visible form be king or majority. It is open to question—I put it mildly—whether it is expedient to touch with the strong hand the impulse of a people to train with earnest thought their young, or the impulse of a people to give light to their fellows. People wish, in the main, that their children be well taught. Without this wish a school system, public or private, would be impossible. This wish is the fundamental fact; that the system is public and tax-supported is the secondary fact; the result, not the cause. People wish also, in the main, to give their fellows and themselves the opportunity for self improvement. This wish is the fundamental fact at the bottom of the free, compulsorily supported public library. It is on these fundamental facts we should keep our eyes and our thoughts, not on the feature of compulsion.

We should work, then, such is my conclusion, for the extension of the public library from the starting point of human sympathy; from the universal desire for an increase of human happiness by an increase of knowledge of the conditions of human happiness; not from the starting-point of law, of compulsion, of enforcing on others our views of their duty.

I have said enough in this line. To the observant eye our libraries are not altogether halls of learning; they are also the haunts of the lazy. They do not always interest parents in their children; perhaps they lead parents to be indifferent to their children.

But really, librarians will say, all this is not our concern. We find ourselves here, they say, loving the companionship of books; desirous of extending the joys they can give to our fellows; embarked in public service, and active—none are more so; zealous—none are more so; honest—none are more so, in our work of making good use of books. Your modern librarian in his daily life is no disputatious economist, idly wavering, like the fabled donkey, between the loose hay of a crass individualism and the chopped feed of a perfectionist socialism. He is a worker. If there are things to be said which may add to the efficiency of his attempts to help his fellows to grow happier and wiser, let us hear them; and for this we have come together.

I have said these things, not with the risk to lessen the zeal of one of us in our chosen work. A moment's look at the case against us cannot anger us—that were childish; cannot discourage us—that were cowardly. It may lead us to look to the joints of our armor; it should lead us to renew our efforts. If the free public library movement be not absolutely and altogether a good thing, and he is a bold economist who vows that it is, how urgent is the call to us to make each our own library and corrective, as far as may be, of the possible harm of its existence. A collection of books gathered at public expense does not justify itself by the simple fact that it is. If a library be not a live educational institution it were better never established. It is ours to justify to the world the literary warehouse. A library is good only as the librarian makes it so.

Can we do more than we have done to justify our calling? Can we make ourselves of more importance to the world, of more positive value to the world? Our calling is dignified in our own eyes, it is true; but we are not greatly dignified in the eyes of our fellows. The public does not ask our opinions. We are, like the teachers, students; and we strive, like them, to keep abreast of the times, and to have opinions on vital topics formed after much reading and some thought. But save on more trivial questions, on questions touching usually only the recreative side of life, like those of literature commonly so called, our opinions are not asked for. We are, to put it bluntly, of very little weight in the community. We are teachers; and who cares much for what the teacher says?

I am not pausing now to note exceptions. We all know our masters and our exemplars; and I shall not pause to praise the men and women who have brought us where we are; who have lifted librarianship, in the estimation of the wise and good, to a profession, and have made it comparatively an easy thing for you and me to develop our libraries, if we can and will, into all that they should be, and to become ourselves as librarians, men and women of weight and value in the community.

I have said that your library is perhaps injuring your community; that you are not of any importance among your own people. And these, you tell me are hard sayings. In truth they are. I am not here to pass you any compliments. If for five minutes we can divest ourselves of every last shred of our trappings of self-satisfaction, and arouse in ourselves for a moment a keen sense of our sins of omission, of things left undone or not well done, I shall be content, and shall consider that we have wisely opened these Cleveland sessions. I would wish to leave you, here at the very beginning of our discussions, not, indeed in the Slough of Despond, but climbing sturdily, and well aware that you are climbing, the Hill Difficulty. Others, I can assure you, will, long before our conference ends, lead us again, and that joyfully, to our Delectable Mountains.

Pardon me, then, while I say over again a few of the things that cannot be too often said.

Look first to your own personal growth. Get into touch with the world. Let no one point to you as an instance of the narrowing effects of too much of books.

Be social. Impress yourself on your community; in a small way if

not in a large. Be not superior and reserved. Remember that he who
to the popular eye wears much the air of wisdom is never wise.

Speak out freely on matters of library management; and especially,
in these days, on matters of library construction. In recent years
millions of dollars have been spent on library buildings in this country,
and we have not yet a half dozen in the land that do not disgrace us.
If we have stood idly by and not made our opinions, our knowledge,
our experience, felt by trustees and architects, then is ours the blame,
and we are chief among sufferers. Persuade architects and their
associations, local and national, who ignore us because in our
inconsequence they know they can, that they may wisely and without
loss of dignity consult the professional librarian about the building he
is to occupy. I say persuade them; I might better say compel them. To
compel them will be easy when you have become of importance in
the world. Even now it is not too soon to attempt to confer with
them. You can at once make the beginning of friendly and helpful
relations with the American Institute of Architects. But you must ask,
not demand.

Advertise the A.L.A. and what it stands for. Help to broaden its
field. Support heartily measures which look to a greater degree of
publicity for it. Interest your trustees in it. Interest your friends, and
your patrons and constituents in it. Be ready and willing to do your
share of the work, and there is no end of work that each year must be
done to keep it properly alive and well in the public eye. Call the
attention of your trustees to the difference between the efficient library,
such as the A.L.A. advocates, and the dead-and-alive collection of
books, still altogether too common. Consider the contrast between
the possible public library and the public library that is. If the causes
for that contrast lie at your door, face them frankly and bravely and
strive to remove them.

Do not forget the Library Department of the National Educational
Association, recently established. It gives you excuse, and it gives you
cause to take an interest, more active even than heretofore, in the
introduction of books and library methods into school work, and to
concern yourselves more than ever before with the general reading of
teachers and their pupils. Impress upon teachers the value to them of
your library. Persuade them, if you can, that to do their best work
they must know well and use freely the good books.

See that your local book and news men are heartily with you in the
work of spreading knowledge of the right use of books and encouraging
ownership of books in your community. If you come in contact with
the bookseller and the publisher of the great cities, do what you can to
persuade them that to join in the work of this association of librarians

is not only to benefit the community at large, but to help their own particular business as well.

Be not slow in giving hearty recognition to those who have, in the beginnings of library science, taken the first place and borne the burdens and made an easy way for us who follow. If, perhaps against some odds, a librarian, man or woman, is making an eminent success of some great city library, may you not properly send him, once and again, a word which shall signify that you, at least, are alive to the fact of his good work and are yourself encouraged and inspired thereby? Like words of approval you may well extend to the good men, outside the profession proper, who have given their time and energy, a labor of love, to improve certain features of library work.

Interest in your work in your own community your local book-lovers and book-collectors and book-worms and private students and plodders and burners of midnight oil. Get in touch with the teachers of literature in the colleges and schools of your neighborhood. Expound to such, and to the general reader as well, whenever you properly can, the difficulties and the possibilities of your calling, your conquests in classification and cataloguing, and your advances in bibliography and indexing, and the progress in recent years of general library economy. Remember that all these things can be even better done in a small community, in the village library of a few hundred volumes, than in the large library of the great city.

Note the women's clubs, art associations, historical societies, scientific societies. Do not forget the private schools. In the small town you can gain without difficulty the good-will of the local newspaper. You can often assist the editor in his work, and lead him to help you in return. The clergymen in your town certainly care somewhat for the reading of their young people, and will cooperate with you in any intelligent offer to increase it and improve it. The Sunday-school libraries of your neighborhood are open to your suggestions, if you approach them properly. And the Y.M.C. and the Y.W.C. associations will gladly take from you advice and assistance in the management of their reading-rooms and their libraries.

None are so poor that they cannot give to others; and few libraries are so small that they cannot spare books and magazines enough to make a little library which may be sent out into a still smaller community and there do good service.

Do the business men and the business women, the active people, those who feed us and clothe us and transport us, those who have brought about in the last few decades the great increase in creature comforts for every one, do these business people take an active interest in your library? Do they care for you or for your opinion? If not, is it their fault? Is it that they are gross and dull and material and wordly; or is it that you, the wise librarian, know not yet how to bring your educational forces to bear on the life that now is? Our work is but begun so long as we are not in close touch with the man of affairs.

Remember that as you in your town, or in your city, widen the sphere of your influence, grow to be a person of worth and dignity in the community, you thereby add so much to the dignity and to the effectiveness of the whole profession. If in a city or town near you there is a library which, in its general arrangement is not what it should be, which is but a dusty pile of printed pages or but a roosting-place for a flock of cheap novels, yours is in part the fault, and you are largely the loser. When a dweller in that town, one unacquainted with library affairs—and most are such—hears you alluded to as a "librarian." he thinks of you as a person akin to the bibliothecal pagan who fails to manage the library of his own town, the only library he knows by which he can measure your work. He is a "librarian"; you are a "librarian". We wear the livery of our co-workers as well as our own.

Keep these thoughts in mind and you will see how essential it is, would our profession reach the standing we wish it to reach, would we make it everywhere an honour to wear our name, that every smallest library be an effective educational machine, and that every humblest librarian be an active, enthusiastic, intelligent worker.

See that your library is interesting to the people of the community, the people who own it, the people who maintain it. Deny your people nothing which the book-shop grants them. Make your library at least as attractive as the most attractive store in the community. Open your eyes to the cheapness of books at the present day, and to the unimportance, even to the small library, of the loss of an occasional volume; and open them also to the necessity of getting your constituency in actual contact with the books themselves.

Remember always that taxation is compulsion, that taxation is government; that government, among present-day human creatures, is politics; that the end of an institution may not justify its means; that a free public library may be other than a helpful thing. See to it, therefore, the more carefully that your own public library at least is rationally administered, and promotes public helpfulness.

Dana, John Cotton. Hear the other side. President's address to the American Library Association, Cleveland, Conference, September, 1896. In, *Libraries: addresses and essays*, New York, 1916, pp. 3-14. (Reprinted by kind permission of the H. W. Wilson Company.)

CHAPTER 36

# Thomas Mason (1857–1914)

> "His record was one of creditable industry and marked individuality, and the name of Thomas Mason must always hold an honoured place upon our roll of service."
>
> FRANK PACY.

THOMAS MASON, the son of another librarian bearing the same name, was born at Aberdeen in 1857. After working as a mechanic, in 1877 he became assistant in the Mitchell Library, Glasgow, where he rose to become Assistant Librarian. The year 1881 saw his appointment as Librarian of Stirling's Public Library, Glasgow, but eight years later he came to London as first Librarian of St. Martin-in-the-Fields. He retired from that position in 1905 when the parish was absorbed to form the City of Westminster, and was engaged in journalistic work for Messrs. W. Stevens Ltd. He died on March 30th, 1914.

Mason joined the Library Association in 1880, and six years later was elected to the Council. He served as Joint Honorary Secretary with MacAlister for three years, and contributed several interesting papers to the Library Association conferences. These were printed in the *Transactions*, and include "The free libraries of Scotland", 1880 (also published separately in Glasgow the same year); "Fiction in free libraries", 1889; "An alphabetical list of places where the Acts have been adopted, with dates of adoption", 1890; and "A new method of arranging a lending library", 1893. Mason wrote a novel entitled *Adam Dickson; or sae sweet, sae bonnilie*, Glasgow, 1888, and a most interesting volume, *Public and private libraries of Glasgow*, printed for subscribers and for private circulation at Glasgow, 1885. This contains a wealth of interesting material that is not readily available elsewhere.

At the Glasgow Conference in 1888 Thomas Mason read the following paper on Robert Watt, which does justice to the memory of a great bibliographer, and is not unworthy of representing its author's writings.

## REFERENCES

Minto, John. *A history of the public library movement in Great Britain and Ireland*, 1932, pp. 328–329.
Obituary. By F. P[acy]. *Library Association Record*, 16, 1914, pp. 262–263.

## MASON ON ROBERT WATT

If any apology were needed in connection with the presentation of a paper upon the Life and Work of Dr. Robert Watt, the author of the *Bibliotheca Britannica*, it ought surely to be a humble and contrite one on the part of the reading and writing public, for seventy years of comparative neglect and indifference.

The *Bibliotheca Britannica* is in use in every library possessing any bibliographical tools at all, and yet how very little is known about the man who produced it? The best account of Watt is to be found in *Chambers' Dictionary of Eminent Scotsmen*. It is indeed, as far as I have been able to find, the only notice of Watt deserving attention. The rest are scrappy and inaccurate, beyond even the average scrappiness and inaccuracy of biographical dictionaries. The new edition of the *Encyclopaedia Britannica* does not mention Watt, but let us hope that Mr. Leslie Stephen's *Dictionary of National Biography* will make amends and do justice to the memory of an accomplished and notable man.

Robert Watt was born at his father's farm of Bonnington in the parish of Stewarton, Ayrshire, on the 1st of May, 1774. The farm had been in the possession of the family for several generations, but the Watts seem to have been more joiners and wheelwrights than farmers. At the death in 1810 of John Watt, our author's father, the farm was sold.

Watt received very little if any day-schooling. Like another son of Ayrshire, Robert Burns, he was early impressed into the work of the farm. There was little time for schooling and no time for play. The day began early and ended late. With his two brothers, Watt attended an evening school, and what he picked up there he supplemented by study during the odd moments of the day. Whether as herd-boy, plough-boy, or stone-dyker, he seems to have been eagerly bent upon self-improvement, and determined if possible to enter college and study for one of the learned professions. Thus in plain living and high thinking was Watt's youth spent, and so assiduous was he in the acquisition of knowledge, not forgetting the acquirement of a few pounds of the current coin of the realm, that he was able to enter as a student at the College of Glasgow by the time he had turned his eighteenth year. The indomitable perseverance which was afterwards to come to his help in the compilation of the gigantic work with which his name is associated, carried him triumphantly through his early difficulties.

One of the Professors under whom he studied in the College of Glasgow, was William Richardson, author of numerous works, and an intimate friend and ardent supporter of the brothers Foulis— Glasgow's famous printers.

It is not improbable that Richardson may have first directed the mind of his student to the value of a systematic and readily available record of literature, as we know that as early as 1799 Watt began collecting materials, which were afterwards used in the *Bibliotheca*.

At the conclusion of his studies at the University in 1797, Watt gave some attention to theology, but subsequently forsook the church for the hospital. In 1799 he qualified for medical practice by passing the examination of the Faculty of Physicians and Surgeons in Glasgow. The first scene of his labours was Paisley, the birthplace, and the home of many famous men. Fortune smiled upon the young doctor, and his practice increased so rapidly that he was soon obliged to take a partner. He remained in Paisley for the space of ten years. During this period, while busy professionally, he was not idle with his pen, and produced a large number of works on medical and philosophical subjects. One of these, a treatise on cases of diabetes, consumption, &c., with observations on the history and treatment of disease in general, was published in 1808, and created considerable discussion in medical circles at the time. Dr. Watt's other published writings besides the *Bibliotheca* were a *Catalogue of Medical Books, for the use of students attending Lectures on the Principles and Practice of Medicine; with an address to medical students on the best method of prosecuting their studies*, Glasgow, 1812; *A Treatise on the History, Nature and Treatment of Chin-cough; including a variety of cases and dissections. To which is subjoined, An inquiry into the relative mortality of the principal Diseases of Children, and the numbers who have died under ten years of age, in Glasgow during the last thirty years*, Glasgow, 1813; *Rules of Life; with reflections on the Manners and Dispositions of Mankind*, Edinb., 1814. This was published anonymously. Dr. Watt also made several contributions to scientific journals. No kind of literature ages and becomes obsolete so soon as that pertaining to the cure and care of the body, and Dr. Watt's medical writings, with one exception, have suffered the usual fate. The exception is the remarkable appendix to the treatise on chin-cough, an appendix which has been and still is a mine of information to the medical statist.

Feeling the need of a larger field for the exercise of his vocation, Dr. Watt took a journey into England and visited most of the principal towns with a view to settling down, but unable to make a choice, he returned home in the course of a few months, and shortly afterwards removed from Paisley to Glasgow. This was in 1810. His reputation as a skilful doctor preceded his appearance in Glasgow, and when he set up in Queen Street as Physician and Accoucheur, he very soon obtained a large and excellent practice. He had previously received the degree of M.D. from the University of Aberdeen, and local honours crowded upon him in the course of a few years. He was elected President of the Faculty of Physicians and Surgeons in Glasgow, and appointed one of the physicians to the Royal Infirmary. For several years he lectured on the Theory and Practice of Medicine to crowded classes. He was a fluent speaker and an attractive lecturer.

There are two portraits of him in the rooms of the Faculty of Physicians and Surgeons. One represents him when a young man in Paisley; the other, much the finer of the two, had probably been painted four or five years before his death. Both pictures bear out the statement that he was a man of fine bearing, tall and handsome. For the purpose of his classes he accumulated a large collection of medical books, to which he gave his students free access. To enable the young men to readily make use of the collection he compiled a catalogue of it, which he published in 1812. This catalogue consisted of an alphabetical list of authors, with an index of subjects, and was the forerunner of the *Bibliotheca*. The utility of the index was so apparent that Dr. Watt at once set about enlarging its scope, so as to include the titles of all medical books published in the United Kingdom from the introduction of printing into England. When he had done this he again extended his plan, taking in books treating law. As the work grew the scheme of the compiler expanded. After taking in law he embraced divinity, and before he again made a halt the whole body of literature, which for want of another name the librarian still calls "Miscellaneous", was included in the as yet untitled bibliography.

He was now in a position to print. He had finished as far as his means and opportunities permitted him a definite and much wanted piece of work—the indexing for ready reference of the whole body of British literature. He issued a prospectus which received a favourable reception, and thus emboldened, he prepared for publication. On the eve of going to press he once more resolved upon enlarging the work, and resolutely sat down to the herculean task of recording the principal productions of the printing press throughout the entire world.

The labour of compilation soon crushed out all other work, and in 1817 Watt abandoned his professional career, and devoted himself entirely to the *Bibliotheca*. The prosecution of his self-imposed task seriously aggravated a constitutional disorder, and for the last two years of his life Watt was a confirmed invalid. Still he kept manfully on, unwilling to leave the work unfinished. He employed amanuenses, and was also assisted by his two sons. To secure uninterrupted leisure he removed from the city to a house at Crossmyloof, then a village about two miles from Glasgow, but now a part of the city actual, though not yet municipal.

The result of this unremitting labour was that the work made great progress. So alas did the malady which was sapping away the life of the heroic worker. It was a race between work and death. Hoping to improve his health Dr. Watt went from Leith to London by sea, and afterwards made a sojourn in some of the country districts of England, but all to no purpose. He returned to Glasgow in worse health than ever, and took to his bed, from which he hardly ever again rose. Although confined to bed he continued working at the *Bibliotheca*, supervising the work of his assistants, but a day came soon when, finished or unfinished, the labourer's work was done. Dr. Watt died on the 12th of March, 1819, in the 45th year of his age: a martyr to bibliography if ever there was one. He is buried in Glasgow Cathedral churchyard.

Fortunately Dr. Watt left the manuscript of the *Bibliotheca* in an almost completed state (some of the first sheets were printed off), but, to allay any anxiety on the part of the subscribers as to the condition of the work, the family of the deceased bibliographer caused the manuscript to be examined by four esteemed citizens of Glasgow, well able to form an opinion upon the fitness of the work for immediate publication. These gentlemen were the Rev. Dr. Thomas Chalmers, Prof. Jardine, James Ewing, and Ralph Wardlaw. After examining the manuscript they issued the following report:—

"Glasgow, April 14th, 1819.

In consequence of the lamented death of the late Dr. Robert Watt, of this city, we have been requested by his family and his publisher to examine the manuscripts of the *Bibliotheca Britannica*, left by him in the possession of his son, and now in course of publication.

In compliance with this request we have this day inspected the numerous written volumes of this laborious work, going through the contents of each letter *seriatim*, and comparing their relative proportions. It was not, of course, within our commission to form any judgment of the execution and merits of the work itself; but we are happy to have it in our power to assure the subscribers, that, as far as our examination could enable us to judge, it has been left by the author, throughout, in a state of readiness for publication. Nor can we forbear adding our attestation to the striking evidence afforded by it of indefatigable industry and unwearied perseverance, in a department of labour too, which, however useful in its results, must appear to most minds to possess few allurements in the execution. The author, we understand, devoted the greater part of the last twenty years of his life to the collection and arrangement of the necessary materials, and of these *the whole* has been copied *thrice*, and some parts of them even *six and seven times*.

During the last four years his son has been engaged, under the direction of his father, in forwarding and completing the work; and, from the experience he has thus had, as well as in other respects, we have no doubt of his qualifications for perfecting what yet remains to be done, in adding the new publications which may make their appearance during the progress of the work through the press.

It is with sincere satisfaction we thus state our conviction that this important work is not likely to suffer from the decease of its author; and it is, at the same time, our earnest desire and hope that his bereaved family may reap, both in credit and emolument, the fruits of the courage which projected, and the industry which completed a publication which, we are satisfied, will, on several accounts, form a very valuable acquisition to the literary world."

The printing of the work proceeded under the supervision of Dr. Watt's eldest son. The first two volumes were printed at Glasgow and the third and fourth at Edinburgh. The printing of so vast a work necessarily occupied a long time, and it was not until 1824 that the work was published. It was issued in eight parts and was dedicated to George the Fourth, who by the way does not seem to have subscribed for a copy; 505 copies were subscribed for before publication, and the hope expressed by the examiners of the manuscript, that the family of the deceased bibliographer might reap substantial emolument from the publication of the work, seemed likely to be fulfilled. Messrs. Archibald Constable and Co., the well-known publishers of the *Waverley Novels*, agreed to publish the work, and undertook to pay Mrs. Watt the sum of £2000 for the right. Bills to this amount were sent to Mrs. Watt, but before they could be turned into money the great publishing house came down, and the Watts, with many others, were involved in ruin. Misfortune seemed to have marked the family of the unfortunate bibliographer for its own. The whole city was shocked one morning, some months after Dr. Watt's death, to learn that the home of his widow had been entered by a band of robbers and stripped of every removable thing of value. The miscreants, who were nine in number, were so bold and ruffianly as to make the poor lady wrench the rings from her fingers. I have seen it stated that they destroyed a portion of the manuscript of the *Bibliotheca*, and that it took a year's labour to repair the mischief, but it is difficult to see how the missing portion could be replaced and for the present, therefore, I hesitate to hand over the rascals to Mr. Blades for canonisation among the "Enemies of Books". For a time it seemed as if the scoundrels were to escape, but about a year after the date of the robbery four of them were caught, tried, found guilty, and robbery being then luckily a capital punishment, sentenced to death and executed. It was perhaps not inappropriate that the sermon to the condemned men was preached by a Director of Stirling's Library—the principal public library of the city.

In 1821 John, the eldest son of Dr. Watt, died, and the superintendence of the *Bibliotheca* fell to James, the other son. In 1829 he too died, his death, it is said, having been hastened by his severe labours on his father's great work. Mrs. Watt was now in very great straits. The Faculty of Physicians and Surgeons of Glasgow generously granted the poor lady a pension of £45 per annum, which enabled her, with teaching, to keep the wolf from the door. All her nine children save one—a daughter—died before her. After her mother's death this only remaining child of the once prosperous and popular physician was fated to suffer great hardships. The story is a pitiful one. The poor woman eked out the scanty sum left by her mother by sewing; living alone, and brooding over the sorrows of her family, her mind gave way, and she was removed to the asylum as a pauper lunatic. A strong representation was made to the Government of the day in favour of granting her a pension of £100 a year. This memorial was signed by, among others, Alfred Tennyson, Thomas Carlyle, John Ruskin, George Grote, Mrs. Gaskell, and Sir Frederick Madden. No answer was received for many months—not until after the poor lady's death has been intimated to one of the Prime Minister's secretaries. About a week after this another of the premier's scribes wrote enquiring if Miss Watt could be supported upon £50 a year; if so, that sum might be given her. Poor Miss Watt!

Any lengthy description of the *Bibliotheca Britannica* is unnecessary, but some account of it may be pardoned for the sake of rendering this article more complete.

The work consists of four large quarto volumes. The first two contain the names of upwards of 40,000 authors, with full particulars of their works chronologically arranged. A few particulars are usually given, besides the titles and dates of the books, so that the work is something of a biographical as well as a bibliographical dictionary. The lists of works are often extremely full. England occupies 50 columns, Bible 42½, France 29, Sermons 26, Scotland 21, Rome 20, Great Britain the same, Jesus Christ 18, Psalms 17, Parliament 17, Cicero 16, Medicine 15, Ireland 14, Religion 14, Christianity 13, and Church 12. The second part of the *Bibliotheca* contains all the books mentioned in the first part arranged under subjects. Useful as the first part is, the second has doubtless solved many more difficulties for the searcher. In tracing the authors of anonymous books it is invaluable, and not the least merit of the arrangement is that, being chronological, it shows the literature of a subject historically. Not content with authors, Dr. Watt also gave long lists under the names of famous printers of the works which issued from their presses. Dr. Watt also anticipated the distinguished American librarian, Dr. Poole, by indexing a number of transactions and journals of the day. To facilitate cross reference the first part is paged in a particular manner, so as to enable the reader to compare both entries of the same book.

To give those unfamiliar with the *Bibliotheca Britannica* some idea of the gigantic undertaking, the weight and worry of which broke down Dr. Watt's health, I may say that the manuscript consists of 57 folio volumes. It is preserved in the Paisley Free Library. The four volumes of which in its present form the work consists, contain altogether 3179 pages. Each page is divided into two columns so that we have 6358 columns of print. Each column contains 86 lines averaging a dozen words each, which gives us 546,788 lines and 6,561,456 words in the whole book. A bibliography of all books is very liable to error, especially when as in Watt's case many of the descriptions had to be taken at second-hand. The *Bibliotheca* is frequently not to be wholly trusted, but on the other hand its positive merits are many. Its utility is proved by every-day use. The more one knows of the book the more one wonders how one man—and in a short life too—could have accomplished so much. It is an amazing performance—a performance which proclaims its author a king amongst bibliographers. Stupendous as was his work, an even more stupendous task remains to be done. Our young men are fond of complaining that all the great men have lived before the present time, and that all the great things have been done. Railways, the telegraph, the telephone, and steam navigation are accomplished facts. Gibbon has written his *Decline and Fall*, Lord Macaulay his *History of England*. The Battle of Waterloo has been fought, and Donnelly has invented his Shakespeare-Bacon cipher.

What is there for the poor young man of the present period to be ambitious about? For the young man of a bibliographical turn, a great task lies at hand in the consolidation of existing bibliographies. A single bibliography, combining the stores of Watt, Allibone and Lowndes, with all their merits and none of their imperfections, is an achievement well worthy of a life's devotion. He who embarks upon it must be prepared for many years of arduous, unappreciated labour, and, if he expects to make a fortune out of his exertions, he had better turn to any other employment under the sun. This touches an important point. So large a work would require, not the intervals of other occupations for its accomplishment, but the whole time of at least one man with the leisure of as many more as he cou ld gather round him. And how would the editor live while the work was in progress?

Bibliographers are modest men or they would not pursue bibliography, but, however willing they may be to abjure Fortune, they cannot cheat Nature; and if they are to live and work, must at least eat.

To provide the sinews not of war but of peace, I would propose that, in the absence of wealthy patron of literature willing to bear the expense, a British Bibliographical Society should be formed. A society formed upon a broad and liberal basis, having for its object the compilation of a bibliography of everything written by, printed by, or about English-speaking people throughout the world. Such a society, with a capable editor, would seem to me to provide a very practicable method of obtaining this most desirable end. Let us pray that the work may soon be undertaken and that it may fall into competent hands.

From, Mason, Thomas. A bibliographical martyr – Dr. Robert Watt, author of the *Bibliotheca Britannica*. *The Library*, 1, 1889, pp. 56–63.

# CHAPTER 37

# John James Ogle (1858–1909)

"Shades of Edward Edwards and William Ewart! little did you dream of the fertility of the land where you sowed in hope, where we reap in gladness. Small space at present do your biographies fill in the national chronicles; large space will you occupy in the estimation of generations yet unborn!"

J. J. OGLE.

JOHN J. OGLE was born at Carlton, near Nottingham, in 1858, and joined the staff of Nottingham Free Public Libraries in 1881, where he worked for six years under John Potter Briscoe. He also studied at University College, Nottingham, matriculating at the University of London, but did not proceed to a degree.

In June, 1887, Ogle was appointed first librarian and curator to Bootle Public Library and Museum, which position he was to hold for thirteen years. From June, 1891, he was also organizing secretary for technical instruction, but in 1900 severed his connection with librarianship to become Director of Higher Education at Bootle Technical School.

Ogle joined the Library Association in 1883, and was for many years an active member of the Council. In 1892 he read a paper on "A summer school of library science" (here reproduced), which led to the foundation of summer schools. Ogle contributed numerous papers to librarianship periodicals, and his more important publications include: *Library legislation (1855–1890)* (with H. W. Fovergue), which forms Part 1 of the Public Library Manual edited by J. Y. W. MacAlister and Thomas Mason, and which was based on an essay for a prize awarded by MacAlister for the best draft of a Consolidating Libraries Bill; *The free library movement: its history and present condition*, 1897, a most interesting volume devoted to the history of the public library movement during the critical years following the Act of 1850; *Education Department. Special report of the connection between the public library and the public elementary school* (Sectional reprint from Vol. II of *Special reports on educational subjects*), 1889, which gives details of the development of public libraries and their contact with schools in the library systems of Great Britain and the United States; and numerous papers in professional periodicals. In 1898 he inaugurated the "Library

Assistants' Corner" in *The Library*, and contributed this feature for two years.

The year before his death on December 19th, 1909 Ogle was elected an Honorary Fellow of the Library Association. He was deeply religious, modest, a keen administrator, and possessed of a strong character. He had many public interests, and when Ogle reluctantly left the library profession, librarianship lost an enthusiastic advocate and an unselfish protagonist who had done much towards initiating an education programme for librarians.

### REFERENCE

Obituary. By W. E. D[oubleday]. *Library Association Record*, 12, 1910, pp. 31–33.

## OGLE ON A SUMMER SCHOOL OF LIBRARY SCIENCE

Most British librarians have been brought into tolerably close contact with the University Extension movement these few years past, and many are familiar with the "Summer School" development of that movement, but one may be pardoned for leading up to the subject of this paper by a brief account of the movement which suggested it to the writer's mind. The facts are chiefly drawn from Messrs. Mackinder and Sadler's "University Extension, past, present, and future", and they are given, as far as possible, in the words of that book.

"Oxford . . . started the summer meeting in 1888. . . . The idea of a general summer meeting of University Extension students derived from the assembly held at Chautauqua in the United States. The application of the idea to English conditions was due to a suggestion made by Mr. Charles Rowley, of Manchester, to a small committee which, at the instance of Dr. Paton, of Nottingham, had met to consider the possibility of introducing into England a system of Reading Circles, similar in point of arrangement to those which centre in the assembly at Chautauqua."

"It was at once felt that, by means of a summer meeting in one of the University towns, the Extension movement would be able to avail itself of the services of those resident teachers who, though friendly to the work, are prevented by their University duties from taking any active part in it as lecturers. The plan would furnish an opportunity for an excellent use of the scholarships previously offered by Mr. J. G. Talbot, M.P., and others, to enable deserving University Extension students to reside in Oxford for a short period of vacation study. The students would enjoy the great advantage offered by the University museums, collections and libraries, and would gain stimulus from their intercourse with one another. In short, the meeting would introduce into University Extension the one element in which, from the University point of view, it had been chiefly lacking—the element of 'residence'."

"The idea of the Summer Meeting was at once taken up in Oxford, where already on a small scale arrangements had been made during the Long Vacations of some previous years for the accommodation within college walls of elementary schoolmasters and others."

"The first University Extension Summer Meeting was held in August, 1888. In 1890 Cambridge commenced similar meetings. According to Dr. Roberts (*Eighteen Years of University Extension*), the first Cambridge Summer Meeting 'included practical work in the chemical and physical laboratories on alternate mornings, a practical class on palaeontology for geological students, and courses on Greek art, architecture and other branches that could be illustrated by the collections in the University Museums. . . . The design of the Oxford Delegates has been somewhat different from that of the Cambridge Syndicate. While only forty-one students assembled at Cambridge, the number of persons who attended the Oxford gatherings has been about nine hundred, for whom a large number of short courses of lectures on a variety of subjects, together with conferences, excursions, and social meetings, were held. . . . Oxford welcomes all who care to come to her summer gathering. . . . The courses of lectures are of general interest and designed to meet the most varied tastes. The plan of Cambridge, on the other hand, is to limit her invitation to those most earnest students who, having obtained certificates in connection with the courses of lectures during the winter, desire to supplement their theoretical knowledge by practical work in the laboratories and museums.' This difference in the plans of the two Universities, however, seems less marked now than formerly, for Oxford has latterly divided her meetings into two parts, the second part being reserved for students of the kind formerly catered for by Cambridge only. Oxford has also improved her scheme by grouping the courses of instruction into sequences extending over four years."

"But," says Messrs. Mackindler and Sadler, "by far the most striking advance of the year 1890–91 has been in America . . . with characteristic enthusiasm and energy . . . Pennsylvania and New York have, in a single session, done such work as entitles them to rank with the Oxford, Cambridge and London organisations." Librarians will be pleased to learn that a librarian whom we all know and respect, Mr. Melvil Dewey, is one of the principal leaders and workers in this Transatlantic University Extension Movement. Hence no one need be surprised that "Summer Schools of Library Economy" have been established in several of the larger Public Libraries of the United States, where persons are received on certain conditions for a few weeks' instruction and practice in library methods and library work, with a view to fitting them to discharge efficiently the duties of library assistants in the future, and eventually to take up the profession of a chief librarian.

The imperfect information to hand prevents any description being given of the American Summer Schools for Librarians, but instruction in cataloguing seems to hold a prominent place in the curriculum of each, and from what we know of the School of Library Economy we may be sure that a thorough knowledge of the material equipment of a library is aimed at in all the teaching given. Then, why may we not have in England our Summer School of Library Science, with its courses of lectures and demonstrations to librarians and library assistants? But those parts of library science—concerning which the librarian of a public library feels it a disgrace to be ignorant—although under present circumstances it is difficult for him to amend his ignorance —those parts of library knowledge, rather than the mechanical part thereof, should have the first place in our "Summer School" courses. Could there not be something established on the lines of the "Summer School of Theology", which has lately been brought to a successful termination in Oxford?

Towards the end of last July a large number of men who had been already trained to the business of preachers and pastors, and many of whom had been years in active work, assembled in Oxford to hear some of the most advanced thinkers of the day discourse on the Higher Criticism, and the many theological questions which have been fermenting in men's minds of late years. The prospectus announced that "lectures will be delivered, designed to meet the wants of men who feel that the ordinary work of the ministry has not allowed them to keep abreast of the later inquiries and discussions in the field of Theology, Biblical, Apologetic and Dogmatic." Canon Driver, Dr. Marcus Dods, Dr. Sandy, Dr. Fairbairn, and others equally eminent, occupied the lecture halls and pulpits of Oxford for this purpose, and the meetings were a great success.

Specialised vacation studies have also, for the sixth time, been lately provided for an Edinburgh University. The subject of education has been comprehensively treated, including the much talked about and little understood subject of Technical Education, in a series of lectures and visits extending over several weeks.

Surely, then, it is practicable for the Library Association to arrange for similar work adopted to the needs of public librarians, and if practicable, desirable also. Let it be supposed this is agreed to, and that the Council has received its instructions and has organised a Summer

School of Library Science. We are now, let us suppose, at the year 1897. It is June: thirty or forty young men and a few young women, all library assistants in big towns, or librarians in smaller towns, have come up to London for a week's instruction. The Committees of the various libraries represented have agreed to pay their expenses on production of certificates of attendance at the lectures upon their return. It is Monday morning and 10 o'clock: Dr. Garnett of the British Museum is just commencing a lecture on the "Great Libraries of Antiquity." At 11 o'clock he will be followed by Mr. H. R. Tedder on the "Growth of the Modern Public Library Movement." At 12 o'clock the students will disperse, to re-assemble at 2.30 p.m. for visits to the Guildhall Library and to a typical Metropolitan Free Library. On Tuesday morning Dr. Maunde Thompson will discourse on "The Leading Principles by which the Age of Manuscripts is Determined", and Mr. Pollard on "Some Features of Early Printed Books". The afternoon will be devoted to a personal inspection of a few selected MSS. and incunabula at the British Museum.

Wednesday morning is set apart for a lecture by Mr. Gordon Duff on the "Invention and Early Spread of Printing", and another on "Fifteenth Century Types" by Mr. Talbot Reed. The afternoon will be occupied in a visit to the "Blades Library", which by this time it is supposed will be accessible to the public.

On Thursday our students will assemble to hear Mr. Trueman Wood on "Modern Methods of Book Illustration", and Mr. W. M. Conway on "Fifteenth Century Blocks". The afternoon visit on this day will be to a large engraving and lithographic establishment. Friday will be given up to lectures on the History and Manufacture of Printing Paper, Stereotyping, and Modern Improvements in Printing, with visits to a paper mill and a printing office. On Saturday morning the course is to be concluded by lectures on "Historic Styles in Bookbinding", by Mr. Salt Brassington, and on the "Proper Decoration of a Book Cover", by Mr. William Morris.

It may be objected that an hour is too short a time for any profitable instruction in certain of the subjects named for lectures. Yet surely some good elementary principles can be inculcated in that time, and, which is equally important, a mental stimulus given to the prosecution of the subject dealt with in ways which the lecturers could very well indicate to those who attend their lectures. The afternoon visits would certainly be the very best of object lessons, and would inspire a respect for the written roll or printed book, which could not but have a wholesome influence on the management of the libraries to which the summer scholars were ultimately appointed.

From, Ogle, J. J. A summer school of library science. *The Library*, 4, 1892, pp. 319–323.

# CHAPTER 38

# Herbert Putnam (1861–1955)

"Herbert Putnam was born with a book in his mouth."

D. C. MEARNS.

LIBRARIANS of prominent libraries must come under public scrutiny, and their fitness for their respective posts is measured by the results of their activities. The more important the posts the greater the achievements expected. Only great men acquit themselves with credit in these circumstances, and Herbert Putnam, "the Panizzi of the twentieth century, one of the two great formative lives of the library profession", more than justified the confidence placed in him when he was elected Librarian of Congress.

Born in New York on September 20th, 1861, (George) Herbert Putnam was the son of George Palmer Putnam, founder of the publishing firm of that name. After studying at Harvard, Herbert Putnam graduated in 1879, and then attended Columbia Law School. In 1884 he went to Minnesota as Librarian of the Minneapolis Athenaeum, and three years later became City Librarian of Minneapolis. Putnam resigned this post in 1891 and practised law until he became Librarian of Brown University (1893), followed by a similar position at Boston Public Library in 1895. The year 1899 saw Herbert Putnam's appointment as Librarian of the Library of Congress, where he remained actively engaged for forty years. At the Library of Congress Putnam introduced the printing and sale of catalogue cards, he drew up the Library of Congress classification scheme, and built up the collection and its services until it became foremost among national libraries of the world.

Despite Herbert Putnam's outstanding success at the Library of Congress, his successor was nominated from outside the library profession, producing a large number of protests. Putnam's work had extended far beyond the walls of the institution of which he was head, and he was honoured by numerous governments and institutions. He was President of the American Library Association in 1898 and 1904, and from 1917 to 1919 was General Director of the American Library Association, Library War Service, for which he was awarded the Distinguished Service Medal, and in 1929 also received the Roosevelt Distinguished Service Medal.

On the thirtieth anniversary of Putnam's election as Librarian of Congress his friends presented to him *Essays offered to Herbert Putnam*, 1929, and when he retired ten years later, he was elected Librarian Emeritus. Putnam continued his activities for many years, and when he died on August 14th, 1955, he left the Library of Congress as his chief monument. His name will always be associated with that institution, with printed catalogue cards, and with library classification.

## REFERENCES

Bishop, William Warner, and Keogh, Andrew, *Eds. Essays offered to Herbert Putnam by his colleagues and friends on his thirtieth anniversary as Librarian of Congress, 5 April 1929*, New Haven, 1929. Portraits.

*Herbert Putnam, 1861–1955: a memorial tribute*, Washington, Library of Congress, 1956. Appreciation; bibliography of writings and addresses by Putnam, and books and articles about him; chronology of his life; portraits.

Mearns, David C. Herbert Putnam: Librarian of the United States. The Minneapolis years. *Wilson Library Bulletin*, 29, 1954–1955, pp. 59–63. Portraits and references.

Obituary, by Arundell Esdaile. *Library Association Record*, 57, 1955, pp. 420–421.

### Putnam's Reflections from Ingonish

To the Friendly Editors:

This is addressed to you because at this date I cannot address to Dr. Bishop himself a message certain to be valid at the date, a year hence, which you are proposing to commemorate. Those of you who are attempting it are doubtless—as is usual in such symposia—selecting themes either historic, or scientific, or abstract, or in some other way remote from the agitations with which our convictions and emotions are now struggling. I have at my command no such theme. So, in lieu of it, I have awaited a *point of departure* (for a message) at least physically detached. I seem to have found it here at Ingonish.

The detachment isn't mentally complete. There are nagging professional reminders in some books, mostly mummified. My window is even propped with a copy of *Ivanhoe*, which bends beneath the adversity, but like the author, does not break. And there is intrusion from the world at dispute in daily broadcasts from London. Still, there are many of the requisites: geographical remoteness, Ingonish being, as you know, at almost the northern tip of Cape Breton. A step beyond would bring you to an area under patrol. But you need not take it, and, unless conscripted, the native never does. His activities are purely local, concerned, not with the sword, but only with the swordfish, and, at intervals, some tilling of the soil. All of them involve work with the hands, pursuing, unquestioned, the principles and practice of preceding generations. No dependence upon books, nor interest in the doubts raised by them. And, at large, *Nature*, which is never controversial, which states—inexorably—but does not argue.

So this noble bay, and the sea beyond it, the domed island, and the long double ridge of mountain forming the western shore: all make for the serenity resident in aloofness—not merely from the quarrels of men but from the disturbances of literature.

The human element—so far as native—does not disturb it; for if not dumb, it is reticent. Not ambitious, it is not uneasy. It is content with the established order, the orderly way. The individual human is secure in a livelihood, a home, a family, the respect of his neighbors responding to his respect for them, with little of grace, perhaps, but much of substantial kindness. And when, an Octogenarian, his efforts conclude, and he is past the ability to repay attentions, his entire community will lay aside its affairs, and, donning black, convoy his flowered casket to its pre-destined lot.

There was glee in Scotia on Registration Day when a dame, asked if she had sons, replied, "Yes, three: two living and one in Cape Breton."—But the glee had no substance. The Breton is unpretentiously but very definitely alive. His life is shaped to a plan; he pursues it calmly, but obstinately; and he reaps from it rewards that fully satisfy his requirements. He has every freedom, every opportunity, every appreciation within his own horizon.

What does he lack that books could supply?

"But his horizon is so *limited*." Yes, it isn't wide, but its depth is considerable.

"Idealism?"

He is already an idealist. Only his ideals, except of a duty in human relations, are of a concrete product from his effort. In that sense he is a materialist; concerned with the substance rather than with the form or the justifications. His mind is ever upon the doing, not upon the thinking. He has no concern with the symbols with which the intellectual is constantly fussing. Yet in certainty, and in ultimate contentment no merely intellectual life is the equal of that which he fashions by his native wit and modest industry. If he has no dreams, he escapes all nightmares. And in religion he has the superior convenience of a faith that, in proportion as it is unchallenging, is firm, uncomplicated, and suited to his requirements.

"But such a lack of *vision*!"

At a corner in St. John sits a blind singer with an accordion. He invites contributions for his son, but no *alms*. His moustache is defiantly waxed; and a placard on his breast declares: "I am Blind, but *Happy*."

So the life of the Breton, modest as it is, has personal contentment, civic sufficiency, and a certain symmetry. In contrast, the life of the intellectual, groping among intangibles, even if equally honest (and it isn't apt to be) is dubious in its aims, imperfect in its attainments. It is a life of incessant frustration. Why then urge it upon the unlettered, or try to wean his offspring to it?

Indelicate questions! And, one might say especially inapposite to the celebration of a career devoted to the promotion of the intellectual life, and the complacencies of the scholar. And a near heresy: for the Breton might be taken to represent the unlettered generally, to whose salvation by literature the effort of librarians has for eighty years been directed.

But the sufficient inference is that we may have gone too far in assuming that books are a universal specific, indispensable to the conduct of a useful, happy, and symmetrical life:—that all virtues lie in them, and all solutions; and the rectification of all that is wayward in the human spirit.

An illustration quite complementary is now being forced upon the attention of a bewildered world. It is in the spectacle of the most "bookish" people of our time discarding *all* the symmetries patterned upon religion, common sense, and the simple moralities; denying to the rest of mankind any freedom of design in living; and proposing to substitute a *rule* of its own, for its own exclusive benefit.

This is certainly disconcerting. Of what avail Learning if it include no safeguard against a selfishness so monstrous?—Of what profit the efforts of Dr. Bishop and others of us—to promote it at large, in the belief that in making for general understanding it would make for mutual respect, sympathy, and forbearance? In aiding the scholar, have we been assuring a baleful efficiency in the class under whose control society is *least* safe, and humanity *least* likely to be regarded?

Such, I suppose, are the present reflections of Dr. Bishop himself, preëminent among us librarians in international endeavor. I hope they will not induce in him either repentance or discouragement.—There is this to be said for learning: that if, by its own perversities, it develops maladies within itself, it has also within itself the remedy for them. Discovered and applied, Learning may resume its fit authority over the conduct of society. And there may remain of the experience only the mortification that, in a crisis imperilling the social order, society was saved, not by the refined intelligence of the scholar, but by the homespun qualities of the common man: that it was he who was least confused, his conscience never having been regimented by his reason, and his judgments, fibred by the exercise of the minor moralities, stretching easily to the defence of the major ones, when they came into issue.

May that consideration, Dr. Bishop, give you upon your retirement the satisfaction that it is now giving me in making his nearer acquaintance.

Discovery of his qualities need not imply disloyalty to the cultural studies which you have been assisting and personally pursuing; nor your faith in our calling; nor your zeal in the preparation of those wishing to embark upon it. The demands for your aid and counsel will increase rather than diminish with your supposed freedom, and you cannot abruptly slough off your habit of cheerful acquiescence.

They will interfere with those plans you are cogitating for delectable scholarly research; and even your tenser reading will relax into Trollope. But you may take comfort in the reflexion that if there were a possibility of exactness in History, conclusions in Education, perfections in Culture, equilibrium in Society, achievement of it does not rest upon the men past seventy.

That relief will be yours when you join the company of the Irresponsible Elders. As an ancient colleague, a sometime associate, and a long-time friend, I shall offer no condolences in welcoming you to it.

HERBERT PUTNAM.

The Spruces,
  Ingonish, Cape Breton.
    August 20th, 1940.

From, *William Warner Bishop: a tribute, 1941*. Edited by *Harry Miller Lydenberg and Andrew Keogh*, New Haven, London, 1941, pp. 5–10.

# CHAPTER 39

# James Duff Brown (1862–1914)

"He was in truth a modest man, but he had fire and faith which never spared him."

E. A. SAVAGE.

THE name of James Duff Brown is better known to modern librarians than that of any of his contemporaries, chiefly on account of the fact that his *Manual of library economy* is maintained up to date as the standard textbook on the subject, and because his Subject Classification is still of interest. A third edition to the latter, revised by James D. Stewart, appeared as recently as 1939, and might even have gained more popularity but for the outbreak of war. First published in 1906, a second edition was published in 1914, and the scheme has many interesting features which prompted J. D. Stewart to describe it as "a highly practical scheme for application to the collections of any normal library."

Brown was born in Edinburgh on November 6th, 1862, and after a brief period as apprentice in the publishing business, became a member of the staff in the Mitchell Library, Glasgow in December, 1878. Ten years later he went to Clerkenwell Public Library as Librarian, where he later introduced safeguarded open access. In 1892 his anonymous paper "A plea for liberty to readers to help themselves"[1] had been published, and two years later Brown visited America, where he found open access in several libraries, but safeguarded open access was his own innovation. He introduced many ideas for the development of library organization, and several library appliances were invented by him. He advocated county libraries and library schools, and commenced a museum of library appliances for the Library Association, but the material then vanished. Brown was the staunch friend of Jast, but was disliked by Cotgreave, the inventor of the indicator and other fittings, who lost substantial royalties as the result of the introduction of open access.

Among Brown's contributions to library literature should be mentioned his *Guide to the formation of a music library*, 1893 (Library Association Series, No. 4); *Characteristic songs and dances of all nations*, 1901, written in collaboration with Alfred Moffat; *Biographical dictionary of musicians*, 1886; *Handbook of library appliances*, 1892; *British musical*

[1] *The Library*, 4, 1892, pp. 302–5.

*biography*, 1897, with Stephen Stratton as joint author; and *Manual of library classification and shelf arrangement*, 1898. His *Manual of library economy* was first published in 1903, and was maintained up to date under the capable editorship of W. C. Berwick Sayers, and then R. Northwood Lock. In 1897 Brown planned and edited *Greenwood's Year Book*, and in the following year founded *The Library World*. The first issue was published in July, 1898 under the anonymous editorship of James Duff Brown as an independent organ, unhampered by official connections, and in opposition to the *Library Association Record*, then edited by Henry Guppy. Brown owned, edited and wrote most of the contents of the *Library World* until 1911, when these responsibilities were taken over by J. D. Stewart. A few of Brown's aphorisms gleaned from that journal indicate that he had a lighter side to his character. For example:

If you cannot classify a book—don't buy it.

A book in the hand is worth two at the binders.

A misguided ambition to get married is the main cause of the zeal of library assistants for advancement.

The librarian who invented everything before anybody else was born, is generally a man with a strongly developed inventive faculty.

James Duff Brown became the first Borough Librarian of Islington in 1904, and died on February 26th, 1914. He had been a Councillor of the Library Association from 1890 to 1911, and librarianship owes much to his progressive foresight and boundless energy, which enabled him to contribute so much towards the advancement of all subjects covered by the term library organization.

## REFERENCES

Savage, Ernest A.  James Duff Brown after fifty years. *Library Review*, 135, 1960, pp. 489–495.

Stewart, James D.  Brown's "Subject classification". *Review of Documentation*, 17, 1950, pp. 56–63.

——. James Duff Brown and the 'L.W.' *Library World*, 63, 1961–1962, pp. 56–58.

There is a Memoir of Brown in his *Manual of library economy. . . . Third and memorial edition, revised and rewritten by W. C. Berwick Sayers*, [etc.], 1920, pp. 1–10. Bibliography and portrait. See also *Library Association Record*, 16, 1914, pp. 239–262 for tributes by James D. Stewart, T. Aldred, E. A. Baker, C. H. Benn, Olive E. Clarke, H. T. Coutts, L. S. Jast, E. A. Savage, W. C. Berwick Sayers, H. R. Tedder and many others.

### BROWN'S "A PLEA FOR LIBERTY" TO READERS TO HELP THEMSELVES

There has been so much discussion recently about charging or lending systems in public libraries, that a brief note on the subject from an unusual point of view may not be thought amiss. We call it "unusual", because it is rather that than novel, having over a century's antiquity to boast of; and the idea for lending library management about to be described, is, therefore, only to be considered as a fresh application of a good old method. The original lending library, or circulating library as it was commonly called, had no counter to speak of, and subscribers were allowed direct access to the books on the shelves. This plan is in vogue at the present time in all kinds of commercial and proprietary subscription libraries. It is the plan now worked in various reference libraries, to which readers have access under certain restrictions, and may be seen in operation in the British Museum, Sion College, London, and various collegiate and other libraries. Most important of all for the purpose of this note, it is in operation successfully in various town libraries in England, the Colonies, and the United States, and *any person from the street*, being clean and of proper age, may have unrestricted access to the books on open shelves. This being so, why is it that borrowers in Public Lending Libraries are kept at bay by barriers and all sorts of mechanical contrivances, notwithstanding that they are all guaranteed, and, to a large extent, well known to the staff? If Tom, Dick, and Harry, minus any credentials whatever, can enter reference libraries at Bradford, Cambridge, Melbourne, and elsewhere, to select his reading, why is it that Thomas, Richard, and Henry, fully vouched for and carefully selected, cannot exercise a similar privilege? It is simply because of the RULES AND REGULATIONS! and also because a certain traditional distrust of the public makes librarians and their masters dread an annual loss of half-a-dozen volumes in the effort to make their readers thoroughly satisfied, by permitting the right of free selection unhampered by bad catalogues, and indicators which save trouble only to the staff. The outstanding fact and universal cry in all popular lending libraries, is not only that borrowers cannot get the books they want, but also that they cannot chance upon any book likely to suit them, owing to catalogues being mere inventories, and the existence of all sorts of barriers, which make the selection of books a heart-break and a labour tinctured with disgust. The number of persons who leave our lending libraries with the conviction that they are impositions is too great to be easily calculated, and for the credit of modern librarianship, it is perhaps best that nothing definite should be known. What lending libraries want, in addition to a less suspicious method of dealing with the public, is a better means of making their book-wealth known, while giving a less elaborate system of charging and service. To some extent the proposal about to be made meets every want which can arise in the public use of a library, while it also sweeps away the artificial intermediaries, which have been gradually adopted to meet the requirements of small staffs, and the various exigencies of charging systems designed for speed in issues and accuracy in recording. In short, the proposal simply amounts to this: *Let the public inside, and place the staff outside, the counter.* The book shelves are ordinary standards about seven feet six inches high, raised nine to twelve inches from the floor by a narrow step, and spaced about six feet apart. In these the books are closely classified according to subjects and authors (in the case of fiction), and properly numbered and marked as in libraries where public access and close classification go hand in hand. Each class would have a differently *shaped* location label, and each shelf of a tier a different *colour* of label, to get over the disarrangement difficulty. The movable location would be used, and the backs of the books would simply bear a label, according to class and shelf number conspicuously marked on it, the classes to be arranged so that fiction would go all round the walls alphabetically, and subjects so distributed that crowding would be reduced in the different divisions. The whole to be so plainly labelled and marked, that only the blind would be unable to find a given subject—author or number. There are many ways of doing all this, which need not at present be entered upon. Each borrower on joining receives an identification card, which he retains till it expires, and in addition a small pass-book, bearing his name and number, and ruled to show the numbers of books read and dates of their issue, is kept at the library. When he enters to get a book he simply shows his identification ticket bearing his number, and the assistant hands over the pass-book, and allows him to pass the turnstile on the left of the plan. At this turnstile umbrellas, hand-bags, etc., must be left, and unsatisfactory messengers and non-registered borrowers stopped. The reader proceeds to the shelves and makes his selection, probably contenting himself with Hooker's *Ecclesiastical Polity*, on finding Mrs. Henry Wood all *out*! He then goes to the turnstile on the right of the plan, and hands his book and pass-book to the assistant, who simply enters the book number in it, and dates both book and pass-book. The reader then goes out, leaving the pass-book. A simple card-charging system enables the librarian to tell all the books out, and who has them; who among the borrowers have books out, and who have not; as well as when any given book is due back at the library, and the issues of a given day. When a book is returned the same routine is observed, except that the assistant goes to a dated tray for the pass-book instead of to the stock of unclaimed tickets. In this way a complete and simple plan is worked, which has advantages in economy to the library and real usefulness to the public, not to be gained by any other lending library systems now in use. The educational value to the readers would be enormous, and the popularity and standard of reading of every library would be largely increased. The arrangement of the plan provides for such a degree of supervision that thefts would probably be less common than at the first glance seems likely; while the presence of an assistant, free to help readers, and keep order among both books and people, would add to the value of the whole scheme. It is not for the writer of this to suggest weaknesses in it, nor to affirm that the arrangements of old-established libraries could easily be altered to admit of the plan being adopted; but it is for him to claim some consideration for the scheme, especially from those who have it in their power to make it a feature in new buildings. The subject is one which deserves the best thought which librarians can give, and it may be that the plan is actually less revolutionary and dangerous than it may seem at first sight. In any case it is felt necessary to safeguard the position now taken up, by stating that all the possible arguments in favour of the plan have *not* been advanced. On the other hand, three points are admitted as possibly, though not probably, adverse to the general adoption of the scheme, and these are—possible thefts, possible disarrangement, and the possible increase of the idler. But are these, and even the somewhat more probable objection of additional wear and tear to the books, to be set against the enormous advantages to the public of proper access to their own libraries?

"THE OTHER SIDE OF THE COUNTER"*

* The plan accompanying this article is omitted. [J.L.T.]
From *The Library*, 4, 1892, pp. 302–305.

## BROWN'S PREFACE TO HIS MANUAL OF LIBRARY ECONOMY

This work is an attempt to provide a text-book of advanced library practice, on more comprehensive lines than anything of the kind yet published in English. There is no single work on modern library economy which gives a general account of the principal methods which have survived the test of continuous and widespread trial, nor one which considers these methods and principles as affected by the rate limitation imposed by the Public Libraries Acts.

Librarianship in Britain has suffered to some extent from the lack of anything in the way of classification of its essential elements, and it differs from most other sciences in having no generally recognised series of established facts to form a basis on which to erect a properly developed science of library economy. Perhaps it is fortunate that British library practice has progressed on freely experimental lines, allowing for improvements and readjustments at any point, as it will thus avoid all risk of becoming stereotyped, or running into grooves which may tend to check the growth of original ideas. The hampering effects of too much uniformity are to be seen in full operation in France and the United States. In the former, a government bureau has ordained that the communal libraries shall be organised according to a narrow and very elementary code of rules, drawn up nearly twenty years ago, in which every detail of library management is made the subject of a cut-and-dried ordinance. Naturally, this effectually stifles improvement and produces a monotonous uniformity which rejoices the official mind without, however, attracting or satisfying the public.

In the United States a much higher level of attainment has been reached, but here again the paralysing hand of uniformity has arrested progress after a certain standard of efficiency has become general. American libraries are conducted on lines which closely resemble those of ordinary commercial practice, in which everything is subordinated to the furtherance of profits and economy. Their methods are standardised, and everything is more or less interchangeable, with the result that in America we witness practically the same phenomenon as in conservative France. Where methods are run on codified lines, there is always this danger of everything becoming fixed, and all the advantages arising from adjustability and the power of revision being lost in the unprofitable pursuit of the unalterable. In British libraries most methods have been in a state of flux for fifty years, and there is little immediate danger of any process crystallising into a fixed and unalterable condition. For this state of things we have to thank our freedom from too much state interference, and the comparative absence of commercial syndicates which profess to supply libraries and librarians ready made. The only fixed principle from which British libraries suffer is the rate which may be levied for library purposes, and for this our Government is entirely responsible, having been smitten for once with the French bureaucratic craze for a mediocre uniformity.

This manual does not attempt to record all the conventions and traditions of the older librarianship, nor does it pretend to describe all the ideas and methods of librarianship. It endeavours to collect and summarise some of the best and most vital methods which have been adopted, and to arrange them in such divisions as may tend to give the book a systematic form, and so place the study of library economy on a more consistent and scientific basis than heretofore. For the first time, too, an effort is made to consider questions connected with buildings, finance, books, etc., from the standpoint of the limitation of the Library Rate. This brings out in full relief the crippling influence of the plan of financial restriction placed upon every department of British library work by Parliamentary limitations, and shows the difficulty of further developments and improvements in library equipment and practice, without additional means. . . .

JAMES DUFF BROWN.

Clerkenwell Public Library,
   Finsbury, London.
*May*, 1903.                                         [pp. iii–v]

.    .    .    .

## BROWN ON LIBRARIANS

Like the prominent members of every other trade, profession or branch of learning, good librarians are born, not made. No amount of training or experience will create such natural gifts as enthusiasm, originality, initiative and positive genius for the work; but training in sound methods will help to provide a passable substitute for natural aptitude. Experience alone will not prove equally valuable, because it may not have been associated in its course with training in effective methods, and consequently may only represent knowledge of an effete and inefficient class. If all library methods were identical, and of the same standard of advanced excellence, experience alone would equal special training; but owing to the very wide difference between the methods of twenty or thirty years ago, and the more scientific methods of today, it is necessary to judge the experience of any librarian by the school in which he has been trained.

[p. 53]

.    .    .    .

## BROWN ON INTER-LIBRARY LOANS

This is a method of book distribution which has not been tried to any extent among British municipal libraries, and some organisation would be required to place it on a working basis. Briefly, the idea is to enable a public library which has not got a particular book to borrow it from some library which has, assuming all the responsibility for its safety and due return, and making its own arrangement with its borrower for the cost of carriage. This kind of exchanging could be managed better in London than anywhere else, but it could be applied to any group of libraries, such as those of Lancashire, Wales, Yorkshire, Staffordshire, etc. Each exchanging library would require to possess a complete set of class lists and bulletins, or other catalogues, of all the other libraries, and when a demand was made for a book which was not in its possession the assistant could look through the catalogues of the other libraries till he found a copy, and it could then be written for, the borrower paying all resulting expenses. Of course, this arrangement would only apply to non-fictional works. We have done this on several occasions, often with excellent results, and certainly to the amazement and joy of our borrowers, whose admiration for our resources and command of literature in other libraries has made them devoted life supporters of the library! There would be an undoubted advantage, too, if such a privilege could be obtained for public library borrowers from some of the proprietary libraries with huge stocks of practically unused books which municipal libraries would not buy in the ordinary course. Arrangements whereby books from special scientific or other libraries could be borrowed for the use of local borrowers would benefit a greater number of students and other persons than at present. But, of course, there would be very serious difficulties in the way of inducing the owners of valuable special libraries to lend books for the use of strangers introduced by municipal library authorities. Meanwhile, because of these difficulties thousands upon thousands of valuable and useful books are lying idle and neglected in every part of the country; a waste of power which it is sad to contemplate.

[pp. 412–413]

From, Brown, James Duff. *Manual of library economy*, [*etc.*], 1903.

CHAPTER 40

# *Frank Pacy (1862–1928)*

"Amongst these new librarians were also many who entered our calling
without any previous service in its lower degrees. Some library committees were dazzled by showy academical qualifications. Others, strong
in parish patriotism, resented 'furriners'."

FRANK PACY

FRANK PACY was born on May 26th, 1862, at Wishaw, Lanarkshire,
and was educated at Wigan Grammar School. At the age of sixteen
he became an assistant under H. T. Folkard in Wigan Public Library,
where he was appointed Sub-Librarian at the age of twenty-one with
a salary of £50 per annum. After a short period, he joined the cataloguing staff at Birmingham in 1883, but the following year became
Librarian at Richmond, Surrey. The year 1891 saw his appointment
as first Librarian of St. George, Hanover Square, and in 1905 he finally
removed to the City of Westminster.

Pacy became a member of the Library Association in 1880, and in
1898 succeeded MacAlister as Honorary Secretary, to resign after
three years owing to dissension on the Council. But in 1915 he re-
occupied this office, which he held until his death on June 24th, 1928,
shortly after his retirement from Westminster.

Frank Pacy did not spare himself in the service of the Library
Association, and was very capable and statesmanlike. His judgment was
reliable, and his opinions much sought after. He sometimes differed
from his colleagues, as in the 1927 Report,[1] where his Reservation is
principally concerned with library service in London, which was
divided into twenty-eight sections. He suggested that there should be
one authority, and that the area should be subdivided into six or eight
districts, with a uniform rating over the entire area. The lack of commercial and technical libraries in London was deplored, as was the
fact that no single borough provided adequate reference library
facilities. Pacy did not hesitate to differ from his distinguished fellow-
members of the Committee, which included Sir Frederic Kenyon
(Chairman), Sir John Ballinger, E. Salter Davies, Albert Mansbridge,
Col. J. M. Mitchell, S. A. Pitt and A. E. Twentyman.

As delegate to many Library Association conferences Pacy con-

[1] *Public Libraries Committee. Report on public libraries in England and Wales,* [etc.], 1927.
Reservation by Mr. Frank Pacy. Chapter V, pp. 215–216.

tributed several papers to the *Transactions*, but his paper on the development of the Library Association printed below is possibly the most important of his writings, for in his day Frank Pacy *was* the Library Association. (Portrait, Plate 14.)

## REFERENCES

Minto, John. *A history of the public library movement in Great Britain and Ireland*, 1932, pp. 334–336.

Obituary, by W. E. Doubleday. *Library Association Record*, 2nd Ser., 6, 1928, pp. 221–223.

## PACY ON THE LIBRARY ASSOCIATION

Youth looks forward and age looks back, particularly when passing the milestones; and the impulse is irresistible, when one arrives at such a notable point as a jubilee, to cast a glance over the long years, now so strangely shortened; to recall impressions, revive memories, review judgments, and, before the dust of oblivion covers them, live once more through the high moments that stand in memory or record.

The jubilee of the Library Association so nearly coincides with my own fifty years of librarianship, that I may be excused if, in these reminiscences, the personal element becomes obtrusive. The Association has been so much a part of my life that I now find some difficulty in remembering that, after all, I am also a librarian as well as your secretary.

I do not really pretend that, in the year 1877, I was in a position to take such a personal interest in the newly-born society as did my old friend, Henry Richard Tedder, who was so active as its midwife; but at times, such is the effect of long intimacy, I almost feel that I was there with him, even as King George IV believed that he commanded a division at Waterloo.

However, due respect must be paid to facts, and honour given where it is due, so it behoves us to admit that the real *fons et origo* of our Association was in America, where the sister society anticipated us by a year, as indeed they had held a preliminary conference a quarter-century before that even. We precipitately hurried from Conference to Association within one fateful week, the first week in October, 1877. It was in the old London Institution, that Mecca of Victorian culture, better known to us perhaps through its famous first librarian, Porson the Grecian, a great scholar but a bad librarian: for did not his managers complain that they only knew he was their officer through seeing the receipts for his salary?

There was a notable American delegation to this Conference including Cutter of the "Rules", our first pandect; the American Nestor, Poole of the Index; Dewey of the Decimals, that great classification which is swallowing up all others; and Justin Winsor. Great names! Is it fancy or false perspective that makes me think we have few to put against them now? The almost legendary Dr. Garnett was there, the almost mythical Dr. Crestadoro; William Blades, Robert Needham Cust, R. K. Douglas, W. S. Jevons, Stirling Maxwell, Henry Morley, Mark Pattison, Bernard Quaritch; name after name has earned place in our Valhalla, "The Dictionary of National Biography". How many of us, I wonder, will attain that degree of immortality?

To read the proceedings of this Conference is to renew one's youth. Every subject is fresh, every question new, every point novel. Here and there simplicities and naivetés that make us smile, but mainly we can only feel abashed at the thought of how little we have progressed. The ambitious young librarian who seeks distinction by some address or thesis on matter of his profession should read the transactions of these early conferences. He would arise a sadder and a wiser and a much more silent man.

At the last session of this epoch-making Conference, after nearly every-thing had been said that, in the ensuing fifty years, we have been re-saying and repeating, the Library Association was founded. The reason of its being was that proclaimed at the almost-forgotten Conference of 1853: "for the purpose of conferring together upon the means of advancing the prosperity and usefulness of public libraries, and for the discussion of topics of importance to book-collectors and readers."

An organizing committee had already drafted the Constitution, which was largely the work of Henry R. Tedder and E. W. B. Nicholson. The first Council was formed: there was no election; no doubt it was difficult to improve upon the list of names, for the President was the Principal Librarian of the British Museum, the Vice-Presidents were the Librarians of the Advocate's Library, the Bodleian, and Trinity College, Dublin. Glasgow, Liverpool, Manchester, Birmingham, Leeds, sent their men; the joint Secretaries were E. W. B. Nicholson, then of the London Institution, afterwards to become Bodley's Librarian, and H. R. Tedder, even then of the Athenæum; the Treasurer, the courtly and venerable Robert Harrison, of the London Library. Our Association was bravely launched, and the great Conference concluded with the congratulations of the distinguished foreign representatives.

The first ordinary monthly meeting was on March 1st, 1878, at the London Institution, our earliest home in a long series of migrations. The first annual meeting was at Oxford, which emulated the London conference in producing a noble volume of Transactions and Proceedings.

The first change of officers was the replacement of Mr. Nicholson by Mr. E. C. Thomas as joint secretary.

The early meetings provided a continuance of the good things of the first conference. The supply of meaty material then seemed inexhaustible. Open access, percentage of fiction, quality of bindings, periodical indexes, all our stock dishes were on the menu and appetite was keen. An early *pièce de résistance* was the "General Catalogue of English Literature". Bodley's reverend librarian, presiding at the Oxford meeting, in the true Bodleian tradition deprecated this undertaking, thinking that there was much in English literature, the record of which he did not care to see perpetuated. This must have been before they bought back their discarded Shakespeare folio!

The second annual meeting was at Manchester, in that grandiose new town hall they were so proud of. The lovely old Greek building, discarded for the Victorian Gothic, now housed the library, under that gentle soul Charles W. Sutton, who had done all the organizing work of the meeting, but *more suo* shrank from recognition. The gathering was rather overpoweringly Mancunian, but very profitable to the Association in increased membership, as the black-letter school was eclipsed by the modern municipal.

Indicators were more popular than incunabula.

With somewhat excessive modesty and self-effacement the young Association had adopted the American *Library Journal* as its official organ, but, not surprisingly, soon found it inconvenient to await from America accounts of its own proceedings and notices of its meetings: so in 1880 a tentative leaf of *Monthly Notes* was put out, as an inset or supplement to the trade circular of Trübner, the publisher, one of the original members.

The annual meeting of 1880 was at Edinburgh. Mr. Tedder had resigned his joint secretaryship to Mr. Charles Welch of the Guildhall. It was not so well attended as the Manchester meeting, in spite of the influx of a strong body of Macs, but amongst these was one MacAlister, who later proved to be a host in himself. A strange feature of this meeting was a tactless attempt to pass a resolution approving of the Sunday opening of libraries and museums—the ill-timed proposal being, very properly, severely defeated and snubbed by a shocked assembly. The *genius loci* may further have been responsible for a curious crop of papers upon economical but incongruous binding materials, such as linoleum, cretonne, chintz, etc. The great Indicator war had also flared up into an activity which was to rage for a generation. Some shouted for Elliot, some for Cotgreave, the Bonner, or the Duplex. The ambitious and ingenious sought cunning inventions, gadgets and notions, proudly to bring them to the lap of the

Association as a cat would bring its kittens: but, thanks be, we were never really dominated by the craze for mere technique as then were our trans-Atlantic brethren. The fever passed.

In 1881 Sir John Lubbock's Public Libraries Bill was the principal subject to occupy the minds of members; the present Council will be appalled to hear that twenty-five long meetings of their body were held that year; but they were also gravely concerned about the many rejections by apathetic and irresponsive electorates of proposals to establish town libraries. The fair but fickle Edinburgh had been ungrateful, rejecting the Acts a second time. Indeed, all broad Scotland then had fewer libraries than the English county of Stafford. They were not long to wait for a revulsion of popular feeling. London was stirring. The Richmond library, with Mr. Alfred Cotgreave of the famous indicator as its first librarian, spoiled Westminster's unique claim.

The President, the Rev. H. O. Coxe, Bodley's Librarian, died; and we also mourned the loss of our first President, Mr. Winter Jones: the proposed Conference at Cambridge was deferred and a hurriedly arranged annual meeting held at Gray's Inn. This meeting saw the first step towards what is now perhaps the most important and certainly the most onerous of the activities of the Association; the education and examination of library assistants. The constitution was revised, the provinces being allotted their quota of representatives on the Council. We were pleasantly entertained at Richmond by a lady whose popularity had certainly not suffered at our hands, Miss Braddon. This year showed a large increase of members, and somehow I myself managed to slip in with the crowd, although the editor of the *Monthly Notes*, in recording the elections, apparently thought that incident too trivial for mention.

In 1882 the *Monthly Notes* began to expand into quite a little journal, and gradually to acquire the characteristic features which later on became so familiar to us. News came thick of polls and adoptions, the decade of growth had arrived, the era of Carnegie and Passmore Edwards. Public libraries were springing up all over the country like so many mushrooms; new appointments, promotions, changes, made a yeasty bubbling in our membership. Prospects were bright.

> Bliss was it in that dawn to be alive,
> But to be young was very heaven!

In 1882 the *Library Journal*, an austere parent, disclaimed further responsibility for us, and Messrs. Trübner also felt that we were getting too big for the nest. The Cambridge meeting closed the first lustrum, with a membership of nearly 400 and an awe-inspiring record of activity and zeal. It was very academical, and possibly at that time began the first symptoms of revolt against the too antiquarian tendency. There were signs of schism; the bibliophiles protesting against the aridity of the exclusive diet of professional topics which characterized the A.L.A. In fairness to the black-letter men it must be said that the catholicity of the appeal of the Association had resulted in a membership which at that time had far outgrown the A.L.A., and contained names that any learned society would have been proud to claim.

Mr. Welch relinquished his share of the secretariat, and for a time Mr. Thomas carried on alone. Through 1883 the *Monthly Notes* continued, rather timorously, hiding the nakedness exposed by the withdrawal of Trübner's fat catalogues with a depressing blue cover of the true Seidlitz-powder hue. It was bright enough inside though, and an amusing little feud with out contemporary, *The Bibliographer* pleasantly relieved the inevitable stolidity of the usual matter. There was quite a touch of the brotherly greetings of the *Eatanswill Gazette* to the *Eatanswill Independent*, and the sparring only concluded with a triumphal but heartless crow in December, 1884, over the demise of *The Bibliographer*.

But it was clear that the title, *Monthly Notes* lacked distinction, and late in the year members were thrilled by the imposing yet dignified prospectus of *The Library Chronicle: a journal of librarianship and bibliography*, promised for March, 1884. This was largely the outcome of the Liverpool Conference, which, as it was the first annual meeting that I attended, lingers in my memory as a most successful and important gathering. My neighbour and colleague of later years, Thomas Mason, then at Glasgow, was almost lyrical in a newspaper account of its sustained festivity.

The first meeting of 1884 saw the election of a Scottish library assistant who was destined to have great influence upon our calling, James Duff Brown. In March *The Library Chronicle* came as promised, under the editorship of Ernest Thomas, and I think that its five volumes with their noble page, fine printing, delightful devices and ornaments, need not shrink even from Mr. Esdaile's critical glance. He may perhaps be envious when I tell him that the first number ran into a second edition! I doubt whether that has ever been equalled in our *Record*.

The *Chronicle* indeed deserved to be a best seller; it is eminently readable to-day. I should like to see some of those old papers reprinted. Dr. Garnett on "Librarianship in the Seventeenth Century" for instance; or Ernest Thomas on "The Libraries of London in 1710". The learned Germans have commenced to visit us again; I hope they will be candid in recording their impressions as was Conrad von Uffenbach. May I quote from him? "The person in charge of the library is an Englishman which is as much as to say a man who troubles himself very little about it." "Whenever I examined books in London I always made my cuffs as black as coal." "The man who showed us the library knew nothing about anything." (This was at Sion College, our ex-president will be grieved to head.) The Westminster librarian "not only looked like a chimney-sweep, but was very deaf". I hasten to point out that this was at Westminster School. Herr von Uffenbach wasn't a bad sort though, he thought Archbishop Tenison's library near St. Martin's Lane, "the handsomest and most numerous of all the libraries in London", and this of course was the Westminster Public Library of that time. Also he offered another librarian a tip of two crowns. O! si sic omnes!

The Conference of 1884 was at Dublin, and attracted a remarkable attendance of local notables. The Lord Lieutenant, Spencer, the red earl, came especially to hear the paper upon the Althorp Library, contributed by Lord Charles Bruce. It was rather a high-brow meeting, but lightened by a paper by J. D. Mullins on "Some of the Less Pleasant Duties of a Librarian", which led to a discussion that reads quaintly now. The most remarkable statement came from Mr. Peter Cowell, of Liverpool, who plaintively complained that there they used to indicate improper books by an asterisk in the catalogue, and were pained to find that this actually led to people reading them instead of avoiding them as was expected. I wonder whether our friend, Mr. Quinn, then an assistant there, had the difficult and delicate task of making the selection.

The first examination of library assistants was held in July, 1885. I am afraid it was not a great success. The entrants were three in number. However, all but one passed. This standard was not even maintained. A year or two later, after elaborate preparations, not one solitary candidate faced the examiners.

The Conference of 1885 was at Plymouth, and the municipal librarians had their turn. The eloquence of my friend Herbert Jones then, I believe, charmed for the first time, and I also found myself making my maiden speech. In this year we said good-bye to our earliest home, the London Institution, and moved to Gray's Inn. The Benchers were hospitable, but we began to feel the need of some pied-à-terre of our own.

The Chronicle, which was rather a burden upon the slender exchequer of the Association, was turned into a limited liability company.

The next year commenced in gloom. In one short month we lost Edward Edwards, Henry Bradshaw, and Henry Stevens. The youngest of us know the first two names, but I am afraid few are left who remember "the young man from Vermont".

Addressing myself for a moment more directly to our American visitors, I wish I could find words to explain to you the unique position Henry Stevens had attained in our regard. Our elders then were very much of their age, Victorian. Somewhat solemn, perhaps a little pompous, taking themselves always very seriously. Stevens was a type new to them. He was of course a great bibliographer: his knowledge of early American books had amazed and delighted the great Panizzi. But it was the puckish and whimsical personality of the man that at first puzzled and finally captured our hearts, when its underlying sweetness became apparent. It was his humour always to append to his name the letters "G. M. B.", which, he delighted to explain to the dull Britisher, did not cover some degree in our ancient and most honourable Order of the Bath, but stood for "Green Mountain Boy", an esoteric distinction which will no doubt convey more to you than it did to us, and certainly which he prized above his academical and antiquarian honours. He has been dead now these forty years, but still lives in bright and affectionate remembrance, in the memories of those who knew him.

The ninth annual meeting was again at Gray's Inn, under the Presidency of Dr. Bond.

The *Chronicle* about this time was very much a newspaper. Space could hardly be found for all the personal paragraphs, the appointments and changes, and the little items of news; amongst which, many names that in our later years were familiar first cropped up. The editor's eye ranged wide; even the indignant American librarian who was fined twenty dollars for smacking the head of a small boy who made a noise on the stairs was solaced with a paragraph.

The Birmingham Conference came in the jubilee year of Queen Victoria, and our well-loved and remembered friend, the leonine Sam Timmins, had his hour of glory. I can see him now, in the old Red Horse at Stratford-on-Avon, a not unworthy occupant of the armchair that once held Washington Irving, giving his inimitable lecture on "The dark races", or discoursing in Johnsonian manner to his attendant Boswells and his *fidus Achates*, Edmund Tonks. We visited the famous Althorp library in the home where it grew; and I contributed my first paper even as this, I fear, may be my last.

There were many new entrants to librarianship about this time, and as all were not yet subdued to the hue they worked in, the gentleness which marks the true bookman, a certain acerbity was noticeable. Rumours spread of a mysterious "executive" of the Association, a *Vehmgericht* more convivial than terrible; George Bullen, Sam Timmins, Edmund Tonks, with the young MacAlister, were regarded askance—sinister figures wielding unlawful power. We began to quarrel in our annual reports, to read each other's jealously, fiercely to search for over-statements and unfair claims, to hurl statistics at large, making invidious comparisons. If there was a battle of the indicators, there was a veritable campaign of statistics. It became really astonishing what we could prove with them. Bound volumes of pamphlets or magazines scored heavily and unfairly in issues. One famous library return proved that its small reference library stock, in the class of Commerce and Education, was "turned-over" sixty-three times in one year! Ultimately the thing became almost a scandal and altogether laughable, and a Committee of the Association was appointed to draw up some recommendations which would reduce the absurdities.

It was only excess of zeal: a desire to show meanly and mercantilely minded town councils that their new toy was worth the money. For town councils then did not take their libraries for granted, as most of them do now. The remnant of the opposition was going down fighting. The enthusiasts were sometimes indiscreet. We were in the limelight, and local legislators were flattered to find their personal views on the morality or otherwise of the novel of the day a matter for wide comment. If Stow-in-the-Marsh banned *Jude the Obscure* the nation heard of it. When Ealing blushed hotly over *The Manxman*, that blush was not unseen: when again that delicate-minded community condemned Marie Corelli, the outraged novelist, invoking the shades of Shakespeare, Sterne, Swift, Shelley, and Byron, made the Press resound. Small wonder that one library committee I heard of swelled to the number of sixty members.

Amongst these new librarians were also many who entered our calling without any previous service in its lower degrees. Some library committees were dazzled by showy academical qualifications. Others, strong in parish patriotism, resented "furriners". I remember that Croydon, of all places, was deeply moved; the local Press indignantly pronouncing that a local candidate, whose claims for consideration would, in these days, seem somewhat ambiguous, was altogether too good for the librarian's job, he was even worthy of a seat on the Committee! Or the north-country editor who unkindly argued that as "anybody is fit to be a librarian, *therefore* the post should be given to the w—— candidate". True, the day had passed when library appointments were looked upon as suitable endowments for effete clergymen and schoolmasters, but the day had yet to dawn when it was generally recognized that there was in truth an art and craft and science of librarianship. The position was very fairly, sanely, and most humorously put, in a striking paper by MacAlister, "Wanted a Librarian", which attracted much attention, and crystallized the vague ideas and tendencies that, somewhat aimlessly, still were already drifting towards the ideal of a Charter and a Profession.

It was soon after the Birmingham Conference that MacAlister's name appeared jointly with that of Ernest Thomas as Honorary Secretary.

In 1888 we met at Glasgow, under the presidency of Professor W. P. Dickson, Curator of the University Library; a propaganda visit, for Glasgow still held out against taxing herself for "buiks", thrice sternly negatived. The city bailies were duly apologetic, and the members properly tactful. Homage was made at the immortal birth-place in Ayr, and a pleasant junketing "doon the watter".

Late this autumn our financial worries, never far from us in those penniless years, became more pressing. Ernest Thomas had broken down in health, and in his absence we found to what an alarming extent he had been the main support of the Association for so many years. Librarians then were passing poor on a salary of, say, £120 or so. Lack of pelf, as always, vexed the bookish mind. Half-a-guinea subscription was a grave matter; the kindly officers turned a blind eye to many defaulters. But the Treasurer could no longer carry on the Sisyphean task, and early in the next year, 1889, resigned, to be succeeded by Henry R. Tedder, who never more than in that dark moment showed greater faith in the Association. From that day until his death in 1924 he controlled jealously and with skill our precarious finances. His passing is too recent and his great services too fresh in our minds to call for further mention. He was the link between the heroic days of the Association and our own prosaic times.

With the dawn of the new year, 1889, came a more startling change. The gentle and quiet Ernest Chester Thomas was eclipsed by the vivid, forceful, and dominating personality of John Young Walker Mac-Alister. The *Chronicle* faded and died: but immediately sprang up, full of life and vigour, *The Library: a magazine of bibliography and literature*. Less ambitious in form, it retained in full the scholarship and distinction of its predecessor, and was even more definitely our official organ. MacAlister had strong views upon the need for some centre or head-quarters where the Association's business might be carried on, and had previously issued the prospectus of his scheme for the formation of a "Library Bureau", an admirable idea which still lacks its full accom-plishment according to the original programme, although some years later that capable business man and good friend to librarians, Cedric Chivers, borrowed it, with the inventor's blessing.

In this year the Mersey District Association of Librarians was formed, the first of our provincial branches, but for the time unaffiliated.

The twelfth annual meeting was held at Gray's Inn, under the presidency of the Worshipful Richard Copley Christie, Chancellor, not of the Duchy of Lancaster but of the Diocese of Manchester. Chancellor Christie was a lovable and a learned man, and, with perhaps a single exception, was of our long list of distinguished presidents, the one who took the most personal and real interest in his job. He never forgot us and assuredly we shall never forget him, as long as his munificent legacy, our solitary testamentary benefaction, brings in its ever welcome annual tribute to cheer a treasurer's heart.

When I glance over that list I feel that I should like to write an addendum to these reminiscences, entitled "Some Presidents I have known". I assure you it could be made quite interesting. Presidents, of course, are, at any rate officially, all good and great men, but still they are men, with the failings of weak humanity, and—"I could a tale unfold".

But I must put this temptation away, and return to our twelfth annual meeting. Professor Dewey was there again: he must be immortal; 1877, 1889, 1927, these must be figures without meaning to Melvil Dewey. My principal recollection of this meeting has its painful side: the ever-troubling financial question clamoured for notice. The long-suffering treasurer humorously complained that when, at meetings, he hinted at unpaid subscriptions, only those owing one year had the grace to blush, those owing two years kept brazen faces. In timid desperation the Council brought forward a motion to increase the subscription from half-a-guinea to fifteen shillings. An amendment was put to split the difference and make it twelve-and-sixpence, but I, in the extravagance of youth, moved that it be a guinea. This was carried, and, I fear, the shock to the frugal or impecunious was the first cause of the secret unpopularity under which I ever afterwards lay.

In December of 1889 the monthly meeting was held at 20 Hanover Square, an address that was to become very familiar, for in the following spring, thanks to MacAlister, we were able proudly to speak of "our" rooms in that fashionable quarter.

The North Midland Association was formed in 1890, and William Blades died. The conference was at Reading, and we talked a lot about the new Public Libraries Bill. Secretly, we much preferred a pilgrimage to Eversley and a delightful river trip. I remember how the lovely English scenery deeply impressed Professor Justin Winsor, who again was an honoured guest. Thomas Mason, who for some time had unofficially replaced Ernest Thomas as joint honorary secretary, at this election was accorded formal recognition. I think it was at this conference that our now important exhibition-annexe first took shape, organized by the Reading librarian. It was there that

Mr. Cedric Chivers' new inventions and improvements in bookbinding became known to most of us.

The late 'eighties and early 'nineties certainly was the great age of library journalism. The adoptive basis of the Acts, the propaganda on both sides, the polling of ratepayers, had thoroughly aroused the public interest. Each opening of a new library was the occasion of a function and a speech by some notable. The opposition was such that it only added savour to the success of the movement. Had we been serpentlike in our wisdom and employed them as *agents-provocateur*, we could hardly have found better helpers than some of our opponents. There was the gentleman who misquoted John Morley as saying: "Eighty per cent of the books read at the free libraries were of a licentious, lewd and low character". There was the essay on "A plea for liberty", that forlorn attempt to raise the bannerol of a dead individualism. There was the disgruntled professional bookman who announced "The Free Library Failure", in Henley's brilliant *New Review*: he disliked our lending libraries because they were too "light", and our reference libraries because they were too "heavy". My own newly established library in St. George, Hanover Square, provided him with much material. I still feel crushed under the scornful list of the "behemoths" he there discovered. Dugdale's *Monasticon*, Foxe's *Acts and Monuments*, Jeremy Bentham, Barrow's *Sermons*; actually a set of the Camden Society, and "all the rubbish that Pope, Longfellow, Wordsworth, Southey and the rest ever wrote"; in the most expensive editions too! It was dishonest alike to publishers, booksellers, and authors, and to all who depend upon the book-trade for a living. Sixpenny editions might not be everything the bibliophile could desire, but were quite good enough for the public, and the outlay of a few shillings would provide all that the ordinary common man could read in a quarter of a century. How this book-cleric scolded! His voice is in my ears to-day.

It is a true instinct that fears indifference more than dislike. When we have none to condemn we shall have none to praise.

Further, to be quite candid, the right was not always on the one side. Some of those early librarians were rather dreadful. Usually the official organ dealt tenderly with the crude attempts at cataloguing betraying the grossest ignorance of the books as well as of the method; but too often the mild comment exposed *gaffes* that must be read now to be believed in these days of certificates and schools of librarianship. Skeletons hang in many library cupboards. The classic "Ditto on the Floss" does not bloom alone. The editor of *The Library* must have been sadly tempted to compile an anthology of the humours of the "dot and dash" system of cataloguing, but his discretion or more likely his kind heart led him ultimately to decide in a reproachful leader, which contained a few choice final quotations, only to notice good catalogues.

My favourite from MacAlister's gibbet is—

I Puritani, by Bellini;
— say no," by Wilkie Collins;

but there are many rivals. The humours for which the printer might share responsibility are better known, but most of them, I fear, are apocryphal. I have failed to verify Penn's "No cows, no cream!" but I can guarantee the authenticity of Cobbold's "Notes on Infernal Parasites"; Stewart's "Conversations of Energy", and Jevons's "Poetical Economy".

To resume my chronology, in the early 'nineties itinerant monthly meetings were our fashion, most of the libraries in and near London being visited to hear the proud custodian display his charge to his colleagues.

The conference of 1891 was at Nottingham, under the presidency of Robert Harrison. It was very businesslike and severe: we had been rebuked by the more ascetic brethren for the picnics and pleasurings that enlivened the preceding gatherings, and were somewhat chastened. Our noses were kept well to the grindstone, and Messrs. J. Potter Briscoe and J. D. Brown abashed the rule-of-thumb librarian with a frightening exhibition of modern library appliances, almost American in their stark efficiency. The museum afterwards went to Clerkenwell: I do not know what has become of it, but trust that it has been burnt.

In February, 1892, Ernest Chester Thomas died, and we lost the first of our great triumvirate. For twelve years he had been our secretary, for almost as long our editor and his own principal contributor, at any rate the only one he could rely upon with confidence. Of untiring energy and capacity for drudgery, upon his frail frame rested the fortunes of our Association during its precarious childhood, and upon his light purse our financial probity. He grudged nothing to us but everything to himself.

One monthly meeting in 1892 was memorable. Our patron saint, Andrew Carnegie, was in town, and benevolently allowed himself to be led to 20 Hanover Square by Mr. Hew Morrison, who read a paper on the Edinburgh Public Library. Ursa Major was gracious and explained his theory of the economics of the disposal of surplus wealth. Thomas Mason, as to a brother Scot, had the temerity to suggest that the endowment of the librarian was a deserving and suitable complement to the endowment of the library, but the great man was not to be drawn.

Our *bête noire*, the net book agreement, first raised its grisly head at the June meeting, but was light-heartedly shooed away, the members present being too full of anticipatory delights in the forthcoming Paris Conference.

Of that gathering, I regret to say, I have no personal recollections. The President was Dr. Garnett, also an unwilling absentee. The official account of the Conference, of course, tells us nothing of what we would really like to know, but judging by the havoc it created in our humdrum routine, it must have been a devastating success. I am told there was a princely reception at Chantilly by the Duc d'Aumale, that a lady had for the first time mounted our rostrum, that although the papers were long the sittings were short. Anyhow, it was six months before MacAlister was able to bring out another number of his journal. When the dust had cleared away we found that Thomas Mason had dropped off the pillion and MacAlister rode alone as Secretary. Also, a lot of interesting things were happening in the library world. Woman had cast her eyes upon the profession, so Miss M. S. R. James warned us:[1] and a little cloud no bigger than a man's hand had formed in the Clerkenwell district which was to spill disaster and ruin on the trade in indicators. We heard for the first time in an anonymous article in *The Library*, that revolutionary, that anarchistic suggestion, "why not let the public inside and place the staff outside the counter".[2]

I do not propose to say much about the great controversy that raged for a generation afterwards. I never took part; in fact, to this day I have a foot in both camps. One flower I should like to put on the grave of the vanquished. The indicator had the grace to blush redly when it revealed deficiencies—the open shelves stare blankly.

In December of 1892, for some reason I do not recall, our monthly meeting was held at Liverpool. From a paper read there by Mr. J. J. Ogle, the summer schools,[3] now so popular and valuable, had origin, the first being in London, in July, 1893.

To the Chicago Conference of 1893 we sent a small but potent delegation, which included Miss James, J. D. Brown, and Peter Cowell. Brown was, of course, one of the last men to be impressed by imposing façades, and his shrewd dissection of the claim, far too readily admitted over here, that American libraries were much superior to ours, aroused much comment, and was not altogether relished by our friends.

The Conference of 1893 was at Aberdeen, a violent rebound from

[1] See pp. 244–251.
[2] See pp. 292–295.
[3] See pp. 282–285.

Paris. Or perhaps it was regarded as a suitable place to economise, for the Paris meeting had proved expensive, the Association having to bear all local costs as we were self-invited guests. However that may be, it was a highly successful meeting, and I cannot remember any which was more productive of animated discussion and argument. That of course was natural and to be expected in such an atmosphere. The "blacking-out" question, made notorious by Aston, was the principal bone of contention.

The Amending Act of this year abolished the appeal to King Mob, and the Verneys lit their little lamp at Middle Claydon.

The black-letter men budded off and formed their own society. I think we suffered by that; perhaps we had a little too much of the monk of Bury and "rare old Bartholomew" from the ancients, but some sweetness departed with them.

From the increasing complexity of library legislation we fled to Mr. Fovargue, who has ever since guided our steps in the mazes of the law, a fine record of honorary service. Indeed, with of course one obvious exception, we have been fortunate in our officers beyond ordinary.

My memories of 1894 are faint; there was a big meeting at the Royal Colonial Institute, and I think the rise of Edward Foskett of Camberwell as a controversialist became a feature; as also that equally doughty fighter, C. W. F. Goss. In the squabbles that enlivened our monthly gatherings during the next decade, and gave our Society a likeness to that upon the Stanislaus, Foskett was redoubtable and unquenchable. I recall a severe trouncing that he gave to Mr. Charles Welch, librarian of the Guildhall, in reply to a somewhat superior and high-brow condemnation, delivered *ex-cathedrâ* at the Mansion House, of fiction reading, the Guildhall Library being of course happily free from the charge of encouraging the growth of this "evergreen tree of diabolical knowledge". Mr. Welch thought our readers would be much happier if they were permitted to take home Herbert Spencer's huge tomes of *Descriptive Sociology*, Spon's *Dictionary of Engineering*, or Sowerby's *Botany*, works which we had mistakenly placed in our reference libraries. One of Mr. Welch's best sellers for a lending library was Kemble's *Codex Diplomaticus Ævi Saxonici*, a book no doubt deservedly popular, but which I was dismayed to find was not in my library at all. Lacking these delights, the starved reader had perforce to content himself with Ouida and Miss Braddon. Chancellor Christie strove hard in support of Mr. Welch, but I am afraid the sense of the meeting was against him.

We went to Belfast in the autumn, under the presidency of that illustrious Irishman, ambassador and viceroy, the Marquis of Dufferin and Ava. His interest had contributed to the success of the Paris Conference, which took place during his embassy and a seed then sown now bore fruit.

This year died George Bullen, full of years and honour, and in the new year William Lane-Joynt of Dublin, a brilliant orator of the old school and a personality that would have fitted the hero of a Charles Lever novel. Both were original members; the list was shrinking rapidly.

Early in 1895 we first heard, somewhat incredulously, of a dazzling distinction our Secretary held out as a not impossible aspiration—a Royal Charter. He cajoled a fund of reluctant guineas, and persuaded the Cardiff Conference to bless him and wish him luck. The prospect may have unsettled us, for most of the papers at that meeting were taken as read, and we spent the time with the grasshopper, not the ant; Mr. Ballinger and our President, Lord Windsor, better known afterwards as the Earl of Plymouth, conniving.

The Library Assistants' Association was formed this year, but I dare not venture to include any reminiscences of their early days; they are young enough to be sensitive.

Owing no doubt to the editor's pre-occupation with the Charter, *The Library* again relapsed into irregularity, but its brilliance atoned for its dilatoriness. Some of you will remember with me the controversy MacAlister unwisely entered into with a popular pseudo-scientific periodical, upon the alleged danger of infection from library books; his humorous rage at finding his carefully compiled evidence of the negative results of nasty experiments superbly ignored, and his careless words turned against him; when a flippant remark upon the poisonous practice of thumb-licking was seized upon by the unscrupulous journalist, who triumphantly held as finally proved the lethal qualities of the well-thumbed volume. Or his delight in the pious managers who, yielding to a demand for Sunday opening, soothed their uneasy consciences by ordaining that *Punch* should be locked up from Saturday to Monday to ensure against the spiritual danger of an ill-timed smile. I do not know where these casuists gloomed, "O profane one", but for the sake of the Puritan tradition I do hope it was Banbury!

It cannot be denied that MacAlister was at times capricious, and impatient under criticism. Hotly proud of the Association, a keen upholder of its honour, indignantly resentful of the little meannesses of spirit that, alas, seem inevitable cankers in the growth of all such bodies, scornful of the soft answer, he of course made some enemies. But the causes that led to the formation of the schismatic "Society of Public Librarians" in the autumn of 1895 were not entirely personal.

Again we lost a valuable element, and MacAlister's Æsopian fable of "The Goslings" on the parting was—

"Of that nature as to make
"One's fancy chuckle, while his heart doth ache."

The 1896 volume of *The Library* is precious to me through J. D. Brown's article on "Fiction Classification", a gem that should shine in the yet-to-be-compiled "Librarian's Golden Treasury". I think I see his hand also in the "Model Rules for Open Access Libraries" in the same year. From time to time I have come across many evidences that his sly spoofery was taken seriously, even by his compatriots: for instance the following excerpt from an alarmingly technical and laboriously compiled children's catalogue:

340 LAW.

343.—4—9. Crime and punishment in special countries.

343.4267 ESSEX [!!!].

Thorndyke, R. Doctor Syn, a tale of Romney Marsh.

Oh! Dewey: what crimes are committed in thy name!

Brown, even when conveying ideas seriously meant, had a trick of colouring them with his sardonic humour, even to the *reductio ad absurdum*; and when he enrolled that other occasional *farceur* (if he will forgive me), Stanley Jast, in a crusade to spread the religion of the new cataloguing, their success in drawing the heavy guns of the old school in a broadside from Robert K. Dent and others, must have been as much a delight to them as it was to an amused library world. The monumental dictionary catalogue of the old Newcastle, Birmingham, and Manchester type, was then at least moribund from natural causes, and the light-hearted savagery of its slaughtering caused more tears of delight than regret.

At a Special General Meeting, in January, 1896, the constitution was revised, an important change being that providing for branch associations. This poor old constitution of ours was always getting torn, or patched; little can now be left of the original garment. We felt in need of a quiet holiday after the excitements of previous conferences, so went to Buxton to take the waters, without fuss or hospitality. To compliment Manchester upon its success in resisting the tax-collector, we chose Alderman Rawson, Chairman of its Libraries' Committee, for President. It was a soothing, domestic meeting, and the somnolence induced by the continual rain enabled me to creep into the Council.

The Diamond Jubilee year was marked by the great International Conference, for into such had developed the idea of a joint conference between the American Library Association and our own body. Sir John Lubbock presided, and was supported by many distinguished vice-presidents; men of mark in science, literature, and art. Fourteen governments and more than three hundred libraries were represented, in a membership of 641. It was a worthy successor to the 1877 Conference.

Our next annual meeting, following soon after, naturally suffered somewhat as an anti-climax, and we were distressed to learn of the contemplated resignation of the Honorary Secretary. About to see his work crowned in the now imminent Royal Charter, suffering in health, and dismayed at the arrears of his journal, which had not appeared for some months, his violent desire for a quiet life grew into a tumult. It was at a Special General Meeting in February, 1898, called to discuss some tea-cup storm—Mr. Goss, I think had been handling the spoon—that the news of the receipt of the Charter first came to us. It was formally handed to the President, then Mr. Tedder, on May 9th.

Our Education Committee also came early this year with H. D. Roberts, who largely was responsible for it, as its first secretary.

The Conference of 1898 ought really to have been held at Wigan, but fearful lest the undeserved reputation of that much-maligned town should repel, we compromised by including Southport and Preston. The Earl of Crawford, who had become well known to us by presiding at some meetings of the International Conference, was President-designate, and we had the privilege of visiting Haigh Hall and viewing his famous library. We had, of course, been there before, in 1883, but now felt more at home.

Lord Crawford, the possessor of one of the finest private collections in the realm, was not only a great bookman but a great scholar, like his father before him and his son after him. Few could fathom his knowledge of astronomy and Egyptology, to mention two only of the subjects in which he was an acknowledged expert. A dignified and reserved man, he took his duties as our principal officer seriously, even when that duty was the distasteful one of keeping order at a turbulent meeting, or soothing the ruffled plumes of contentious members.

It was at this meeting that I, in the valour of ignorance, first took up the load MacAlister had dropped after eleven strenuous years.

The resignation of MacAlister closed an epoch and marked a change. A Special Committee of Publications had come to the conclusion that it was imperative that the Association's journal should be its property. Delicate questions affecting responsibility had arisen. The great fight of indicators *versus* open access had flared up into a perfect orgy of paper warfare. It was very necessary to treat warily, for more cautious

timorous editors than MacAlister was every like to be fall foul of the
law of libel. So with its tenth volume *The Library* ceased to be our
official organ. Perhaps it was inevitable: the editor was obviously
out of sympathy with much that he had to print. His fastidious taste
could not gladly accept the dull papers that, as Secretary, he had to
invite and even welcome, for lack of better. His wide mind could take
no pride in the minor chronicling of small events. His habit of work
was foreign to the meticulous routine of the office. Relief must have
prevailed over regret when, freed from the harassing of committees
and councils, the heckling of monthly meetings, the disputations of
captious and querulous correspondents. *The Library* commenced a
second series and a new life in December, 1899, as an independent
quarterly review of bibliography and library lore. MacAlister's faith
in the child of his brain has been well justified, and now in its fourth
series, as the organ of the Bibliographical Society, still under the main
editorship of Dr. Pollard, this long familiar journal by its old associations has secretly a place in my affections that its official successor
never reached.

When in later years, we made some tardy acknowledgment of
MacAlister's great services in electing him our President, we honoured
ourselves more. His death, following so closely that of his long-time
colleague, H. R. Tedder, made sharper the severance of past and
present. MacAlister had many gifts of mind and person, but the
greatest was his gift of attracting friendship.

With *The Library Association Record*, our official organ and our own
property, the first number of which appeared in January, 1899, under
the editorship of Dr. Guppy, begins a new era. For nearly four years,
until that library of a dream, the Rylands, claimed him, Dr. Guppy
brought out *The Record* with unfailing punctuality and unfaltering
excellence, so much so that, upon his departure, no one cared to
continue the task. It took quite a number of us, an editorial committee,
and the result was the lowest common denominator of our intelli-
gences. Strange the workings of group psychology—always an amusing
study to a secretary. After plumbing the depths of dullness the *Record*
came to light and life again with Mr. Esdaile. The "sundry and
manifold changes of the world" we have, more than most, been
unable to escape. But, as the Latin poet said: "All things change though
nothing perishes", and in the present dignified yet simple pages we
can feel that the torch bravely lit by Ernest Thomas, brilliantly carried
over rough seas by Sir John MacAlister, gallantly handed on by Dr.
Guppy, stumblingly by the Publications Committee, and now serenely
by Mr. Esdaile, will be a beacon to us for generations.

But these later days I find more difficult to speak of. The events of thirty years ago, in these impetuous times, are fast fading from memory. I have therefore some confidence that even those who could, and there are lamentably few, would hesitate to contradict or correct me; to question my incidents or deprecate my comments. They are such old friends that their hearts if not their minds would maintain me. But with the events of this century I feel less certain of either. One can regard with benignity and complacency the errors of youth, but impartiality becomes more difficult as distance lessens.

This retrospect, therefore, must remain a distant one—I dare not bring my eyes nearer yesterday. For I claim no virtue of judgment— not for me the clarity and final summing of the historian. I have no stomach for the dullness of the recorder: and have we not already the ordered, the monumental roll of transactions and proceedings on our office shelves, mummified for all time. We librarians by nature of our calling see enough and to spare of dusty death.

Just for a span I have endeavoured to live again the winged moments, the pleasant hours, of the days when I was young, when Plancus was Consul.

*The Library Association early days: a retrospect. By the Honorary Secretary, [Frank Pacy]. Submitted to the Fiftieth Anniversary Conference, September, 1927.*

# CHAPTER 41

# *John Minto (1863–1935)*

"Minto contributed a love of order, administrative ability, and technical
and bibliographical knowledge."

E. A. SAVAGE.

JOHN MINTO was a native of Aberdeenshire, and was born in 1863.
He graduated M.A. at Aberdeen University in 1885, and received his
early library training at King's College, Aberdeen, where he was
a member of the staff from 1885 to 1892. In the latter year he was
appointed Sub-Librarian of Aberdeen Public Library, but four years
later went to Perth as Librarian. In 1902 Minto went south as Chief
Librarian to Brighton, where he completely reorganized the library.
However, he returned to his native land in 1906 as Librarian of the
Society of Writers to the Signet, Edinburgh.

Minto served on the Council of the Library Association for thirty
years, was Vice-President for nine years, and from 1930 to 1934 was
Chairman of the Education Committee. As Honorary Secretary of
the British Committee responsible for the compilation of the Anglo-
American Code, published in 1908, he closely collaborated with his
opposite number, J. C. M. Hanson, and did much to bring the task to
a fruitful conclusion. Minto was President of the Scottish Library
Association from 1921 to 1925.

The urgent need for a bibliography of reference books was met
by Minto's *Reference books*, 1929, to which a supplement was issued
in 1931. He also wrote for the Library Association Series of manuals
*A history of the public library movement in Great Britain and Ireland*,
which was published in 1932, and represents a most thorough record of
the development of librarianship within the limits set by the title.

Minto was a great lover of Aberdeen, and did much useful work
for that city. As a librarian he was thorough although cautious, while
his writings indicate a genuine interest in his profession that was of
real value to his fellow librarians.

### REFERENCE

S[avage], E. A. John Minto. *Library Association Record*, 4th Ser., 2, 1935, pp. 322–324;
see also p. 487.

## MINTO ON THE HISTORY OF THE PUBLIC LIBRARY MOVEMENT

The establishment and growth of the public library may be viewed as part of the great social movement for the spread of knowledge among the poorer classes which took place in the late eighteenth century and the early years of the nineteenth century. This movement was characterized by the establishment of various educational agencies, some account of which may here be briefly given.

Sunday Schools which, in their beginnings, were not exclusively religious institutions, and were not confined to children, were the result of the pioneer efforts of Robert Raikes, printer in Gloucester (1780), of the Rev. Rowland Hill in London (1784), of Hannah More, Sydney Smith, and others. Secular subjects were taught in these schools, and evening classes were sometimes held during the week as part of the system. The formation of the Sunday School Union in 1803 gave a powerful impetus to the movement in England. It provided for "the training of teachers, the grading of classes, and schemes of lessons suitable to the various stages of the scholars' mental growth."[1]

The establishment of two important societies, the National Society for the Education of the Poor (1811) and the British and Foreign School Society (1814), carried forward the educational movement for the greater part of the nineteenth century. The moving spirits of these two societies were the Rev. Andrew Bell, D.D., and Joseph Lancaster.

[pp. 15–16]

.        .        .        .        .

In the early part of the seventeenth century the desire to help their less-fortunate brethren led a few wealthy and philanthropic men to present or bequeath their collections of books to municipalities with a view to their preservation for the free use of all.

A public library was established in the Free Grammar School of Coventry in 1601, the initiative being probably taken by Dr. Philemon Holland, "the translator-general of his age." A separate library room was provided in the school. This library existed until 1913 or 1914, when the valuable residue was sold by the governors of the school, much to the dismay and indignation of the citizens when the facts became known. The original donation book of the library, with a list of the first donors, is now in the Cambridge University Library, the authorities of which had the good sense to purchase what Coventry

[1] *Chambers's Encyclopaedia* (Article on Sunday Schools).

PLATE 13

JOHN COTTON DANA

(1856 – 1929)

(From Chalmers Hadley, *John Cotton Dana*, by kind permission
of the American Library Association)

PLATE 14

FRANK PACY

(1862 – 1928)

(By kind permission of the Library Association)

had stupidly sold. Probably this public library and that of Norwich were the earliest municipal public libraries in England.

The municipality of the city of Norwich in 1608 set apart three rooms, "parcel of the sword-bearer's dwelling," and fitted them up for the reception of a library in the south porch of the New Hall (now St. Andrew's Hall). The rooms were to serve the additional purpose of lodgings for preachers coming from a distance to preach in the city. The sword-bearer had to find "bedding, lynnynge, and other necessaries for their lodging." The Mayor, Sir Thomas Petters, set a good example, which was quickly followed, by heading the list of gifts to the new library with fifteen volumes.[1] This early library now forms part of the Norwich Public Library.

In 1615 a city library was opened at Bristol through the munificence of Dr. Toby Matthew, Archbishop of York, and Robert Redwood, a public-spirited citizen. This library, like that at Norwich, was afterwards incorporated in the Bristol Public Library. In 1623 Sir John Kederminster established a parochial free library at Langley Marish in Buckinghamshire. Leicester has had a city library since 1632, and the famous library of Sir Humphrey Chetham[2] was, under the terms of his will, made freely accessible to the inhabitants of Manchester in 1653. The great difficulty in preserving the continuity of these early libraries has been the want of provision for their maintenance and the lack of funds for their growth. The Chetham Library is believed to be the only library in England with a continuous history since its foundation, freely accessible to all. It will readily be understood that these few and scattered libraries could, of necessity, do little to meet the needs of the reading public of England.

[pp. 22-24]

## MINTO ON THE PUBLIC LIBRARIES ACT, 1850

Meantime, on the same day, as it happens, on which the Select Committee was reappointed (February 14, 1850), Mr. William Ewart introduced in the House of Commons his "Bill for enabling Town Councils to establish Public Libraries and Museums." In doing so, he said there was scarcely any country in Europe so inadequately provided with public libraries as England. Generally speaking, on the Continent the rule of accessibility was universal. In Italy and Germany no great town was without a library. Here there was only a sort of small public library in Manchester; but there were none in

---

[1] Article by Albert D. Euren, editor of the *Norwich Mercury*, in *Book Auction Records*, Vol. 10, 1913, p. 25.
[2] Chetham was not entitled to the knighthood here conferred upon him. [J.L.T.]

Glasgow, Leeds, Sheffield, and other great manufacturing towns; whilst in Amiens, Rouen, Lyons, Marseilles, and other towns in France the working-classes resorted in numbers to the fine public libraries that were open to them. The Americans had made far greater advancement in the matter than the people of this country had. In every state of the Union there was a library kept up by the State, and accessible to the public, and from them the people derived immense benefit. His Bill was a brief one. A few years ago his friend the member for Salford (Mr. Brotherton) and himself had introduced a Bill enabling Town Councils to establish public museums of art and science. It was carried unanimously and had proved of considerable advantage to the public. The proposed Bill would consolidate the two Bills and enable Town Councils to found both museums and public libraries. The Museums Act gave power to levy a rate of one halfpenny in the pound. That principle he had adopted to allow Town Councils to purchase land and erect buildings and furnish them out of the proceeds. The property would be vested for ever in the Town Council, thus securing perpetuity. The Museums Act restricted the power to towns of 10,000 inhabitants. He thought it better to extend the power to all municipal bodies whatsoever. He proposed to abolish the charge of one penny per person admitted to the museum which was allowed by the Museums Act. It was a useless impediment. His Bill would not give the Town Council power to purchase books; they relied upon books being supplied by the donations of individuals. There arose the question, Was it called for? It was. It had even been anticipated by the town of Warrington, which had taken advantage of the Museums Act to establish a library as well as a museum. In Salford, too, the Town Council had placed at the disposal of the public a large building which was in their possession, and although it had been in existence as a library only six months they already had 5,000 books in it. One advantage of the museums would be that they would be illustrative of the local and natural history of the places in which they were established. The promoters of the Bill merely asked that these popular institutions might be legally founded by the people, supported by the people, and enjoyed by the people.

[pp. 80–82]

- - - - -

The Act as passed enabled Town Councils to establish public libraries and museums, and repealed the Museums Act of 1845. The operation of the Act was confined to boroughs having a population exceeding 10,000 "according to the last count taken thereof by authority of

Parliament." The procedure in adopting the Act was as follows: The Mayor, upon the request of the Town Council, was empowered to cause a notice to be fixed on the door of the town hall and on the doors of every church or chapel within the borough, and to be inserted in a local newspaper specifying on what day not earlier than ten days after the affixing and publication of such notice, and at what place or places within the borough the burgesses are required to signify their votes for or against the adoption of the Act. A two-thirds majority of the votes given was necessary to secure adoption. The Act, when adopted, gave power to the Town Council to purchase or rent any lands or buildings for the purpose of forming public libraries or museums of art and science, or both, and to erect, alter, and extend any buildings for such purpose, to maintain them in good repair, to purchase fuel, lighting, fixtures, and furniture, to appoint officers and servants with salaries and remuneration, and to make rules and regulations for their safety and use and for admission of visitors and others, *but they had no power to purchase books or specimens.* They were given power to levy a rate up to one halfpenny in the pound of annual value, and to borrow money on the security of that rate for the above purposes. The buildings so acquired were to be vested in the Town Council, or in any committee appointed by them, to be held in trust for ever. Admission to the libraries to be free of charge. If the adoption of the Act was rejected, no further application for its adoption could be made within the next two years.

Thus after a long struggle, and in the face of opposition hardly credible at the present day, the fight was won, and the first Public Libraries Act became law. This result was achieved through the enthusiasm and perseverance of its chief promoters, William Ewart and Joseph Brotherton, with whom must ever be associated Edward Edwards, whose whole-hearted support is fully disclosed in his evidence, and in the carefully compiled statistics which he had gathered over a number of years, and freely put at the disposal of the Select Committee.

[PP. 94-95]

From, Minto, John. *A history of the public library movement in Great Britain and Ireland,* 1932.

## CHAPTER 42

# *Louis Stanley Jast (1868–1944)*

"He was in my view, the most original thinker, the most inventive worker, the best speaker and the most dominant character in librarianship in his day."

W. C. BERWICK SAYERS.

THE progress of librarianship is frequently hampered by the complacent individual who is perfectly satisfied with the *status quo*, and views with scorn any proposed innovation. Librarianship must advance with the times, or perish from stagnation, and it is due to the compelling characters of a few prominent librarians that we owe the stimulation needed to spur on the laggards. Jast was one such forceful character. He inspired all coming into contact with him, revolutionized the library systems with which he was connected, and by his papers and writings spurred on the efforts of those on the verge of discouragement.

Louis Stanley Jast was born at Halifax in August, 1868, with the family name of de Jastrzebski, his father being a Polish refugee. He was educated at Field's Academy, Halifax, and at King's College, London. At the age of 19 he went to Halifax Public Libraries, eventually becoming librarian of the Akroyd Branch Library. From 1892 to 1898 Jast was Librarian at Peterborough, and in the latter year went to Croydon as Chief Librarian. There he completely reorganized the system, and favourably influenced several members of the staff, who have since occupied prominent positions in librarianship. He replaced Brown's Adjustable Classification, then in use in the library, and introduced Dewey; but in October, 1915, he left Croydon for Manchester, where he was Deputy (1915–1920), and then Chief Librarian. Once more Jast reorganized the system, and completed his career at Manchester by planning the monumental library with which his name must always be associated. His services to Manchester were rewarded with an Honorary M.A. from the University.

Jast held several important positions in the Library Association, including that of Honorary Secretary (1905–1915), and was President in 1930. He was a member of many committees, and lectured on classification at the London School of Economics from 1905 to 1908. He was a keen advocate of open-access, card-charging, the card catalogue, subject class lists and of book display, while he invented several useful items of library equipment. Jast assisted Brown in founding *The Library World*, and at Manchester founded the Unnamed Society, a dramatic club which he actively supported. He died on Christmas Day, 1944.

The writings of Louis Stanley Jast are represented by many published verses, including *Shah Jahan*, 1934, a drama in verse; a book on reincarnation entitled *What it all means*, 1941; and he edited the series *Live books resurrected*, of which six volumes appeared. Professional articles and books from his pen are numerous, and he supported many of the Library Association Conferences by contributing papers. The following are among his more prominent publications: *A classification of library economy and office papers*, 1907; (with H. D. Gower and W. W. Topley), *The camera as historian*, [etc.], 1916; The commercial library. *Library Association Record*, 19, 1917, pp. 118–124; Technical and commercial libraries. *L.A.R.*, N.S. 7, 1929, pp. 98–104; *The child as reader*, 1927; *The planning of a great library*, 1927; *The provision of books for children in elementary schools*, 1928; Presidential address. *L.A.R.*, N.S. 8, 1930, pp. 241–256; *Libraries and living; essays and addresses of a public librarian*, 1932; *The library and the community*, (1939), in Nelson's Discussion Books Series; Book selection and the public, [etc.]. *L.A.R.*, 4th Ser., 1, 1934, pp. 343–347; The brains. *L.A.R.*, 41, 1939, pp. 571–576; and, Libraries and publishers. *L.A.R.*, 41, 1939, pp. 5–11.

In drawing public attention to a romantic association between Jast and Ethel Winifred Austin (1875–1918) W. A. Munford reintroduced a notable woman librarian who had been forgotten. Ethel Austin became Secretary and Librarian in 1906 to the Incorporated National Lending Library for the Blind, which in 1916 was rehoused as the National Library for the Blind. They had planned to marry after the war, but unfortunately Ethel Austin died on May 17th, 1918.

Jast's writings are provocative, sometimes seemingly aggressive, but often with strategic use of humour, and always worthy of careful consideration. As a teacher he was an inspiration to the young librarian, as a speaker he commanded the full attention of his audience, and as a librarian and administrator he was the doyen of the profession.

## REFERENCES

Appreciations of L. Stanley Jast by E. A. Savage, W. C. Berwick Sayers, Charles Nowell and others. *Library Association Record*, 47, 1945, pp. 21–24, 43–45, 84. Also, Louis Stanley Jast. (Edited by W. C. Berwick Sayers.) *Library World*, 47, 1944–1945, pp. 107–113, 124–128.

Fry, W. G., and Munford, W. A., *Louis Stanley Jast: a biographical sketch*, 1966.

Munford, W. A. Portrait of a woman librarian: Ethel Winifred Austin (1875–1918). *Library World*, 60, 1958–1959, pp. 166–170; also, Ethel Winifred Austin and L. S. Jast, by Ernest A. Savage. (*Corres.*) pp. 250–251; and note by W. A. Munford, p. 251.

## JAST ON THE PERFECT LIBRARIAN[1]

This meeting, where librarians and assistants forgather on equal terms, is a happy augury of the future co-operation of all sections of the profession. Soon, I hope, we shall cease to divide ourselves into librarians and assistants; we are all librarians, for the only working distinction that I know of between the one and the other, is that the assistant is oftentimes the fellow who does things, and the librarian is the man who says: "Well done, thou good and faithful servant"— or otherwise, as the case may be. The assistants' section of the Library Association will then cease to exist, and its place taken by a juniors' section, for which there may be a practical case, though I'm not very sure about that.

I have chosen for the subject of this address: the perfect librarian. Let me hasten to admit at the outset that the perfect librarian does not exist, never has existed, and assuredly never will exist. But good librarians do, and better librraians may. What is a good librarian? To answer that question we shall have to abstract certain qualities, capacities, etc., and as it is unlikely that all good librarians will possess all these qualities and capacities, or whatever qualities they do possess possess them in the same degree, we must form some sort of a general picture, which will be an ideal picture, and such a picture will be in effect our perfect librarian, as we measure perfection in our imperfect world.

We are quite familiar with the process in classification, not so much classification in libraries, which is, or ought to be, a purely practical affair, where logic and precision must give way to convenience, but classification in science. There we have ideal types, and according as the real objects to be classified agree with or depart from the type, we group them with this or another particular type, the type with which they have most in common. There is, by the bye, a quite wrong conception of this process amongst librarians and students, due to the fact that the textbooks on the subject are quite wrong. Dr. Richardson in his little book on classification seems to have misled everybody else. The mistake—and it *is* without any kind of question a mistake—lies in the assumption that the things we classify are real things. They are not, they are just abstractions of real things. We place a lion under the genus cat, but both the larger group of cats and the smaller group of lions are mentally abstracted bundles of characteristics; there is no general cat in nature, and the natural lion is an infinitely more complex aggregate than the lion of the zoologist. So that when Richardson says that a natural classification *must* follow the evolutionary order he is confusing nature with something which

[1] An address delivered at a meeting of librarians and assistants at Birmingham.

is a product of men's minds, and not in nature at all. Nothing in nature is classified. Nature doesn't classify. Men do.

But I mustn't wander from my subject before I've properly started. Suffice it that our perfect librarian is an artificial animal, whom none of us will ever come across, as nobody will ever encounter the zoological lion. But it strikes me as amusing that we all dislike perfection as if we'd met it and knew it, which, of course, we haven't outside a few things such as food; I've certainly experienced a perfect rice pudding; and Wordsworth described his wife as "a perfect woman, nobly planned," but then poetry, as Shakspere observes, is nothing but a kind of splendid lying.

Now obviously the best librarian in one kind of library wouldn't necessarily be the best in another. Contrast the following:

The librarian of the Laurentian library.

The librarian of a research department of a manufacturing firm.

The librarian of a commercial subscription library.

The librarian of Slocum-cum-Podgham. But he'll probably describe himself as chief librarian, and head his letter paper: "Librarian's office."

The City librarian of the great city of X——.

The librarian of the Laurentian library will be a scholar, learned in manuscripts and incunabula. Rare books to him will be like W. S. Gilbert's "dukes at two a penny."

The research librarian will have special knowledge of the technical side of his subject so far as it is represented in literature, and will spend a large part of his time in working up his material to meet the needs of a very limited body of readers, with highly specialized requirements. His main concern will probably not be with books, but magazines, transactions, reports, and clippings, the *disjecta membra* of books, and the flotsam and jetsam of his particular sea of print. Much of his matter, however valuable at the moment, is on its way to the W.P.B., to which sooner or later it will be relegated. He is a snapper-up of carefully considered trifles—the Autolycus of librarians.

The librarian of the subscription library is a tradesman. Nothing derogatory is intended; the modern world is little else but a colossal trading concern. One might describe him as a book-chef, whose business begins and ends with pleasing the palates of his customers, book gourmets, who want something tasty and easily digested. A good working motto for this kind of librarian is: "Serve 'em quick and serve 'em hot."

The librarian of Slocum-cum-Podgham, or as that really does sound derogatory, than which nothing is further from my intention, the librarian of the small public library, is in many respects our real bed-rock librarian. He buys books, catalogues and issues them, attends to his readers and advises them, guides his committee, does everything, or knows how to do everything. He lives in a small town, has no competitors, or none which count, knows everybody and everybody knows him. It is quite unnecessary for him to follow the example of the librarian of whom it was said by a fellow-townsman: if you see a man in our town with a top-hat, it's either the town crier or the librarian. No, the librarian's top-hat in his case is his job. If it weren't for the facts that his salary is usually too small and his hours too long, he would be the happiest public librarian of us all.

Then there's the chief librarian of X——. Speaking from my own experience only, mind, I assume he doesn't catalogue nor classify, and if he issued a book there would be consternation in the establishment, because he'd probably foozle the charge. He's an unknown quantity to the majority of his readers, for the major portion of his time is absorbed by administrative detail, and he might as well be running a big store as a library, except that he isn't worried by a profit and loss account. He has all the worries and few of the pleasures of librarianship.

Here then are some contrasted types. They are all librarians, but beyond the fact that they are concerned with books, the differences are seemingly as numerous as the similarities. But I don't intend that to trouble me, and for this simple reason: the perfect librarian is, in the very nature of the argument, competent to conduct successfully any and every sort of library. I shall therefore ignore these differences in jobs, important as they are.

I must also ignore another difference. In a medieval natural history, I remember that amongst other remarkable characteristics of the crocodile, it is stated: "He is sometimes male and sometimes female." Well, that is equally true of the perfect librarian. I may in my own secret mind be of opinion that it is long odds that the perfect librarian is a male—I say I may be, I don't say I am—but anyhow that would be mere prejudice, and cannot be seriously maintained, in face of the disconcerting fact that some of the most efficient librarians in this country, on the Continent, and in America are women.

I shall also have to assume the requisite technical equipment. There is, as it were, the common foundation; it is the superstructure of qualities which we erect on this foundation which distinguishes one man from another. Art begins, according to Arthur Symons, where technique leaves off. Librarianship begins where technique leaves off. The perfect workman may perhaps be defined as one who has the utmost skill in the use of his tools; but the craftsman only starts at this point, he must have in addition imagination, skill in design, and taste. There are plenty of librarians who are only workmen;

they may be good workmen, but they are not craftsmen, they are
not leaders. They will never be librarians in the sense in which
we are now employing the term. There are, however, certain
qualities required in the good technical librarian, which are important
elements in the make-up of the perfect librarian, and which it will be
convenient to deal with in relation to technique, which offers concrete
examples of their application. I refer especially to two of the fundamental processes, cataloguing and classifying.

I asked a member of my staff, who is in charge of the central
cataloguing at Manchester, to write down for me the qualities he
considered necessary for a good cataloguer. And, by the bye, there are
very few of him. He gave me a list of twenty-five qualities, and then
requested the return of the list, because he'd thought of some more!
I'm afraid that on that scale the analysis of the perfect librarian would
become absolutely terrifying. But No. 9 on his list is "Ability to
concentrate on essentials, and avoid side-tracking." That is very
much to the point, and I will consider it further in a moment. Another
of his qualities—an unexpected one in a cataloguer—is courage. I
like the example he gives, which is "Not shirking difficult books."
I also commend his No. 19, "Self-control," which is exercised in not
spending too much time reading books in which one is specially
interested. This is not a personal confession of my own weakness, but
if it were, I should have to plead guilty to that. I have endeavoured,
however, to offset it in the way one usually does counter one's own
weaknesses, viz., by being very severe on any member of the staff
who displays the same fault. The criticism that I would offer on these
and similar qualities in the list is that they belong to the basic virtues,
and have no more specific relation to the perfect cataloguer than to,
say, the perfect tram-conductor or the perfect barmaid. In fact I
should say less. The barmaid who didn't concentrate when fifty
people are clamouring for drinks during the three minutes' stop of
a train in a railway refreshment room, and who served a ginger-beer
to the man who ordered a whisky, would be irretrievably lost. As for
self-control, without *that* a barmaid would not only be lost, but damned.

I once heard a distinguished librarian discourse on the characteristics
of a good cataloguer, and I listened in vain for what is to my mind
the one supreme and pivotal quality of the cataloguer, without which
everything else is naught. And that is *accuracy*. Not ordinary accuracy,
but meticulous accuracy. To put a semicolon when the code requires a
colon; to add extraneous marks to a class symbol; to change or misspell
a word in a title; to do anything whatever except exactly what the
code permits: this in a cataloguer is arson, high treason, burglary—
everything that is illegal and wicked.

Yet accuracy is the rarest of virtues. I doubt if anybody is born accurate, as Pooh-Bah was born sneering. It is a virtue which has to be acquired, and comes from rigorous self-discipline. I think it is a compound quality, not an elementary one, and is partly mental and partly ethical. The mental part of it is the faculty of attention, itself an aspect of concentration, and the ethical part, a high sense of duty, duty to your work. Accuracy is needed in all library work, and people who are constitutionally, or from laziness, inaccurate, should try politics or journalism, where accuracy doesn't matter. It is part of the equipment of a tidy mind, and our perfect librarian must be as tidy in his mind as a Dutchman in his house and in his town. An inaccurate scholar is a contradiction in terms; an inaccurate librarian is a bad librarian.

Next to accuracy I am inclined to put that capacity to seize on essentials, already mentioned. It is a capacity perhaps more vital to the classifier than to the cataloguer. Subjects, and consequently books, tend to overlap to such an extent to-day, that the man who can't grasp the essential nature, or discover, so to speak, the spinal column of a book, on which all the bones hang, is hopeless as a classifier.

Another thing that the classifier can't get along without is general information. And here, I think, it will be well to drop associating characteristics with technical processes of any kind, and think in terms of the complete librarian, because there is no job that I know of where general knowledge is so desirable as that of the librarian. Every scrap of information he possesses he is sure to be able to find a use for some time or other. You can be a very good musician without either character or knowledge. You can be a quite good lawyer, and know little or nothing outside your avocation. But a really ignorant librarian is a catastrophe. And it is not altogether, or even chiefly, having a collection of odds and ends of facts that is wanted—valuable as that is— but rather that alert intelligence, based on a true culture, which is able to get quickly on speaking terms with any facts or ideas that present themselves for consideration. We speak of a man of the world, meaning a man who is easily at home in any society in which he finds himself. The librarian must be equally at home in the world of ideas.

This sort of *nous* is the most important to the librarian *qua* librarian of any of the qualities which are his sign manual, and it is precisely the lack of it that constitutes the most serious deficiency of the rank and file of library staffs. The things that so many of them don't know, don't want to know, maybe aren't capable of knowing, are staggering. I suppose that modern mechanized and unduly stressed vocational education is responsible, together with the revolt against the old-fashioned discipline, I speak, of course, from my own experience, and my own opinion has not been hastily formed,

Reverting to the quest and vision for essentials, this is a great need for the librarian as an administrator. Not necessarily to the *successful* administrator, as success in administration is commonly understood and measured. but to the really good one. Otherwise you will have an administrator who is nothing else, and the country abounds with administrators of this type. They never get outside their machinery. Machinery is regarded as an end in itself, and not a means. The good librarian must look beyond his machinery, and ask himself what it is his machinery is doing. If the machine is turning out sausages, are they the right kind of sausage?

In addition to his alert intelligence the librarian—I do not say here the perfect librarian, because the characteristic I am now going to mention should mark all librarians—must have the catholic mind. "My wife is a Presbyterian, but I am an early riser," said Artemus Ward. The librarian in his private capacity may be either, but officially he must be both, nay even an anti-Presbyterian and an anti-early riser as well. Most librarians are; the very nature of their work tends to a wide outlook. Like the aviator, his own little backyard disappears as he surveys the stretching expanse of literary land and sea.

Truly this business of being a librarian worthy of the calling is not an easy one. For the librarian must be born *and* made. He must start with the requisite intellectual, psychological and spiritual make-up, and he must sedulously train himself—I don't mean technically, for that is understood, and if he has the right kind of mind, it is not difficult By "right kind of mind" I imply the cataloguing mind, the classifying mind, etc.; some people haven't got this mind, and no amount of training in that case will turn them into first-class cataloguers or classifiers. But when I speak of training I refer to the larger and deeper things which have been mentioned, and others, which to deal with in this address would lengthen it inordinately. The capacity, for example, to "get on" with people of various natures and temperaments, to understand their point of view, however strange or alien to our own. I should like to point to a man like Edward Edwards, and say to you, *there* was the perfect librarian. But Edwards failed in cultivating the right relations with his committee, and the tragedy of his career was the consequence of that failure. He was a highly competent librarian, but not a highly competent public official, and the perfect librarian must be both, whether he serves in the latter rôle or no. Edwards did not understand his committee, and his committee did not understand him. But after all it wasn't the primary business of his committee to understand him; it *was* his business to understand them. So, as I said in the beginning, we must leave the perfect librarian in the region of ideals, along with the ideal woman and the ideal plumber.

But fortunately, there is no one of us who cannot rise to that view of our profession which was expressed by Dr. Carnegie, in his address to the Library Association, at the meeting in Glasgow in 1907: "Consecrate yourselves to your profession, for it is noble." Great words, that might well be inscribed in the council chamber of the new headquarters of the Association.

There are some professions and occupations which men have ever agreed are in a special sense "noble." Such among the professions are those of the priest and the physician. And if we ask whether there is any reasonable ground why the occupation of the doctor should be esteemed nobler than that of, let us say, the bank manager, the answer must be, I think, that there *is* a reason behind the popular idea on this matter, which I take to be this. The bank manager works for his living, the efficient physician, and still more the efficient priest, work, of course, for their living also, but in addition they work for the work's sake, and that work itself is noble, for it cannot be done rightly without some sacrifice of self. It is true that there are few occupations which cannot be ennobled by the manner in which they are performed, but in the cases of the priest and the physican the work itself is noble even though it be performed ignobly for the mere sake of gain. No priest can lend nobility and dignity to his calling, it is his calling which lends dignity to him and provides him with the opportunity for service. Happy are those who, in doing the necessary daily task which supports them, can find therein ample scope for that unselfish service to the community which every man who has risen beyond the limitations of the personal self and of the family, desires in the measure of his time and capacity and strength to perform. Was Dr. Carnegie then claiming too much that the profession of librarian is worthy to stand alongside those of the priest and of the physician? I think not. The association of the librarian with the physician is familiar to us from the oft-quoted inscription over the library at Alexandria, which I will not quote here. And I heard on one occasion Mr. H. G. Wells compare the position of the librarian of the future to the parish priest in the old days; what the parish priest was to his community, that the librarian will be to his, the successor of the priest of olden time. But this can only be partly true. In so far at the priest was the intellectual purveyor of his flock, *that* the librarian should endeavour to become, but the true sphere of the priest is, of course, that of the spiritual adviser, wherein the librarian may not enter. There are some people who look to see the priest disappear; not long ago a clergyman himself said to me: "I look forward to the time when the only priest will be the librarian." That is not my view. To the priest the spiritual, to the doctor the physical, and to the librarian the intellectual ministry of man. It is a splendid part for us to play. That we are almost ludicrously incapable of playing the part as yet let it be granted. The costume

> "*Hangs* loose about *us* like a giant's robe
> Upon a dwarfish thief"

but the dwarf will grow. There is a fine passage in the work of a curious and fantastic French writer which says that a man should bear himself *as if he were a dispossessed king who shall one day reascend his throne.* Let us remember that in the days gone by the librarian was a priest as well as a physician. And why therefore in the future should he not make good his claim to stand once more beside the physicians of the soul and of the body—one who has become three—but whose work dovetails together and is equally necessary for the building up of the perfect man? Why not?

From, Jast, L. S., *Libraries and living: essays and addresses of a public librarian*, 1932, pp. 83–93.

# CHAPTER 43

# William Warner Bishop (1871–1955)

"Are we as librarians, whatever our own special branch of library work, to incur the just reproach of real ignorance of our wares? Is there any way we may escape the consequences of our calling, our undue outward familiarity with masses of books?"

W. W. BISHOP.

THE influence of most librarians does not extend beyond the sphere of their respective libraries, but a few are able to affect national library policy, and a very small minority can boast of an international reputation. One such man was William Warner Bishop.

Born in 1871 in Hannibal, Missouri, W. W. Bishop had his early education in Detroit, and qualified A.B. and A.M. at Michigan University, studying classical literature, which enabled him to take his first post teaching Greek at Missouri Wesleyan College. In 1895 he went to the Garrett Biblical Institute, Evanston, Illinois as assistant librarian and instructor in New Testament Greek, where he remained until 1898. He then went to Rome as a fellow of the American School of Classical Studies, and upon his return to the United States was librarian and instructor in Latin at Brooklyn Polytechnical Institute, where he remained from 1899 to 1902. In the latter year Bishop joined the library staff at Princetown University as head of the Cataloguing Department, and after two years became reference librarian there. From 1907 to 1915 he was Superintendent of the Reading Room at the Library of Congress, where Herbert Putnam was Librarian, but 1915 saw Bishop's appointment as Librarian of the University of Michigan. There he remained until his retirement in 1941, when he was elected Librarian Emeritus, and a tribute edited by H. M. Lydenberg and A. Keogh was published in his honour.

At Michigan, Bishop planned the new library building opened in 1920, reclassified the collection by the Library of Congress scheme, and established a library school in 1926. He was President of the American Library Association (1918–1919), of I.F.L.A. (1931–1936) and of the Bibliographical Society of America (1921–1923). Many other honours were awarded to him, including honorary doctorates from eight universities and colleges. Bishop made numerous trips to Europe, purchasing books, attending conferences, and making friends wherever he went. Probably the best-known American librarian of his period, Bishop was the author of many books and articles, a list of which has been compiled by David Kaser. The collection of essays published in 1925 under the title *Backs of books* is outstanding, while Bishop's *Practical handbook of modern library cataloging*, first published in 1914, with a second edition in 1924, was translated into Russian and Chinese.

When William Warner Bishop died at Ann Arbor on February 19th, 1955, he left a gap in the profession, for men such as he forged together the bonds of international librarianship.

## REFERENCES

Gjelsness, Rudolph H. William Warner Bishop, 1871–1955. *Libri*, 6, 1955, pp. 3–5.

Kaser, David. William Warner Bishop: contributions to a bibliography. *Library Quarterly*, 26, 1956, pp. 52–60.

Lydenberg, Harry Miller, and Keogh, Andrew, *eds. William Warner Bishop: a tribute, 1941*, New Haven, London, 1941.

Mohrhardt, Foster. Dr. William Warner Bishop: our first international librarian. *Wilson Library Bulletin*, 32, 1957, pp. 207–215.

Obituary, by W. C. Berwick Sayers. *Library Association Record*, 57, 1955, p. 210.

## BISHOP ON THE BACKS OF BOOKS[1]

Few men who are called upon to address graduating classes in colleges and schools can refrain from the temptation to usurp the functions of the preacher. Here is an opportunity too tempting to be missed. The familiar surroundings so soon to be abandoned, the eager students facing their life-work, the parting of teachers and pupils, combine to set the commencement speaker in the way of moralizing on the situation, so well-worn by manifold predecessors, so painfully familiar to every audience of this sort. Try as I may to avoid preaching to you, I too shall probably be found pointing morals, if not adorning tales, for the occasion inevitably lends itself to the giving of gratuitous advice.

There are, however, some differences between the graduation of a class of prospective librarians and the ordinary school or college commencement. There is the obvious fact, which this class shares with all similar classes in professional schools, that you have been prepared for a specific line of work and are about to enter on the actual practice of your profession. The impending change from theory to practice faces likewise the graduates of schools of law, medicine, theology, and engineering. But your situation differs in at least one respect from theirs. For years they (and you) have been hearing lectures, working in laboratories, studying text-books. From books they have chiefly gathered the theory and training they are about to

[1] Address delivered at the Commencement Exercises, Library School, New York, Public Library, June 12th, 1914.

exercise on a more or less unwilling world. But you are to abandon the formal study of individual books as vehicles of knowledge for the practical handling of books in masses for the benefit of other people. In other words, you are to take what you have learned in a few books and apply it to the marshalling and serving of many books in libraries in aid of readers. What you have gained in theory is to be applied in practice to the very material from which the theory has been evolved, only the application is no longer for your own benefit, but for another's.

Your work therefore will necessarily involve a collection of books as a fundamental basis. Without books there are no libraries or librarians. It is occasionally necessary for some of us to speak up and say this plainly, for the library press and the discussion at conventions teem with so much talk about methods, about ways and means, about library extension, about librarians, that one sometimes wonders what it is all about, and where the books come in. So you will, perhaps, pardon an older librarian for speaking, not about his favorite methods in library work, not about the nobility of our calling, nor even the mission of the librarian, but just a bit about our books and the extent to which we know them. "*Die Hauptsache*", said a German scholar to me years ago in discussing libraries, "*Die Hauptsache ist die Bucher zu besitzen*". Absolutely fundamental, but too often neglected, is this cardinal principle of library economy. Without books, many, many books, there is no need for this school, or for this graduating class. The chief defect of our American libraries is, perhaps, the exaltation of method over content. To say this in the very home and citadel of training in method—a library school—may seem strange, even presumptuous; but to say it in the building which houses the noble collection of The New York Public Library is both safe, and, I trust, acceptable.

I wish, then, to speak very briefly on the librarian's knowledge of the books entrusted to his care (particularly in libraries of some size), on his familiarity with his collections. How far may he actually recall even the titles of books, much less know their contents? It is possible for a truly competent person to remember the names of practically all the authors and titles in a good-sized library? Of course definite answers to these questions are obviously difficult. But I call to mind many a librarian who certainly holds in his head many thousand separate titles, who can with an extraordinary quickness name different editions and publishers of books he has consulted but a few times. I once asked my honoured friend, Mr. Anderson H. Hopkins, then assistant librarian of the John Crerar Library, how far he was personally familiar with the books in that institution—I knew they had all passed

PLATE 15

WILLIAM REGINALD BRAY PRIDEAUX

(1880 – 1932)

(By kind permission of Mrs. Ruth Prideaux)

PLATE 16

WILLIAM JOHN BISHOP

(1903 – 1961)

through his hands (for the library was then new), and that he had a very retentive memory, but I was hardly prepared to hear him say that up to the first sixty thousand volumes purchased he could recall practically every title, but that above that number he began to lose track of the accessions. I am convinced that this was no over-statement, for in my own experience I have met not a few librarians whose knowledge of titles equalled his. Such men as Dr. Spofford and Mr. David Hutcheson of the Library of Congress doubtless knew intimately several times that number. And it is the familiar experience of reference librarians that at least appropriate titles, if not always the one best book, seem often to leap into memory to answer a reader's demand. The older choice libraries of about one hundred thousand volumes were probably pretty well held in mind by their directors, particularly when these were men of unusual ability.

It is a curious sort of knowledge, this acquaintance with a library. It is the backs of books that we know; those solemn rows that are seldom disturbed, those less stately ones whose battered appearance and unsteady carriage testify to their popularity. The familiar anecdote of the Kansas legislator who objected to an appropriation for more books for the university library touches peculiarly the librarian. "Mr. Speaker", said he, "I object to spending this money. Why, they've got forty thousand books there at Lawrence now, and I don't believe any one of them professors has read 'em all yet!" Neither have we read ours, and yet we know them, and sometimes know them well.

At least we know them well enough to help other folk to get what they want out of them. In every library in the world persons are constantly seeking material on topics which the librarian has never studied, and which he never will study. Unmoved and undismayed by his ignorance of, let us say, ballistics, or ceramics, or Egyptian tombs, he is somehow able to introduce the reader to the books on these or countless other subjects. And somehow, particularly if the librarian does not pretend to undue knowledge, the reader is often helped materially. He even feels grateful, and occasionally says so in print. (I pass over the times when he doesn't.) One knows the backs of books so well, and somehow has imbibed such a sense of their relative values, that the competent reference librarian becomes one of the most useful folk imaginable.

It should not be forgotten, however, that this knowledge is one of method fully as much as of the books or their appearance. The reader is generally unfamiliar with the order in which the books have been arranged and the means employed to list them. It is the librarian's intimate acquaintance with classification and cataloging which give him such an advantage over the reader in arriving quickly at desired books or information. You know the order in which your books fall. You know the ins and outs of your own catalog. You have at hand all manner of indexes and of catalogs of other libraries. So you give a man at once something to keep him occupied, while you hastily look up the things he really wants. And before he has time to thank you, you begin on the same process for half a dozen others. So it goes, day in and day out. Of course the backs of the books become familiar— you live with them. Of course it is easy to run down "aggravating ladies", and others who have frequently changed their names in print. You do it all the same. Of course you know that the British Museum Catalog enters biographies under the name of the subject. That fact has helped you out of many a tight place. It is this intimate acquaintance with the tools of the trade which makes for speed and accuracy. And precisely those librarians whose memory for the actual volumes on their shelves is most retentive are likely to know best both their tools and the proper method of using them. If we can perform what seem to the uninitiated sleight of hand tricks with cards and books, it is because we know well catalogs, classification, indexes. In fact, a knowledge of the classification in force in the library in which you are working almost takes the place (for practical purposes) of knowledge of the contents of the books themselves.

Let me illustrate this: A friend brought me what appeared to be a genuine manuscript letter of the German poet Schiller. It was addressed to his sister, and all in his handwriting. And yet it looked a trifle suspicious. Despite the appearance of age it had a little the air of a facsimile. But my friend thought it might be an original letter—it had been given to him as a valued possession. Now I am no Schiller scholar. I painfully waded through *Wilhelm Tell* in college, and once, even more painfully, conducted a class through *Die Jungfrau von Orleans*. I had never heard of Fritz Jonas's celebrated edition of Schiller's correspondence. But I did know where the Schiller books were, and that there was among them a set of volumes of letters. In three minutes I went to the place, found the authoritative-looking set, picked out the year and day of the letter, and discovered a footnote to the effect that some one had caused an admirable facsimile of this letter to be lithographed and that efforts were constantly being made to sell it as an original.

Now, this incident will bear analysis. It is typical of much that goes on in our service. The query was not simple. But the means of answering it to the entire satisfaction of the inquirer were really primitive. They consisted merely in a knowledge that there was once a German poet named Schiller, that he had a place in our classification, that his books were shelved in a certain part of our stacks, and that, as a rule, editors arrange correspondence in chronological order. I knew no more about German poetry, or Schiller, or Schiller's letters, when the transaction was over than when it began. But my friend—who is a man of much learning and—I may be pardoned for saying it—one of our foremost scientists, seems firmly convinced that I can find him anything in German literature which he wishes to know. You see on how slight a foundation of real knowledge one can and does perform his daily duties. The backs of books! How they help us! How well do little matters of shape, size, color, location, impress themselves indelibly upon us and aid us to earn our living!

But precisely this facility in helping people to find things has too often a most unwholesome influence on the librarian's attitude toward the world of knowledge. It can not but tend to render him neglectful of that real and sound study which alone gives fibre and substance to his mind. The numbing force of inertia must be reckoned with. We are all busy—too busy. We move along the lines of least resistance. We content ourselves with knowing the backs of our books, with a familiarity with labels and groupings in lieu of ideas. Too soon *you* are likely to discover that executive work absorbs the greater part of your powers. Too soon the habit of doing pretty well in your work without much reading and study becomes fixed. If you can recall titles easily, can locate desired information quickly, can send a reader to this or that place where his books are to be found, and meantime keep an eye on the needs of half a score of others, you begin unconsciously to think well of yourself and to ignore the fact that man does not live by bread alone.

The wisest man I have ever been privilegde to know once said to me: "You can be very useful. You can help a great many people. You can perhaps do a great work. *But*, if you stay in library work, your mind will be an intellectual rag-bag after ten years."

What is the remedy? Are we to be content with this "bowing acquaintance", as Emerson called it, with the books on our shelves? Are we to be satisfied with bright and parti-colored scraps of information, mental confetti? Are we as librarians, whatever our own special branch of library work, to incur the just reproach of real ignorance of our wares? Is there any way we may escape the consequences of our calling, our undue outward familiarity with masses of books?

It is, of course, impossible, even if it were wise, in this day of large libraries to recommend an effort to know the insides of all the books, or even of the better books, in our collections. They are too many even for the most indefatigable reader, to say nothing of the busy librarian. It is equally unwise to urge you to neglect the knowledge of titles and of classification, of the backs of your books. Cultivate that by all means. It means bread and butter, whatever your particular function in a library. But by all means keep yourselves "sweet", as our fathers used to say, by some intensive work which involves study. I have the greatest respect for the man with a hobby—even if he proves a nuisance at times. Without a hobby life is not worth living. You should have one—a real hobby which becomes vastly more important to you than any mere business can be. I would not prescribe the kind of hobby a librarian should ride. My advice, or any one's else for that matter, would be unavailing. A hobby cometh not with understanding, any more than falling in love. But it is sometimes as happy a possession as a true help-meet, and occasionally as disastrous as an unfortunate marriage. A hobby which will refresh in your hours of weariness, attract when you are lazy, and inspire when you are worn, is precious beyond words.

But a hobby, whether golf, or gardening, or bird-study, or collecting china, or any other like expensive and joyous pastime, is not enough to pull a busy librarian from the slough of inertia as regards books. Indeed, it may tend to keep him there, the more if he wisely takes to some sane supreme interest—out of doors. A line of study which is peculiarly your own will do more for you than you can possibly know at this stage of your careers. A small specialty which you have cultivated to the point where you know with almost complete fullness the literature of the topic is worth vastly more to you than the mere knowledge you acquire in it. The very fact of intensive study of a small topic keeps you in touch with methods and men, and is an admirable corrective to the scattering tendencies of our calling. I know a librarian who started in years ago reading everything he could on our Civil War. He kept it up amid purely executive duties until even specialists in military history now come to him for aid, and the government itself seeks his advice in matters of historical accuracy. He is concerned with the purely business side of a great library, but his extensive knowledge produced by steady reading has kept him in touch with the world of letters in a very vital way. The best man I know in matters economic and statistical knows also (purely as a side issue) more about English poetry, particularly the minor poets, than any professor of English I ever knew. And he is an active librarian, a graduate of a library school, and an "alumnus" of the New York Public Library.

No librarian need despair, if only he sets inflexibly this goal before him, of attaining to productive scholarship. We recall Justin Winsor, who administered in able fashion two great libraries, and yet edited the

*Narative and Critical History,* to say nothing of other books; Dr. J. K. Hosmer whose array of volumes in English and American History is more than the product of mere industry, and whose *Color Guard* and *Thinking Bayonet* pulsate with the great struggle of the sixties; Reuben Gold Thwaites whose monument will be the *Jesuit Relations* rather than the Wisconsin Historical Society's library; Dr. Poole who will live in his *Index* long after his other library labors at Yale, Cincinnati and Chicago are forgotten; and last, and greatest of all, Dr. John Shaw Billings, soldier, physician, author, director of great enterprises, yet a librarian who built up by incessant labor the greatest specialized library in the world, and then at an age when most men seek retirement, with unmatched patience, wisdom and zeal wrought the New York Public Library into an organic whole and housed it in this resplendent palace. With these men in mind—and others whom time fails me to mention—who of us shall be content with mere skill in technique, with mere facility of movement among printed things, with mere knowledge of the backs of books?

I said I should probably fall into the habit of the preacher. Full well do I remember that professors of homiletics always urge that the sermon close with an "application". Perhaps some of you are saying —"I am not to go into reference work. I am to be a cataloger, or to have charge of a branch library, or to aid in library extension. These warnings are not for me." But they are for you, and for every one of us librarians. Whatever our peculiar part in library work, we can not escape the inevitable tendency to treat books as the mere vehicle on which we exercise our skill; we can not fail to gain a certain superficial exterior acquaintance with them. The longer we know and live with the back of books, the more we shall need the tonic which comes from our own special line of research. Ordinarily, specialists grow narrow, but deep; librarians too often grow broad, but shallow. Begin now, therefore, when you are starting in to practice your profession, to cultivate intensively some one field. Hold to it as the years go by. Dig deeply and wisely into the accumulated store of wisdom which the ages have deposited in your little area. And give the world the ripened fruit you have grown. Thus will you give the lie to Mark Pattison's often misapplied dictum: "The librarian who reads is lost."

From, Bishop, William Warner. *Backs of books, and other essays in librarianship,* London Baltimore, 1926, pp. 1-14.

# CHAPTER 44

# Septimus Albert Pitt (1878–1937)

"At all times he kept his singularly agile, though cautious, mind alert to assess the value and the possibility of new ideas."

J. M. MITCHELL.

SEPTIMUS ALBERT PITT was born at Low Fell, Co. Durham, in 1878, and at the age of fourteen became assistant in the South Shields Public Library, two years later occupying the position of Sub-Librarian when less than seventeen years of age. He occupied a similar position at Aberdeen from 1898 to 1901, when he went to the Gorbals Library, Glasgow as Librarian. Two years later Pitt became superintendent of branch libraries, but in 1908 went to Coventry as City Librarian. However, he returned to Glasgow in 1915, where he greatly extended the library services. He organized the first municipal commercial library in this country, and was an ardent advocate for their development in other areas. Pitt opened the music department at the Mitchell Library, and issued a union catalogue of the Glasgow libraries which was published in two volumes, 1929–1934.

Pitt served the Library Association as a member of the Council from 1915, Vice-President in 1920, and as President in 1934, but during this latter term of office he suffered severely from ill health. In 1924 he served on the Departmental Committee on Public Libraries, and also reported on the library services in South Africa and Kenya for the Carnegie Corporation of New York.

Septimus Pitt was a very thorough and cautious worker, who rendered great services to the libraries with which he was connected, to the Library Association, and to librarianship in general. Unfortunately he died on August 27th, 1937, at the age of 59, and the inspiration of a remarkable personality was removed prematurely.

REFERENCE

Past-President Pitt. Died August 27th, 1937. *Library Association Record*, 39, 1937, pp. 552–556. Appreciations by E. A. Savage, J. M. Mitchell, A. M. Williams, W. C. Berwick Sayers, and Charles Nowell.

## PITT ON THE LIBRARY ASSOCIATION

The enthusiasm of the original members of The Library Association was most notable. All sorts of projects were suggested and considered:

A General Catalogue of English Literature, A Book Classification Scheme first suggested by Dr. F. T. Barrett, A Manual of Librarianship, first mooted by Sir John MacAlister, and other schemes, small and large, some very large. All these projects came to nothing for want of money and workers. In its middle period the Association became little more than a debating society on library topics, sometimes a rather ill-tempered debating society, and during this period very little constructive work was accomplished. Probably the Sound Leather Committee, under the guidance of E. Wyndham Hulme, gave some of the best results, but apart from this and a few other very minor activities, and apart from its debating opportunities, the work of the Association was barren for many years. Now there are many branches of librarianship in which it is essential that research should be undertaken and that data should be collected. It is not desirable, now that an increased membership gives us strength and increases the number of our workers, that some of this work which is waiting to be done should be tackled? The attainment of maturity has brought with its greater opportunities and wider responsibilities than those given to the Association in its infant and adolescent stages, and we shall be judged according to the degree to which we initiate and stimulate the essential activities and developments made possible by our growth and increased resources.

Very important changes have taken place during the last two decades, and never were the opportunities greater and more numerous than they are today for those interested in the library movement. But it is clear that the need for wise direction is equally emphatic. Just as the Royal Commission of 1849 indicated a great and fallow field, so did the Departmental Committee's Report of 1927 describe conditions and suggest advancement. Stimulated as public libraries were during the later years of last century and the earlier years of this by the princely gifts of generous benefactors, they have been equally aided by the liberal and systematic policy of the Carnegie United Kingdom Trust which has carried out with knowledge and vision its founder's views.

· · · ·

Fifty-seven years ago The Library Association was inaugurated at the First International Conference of Librarians held in London. Two hundred and sixteen persons were enumerated as Members of the Conference, including overseas representatives, and 114 of these came from libraries in Great Britain and Ireland. The foundation of the Association, with its object "to unite all persons engaged or interested in library work, for the purpose of promoting the best possible administration of existing libraries, and the formation of new ones where desirable," . . . and "the encouragement of bibliographical research," was very properly claimed by Mr. H. R. Tedder to be a practical result of the Conference which left to the Association the task of continuing the good work the Conference had commenced.

The Conference met in the London Institution by the hospitality of the Board of Management, and during the fifty-six years following the Association continued to carry on its work in rooms either lent or rented.

Many of the most significant changes which have influenced recent development date from the year 1915. In that year the Carnegie United Kingdom Trustees issued the Report prepared at their request by Professor W. G. S. Adams, which included recommendations resulting later in the establishment of county libraries. In the following year the fore-runner of the National Central Library had its origin in the Central Library for Students. The years 1918–1920 will remain outstanding for legislative measures, *inter alia*, those constituting Counties as library areas and extending or removing limits on the rate for the support of libraries. In 1927 we had the Report of the Departmental Committee on Public Libraries in England and Wales, followed two years later by a similar publication for the Libraries of Northern Ireland. Then last year, largely as the result of the benevolent aid and encouragement of the Carnegie United Kingdom Trust—exercised continuously throughout the period under review—Chaucer House and the new premises for the National Central Library were opened.

Other events and projects encourage us to be hopeful about future progress. The new Manchester Library, the nearly completed Cambridge University Library, the projected huge extension to the Bodleian, and the emergence of the Leeds University Library as one of the most important in the country, justify me, I think, in describing this as a time of great library building—such a time as we have not seen hitherto in the history of the Association. Among other events of the same hopeful kind I note the success of the fund for purchasing the *Codex Sinaiticus*. The fact that so large a sum of money has been raised so quickly in these times is heartening testimony to the foresight of our past President, Sir Frederic Kenyon, to the public's belief that the British Museum should continue to remain the chief literary treasure house of the nation, and the result is a complete answer to those few critics who received the project with so little faith and even less judgment.

.        .        .        .        .        .

Under greatly improved conditions what is to be our future programme? The Report of the Departmental Committee, based on official replies to systematic enquiry, made important pronouncements regarding existing conditions and offered suggestions toward betterment. It not only revealed the absence of library provision from many urban districts, but indicated that half the county population of 12,000,000 was similarly unprovided for eight years ago. Where services had been established and were ineffective, recommendations were submitted with the object of bringing about improvements to enable them to meet reasonable requirements. Schemes were outlined with a view to securing the better selection of books and the establishment of a central cataloguing agency. The recruitment and training of staffs was carefully considered and suggestions for future practice were made. And, among other important features of the Report, the ideal of an organized national library service was set forth with the proposed changes in legislation to make such a service effective.

Unfortunately, as an Association, our reactions to the inspiration offered by the Report have proved disappointing. A glance at the "Annals" discloses the fact that, although the Council have incidentally made slight progress affecting some of the Committee's suggestions, no definite and systematic action has been taken to bring about the conditions envisaged by the Report. Indeed, we have evidence that on some matters, regarding which the Report is very explicit, recommendations have either not been adopted or have been only partially accepted. This, however, need not affect the attitude of the Association on the question of its future policy and programme. Responsibility for the extension of the relevant acts to areas unprovided with library service remains one of the objects of the Association stated in the Royal Charter, and continues to be an important function of the Association.

Nor can the Association conscientiously remain inactive in regard to those areas in which a library service exists in name rather than in practice. Local acceptance of a low and inadequate standard of provision is one of the worst possible advertisements for the movement generally, and the library service, as a whole, cannot even approximate to present day requirements until much improvement has been made in the backward areas.

    .       .       .       .       .

The training of staff is an ever pressing problem which demands continuous attention, and it is perhaps well that we should not lose sight of the fact that some of the difficulties involved are largely of our own creation. At the moment, professional educational provision and examination falls into two separate and unrelated forms. The first, which was founded in the earlier days of The Library Association, offers the student of library practice and associated subjects tuition by correspondence and short term summer schools, and provides professional examinations, the ultimate aim of which is the Diploma. The second is the University of London School of Librarianship, which was established on the representations of the Library Association, in 1919. It is not without interest to note that during the last year more than 1,600 candidates sat at the examinations of the first, while 128 students enrolled in the second. The two examination systems are now equated, but each body continues to issue its own Diploma—a state of affairs which is not desirable. Inevitably, questions of the comparative value of the diploma must arise, and wisdom suggests a thorough and early analysis of the situation if the bitterness of professional partisanship, with all its distasteful concomitants, is to be avoided. In my opinion the remedy lies in the establishment of a joint examinational board representing the University, the Association, and Employers of Librarians.

.    .    .    .

For the first time in the history of the Association it has become possible to establish in premises of our own a centre for the collection and dissemination of information regarding every branch of library work. The establishment of an efficiently organized information bureau, reinforced by a well-equipped library, should prove an invaluable centre for the accumulation of records and data on all topics embraced by library interests. To it, we should hope, the librarian would turn as a matter of course when seeking guidance on any of the many problems to which the desire for progress gives rise. Records relating to new and altered buildings, systems of heating and lighting, designs for furnishings and decoration, and notes on new and unusual materials should all be readily accessible to the members. There should be concentrated in the Bureau the maps of library areas showing how the units of service are co-ordinated, and with them should be seen the plans of the libraries themselves, with particulars of cost of sites, of erection, and of maintenance, and such information about service as might be helpful to others likely to be faced by questions of a similar nature. In this connection it is worthy of note that a Committee of the Council has been appointed to pursue enquiries with a view to the publication of serviceable facts relating to library buildings and their equipment. The first of a series of papers will deal with the subject of "Sites," and this and subsequent publications will, it is believed, make valuable addition to the information otherwise available, and bring it up-to-date. Recent developments in the design, materials, and methods used in the construction of buildings and their equipment, have almost revolutionized what was not long ago accepted as standard.

The Bureau should also aim to be the repository of information on the diverse methods of library operation, of classification, cataloguing, and the treatment of stock, of the filing of maps, plans, pamphlets, papers and cuttings, and of the preparation of statistics.

At each annual meeting a display of new materials and methods would form an attractive and valuable practical exhibit offering all who wish to note improvements an opportunity of familiarizing themselves with recent progress.

At the Headquarters there should be accessible the technical library for librarians, which should include the literature published not only by our own Association, but by similar bodies elsewhere, all works about the library movement, and kindred publications.

The productions of our own Publications Committee should be prominently exhibited there. In his remarks at the Harrogate Conference Mr. Savage referred to publications of a kind which might properly engage the attention of our Publications Committee. He instanced particularly the series *Reading with a Purpose*, issued by the American Library Association and gave figures indicating that they met with a ready sale in America, largely through public libraries and very probably to readers using those libraries. We certainly have a similar need and, I believe, a relatively good market for productions of the same kind suitable for our public. In the absence of something more ambitious I would stress the need for guides to the best standard works which are looked for in every public library.

In addition to its technical library the Association now has accommodation for the exhibition of selected current literature. It may not be possible to maintain such a display on a large scale, or to incorporate from week to week the most recent additions, but by periodical revision of the selection and the showing of such new publications as merit exhibition, a really useful purpose might be served.

Much valuable work is being done up and down the country by the provision of guides to the literature of special subjects, and it is a matter for regret that the publications as a rule are available only to local readers. It takes little effort of the imagination to calculate how the value of this work would be increased inordinately if the outcome of it were available to every reader in the land. The correlation and distribution of such guides is a task that might well fall within the purview of the Publications Committee's activities. I have in mind such guides as those on Music and other subjects produced by the Leeds Public Libraries and sold at prices bringing them within the reach of almost any reader. These must have provided invaluable guidance to large numbers of student-readers in Leeds. If, by agreement, the Publications Committee could have issued these guides and given the benefit of their production to readers in different towns and countries, where the books included in the prints are available, the benefits would have been greatly extended.

In reviewing the situation as it exists to-day, notwithstanding the improved position of libraries and their greater potentialities individually and collectively, it is necessary to keep before us the need for further legislation. From a comparison of the powers vested in County and Borough authorities in England and Wales, it is clear that there is considerable room for amendment and extension which would result in improved administration. On many of the points raised in the Report of the Departmental Committee suggestions are made for the betterment of library service by alteration of, or addition to, library Acts. In Scotland there is urgent need for the additional powers which have been granted to England and Wales. To mention only the most important of these, I would draw attention to the fact that, while county libraries are empowered to co-operate with public libraries, no such right is conferred on the burghs; and that the amount of rate which may be fixed for the support of libraries in counties is left to the discretion of library authorities, while in towns the restriction on rate—removed in England and Wales—still remains. Although regional service has been established and makes good progress south of the border, it is impossible under present conditions on the Scottish side.

As Regional co-operative services throughout the country must necessarily form the foundation of an organized national service, no petty legislative obstacles should be allowed to prevent progress. The ideal of the national service should be ever in the minds of all who have the interest of libraries at heart and towards its achievement every member of the Association should be ready to contribute his share.

Omitting reference to activities in which the Association should engage jointly with other bodies, I have attempted to point out the form and direction which some of our efforts should take, and here it may not be inappropriate to say a word about ourselves in our constitutional relations.

I have not discussed our internal organization, although I am well aware of points of weakness that could hardly fail to develop in conditions of our rapid growth in recent times. As membership continues to increase and the strength of the various sections grows—often disproportionately—there will arise the possibility of disruptive tendencies through divergent and necessarily partisan views. This is a danger that must be guarded against if we are to retain and consolidate our improved position. The weaknesses that emerge will, in due course, be eliminated by time and the patient tolerance of those affected by them. And so I end with an appeal for the development of the spirit of unity which has brought us where we are—an appeal to every member of the Association to devote himself, or herself, to its main objects, and to contribute through sections of the Association the maximum effort towards that ideal of national service to which our present position is such a long step forward.

From, Pitt, S. A. Presidential Address. The Library Association: retrospect and prospect. London Conference, September, 1934. *Library Association Record*, 4th Series, 1, 1934, pp. 297–301.

# CHAPTER 45

# William Reginald Bray Prideaux (1880–1932)

"He is particularly remembered for his lectures on cataloguing, and was instrumental in procuring the preparation of a register of professional librarians by the Library Association."

WHEN he died on June 19th, 1932 W. R. B. Prideaux numbered many past students of the University of London School of Librarianship among his friends, for he had lectured at the School since its foundation in 1919. All librarians respected him, for he was modest and helpful, and did thoroughly everything to which he set his hand.

Prideaux was born in London on September 20th, 1880 and went to New Zealand at the age of six. He was educated at Auckland Grammar School, and returned to London in 1898. In 1904 he took a B.A. degree at the Royal University of Ireland, and his first library appointment was that of assistant in the Royal College of Physicians Library, London. In October, 1905, he became Librarian of the Reform Club, and spent the remainder of his professional life in that capacity, although for a period after the first world war he was also part-time librarian to Henry S. Wellcome, whose collection has grown into the Wellcome Historical Medical Library. Prideaux served on the Library Association Council and on various committees. His advice was never sought in vain, and he was always interested in medical librarianship and in early printing.

As a lecturer Prideaux appeared to lack self-confidence, but the theory of cataloguing was not a very inspiring subject to teach. On one occasion he talked to his class for ten minutes, and then suggested that there was something better to listen to at the London School of Hygiene, where C. C. Barnard was lecturing on the Library. Prideaux proceeded to lead the way to Keppel Street, and indulged his interest in medical librarianship, to the great satisfaction of at least one member of the class.

He wrote little, but his papers were carefully compiled, and include "The medical libraries of London" (*Library Association Record*, 8, 1906, pp. 405–422); "Professional education and registration: some suggestions" (*Ibid.*, 8, 1906, pp. 1–6, discussion pp. 20–27), which led to the formation of the Register of qualified librarians and is reproduced below; "Library economy (chiefly Continental) at the end of the seventeenth century" (*Ibid.*, 6, 1904, pp. 129–138); "Library economy in the sixteenth century" (*Ibid.*, 11, 1909, pp. 152–174, also reprinted in the same year); "Some thoughts on indexing" (*Library Association Record*, 2nd Ser., 3, 1925, pp. 160–169); and "Cataloguing codes and card printing" (*Ibid.*, 3rd Ser., 1, 1931, pp. 41–51), based on a lecture delivered at University College, London.

W. R. B. Prideaux was of the type forming the salt of librarianship. Unassuming, but knowledgeable, he was ready to help all in search of advice, and a friend contributing an obituary notice wrote, "he was a good friend and ally, and had an instinct for being on the side of the angels." (Portrait, Plate 15.)

### REFERENCES

Obituary. *Library Association Record*, 3rd Ser., 2, 1932, p. 227.
Obituary. *Library World*, 35, 1932–1933, p. 18.

## Prideaux on Professional Education and Registration

You are all doubtless well aware that there are at present two schools of annotators—namely, annotators proper and evaluators. I hope that you will all belong to the latter at the end of this paper. Both schools are agreed in one particular, namely, that the special qualifications of the author should always be stated. The only special qualification for dealing with the education question that I can put forward is, that it has been my good fortune to have attended one or more courses of lectures arranged by the Education Committee every year since 1899. I am, in short, an *experimentum in corpore vili*.

The subject has thus occupied my attention in a practical way for some years, and I venture to submit to your judgments the results of my cogitation thereon.

I must begin by stating that this paper is not so fully worked out as I had wished, but I plead in extenuation that it has been put down for a much earlier date in the session than I expected.

We are all of us agreed—theoretically at least—that one of the principal objects of this Association is the professional training of librarians and the words of our Charter are explicit on the subject: "The purpose of the Corporation are: (3) To promote whatever may tend to the improvement of the position and the qualifications of Librarians."

Charters are granted to promote the organisation of a given sphere of work and we should be neglecting our plain duty if we did not keep this question of education in the forefront. The cynic may say— in fact has frequently said—that the Council has done practically nothing so far in this direction. This is simply not true. It is not my purpose to detail here what has been accomplished, but I refer any one interested to the paper prepared by Mr. Roberts for the St. Louis Conference. I may also point out what an enormous advantage it is to have regular courses of instruction, especially if delivered in connection with a recognised educational body. To have worked through even an imperfect scheme of instruction is far more valuable than to learn little bits haphazard.

No one who has gone into the matter can fail to recognise the good work done by the Council in the face of great difficulties, but it must be admitted that there still remains a great deal to do. The leaven is working slowly, for only a small fraction of library assistants have as yet risen to the opportunities of technical instruction now offered them. For the future of the profession it is necessary that the numbers undergoing a proper course of training should be largely increased, in fact this should be regarded as the normal qualification for any one seeking positions of responsibility in the library world.

Why then have the numbers been comparatively so few up to now? First because we do not really believe in the value of education—for the most part we but pay it lip service. Belief is the ground of all action. We act on what we believe. I simply ask in this connection what proportion of the members of this Association press on their subordinates the claims of technical training? If even one-half or one-third of the members on our roll were to draw the attention of those working under them to the classes organised for their benefit, and were to give a little encouragement to aspirations towards fuller knowledge, there can be no doubt that in a short while the numbers undergoing systematic training would be largely increased.

There are several reasons why heads of libraries do not press this matter on their assistants: indifference, mental lethargy, disapproval of the present scheme, and many others. Among them in some cases there will, I think, be found on introspection a slight twinge of jealousy that juniors should have an opportunity of obtaining certificates and such-like adornments which were not open to older members of the profession, and which, taken in the wrong spirit, might interfere with the proper maintenance of discipline and obedience. I am not prepared to say that this feeling is altogether unjustifiable, while it is manifestly absurd that the very teachers of library subjects should be without the hall-mark of technical experience obtainable by their pupils.

It will be readily conceded that membership of this Association is not in itself a guarantee of ability to administer a library. We count among our number—and are proud to count among our number—many interested in the library movement, but who lay no claim to the qualifications necessary for the conducting or large institutions. We are, in short, not an Association of librarians—but an Association "to unite all persons engaged or interested in library work."[1]

On the other hand, it is one of the recognised duties of chartered institutions to indicate to the public in a general way those who are qualified by training or experience in the particular branch of knowledge concerned. Thus the Institute of Chemistry indicates those who are qualified to hold the position of analyst; the Medical Register is a list of those who have undergone special training to fit them for the practice of medicine.

You will doubtless see by this time the suggestion I have in my mind —the establishment of a professional register of librarians. It does not seem to me an impossible task. I believe we should have under our present Charter powers to establish a "Register of persons considered competent to administer a library." Of course compulsion would be out of the question, but a very good beginning could be made with optional registration, as in the case of many other institutions.

It is of first importance that the qualifications for admission to the register should be laid down clearly and definitely, and afterwards they should be adhered to firmly in every case. Of course all those who have passed the three sections of the examination should be entitled to registration, provided they have had at least three years' practical experience in a library, but in addition it will be necessary to create the main body of registered librarians. This might consist I think, of the heads of the libraries of over (say) 20,000 vols.[2] who have been engaged in library work for at least three years previously. After registration had been on this footing for a given time, for example a year, no one should be admitted except in the ordinary way of examination.

The diploma might be, not a registering, but an honours qualification, obtainable by those who have passed the three sections of the examination, on presenting a thesis on some subject agreed to by the Education Committee, provided they have already passed some general examination such as the London Matriculation, the Oxford and Cambridge Senior Local, or others of like standing. The latter is an important provision, for it would not be creditable to the Library Association if its honoursmen were lacking in general education.

I venture to suggest that the standard of the pass examinations be not at first placed impossibly high. The standard can be raised later by little and little—a process which has been going on for example in the medical profession since 1858. The training should be as practical as possible, so that others outside the ranks of librarians might find it

---

[1] See words of Charter.
[2] This suggestion was withdrawn in the course of debate. See supplementary note.

worth their while to take one or more of the certificates. For example, classes might be instituted in book indexing, and if those who do this the publishers could be induced to attend, I feel sure that a notable advance in the practice of this art would result, much to the benefit of librarians and authors alike.

The formation of a register in the way I propose is not by any means without a precedent. I will cite one analogous case, but there are many others. In 1878 the Dentists Act was passed, which provided for the formation of an official register of dentists. In the first instance the body of registered dentists was to consist of all those who had received a licence in dental surgery from certain colleges, together with all those who were *bona fide* engaged in the practice of dentistry, at the time of the passing of the Act. After that date only those licensed by the various colleges were to be admitted. If in such an important matter as dentistry the Government saw fit that the actual practice of a profession should in the first instance be sufficient qualification for entrance to the register, surely there can be no impropriety in drawing up an optional register of librarians on the same principle.

Now let us consider for a moment what would happen if a register as outlined above were established. The large State and copyright libraries will almost certainly stand aloof, as they have their own methods of examination and entrance, but a large percentage of municipal librarians should become enrolled. This being the case, if they will only pull together for once, it ought to be possible that in a few years' time all important appointments in public libraries should go to registered librarians. The library authorities of universities, colleges and learned societies would no doubt at first be absolutely indifferent on the subject, but they would probably in time get to see that, other things being equal, trained and registered men were better than untrained men, and the competition of the labour market would soon tend to make those applying for such posts become duly enrolled and qualified.

With regard to title, I fear that "Chartered Librarian" on the model of "Chartered Accountant" would be inadmissible, as no special provision for a register is made in the charter; but no objection could be taken to "Registered Librarian", which would be quite sufficient to distinguish those on the roll—who will not necessarily be members of the Association—from ordinary members. Of course a fee of greater or less magnitude would have to be paid for the privilege of registration, and I do not fancy that our Treasurer would have any objection to that. In passing, I may say that the plan of allowing candidates to enter for examinations and gain certificates for nothing seems to me a bad one, and not calculated to raise them in the estimation of the public. At the very least, written certificates, if required by successful candidates, should be charged for, even though bare notification be included in the examination fee. This is done by many educational bodies.

Finally, the advantages of registration may be thus summed up:—

(1) A homogeneous body of working librarians would be formed who would feel that they have interests in common and would act accordingly.

(2) The Library Association would be more free to press its membership on owners of private libraries and those interested in library work. The development of this side of its membership would give it greater financial and intellectual stability, and more influence on legislation.

(3) An enormous impetus would be given to the examination scheme, the classes of the Association would become recognised as the normal training school of librarians, and the efficiency of the profession at large would be raised.

Fellow members, I do not pretend to show you the way things should be done. I leave that to leveller heads and riper intellects than my own. I simply present to you for what they are worth my own ideas on the subject of education and registration.

## SUPPLEMENTARY NOTE

It came out clearly in the course of the debate that the number of volumes in a library did not form a good basis for registration. The suggestion is therefore withdrawn, and the annual amount expended on the library offered as a substitute. Another point, accidentally omitted from the paper, is that assistant librarians of important libraries should be eligible for registration. This might also be arranged on an income basis.

Prideaux, W. R. B. Professional education and registration: some suggestions. *Library Association Record*, 8, 1906, pp. 1-6.

# CHAPTER 46

# *Arundell Esdaile (1880–1956)*

"One thing is sure. If boys and girls do not get the reading habit in their teens they never will. Even if they do when they come to middle age they will have too little time, but will forever promise themselves a retired old age of making up for lost time by reading the unread books. And who shall say if that time will be theirs?"

ARUNDELL ESDAILE.

ARUNDELL JAMES KENNEDY ESDAILE was born in London on April 25th, 1880 and was educated at Lancing and Magdalene College, Cambridge before entering the Department of Printed Books at the British Museum in 1903. His professional life was served at the Museum, of which he was Secretary from 1926 to 1940, but his numerous other activities made him world-renowned as a bibliographer, a keen student of literature, a poet, and a man with a fund of deep-seated knowledge at his command. This knowledge was freely available to those in search of information, and despite his rather formidable appearance, his friendliness was extended to even the most junior member of the profession seeking advice. Esdaile is remembered by large numbers of students who attended the School of Librarianship at University College, London, where he was Lecturer on Bibliography from 1919 to 1939. His book *A student's manual of bibliography* was written primarily for these students, and was published in 1931 as the first of the Library Association Series with a nominal second edition printed a year later. The third edition, edited by Roy Stokes and published in 1954, maintains this important textbook up to date without obliterating all traces of the original author's personality.

The honours accorded to Arundell Esdaile are recorded elsewhere, and appreciations also catalogue his achievements and publications. He was Prior of the Johnson Club (1925–1926), and Sanders Reader in Bibliography at Cambridge University (1926–1927), his lectures there being published as *The sources of English literature* in 1928, with a second edition issued in 1929. He edited the *Library Association Record* from 1923 to 1935, and the *Year's Work in Librarianship* from 1929 to 1939. In the latter year he was elected President of the Library Association, and continued in that office until 1945.

In addition to the above-mentioned books, Esdaile was the author of *Verses and translations*, 1906; *Bibliography of George Meredith*, 1907;

*List of English tales and romances printed before 1740*, 1912; *National libraries of the world*, 1934, of which a new edition revised by F. J. Hill was published by the Library Association in 1957; *Autolycus' pack*, 1940, a collection of Esdaile's essays, addresses and verses; and *The British Museum Library*, 1946. His bibliographical and literary studies are numerous, and the result of deep scholarship, while his many contributions to the *Library Association Record* and similar library journals are thought-provoking, and typical of Esdaile's wide interests.

Arundell Esdaile was a big man in every respect; he stood almost six feet six inches, and his long white hair gave him a leonine appearance, but if he was sometimes fierce in appearance, he was always ready with a humorous anecdote. In 1907 he married Katharine Ada McDowall, and she died in 1950. Esdaile shared his time and experience between the British Museum, the Library Association, the Bibliographical Society, the students at University College, and librarians in general. He actively supported the formation of I.F.L.A., and was recognized as an international figure in librarianship. A forceful speaker, his views commanded respect, and his advice was freely given at committee meetings and in personal communications. Much of his work cannot be evaluated; it was that of a friend and adviser to many professional bodies and individuals. It will be more deeply appreciated when the passing of time records it in the history of librarianship and bibliography. (Portrait, Plate 12B.)

### REFERENCES

Sayers, W. C. Berwick. Arundell Esdaile, C.B.E., M.A., Hon.Litt.D., F.L.A., April 25, 1880–June 22, 1956. *Library World*, 58, 1956–1957, pp. 25–28.

Obituary notices by H. M. Cashmore, F. C. Francis, J. H. P. Pafford, T. P. Svensma and W. Munthe. *Library Association Record*, 58, 1956, pp. 321–325.

### ESDAILE'S CONFESSIONS OF A VICTORIAN[1]

My claim to address a gathering of school librarians seems to me to be rather tenuous. It is true that I am, or rather have been, a librarian. But the library of the British Museum presents almost fewer features of similarity than of dissimilarity to that of a school. One of its chief regulations debars from access, except in special cases, those under twenty-one years of age; and another treats reading for examinations as a disqualification. In fact, except that both contain books and entertain readers, it is not easy to find common ground.

If, however, my experience as a librarian is little recommendation, I can claim that for twelve or fourteen years, ever since I became active

[1] A paper delivered at the Easter Course in School Library Work at Bedford School, April, 1937.

in the Library Association, I have seen and expressed the need for some organisation of school librarians, such as I am glad to have at last been able to have some hand in bringing into being.

And, after all, we all, whether librarians or teachers, or neither, have been their victims. I may, therefore, perhaps find something useful to you in some discursive remarks and memories of my own days in a school library at the end of that remote Victorian era when people were not so Victorian as their Sexto-Georgian children like to imagine —when I was what I may call, in the modern idiom, library fodder.

Not that anyone actively so regarded us. The library was there, and a certain rather lax control of its use; but no form-master ever suggested to me or anyone else that I know of that we could find a relevant book in it. As a matter of fact it was not at all bad, though not what it is today, and I still wonder at the waste involved of money and librarians' time—the latter voluntary, of course!

I did use the library a great deal, and so did many others; especially before I had a study it was a relief from the tumultuous house room. And here I would like to insist on one thing about school life of those days, whatever may have been the truth about earlier decades. This is that the bookish boy suffered no contempt, still less active ill-usage. It is true that I was even then large and neither wholly unathletic nor at all uninterested in school affairs. But I am thinking of others as well as myself, and I never heard of any such thing. Perhaps the pure athlete regarded the scholar with a certain wonder and a good-humoured shrug of the shoulders—but often with respect. The literary youths who write about public school life are, of course, either over-imaginative, or are Rip Van Winkles returning from half a century earlier.

If love of books was not discouraged at school, it was not created there; and this is where the opportunities of the place were lost. Bookish boys were those who came from bookish homes, who, like myself, had grown in childhood to delight in browsing in their father's library. I was, though, of the two classes of children—those who read and those who draw—much more a member of the latter than of the former. Alas, I now cannot draw at all—reading drove drawing out. The trouble is that there are, and I suppose were, so few bookish homes in proportion to the mass. This has been borne in on me since I came to man's estate by my experience on the few, but even so too numerous, occasions when I have moved house. Every time the remover's men have not only shown, at the same time as their experience and competence in handling such things as furniture and china, their inexperience in handling books, but they have shown it in repeated expressions of wonder at one's having any number of books at all. I have been asked, of course, whether I had read them all, and also whether I were a dealer in them. I found the most satisfactory answer to be that I had *used* nearly all, and that they were tools. In fact that I merely had a rather large bag.

As I was saying just now, no one guided me in the library, nor was it used in school work as it should have been. As a result I grew up largely ignorant of the very notion of historical or textual sources. Mommsen and John Richard Green might for me have been present at the scenes they described; Munro might have taken Homer down in shorthand from the poet's mouth. Criticism of texts and sources should not bulk large in school days, I think; other aspects are more vital. But their existence should be made clearer than it was to me.

The use of books of reference is generally necessary to an intelligent existence, if that of texts and sources is not. And it needs teaching. As you all probably do teach it, I will not waste your time in suggesting methods of doing so to you. A measure of the need of such teaching can be found in the newspaper correspondences in which some matter of fact, easily to be settled by reference to well-known books, is gravely debated, with the production of scraps of fact, by apparently educated and well-to-do people, who have no idea how they are giving themselves, and their masters and mistresses in their youth, away. I only differ from them in having learned, largely from my later professional experience, how to use books of reference. How to use them, but not the need of them. I learnt that early. I have known a very argumentative family which debated matters of fact so fiercely at meals that they had to keep an encyclopaedia permanently handy.

There is one aspect of the choice of books of reference, and indeed of books on important subjects generally, for the top forms, where I would counsel a certain audacity. I would say, do not be afraid of occasionally getting books in French—and more occasionally still in German. There are first-rate books in quantity, the best books on their subjects, which have never been and may never be translated. And to be turned on to look up some point in a French book kills two birds with one stone. The extra difficulty of getting at it helps to drive it in, in the first place. The celebrated Dr. Spooner attributed his fine memory for Greek and Latin etymology to the fact that, being nearly blind, he found looking a word up so painful that he took care never to have to look the same one up twice. Secondly, there is no better way of getting used to a foreign language than to use it not in order to learn it but in order to learn some subject. Like happiness, in fact, it is best attained by aiming at something else. I wish I had been put on to French in this way at school, for ordinary school French is enough for a start, and the rest is nothing whatever but practice—at least, so far as reading is concerned. Rather later did I learn Italian in this way. I had dutifully struggled with *I Prometti Sposi* and *Le miei Prigioni*, but struggled in vain. I kept finding that although I understood every word I somehow did not understand what it was all about. You will remember that maddening sensation, something like trying to hold a train of thought as one is falling off to sleep. Well, I fainted and fell by the wayside. Some years later, I had occasion to read on the traditions of Classical Rome in the Middle Ages. One of the best books on that subject is that of Arturo Graf—*Roma nella memoria e nell' immaginazione del medio evo*. It is in two large volumes of some 500 pages each. I read it straight through without the slightest difficulty, for no reason that I know of except that I really wanted to know what Graf had to say on a subject I was interested in and already knew a little about.

Library administration is not my subject here; I have talked too much about it elsewhere, among librarians in whose experience the tricks of the trade bulk too large instead of, as is the case with most school librarians, too small.

But there are just one or two points of organisation which I recognise as having been important to me. One is the invaluable experience of having been a boy-librarian. I believe it would have been invaluable even had I not afterwards become a librarian by profession. And that though I was not put on to catalogue, for example, as I might have been. Not that there was anybody qualified to teach anybody else to catalogue.

Then we had no house libraries, as they do now. Perhaps they are necessary, as the school has grown larger, but I think we were more fortunate. The house library should be a place to begin in. It may very easily become one to end in. It is often a little too good for the former function; it can never be nearly good enough for the latter. In its absence nothing stood between the boy who wanted to read and the place where there really were—with all deficiencies—a large number of first-rate books.

The deficiencies were pretty glaring in modern languages and science, for example. But then, we made no account of the modern side or of "stinks". In classics the library was pretty good, and in English literature I think quite good.

That was where I found my *pabulum*—in the English poets in particular, and to a certain extent in the classical and near-classical novelists, as well as in some popular novelists like Besant and Rice, who can hardly be put in the latter class, yet who were worth reading, even if they are forgotten today. Stevenson I hardly touched till later. He died in my first school year, but I do not suppose I heard of the fact. I had read *Treasure Island* at my preparatory school, where it had been a good deal spoilt for me by my having previously read in the *Boy's Own* and elsewhere so many imitations that (except for the thrill of Pew, the blind beggar, and the tapping of his stick, of which I well remember the impression, and which I still think a marvel of art) I was unable to appreciate their great original when I did encounter it, and I have never been able to get the proper "kick" out of the idea of heaps of doubloons and pieces of eight. Mine the loss.

To keep to what with me was the preparatory school stage—though I do not think it was with all my contemporaries—I had very soon waded through the shallow waters of Henty and come out on the other side. But Rider Haggard, who came next, I still read occasionally. When he tries fine writing, as in *She*, he is, of course, dreadful. And on the female sex, from mysterious white queens down to missionaries' little blue-eyed daughters, he is quite incredible. At least on modern standards. Somehow we did not much notice that sort of thing, though I always revolted against Dulcie Grimston as the one blot on a perfect book, on which I have in my time scored—and possibly could still score—full marks in a searching examination. Rider Haggard's great merit of style is that his diction is dramatically true; he writes as his Allan Quatermain would have spoken in real life, a sort of Nestor of the velt. Another writer of that day who had just this merit of dramatically true style was Rolf Boldrewood, whose *Robbery under Arms* would be a great book were the volume of its sentiment and piety reduced by ninety per cent.

If Allan Quatermain was Nestor, Umslopogaas and Sir Henry Curtis also were heroes worthy of Homer. Andrew Lang was well inspired when he wrote his Greek verses on Umslopogaas. Sir Henry was, I believe, the secret inspiration of most normal English boys of that generation. Was that regrettable? I do not think so. Probably there is some present-day successor to him who unites in himself the best parts of the old ideal of chivalry. "Empire-builder" is now a term of contempt, I believe. But I am delighted to see that certificate of a wide circulation, appearance in the Penguin Series, attached to a combination of Sir Henry Curtis and Allan Quatermain of real life, the late Captain Monkton's *Experiences of a New Guinea Resident Magistrate*. Monkton's astounding adventures and escapes are only a part of his simply-told achievement. He made notable additions to scientific knowledge; and, more than all, he had the sympathetic imagination which enabled him to understand the ways of thought of his tribes, and, by something closely resembling the perfect system, to govern them practically single-handed. His book fills me with a warm pride of race of which I see no reason to be ashamed.

Books for school libraries may be classified (better than by Dewey) into three classes; the books no boy will read; the books a boy may be induced to read; and the books no boy can be prevented from reading. Those I have been thinking of belong to the third class; the librarian's task is easy here, for all he has to do is to see that enough of the books are provided, the boys themselves will do the rest. Similarly with the first class; it is necessary to have some of these, no doubt, such as dictionaries, to be used, not read, and also some books which the staff will want. The problems are, of course, all with that great second class, of the books a boy may be induced to read. Practically all first-rate literature is to be found in it. May I offer one or two apparently trivial hints. Young people are intimidated by old leather bindings, and never get so far as the contents. Similarly they are repelled by dull or uniform bindings. Vary your colours and styles of bindings. Do not just accept a single pattern from Messrs. So-and-so and let them go on with till Domesday. But you will have a certain number of books in dull or old bindings. I remember a whole shelf of Aldine editions of the English poets, mostly well enough edited and all beautifully printed, as I now know; I read all the other English poets in the library, but I never opened one of that series. Again, not only are old leather bindings awe-inspiring; the old type with the long "s" confounds. This is why I used the phrase "may be induced". Occasions should be manufactured to drive the young person to *use* these books and to get over that quite absurd first repulsion of bewilderment, and to be thereafter free of books of all sorts. I do not think it necessary to introduce him to black-letter, which he may hardly ever see again.

There are certain very great writers, a knowledge of whom is a lifelong possession, a κτῆμα ἐς ἀεί, whom, for reason of their slow-moving bulk, the young must be induced to read. I think of Thackeray, Jane Austen, Scott and Johnson, or rather Johnson-in-Boswell. I found that my own children could appreciate *Vanity Fair* before the rest of Thackeray, which may seem curious. Neither Thackeray nor Jane Austen should be tried too early, however, nor if it comes to that, Boswell. *Everybody's Boswell*—like the companion *Everybody's Pepys*—is an invaluable introduction. To know Johnson is an almost complete equipment for life; for he hardens the head at the same time that he softens the heart.

Scott is the real crux. North of the Border, I am assured, he is still driven into the Caledonian young, but no longer is he read on the wrong side of Tweed. It is the penalty of his date, for he was the great pioneer of story-telling; it is the penalty of his uncertain artistic conscience, which allowed him to write on and on, page after page of heavy, clumsy English, instead of coming to grips with his characters;

and it is the penalty of his passion for historical tradition which induced him to load his novels with introduction within introduction like Chinese puzzles. Scott's amassing of oral tradition for Scottish seventeenth and eighteenth-century history was of immense value, but I would like to see an edition of the Waverley novels with the introductions not omitted, but printed *at the end*. Then anyone interested enough could read them after finishing the tale. On opening the book one would at once come upon the horseman on the lonely moor, or whatever it is, and would read happily on. There is one method, outside your professional scope, and that is to read Scott aloud to small children, generously skipping as you go, and then, not as men and women without hope, to leave the books in the nursery and ask no questions.

One thing is sure. If boys and girls do not get the reading habit in their teens they never will. Even if they do, when they come to middle age they will have too little time, but will forever promise themselves a retired old age of making up for lost time by reading the unread books. And who shall say if that time will be theirs?

From, *School Library Review*, 1, Summer, 1937, pp. 134–138; also in Esdaile's *Autolycus' pack*, [etc.], 1940, pp. 139–148.

# CHAPTER 47

# James Douglas Stewart (1880–1965)

"It has long been accepted, implicitly if not explicitly, that the bounds set to the work of a librarian are in the main set only by himself."

J. D. STEWART.

SUCCESSFUL librarians have seldom been those who hold themselves aloof from their fellow men, the whole essence of practical librarianship being the sharing of knowledge, and companionship in the fellowship of books. One of the most friendly, modest and helpful librarians of modern times was "Jimmy" Stewart. Ever-ready to assist younger colleagues, a fount of invaluable advice based on lengthy experience, with a ready smile and a fund of anecdotes to encourage conversation, he continued his active career long after the normal age for retirement.

James Douglas Stewart was born on August 24th, 1880 in Glasgow, and was a nephew of James Duff Brown. He began his career at Croydon Public Libraries, where Jast was in charge, and he was very much concerned with the activities of the Library Assistants' Association, afterwards the Association of Assistant Librarians. Stewart was a practical committee man rather than a public speaker, and he actively supported open-access. When Brown went to Islington, Stewart also joined the staff there, until in 1927 he became Borough Librarian of Bermondsey. There he remained until his retirement in 1950. He then became editor of BUCOP, continuing the task until it was completed, when he finally retired to Guernsey in September, 1962. He died there on May 5th, 1965.

J. D. Stewart was a member of the Library Association Council for many years and served as Chairman, but unfortunately was never elected President of the Association. He was Vice-President from 1948 to 1962. He was elected an Honorary Fellow in 1959, and his activities on behalf of the London and Home Counties Branch resulted in the establishment of the J. D. Stewart Travelling Bursary in 1956, Stewart having served on the Committee of the Branch since 1923.

The writings of J. D. Stewart extend over a long period. He was the author of *The sheaf catalogue*, 1909; *How to use a library*, 1910; (with W. C. Berwick Sayers) *The card catalogue*, 1913; *A tabulation of librarianship*, 1947; and he edited *The reference librarian in university, municipal and specialized libraries*, 1951. He prepared the third edition of Brown's

*Subject classification*, which was published in 1939, and which would have attracted more attention but for the outbreak of war. Stewart also edited the *Quinquennial Report of the London and Home Counties Branch* for many years, and at one time owned and edited the *Library World*. He wrote "The last twenty years of the Association" (*Library Association Record*, 52, 1950, pp. 338, 343–345), and an interesting account of BUCOP, which is reproduced below. The British Union-Catalogue of Periodicals will remain J. D. Stewart's main achievement, but his initial early work on behalf of librarianship continued to interest him throughout his life, and he remained infectiously enthusiastic in the encouragement of his younger colleagues. (Portrait, Plate 12C.)

<h2 style="text-align:center">REFERENCES</h2>

Harrison, K. C. Mr. J. D. Stewart. Obituary. *Library World*, 66, 1964–65, p. 311.
Thorne, W. Benson. Obituary of James Douglas Stewart. *Library Association Record*, 67, 1965, pp. 210–211.

## STEWART ON THE BRITISH UNION-CATALOGUE OF PERIODICALS

The British Union-Catalogue of Periodicals owes its existence to the initiative and energy of Mr. Theodore Besterman. In a paper which he read at the 17th Aslib Conference in 1942,[1] he argued the case for a really comprehensive union catalogue of the periodicals held in British libraries to replace the various sectional and small regional ones which then, as now, existed. Mr. Besterman succeeded in interesting a number of important bodies in his project; and when the Rockefeller Foundation agreed to make a generous grant for the purpose, the British Union-Catalogue of Periodicals came formally into existence early in 1944. A Council was appointed consisting of representatives of Aslib, the Bibliographical Society, the British Academy, the British Council, the British Museum, the Joint Standing Committee on Library Co-operation (of the university libraries), the Library Association, the National Central Library, the Rockefeller Foundation, the Royal Society and the Science Library; with the late Luxmoore Newcombe as its first chairman. The Trustees of the British Museum have taken a lively interest in the undertaking, and have made a considerable contribution towards its success by providing the necessary accommodation and many facilities. Mr. Theodore Besterman was appointed editor and executive officer and held this post until his resignation in 1947. He was succeeded by Dr. A. Loewenberg, who carried on the work until his most untimely death at the end of 1949. The present editor took office early in 1950. During the whole period Aslib has acted as the secretariat for BUCOP.

[1] Afterwards revised and published as *Aslib offprint No. 10*.

The procedure suggested for the compilation of BUCOP was set out by Mr. Besterman in his original paper:

"The mechanics of such an undertaking are quite simple. The largest possible list that can be compiled in one place is printed and distributed, either simultaneously or by a circulatory method, to the participating libraries, whose returns are collected and reduced to order (not so easy a task as it sounds, admittedly), and the work is ready for publication."

He then goes on to suggest that the basic list of periodicals to be circulated could consist of a consolidation of the appropriate heading from the British Museum catalogue, the *World list* and the *Union catalogue of periodicals in university libraries.*

This in effect was the plan put into operation, and the compilation of the huge basic list intended for printing and preliminary circulation as a check-list was pressed on vigorously. However, by the time the compilation of this list was sufficiently advanced to enable the question of printing to be considered, the cost of printing had risen to such an extent as to make the proposal impossible with the resources that were available. The Council was thus faced with a difficult position. Owing to its sheer size and costliness, the utilization of a printed check-list, against which libraries could note their holdings for consolidation in the final union catalogue, had reluctantly to be abandoned; and the Council decided to put into operation the alternative method of asking each co-operating library to compile a list of its own holdings of periodicals for incorporation in BUCOP. This decision, forced upon the Council by economic pressure, has had the effect of increasing very greatly the labour and time needed to incorporate the library holdings in the final work. It has also led to the inevitable result that, in spite of most careful definition, libraries have varied considerably in the scope of the material they have reported as "periodicals". On the other hand, this method of asking libraries to report individually instead of conforming to a circulated list has had some most valuable benefits; of which the chief has been the securing of the particulars holdings of many thousands of items that would never have been and included in any normal check-list. A large proportion of these holdings are unique in the United Kingdom, and represent a hitherto generally unknown body of research material that should be of great value. It is to be expected that such specialized libraries as those of the R.I.B.A., Kodak, the Royal Geographical Society, the St. Bride's Institute, the Schools of Oriental and Slavonic Studies, and the Warburg and Wiener Libraries, should report holdings of periodicals in their special fields not possessed by anyone else; but this flow of unique or scarce material has also come from most unexpected sources. For example, the Bath Public Library contains holdings of about 120 periodicals of Napoleonic times that are to be found nowhere else in Britain; and all public libraries of any size are comparatively rich in locally published periodicals.

All the important libraries of all kinds in the country were requested to co-operate by completing lists of their permanent holdings of periodicals, and the response was most satisfactory in view of the obvious difficulties. A good many libraries, however, were unable to help in this way owing to such factors as shortage of staff, war-time disorganization, and so on. For the more important of these libraries arrangements have been made for the work to be done on a paid basis by suitable workers in the field; but, of course, there are limits to this. The whole of the work on BUCOP has been done during the war and post-war years; in other words, during a period of much difficulty both in finance and personnel. It is, therefore, a source of gratification, and a tribute to British librarianship, that so many libraries of all kinds have willingly undertaken the considerable task of providing detailed lists of their holdings in spite of many administrative difficulties. The lists received vary very greatly in their quality however, ranging from perfect bibliographical clarity to the utterly incomprehensible.

The cataloguing of periodicals is one of the most neglected among the techniques of librarianship. Only a handful of our more considerable libraries have ever succeeded in cataloguing the periodicals they hold. The great majority, including many of the university libraries, do not catalogue but merely make inventories of such material. Thus in existing catalogues there will be found endless columns of entries under such words as "Journal", "Proceedings", "Transactions", and their equivalents in other languages. More ludicrously, lists just as lengthy appear under "Report", "Annual report", and entries have even been made under "Honorary secretary's report". Codes of cataloguing rules (including the Anglo-American code) may have been a little vague to the uninitiated on this point, but surely their authors never envisaged any result so crass as that!

There are, of course, plenty of entries that should appear under, for example, the word "Journal". Such publications as the *Journal of documentation, Journal of ecclesiastical history, Journal littéraire*, etc., are properly so entered. But the *Journal of the Chemical Society*, or of the Child Study Society, or the Town Planning Institute should be entered under the name of the society. Any other course results in the publications of a society or other corporate body being spread all over the alphabet; and it must be remembered that a society's publication which commences as its Journal very often becomes its Proceedings or Transactions, or takes on some other guise.

BUCOP has its own code of cataloguing rules, formulated by Mr. Besterman and printed in the *Journal of documentation* for September,

1946. Though an individual code, it follows in the main the lines laid down by the standard codes. One important point on which codes differ is whether to enter a periodical under its earliest or latest name. Either method has its advantages and disadvantages. The BUCOP rule is to enter under the earliest name, setting out the various changes in their historical sequence with, of course, references from all the later names. This method has the benefit of showing clearly everything that has happened to a periodical, and also enables the holdings of libraries to be set out more definitely. There are some unexpected results, such as entering *The Times* as the *Daily Universal register*, and *Flight* under its first title of *Automotor and horseless vehicle journal*. But such occasional minor eccentricities are more than compensated for by the advantages gained when tracing the evolution and convolutions of the publications of the continental academies—many of which we believe to have been now really catalogued for the first time.

During the progress of the work it became more and more obvious that the net spread by BUCOP was both too extensive and too small-meshed; with the result that the amount of material drawn in (and what was worse, still to be drawn in) was so immense that eventual publication and even reasonable completion in manuscript, was improbable and remote in view of the resources available. The original scheme brought in, amongst many other things, such publications as the annual reports of every kind of public or private organization, in every part of the world; diaries, almanacs and desk-books; practically the whole of the government publications of all countries; local directories, guides, time-tables, etc.; company reports; and "series" of all kinds from the monographs issued by a university to the "Little one's story books" of an enterprising publisher. Admittedly there must be much among such material that would have value for some purposes. Admittedly also, the perfect record would include everything. But the factors of time and money alone were sufficient to convince the Council that, if BUCOP were ever to see the light, some narrower limit must be imposed on the types of material to be included. By direction of the Council, therefore, the files of BUCOP were examined carefully, and a great mass of entries transferred to a reserve file. These transferred entries are mainly for such material as purely administrative reports, the non-periodical and business publications of governments, guide-books, local directories, time-tables, minor annuals, and publishers' series. It is not now proposed to print the entries in this reserve file, but they will be preserved in manuscript for permanent reference, probably at the National Central Library. It is hoped that the selection of the material to be published has been made with due regard to the real needs of readers and research workers. For example, annual reports, which embody the results of research, and the series issued by universities and societies, still remain in the main file for inclusion in BUCOP.

Now a few words on the scope and extent of BUCOP. It includes periodicals (in a very wide sense) published in any part of the world, dealing with any subject, and in any language, so far as they are represented by holdings permanently preserved in the libraries of the United Kingdom. It is estimated that there are at present about 130,000 entries in the active files, and that as those entries are "historical" in character (setting out successive changes of name), somewhere around 160,000 different titles are recorded. Those totals are being constantly increased as holdings of titles hitherto unrecorded in BUCOP are reported by the co-operating libraries. At least another year is needed to bring the work of compilation to a stage of completeness suitable for publication. By that time the holdings of over 300 libraries will have been recorded. BUCOP is comparable in size with the great American *Union list of serials*, and will probably appear in four volumes of something over 1,000 pages each.

A spot-check (admittedly not final) suggests that as many as 40 per cent of the entries already in BUCOP do not appear in the *Union list of serials*. This rather remarkable result points to the fact that the two works are complementary, and between them will provide a most extensive view of the periodicals of the world.

The task of compiling a work of this kind and magnitude is exacting. I came to it from the carefree activities of public librarianship with much trepidation—to find that I was indeed fortunate in my colleagues. Miss Muriel Hammond, a Fellow of the Library Association, has gifts amounting to second sight that enable her to combat the inward cussedness of both periodicals and librarians; and she has infinite patience with my deviations from BUCOP cataloguing rules and traditions. Dr. Erwin Saenger, a doctor of laws, of Heidelberg, can match his wits against the most eccentric of the German and Italian academies, and guides my stumbling way in German and Russian and other monstrous languages.

Many librarians under-estimate the importance of the periodical in the presentation of their libraries' resources to the public. The needs of all who require up-to-date information are much more likely to be satisfied by periodicals than by books. Contemporary periodicals of any period present the most vivid picture of their times and interests; and an enormous range of literary and research material remains in the files of periodicals and never reaches book form. BUCOP will provide a key to this immense storehouse of interest and information, and I am proud to be associated with so great a work.

From, *Library Association Record*, 55, 1953, pp. 248–250.

# CHAPTER 48

# William Charles Berwick Sayers (1881–1960)

> "Sayers has shaped the outlook of the last two generations of librarians in the English-speaking world."
>
> S. R. RANGANATHAN.

IT will be many years before the true significance of the influence of Berwick Sayers on librarianship is fully appreciated. His interests were so wide, yet apparently so concentrated that each subject appeared to have his undivided attention. Time may result in the conglomeration of the results of his activities into a perspective that can be interpreted by an individual, yet much of his influence must remain undetected. It is the effect of his teaching and of his character on thousands of students and young librarians.

W. C. Berwick Sayers was born at Mitcham, Surrey on December 23rd, 1881, but at the age of five moved to Brighton, where he first entered public librarianship in 1896. In 1900 he was appointed Sub-Librarian there, but in 1904 succeeded E. A. Savage as Deputy to Jast at Croydon. Berwick Sayers became active in the Library Assistants' Association, becoming Honorary Secretary in 1905, President in 1909, and being elected an Honorary Fellow in 1913. In 1915 he was appointed Chief Librarian of Wallasey, once more succeeding E. A. Savage, but a few months later he returned to Croydon to succeed Jast as Chief. Berwick Sayers proceeded to serve Croydon in that capacity with distinction for thirty-two years, until his retirement in 1947, and continued his interest in the history of the borough until his death.

Berwick Sayers became a member of the Library Association Council in 1912 and continued to serve it meticulously to the end of his life. He was President in 1938, and was elected an Honorary Fellow in 1947. He had gained the Diploma as early as 1908, when he was so anxious to obtain it with honours that he took several parts again the following year. In this he was successful, and he was for many years the only person holding the Honours Diploma. His work for the Library Association is inestimable, for he gave freely of his knowledge gained by wide experience of people, of committee work, and from books. He was quiet, courteous and tolerant, but when he spoke it was effectively, and to the point. He was listened to with respect, for he did not lightly plunge into wild speculations, but with slow, deliberate, carefully contrived phrases presented the results of painstaking consideration. Some thought his manner pompous, but Berwick Sayers was the most modest of the eminent librarians of this century. He was keenly interested in education, and in students of librarianship of all ages. He included himself as a student in a conversation held shortly before his death, and it was an apt description of a mind that always remained receptive to new ideas.

The National Central Library was one of Berwick Sayers' main interests, and he became its Chairman in 1947. He was an examiner for the Library Association from 1912, and taught first at the London School of Economics and then at the School of Librarianship at University College from its foundation in 1919. There he taught classification to hundreds of students, explaining the subject so that the most simple mind could grasp the basic essentials, yet maintaining its primary significance in library administration. Basic terminology encouraged those who now deplore the recent trends in writings on the subject, and which contrast so strangely with Sayers' own pioneer writings: *Canons of classification*, 1915; *The grammar of classification*, third edition, 1924; *An introduction to library classification*, 1918, ninth edition, 1954; and *A manual of classification*, 1927, with a third edition in 1955. These saw numerous students through the necessary examinations, and inspired some to pursue the subject further, forming the basis on which more recent developments have been fostered.

Numerous other publications came from the ready pen of Berwick Sayers: *The children's library*, 1913, a subject in which he was a pioneer and remained a keen enthusiast, followed by *A manual of children's libraries*, 1932; *First steps in annotation in catalogues*, new edition, 1955; *Samuel Coleridge-Taylor; musician: his life and letters*, 1915 and 1927, and four editions of Brown's *Manual of library economy* between 1920 and 1949. He was associated with *The Library World* for over thirty years, contributing numerous anonymous and pseudonymous regular features, and was Chief of the Editorial Committee. His published articles are innumerable, and demand a separate bibliography.

Berwick Sayers was keenly interested in poetry and music. In 1915 he married Olive Clarke, a librarian who remained a keen supporter of her husband in his work, and they had three sons. One of Sayers' most interesting articles gives fascinating autobiographical information and it is reproduced below. The Classification Group had decided to publish a *Festschrift* for his eightieth birthday, but unfortunately Berwick Sayers died on October 7th, 1960, and the handsome volume was issued as *The Sayers Memorial Volume. Essays in librarianship in memory of William Charles Berwick Sayers. Edited by D. J. Foskett and B. I. Palmer*, 1961. Royalties are to be used for Sayers Memorial Prizes to be awarded to outstanding students, and the book contains fascinating articles dealing mainly with work in which Sayers was interested—a wide and varied field. The first chapter is a biographical study of Sayers by James D. Stewart, and most of the chapters reflect the influence of W. C. Berwick Sayers on the development of modern librarianship.

REFERENCES

Foskett, D. J., and Palmer, B. I., eds. *The Sayers Memorial Volume. Essays in librarianship in memory of William Charles Berwick Sayers*, 1961.

McColvin, L. R. W. C. Berwick Sayers. *Library World*, 62, 1960–61, pp. 141–144; see also p. 103.

W. C. Berwick Sayers, 1881–1960. Obituaries by H. M. Cashmore, J. D. Stewart, S. R. Ranganathan, Archibald Sparke, and W. Benson Thorne. *Library Association Record*, 62, 1960, pp. 381–383, 419–420.

## BERWICK SAYERS: A BOOKMAN'S BROWSINGS

Almost every author is to some extent autobiographical in his writings, and if he be also a librarian, they are necessarily somewhat undramatic; indeed, were it not for books and the love of them, he would be better for being silent. When, however, one is a book-lover, every day has its possible discovery or at least adventure.

My father was the artistic decorator who placed amongst stars on a blue ground the inscription: "This is none other than the House of God", if I remember aright, around the chancel arch of the parish church of Mitcham in which, then a village, I was born; and, as a small child, I believed that he had painted the stars in the sky also. He had been a student at the Croydon School of Art. My mother, after some training at a school in Brentwood, Essex, taught for a while in the Croydon Parish Church School. I have still the copy of Milton which she used in her studies, the first two books scored with her "parsing" of passages, an enduring souvenir of the unimaginative treatment of a classic. She sang her way through her home life, for she had a beautiful soprano voice and knew all the popular songs which were current when "Just a song at twilight" was new. My memories of Mitcham are few; then a place on the bright little Wandle river with its many mills and with trout and a margin where tiddlers could be caught; its lavender and mint fields; its cricket green whence Dr. W. G. Grace hit a ball into the face of the vestry clock in its tower, and Richardson's demon bowling made fame. And on this green when I was five a grazing donkey's hind hoofs kicked me in the stomach into cataclysmal but fortunately for me transient chaos. But more, I remember the little school nearby and my tiny futile indignation at five when my teacher laughed at me before the class when, directed to read aloud an anecdote, "The busy bees", I pronounced the key-word "bushy". I think that incident was more corrosive, and perhaps taught me more, than anything I remember in my childhood.

The Wandle ran at the back of our house, which was low lying and often misty and damp. The common, half a mile away, was blanketed at times although the summers were lovely. My father was a bronchial-asthmatic and, when he was twenty-nine and I still five, we migrated to the small seaside town of Bournemouth, in search of health, "where", a local poet wrote, "folks lived on who came to die"; not the Bournemouth of today, a somewhat flamboyant mistress amongst watering places, but then with less than ten thousand people amongst its acres of pines and flower gardens, innocent of cars, buses and coaches and without the long promenades. There I was to live for sixteen years. Our home was built in a pine wood, the trees being destroyed ruthlessly as the building progressed; behind was a long narrow cornfield, memorable to me for its singing larks; and beyond the East Common, acres of grass and harebells and golden for months with gorse, where were lizards, grass snakes, an occasional adder and a tadpole pond, called because of its disappearance in summer, Dry Pond. Common, woods and heath could be transformed by a little imagining into unexplored forests such as we found in our books and much of my life was spent in exploring them in what seems to have been perpetual sunshine. At six I became a pupil at St. Clement's Church school, and at seven became a choirboy in the adjacent church. This was important, as the continued rehearsal of collects, psalms and *Hymns Ancient and Modern* made them part of the texture of my English education, such as it is. When I reached the Big Boys' school I came under the influence duly of a remarkable headmaster, with curly red hair, who lived with and for his boys; just, a good sport who put pennies on the stumps to be taken by the bowler who could knock them off. He taught us the three Rs assiduously and was discerning in literature, read Shakespeare with us on sundry afternoons, and gave me a special book prize at ten because within three days I could repeat Tennyson's "Revenge" before the class.

I am unable to remember when or how I learned to read; everybody read or was read to at home. There I got the reality of books. I see even now the room with the bright fire, the round table with the velvet plush table cloth and the brass "Aladdin" lamp in the centre and my sister and I sitting to hear my father or my mother reading aloud from so many books; some of which I have not read, but remember intimately; there was *Pickwick, David Copperfield, Uncle Tom's Cabin* (I have not read that, but recall our weeping over the death of Little

Eva and shivering at the brutalities of Simon Legree), and *Robinson Crusoe* and *Ivanhoe* and even the adventures of Becky Sharp. Of course, of my own volition I read, as all sane boys do, every penny dreadful I could lay hands on—they were a penny then, and dear enough, for at one time it was the whole of my income. The usual ones of course: Buffalo Bill, Frank Reed's wonderful predecessor of all motor cars which cruised the prairies and so on; and there was then a weekly, *Nuggets*, to which my elder brother subscribed, carrying in every issue a serial of tourneys and clashes of armoured heroes who fascinated me. Later there arrived three or four halfpenny weeklies. *The Gem*, *The Halfpenny Marvel*, and *The Union Jack* with stories of heroic virtue that ranged from Pole to Pole. But the author who first incited me to try my own hand at story writing was Edward S. Ellis, the creator of Deerfoot the Red Indian friend of the settler, repudiated later by American librarians, who no doubt romanticised the Redskin as later discovered Fenimore Cooper to do. With him I roamed the banks of the Ohio, finding in my own solitary pine woods and wide heaths something out of which I could create my own romance. When I had any leisure I would write, worried only by the evident truth that my vocabulary was not big enough and my pen could not keep pace with my adventures. And, in my early teens that now forgotten writer of Indian yarns, Dr. Montgomery Bird, made my spine creep with his ghastly *Nick of the Woods*. At this time in another vein I was enthralled by one of the best boys' books ever written, James Greenwood's *Reuben Davidger*, whose adventures among the head-hunters of Borneo fascinated me as I learned many years later they did Henry R. Tedder, once Honorary Treasurer of the Library Association.

Versifying, however, was a much more fascinating exercise. I had a chorister friend, John, son of John Trafford Clegg, who wrote *David's Loom*, a Rochdale weaver story in the nineties. He, the son, had like myself a facile speed in rhyming, a gift quite common which we used to exercise in walking, inventing alternate lines and rhymes. Both of us were in the St. Augustine choir then; a church built and vicared by Canon Henry Twells, a delightful little grey man with straggly uncertain whiskers who long before, when as schoolmaster at Uppingham, wrote the hymn "At even ere the sun was set", while supervising the boys detained to do impositions. No doubt they would, had they known, then have appreciated

"O, in what divers pains they met!
O, with what joy they went away!"

He often preached on hymnody and had a way with boys and influenced our reading and activity. Alas, came the breaking of our voices; our rhyme-capping ceased. Clegg went to electricity; I to the new public library.

When this opened its doors I was too young by about two years to join it. At 14, however, I ceased to press an inadmissible nose against the glass front door of the long narrow shop, in which elysium was represented by wall cases on either side of it and two standard cases running the length, all about eight feet high. It competes for the position of first open-access library to be opened after Brown's pioneer one at Clerkenwell. I have never worked in or used an indicator or other "closed" library. When I got my first reader's ticket I spent an ecstatic two hours amongst, probably, 10,000 books, more than I had ever encountered before, with complete freedom to take away any *one* I liked. I cannot now explain why Craik's *English Language and Literature* was my choice, externally one of the ugliest books I have ever seen, but in its day of scholarship and good judgment it gave me some sense of the infinite range of our speech and writings. I carry to this day an extract in it from Warner's *Albion's England, 1586*, about the old man, boy and ass who passed through the city, the boy riding until the unlookers objected; then boy and man changed places, and again the onlookers objected, and then they rode together, which produced condemnations for cruel overloading of the beast. They solved the problem by drowning it in the seas, and so Warner proves:

> "The good are envied by the bad,
>     and glory finds disdain,
> And people are in constancy
>     as April is in rain."

The exalted Craik influenced me for many years, but the immediate pleasure in such a teacher soon faded. In a corner, only a corner, of the library I found Ballantyne, Fenn, Henty, Kingston, Mayne Reid, Talbot Baines Reed, Harry Collingwood and other natural stuff for fourteeners and read as many as I could get.

School over, there was a job to be found and in Bournemouth there were few choices; only the building trade, shop and hotel activities. Someone, knowing my propensities, suggested "printing" and had my father not stamped on that suggestion, I might have had the experiences Dr. Savage had in his fortunately transient spell as printers' devil at Croydon a few years before. Luckily, a junior assistant was wanted at the library, and the Chairman of the Libraries Committee was Canon Eliot who had been the judge in an essay competition in which I had won the first prize. So, at the current wage of six shillings weekly, I entered work which, a Borough Treasurer explained to me later, "allowed one to pursue one's hobby all day without personal expense";

I was now able to live with books. Charles Riddle, the librarian, aged 28, had been J. D. Brown's sub-librarian at Clerkenwell; his own sub-librarian was Rowland Hill, afterwards librarian of Blackpool, Joseph Faraday, later librarian of Hornsey, Arthur Waterhouse, who to my astonishment left us to become a carpenter, and was replaced by W. G. Wilding who was to be librarian of Finsbury and late-comers A. J. Hawkes, W. G. Fry (to be Nowell's deputy at Manchester), and the last junior before I left was Edgar Osborne. It seems a fine list. Riddle was a clever man, well-read, a disciplinarian, who organized well in a limited field; he had imbibed from Brown that librarian meant primarily bookman and set us on the trail with Stopford Brooke's little *Primer*. Is it much used now? Matthew Arnold recommended it, and from it at least its superb opening went to one heart anyway. It gave that cinematographic view of our literature from Caedmon to Tennyson which every librarian of the general kind ought to possess. But I soon saw that to read about books and not to read them was to learn labels and be ignorant of goods. The pattern of our own and indeed of world literature showed that almost every nation has authors who tower above others as Everest over the Himalayas, and each of these has a chief work—*The Iliad*, *Oedipus*, *The Phaedo*, *The Aeniad*, *The Divine Comedy*, *Don Quixote*, *Faust*, all Shakespeare, *Paradise Lost*, and *War and Peace*—you can add to them. These were additional to the severer drill studies in languages, mathematics, logic and history which had to be pursued. To say more than that would be priggish and a pose; the things were real to me. Shakespeare and many of the others I confess I read for the stories in each of them; the real understanding was to come in maturer life. No one, however, can exist solely on such a diet: and each of us must live in his own age. My own middle teens were years everywhere in England under the influence of the Romantics, and Tennyson, Browning, Matthew Arnold; and Scott still ever dear supreme novelist, although Dickens was even then more popular, and Thackeray's *Esmond* was a particular joy, for me then, exceeding even *Vanity Fair*. Hardy had practically ceased to write, but we living in Wessex thought him absorbing for all his stoical gloom, and Meredith's *Diana of the Crossways* simply had to be read.

This could be prolonged indefinitely, but if I were asked what writers meant most to me, I would select Jane Austen, Scott, Hardy, and to drop back, Thomas Love Peacock. But above all I was absorbed by the poets and feel merely irritation when later poets, some of whom are admirable, attempt to ridicule the great Tennyson who completely absorbed me, and Wordsworth the very voice of nature at his best; and Keats as I developed took his place as the most humanly poet of poets, having much of the magic of Shelley and nearly his supreme lyrical gift.

When I look again over what I have written I realize its inadequacy and complete incompleteness. I read always; never left the house without some book or other, usually of verse. To mention even a hundredth of them would be to make merely a catalogue with meaning only for myself. Such advice as I could give, if any, would be:—read only to enjoy—only that remains with you; read to be able to remember—nothing else can really be worth reading; remember that you cannot read everything, so be very selective in what you read; and remember, too, that books mirror, but are not themselves Life, and find time to live. Above all, remember that tastes, like books and men, are diverse. But also, if generation after generation has proclaimed a book, and *you* find it dull dry and lifeless, are they all wrong?

From, *Library Review*, 134, Summer, 1960, pp. 399–403.

## BERWICK SAYERS ON CLASSIFICATION

The foundation of the library is the book; the foundation of librarianship is classification. Without classification no librarian can build up a systematic library; one, that is to say, which represents adequately the field of human learning as it is recorded in books. Think of the difficulties facing him—if he is honest in his work—in an unclassified library. He must gather together temporarily all the books on any given subject from all parts of his library, every time he wants to add to the strength of that subject or—what is equally important in all but the greater libraries which aim at completeness and never discard books on account of age or for the usual reasons which prompt withdrawal in libraries of more modest size—weed out books which have become obsolete. We fear that much inefficient work has resulted from want of classification. Librarians of larger libraries sometimes advocate the close classification of book entries in catalogues, but reject it for their shelves in favour of no classification or at the best broad classification. The reasoning on which this advocacy is based is not convincing. At any rate libraries arranged upon the open-access system, which in a few years may be the only system in popular libraries,[1] are impossible to work without adequate shelf classification. Readers would be lost hopelessly in an unclassified welter of books.

If, then, a library cannot be built up, or revised, without classification, and if students and readers can get no comprehensive view of the literature of subjects without it, the vital character of our subject is

---

[1] Perhaps, I should say, in small or moderately sized libraries. Open access to entire collections would rarely be advisable or even possible in large libraries.

easily demonstrated. Our purpose in this volume is to study the methods by which the contents of a library are arranged both on its shelves and in its catalogues. The methods which the librarian comprehends as classification, are derived from a consideration of the many ingredients which go to make up the book, an enumeration of which in quite incomplete form would include the size, subject, form, mode of treatment, binding, and printing type used in it. Such classification is of distinctive character. It is specially designed for application to books as an economy in library management, enabling us to determine as rapidly as possible what the book is, to relate it to other books like it, and to enable us to house it with some permanence and to find it for service with ease. It may seem to be superfluous thus to stress this obviously purposive nature of a library classification, but in recent years writers on the subject have busied themselves to a quite unnecessary extent in trying to prove what has long since been proven. In doing so, they have protested too much, even to the extent of alleging that a classification of books is so special that it has no relation to the classification of knowledge, but is an artificial experiment of the librarian. Much in a classification system is necessarily artificial and mechanical, but the basis of the practical schemes which are most likely to endure is the order which workers in the various fields of knowledge have arrived at in their subjects; they are, as Henry Evelyn Bliss has affirmed, "in consistency with the scientific and educational concensus."[1] It is unfair to plunge the reader at this stage into one of the controversies of modern classification method. The reader who can settle the problems involved has no need of this or any book on classification theory. The beginner, however, must become acquainted with the way in which the classifier looks at things and tries to co-ordinate them; and for him the next chapter or chapters repeat quite elementary notions which indeed are available in a hundred textbooks but which he may find it convenient to have brought together. Finally, our definition indicates that when we classify things we do so by some principle which binds them together. This may be one of several features possessed by every member of the class we make. This constitutes the likeness in these things. This likeness is the union of properties in the class. A classification, then, by arranging objects according to their likeness, throws into relief the features which make that likeness—the unity which there is in things.

From, Sayers, W. C. Berwick. *A manual of classification for librarians and bibliographers. Third edition, revised,* 1955, pp. 10–11.

[1] Bliss. *Organization of knowledge in libraries,* p. 42; and *Organization of knowledge and the system of the sciences,* pp. 16, 300, 301.

CHAPTER 49

# Cyril Cuthbert Barnard (1894–1959)

"One should start from the books themselves and build up a classificational structure to fit them, rather than construct a theoretical scheme
into which the books must afterwards be fitted as best they can."

C. C. BARNARD.

CYRIL BARNARD will be remembered internationally among medical
librarians as the author of the Barnard Classification, and with this will
be associated the name of the London School of Hygiene and Tropical
Medicine, London, where he was Librarian for thirty years. He was
born on July 23rd, 1894, and after attending the Stationers' School, he
held appointments in the libraries of the Reform Club, the Royal
Society of Medicine, the Wellcome Historical Medical Library, and
from 1921 in the London School of Tropical Medicine, which in 1929
was incorporated in the London School of Hygiene and Tropical
Medicine. In 1922 Cyril Barnard had gained the B.A. of the University
of London with Honours, as an external student, and he also studied at
the School of Librarianship. In 1931 he was awarded the Diploma
(with Honours) of the Library Association for his *A classification for
medical libraries*, first published in 1936, and which went into a
thoroughly revised second edition in 1955 with the title *A classification
for medical and veterinary libraries*. This was altered to cover the needs of
general medical libraries, and resulted in its adoption by many more
librarians, the first edition stressing hygiene, parasitology and tropical
medicine. Although classification was his main interest, Barnard was
a pioneer in the formal instruction of students in the use of the library
and the exploration of bibliographical materials, and he fostered co-
operation between libraries. He was interested in foreign languages,
and keenly supported conferences and gatherings of librarians.

Cyril Barnard was a member of the Society of Friends, and although
modest and peace-loving, he stoutly supported his principles, and was
enthusiastic in pursuing his special interests. The Medical Section of the
Library Association was one of these, and after his death the Section
established the Cyril Barnard Memorial Prize in his memory. Barnard
was responsible for building up the collections at the London School of
Hygiene and Tropical Medicine into a library that now commands an
international reputation. He compiled a *History of the Library*, published
in 1947, which largely reflects the result of his own activities. It con-

tains a list of his publications up to that date, and indicates a wide range of interests. He contributed the section "Special libraries" to the *Year's Work in Librarianship*, 1935, jointly up to 1938, and single-handed for the volume covering 1939 to 1945 published in 1949. Barnard was always ready to help, and his keen sense of humour, with the accompanying unique chuckle, endeared him to his fellow librarians. Unfortunately he was killed in a road accident on March 6th, 1959, shortly before he was due for retirement.

## REFERENCES

Barnard, Cyril C. *London School of Hygiene and Tropical Medicine. . . . History of the Library*, [etc.], 1947. Publications by members of the staff, pp. 23–24.

Obituaries, by V. G. Glanville, and by Ronald Sturt. *Library Association Record*, 61, 1959, p. 108.

## BARNARD ON THE REVISION OF THE BARNARD CLASSIFICATION[1]

In the time at my disposal I cannot attempt any general exposition of the *Classification for medical libraries*, published in 1936. I must assume that you are to some extent familiar with that first edition and confine my remarks this afternoon to an outline of the changes to be made in the second edition.

It may be of interest first to describe the procedure adopted in carrying out the revision. Within five years of its publication the whole first edition sold out, and for the last ten years I have been turning over in my mind ideas for a new edition. Serious work on the revision began about two years ago. First of all I made a detailed examination of the actual book-stock of two fairly general medical libraries classified by the Barnard scheme, viz. those of the Royal College of Surgeons of England and the Liverpool Medical Institution, noting any subjects represented there for which no adequate place existed in the scheme. I also noted the proportions of the stock in each of the main classes. The reason for this will appear later. Similar stock examinations were made in the three specialized libraries of the Royal College of Veterinary Surgeons, the Royal Veterinary College, and the British Dental Association. The first of these uses the Universal Decimal Classification, the second the Barnard scheme, and the third a very free modification of the latter.

A practical library classification scheme should, in my opinion, be compiled mainly, though not exclusively, on the inductive rather than the deductive principle: in other words, one should start from the books themselves and build up the classificational structure to fit them, rather than construct a theoretical scheme into which the books must

[1] Read at the First International Congress on Medical Librarianship, London, July 20th–25th, 1953.

afterwards be fitted as best they can. This, I believe, is what the classification experts now call "literary warrant". Working on this principle, I found the surveys of actual library stocks described above very helpful as far as they went, but I lacked the time and opportunity to make the many more similar surveys that were really needed. Instead I adopted another method which I could use without travelling about to visit numerous libraries. Assuming that the *Index-Catalogue of the Library of the Surgeon General's Office* and the *Quarterly Cumulative Index Medicus* represented between them a pretty fair proportion of the medical literature of the world, I worked through all the volumes of the four series of the *Surgeon General* and through a few specimen volumes at about five-year intervals of the *Q.C.I.M.*, noting any topic on which there is a considerable bulk of literature and, if it had not already a place in the classification I made one or wrote it down for later consideration. This was done not only for main topics but also for subheadings, for which I intend to provide a series of auxiliary schedules to be described later.

After rather more than a year I had completed all the main schedules and ten out of the eleven auxiliary schedules. Most opportunely at this time came an invitation from the World Health Organization for me to undertake the classification by the Barnard scheme of its library in Geneva. Although this meant a delay of three months in the progress of the revision, it was a delay well worth while, for in the process of classifying about 10,000 books I had a unique opportunity of testing the revised scheme in practice. It stood the test far better than I had dared to hope, but at the same time I obtained many extremely valuable hints for improvements that could hardly have been obtained in any other way.

I will now describe briefly the chief ways in which the second edition of the Classification will differ from the first. They may be grouped under three heads: (a) general revision and expansion, (b) the auxiliary schedules, and (c) the alternative notation.

(a) *General revision and expansion:* The main schedules have been thoroughly revised, brought up to date and where necessary expanded by the methods described above. There are now about twice as many topics entered in the main schedules and allotted separate notation, as there were in the first edition. The respective figures are about 2,800 and 1,400. By the use of the appropriate auxiliary schedules, however, this number can be multiplied many times over. Some of the divisions and subdivisions have been expanded by the addition of a third or fourth letter to the notation. The limit of four letters has not been exceeded except where the auxiliary schedules are brought into use. In practice I believe it will be found that any but the most highly specialized collection of books or even of reprints can be adequately classified by the scheme using symbols of not more than nine or ten elements. For most book collections no more than six will be needed; the majority of books in fact needs no more than two or three. The following are the only major changes in arrangement. Spirochaetes have been taken out of class K and put into class J Bacteriology, where they belong. This leaves the whole of K for the important new subject of Virology, including also Rickettsiae. It has been completely rearranged. The removal of Spirochaetes to Bacteriology has also necessitated some rearrangement of this class, the overcrowding in which has been relieved by transferring Immunology, now a large and important subject, to class H. Infectious Diseases, formerly somewhat incongruously placed at UD, have also been transferred to class H, which now becomes Immunology and Infectious Diseases. The former contents of class H, never very large, have been transferred to the beginning of class L which is used for Parasitology in general as well as Protozoology. Two subjects that have grown in importance since the first edition was published are Radiology and Atomic Energy, and Aviation Medicine. These have been allotted new divisions at BR, and at UA. The Division UD vacated, by Infectious Diseases, has been allotted to Industrial Medicine, as an alternative to SQR. Such alternative placings have been provided much more freely than in the first edition. The treatment of Veterinary Medicine has been drastically changed. I find that both in general medical libraries and in veterinary libraries readers prefer to have veterinary diseases, parasitology, physiology, etc., alongside related human diseases, parasitology, physiology, rather than segregated in a special veterinary class. I have therefore removed all such subjects from class X to the appropriate places in the main scheme, leaving in class X only purely veterinary topics that would have been out of place elsewhere. I find also that readers like to have together in one place everything about special animals, whether it relates to their diseases and treatment, or only to their management in health. All the special divisions of animal industry have, therefore, been transferred from class Y to class X. Thus everything about the horse will be collected together in XXM instead of being partly there and partly in YM.

(b) *Auxiliary schedules of common subdivisions:* In the first edition the only true auxiliary schedule is the Local List, which uses numerals for geographical subdivisions under any topic where needed. Apart from this, common subdivisions are provided by various makeshift devices described in the Introduction under the heading Mnemonic Features. They consist of the addition to the main symbol for the subject of certain symbols taken from other parts of the main schedules. Thus class A is used for form divisions; the main class letters alone are used for subdividing specific diseases; the divisions UE–UV for anatomical subdivisions; and so forth. When used without any sign to mark off the common subdivision from the main symbol, these devices considerably restrict the possibility of future expansion. For instance, if the form divisions of class A and the main class letters have been used for subdividing a specific disease, let us say tuberculosis, then JC cannot be any further subdivided, as it will be in the second edition. It is true that I allowed for this contingency by suggesting that the mnemonic devices could be marked off in some way, e.g. by placing them after a dot or in parentheses, but I added that in my opinion such complication of the notation is undesirable and seldom likely to be necessary. I have since, as the result of a further 16 years' experience with the scheme, changed my mind to the extent that, while still regarding complications of the notation to be in themselves undesirable, I now think that some marking-off sign is quite often necessary and that the great advantages of using just one such sign, e.g. a dot, far outweigh the disadvantages. In the new edition therefore there will be eleven tables of auxiliary schedules, the symbols of which will be marked off by a dot from the main symbols. For the purposes of arrangement, of course, this dot may be regarded as an additional letter of the alphabet coming before A.

Table 1 is a systematic schedule of general subdivisions for use with almost any class, division, or section throughout the scheme. It combines the use of the first edition of class A for form divisions and to some extent that of the main class letters for such subdivisions as history, geography, public health aspects, legal aspects, etc. Table 2 is our old friend the Local List with only a few minor alterations to bring it up to date. It is the only table which uses arabic numerals instead of letters of the alphabet. The remaining tables 3–11 are for special purposes, e.g. anatomical subdivisions, pathological conditions, therapeutic procedures, etc. Although they all use letters of the alphabet in the same way as table 1, they are so devised that, if used only in the appropriate places of the scheme, they will not, I believe, be confused either with table 1 or with each other. In many cases it will even be possible, should the need arise, to use two or more auxiliary schedules at once. To take Tuberculosis again as an example, this can be subdivided first by table 3, e.g. .R, treatment, then by table 7, e.g., RS, artificial pneumothorax, then by table 1, e.g. .D, history, and finally by table 2, e.g., .394, Norway. We thus get a symbol JC.RRS.D.394 for the history in Norway of the treatment of tuberculosis by artificial pneumothorax. This is a far longer symbol than I like, but even so it consists of only nine elements, which compares very favourably with most other schemes for such a minute degree of subdivision. One question that arises here is the order of priority of the various tables when thus used together. I have thought a good deal about this problem, but so far have found no solution. I am inclined to think that no hard and fast rule can be laid down but that different orders of priority may have to be adopted in different subjects.

(c) *Alternative notation:* The scheme was originally devised for a highly specialized library, that of the London School of Hygiene and Tropical Medicine, and one of the commonest criticisms of it has been that it is less suitable for a general medical library. Whereas in the library of the L.S.H.T.M., the book-stock is fairly evenly distributed over most of the main classes, the surveys of the two general medical libraries mentioned earlier, showed that nearly half their whole stock falls into the one main class U, while all the classes from F to O have between them less than one-tenth of the stock. This is obviously a wasteful use of notation for such libraries and to suit their needs I have provided, besides the original notation, which suits the type of library for which the scheme was originally intended, a new alternative notation in which the original classes F to O are compressed into one main class and the original class U is expanded into eleven main classes in accordance with the proportion of books found in these subjects in general medical libraries. The notation for classes A–E, V–Z, remains unchanged and the schedules themselves are exactly the same whichever notation is used. It is unlikely that libraries already using the scheme will wish to alter their notation, but any library adopting the scheme in the future will have the choice of the two systems.

In revising this, as any other practical library classification, two conflicting interests have had to be considered, that of the librarians already using the scheme, who do not want to have any more changes in notation than are necessary, and that of the librarians who will adopt it in the future, who wish to have the scheme as perfect and up to date as possible. Where the two have been irreconcilable I have ruthlessly sacrificed the former and offer no apology for so doing, because I believe it is the wise thing to do. To those who will suffer thereby I would say, though it is no consolation, that probably no library will have to make more alterations of class-marks than my own.

From, *Libri*, 3, 1954, pp. 109–113.

CHAPTER 50

# William John Bishop ( 1903–1961 )

"The librarian without an intimate knowledge of the literature is a mere mechanic. The properly trained assistant will not place undue reliance on techniques and gadgets; he will not regard classification as an end in itself but only as a means; he will realise that everything that is done in the library should subserve the one end – proper service to the readers."
W. J. Bishop.

Most outstanding medical librarians have spent their entire professional careers in medical librarianship, and few have achieved recognition outside that speciality. The subject is a vast one which constantly changes as it develops, and it is necessary to master the literature of a wide range of related subjects. An historical appreciation of the subject is useful in most medical libraries, even where current awareness is of vital necessity, and the longer one works with the literature the more one appreciates the impossibility of keeping abreast of current advancement, or of delving deeply enough into it historically. Several medical librarians have contributed significantly to medical history as well as to medical bibliography and librarianship, and prominent among these was William John Bishop.

W. J. Bishop was born in London in 1903, and began his professional career at the age of seventeen as a junior assistant in the London Library. There he read widely and began furnishing his retentive memory with facts which would prove invaluable in historical research. After four years Bishop was appointed Assistant Librarian to the Royal College of Physicians of London, where he collaborated with Arnold Chaplin, then Harveian Librarian, in several useful projects. His antiquarian interests were further developed in the richness of an outstanding medico-historical collection, but in 1934 Bishop moved to the Royal Society of Medicine where he was appointed Sub-Librarian. The move brought him into contact with current medical literature and the constant demands of an increasing number of readers, but his historical interest persisted, and in 1946 he became Librarian of the Wellcome Historical Medical Library. It might be thought that W. J. Bishop would then have had the opportunity to indulge his own interests and exploit the wonderful collection under his care, but this was impossible. Although fully employed with several important projects, he found himself overwhelmed by the demands made upon his time by research workers throughout the world, and he retired at the age of fifty-one to work on his own initiative. Unfortunately his sudden death on July 27th, 1961 left much of his work unfinished, but he left behind a reputation for scholarship, industry and friendliness that is the envy of his contemporaries.

Elected F.L.A. in 1935, Bishop was keen on the adequate education of medical librarians, and was one of the founders of the Medical Section in 1947, serving first as Honorary Secretary and later as Chairman. He stimulated an interest in the Section, which rapidly grew in membership, and he was a worthy representative of British medical librarianship when he visited the United States. He was Consultant Librarian to the Royal College of Obstetricians and Gynaecologists, and prepared its *Catalogue of the Library up to 1850*, published in 1956. A bibliography of W. J. Bishop's published writings has been compiled by S. H. Watkins, and includes: (with Hamilton Bailey) *Notable names in medicine and surgery*, 1944, 2nd edition 1946, 3rd edition 1959; (with N. M. Matheson) *Medicine and science in postage stamps*, 1948; (with F. N. L. Poynter) *A seventeenth century doctor and his patients: John Symcotts, 1592?-1662*, 1951; *Bibliography of international congresses of medical sciences*, 1958; *A history of surgical dressings*, 1959; *The early history of surgery*, 1960; and *A bio-bibliography of Florence Nightingale* which was published posthumously in 1962. Bishop was the editor of *Medical History* from its foundation in 1957, and was responsible for the maintenance of consistently high standards. He contributed numerous biographical studies to medical periodicals, and to the *Dictionary of National Biography*. His historical writings were the fruits of painstaking research, and reflect such varied interests as "English physicians in Russia in the sixteenth and seventeenth centuries"; "Notes on the history of medical costume"; "Some medical bibliophiles and their libraries"; "Medical caricature"; and "Medical book societies in England in the eighteenth and nineteenth centuries". Bishop planned a "Dictionary of British medical biography", and was also engaged on the preparation of a complete calendar of the letters of Florence Nightingale. It is hoped that these will eventually be completed. He excelled as an indexer, and will be remembered for his encyclopaedic knowledge of medical bibliography and history, and for his readiness to share that knowledge with colleagues throughout the world, to whom he was a constant source of information and inspiration. (Portrait, Plate 16.)

## REFERENCES

Poynter, F. N. L. William John Bishop, F.L.A., 1903-1961. Obituary. *Medical History*, 5, 1961, pp. 306-308; portrait opposite p. 305.

Watkins, S. H. A bibliography of W. J. Bishop. *Medical History*, 5, 1961, pp. 309-312. Obituary notices by G. R. Pendrill, and by John L. Thornton. *Library Association Record*, 63, 1961, pp. 319-320.

## BISHOP ON THE MEDICAL SECTION AND ITS WORK

Two years ago I had the privilege of attending the 49th Annual Meeting of the Medical Library Association of America and of conveying fraternal greetings from the Library Association and its Medical Section to our colleagues in the United States. The opportunity to attend that meeting is one of the many things for which I personally have to thank the Medical Section, because I think it is unlikely that any British medical librarian would have received such an invitation had it not been for the interest aroused in America by reports of the Section's activities. The address which I gave at Boston[1] was largely devoted to an account of the Medical Section and of its short-lived predecessor, the Medical Library Association of Great Britain, which existed from 1908 to 1911. On that occasion I had an easy task because few members of my audience had any prior knowledge of the subject and also because any audience of American medical librarians is not only one of the most decorative but also one of the most tolerant in the world. I do not wish to imply that this audience is less easy to look at, but I do feel that my task this afternoon is a much more difficult one. Most of you know all about the Section and many of you know a good deal about me, so I must tread warily.

My main task is to talk about the origin and development of the Section, but I will make this historical excursus as brief as possible because I wish also to consider some of the wider aspects of the Section's work and future plans.

The idea of reviving the Medical Library Association had been mooted by some London librarians for years, and throughout the greater part of the late war a small group had been meeting regularly on Thursday evenings. At these meetings medical library news was exchanged and discussion ranged over a wide range of "shop"; the little group gradually took on the character of a regular club or society. Just as the Royal Society had its forerunner in the "Invisible College", so the Medical Section of the Library Association had its immediate precursor in the little group which met in a restaurant close to No. 1 Wimpole Street. In the summer of 1947 the founding fathers—the most faithful of whom were Messrs. Hipkins, Morton and Tubbs— took active steps to enlist the aid of other medical librarians. Among the earliest to give their support were Miss Wigmore and Messrs. Cyril Barnard, W. A. Lee, W. R. LeFanu, F. N. L. Poynter, T. J. Shields, and George Wilson.

The Inaugural Meeting was held at Chaucer House on October 14th,

[1] Bishop, W. J., Medical libraries and librarianship in Great Britain. *Bull. Med. Lib. Assoc.*, 1950, 38, 296–311.

1947, when 33 librarians were present from medical institutions in all parts of the country. The new group was formally constituted as a Sub-Section of the University and Research Section of the Library Association. Mr. Cyril Barnard was elected as the first Chairman and he was to be assisted by an Honorary Secretary and a committee of five other members. The most important question that had faced the founders was whether it would be better to form an entirely separate body on the lines of the M.L.A., or to organize a group within the Library Association; and here a valuable lesson was drawn from the history of the old Medical Library Association of Great Britain, which had petered out after a struggling existence of about four years. The old Association was set up as an independent body in spite of the strongly expressed opinion of the great John MacAlister that it should be constituted a branch of the Library Association, and the canny Scot's withdrawal of support was probably one of the main causes for the Association's early decline. Another great mistake made in 1908–11 was to conceive of the M.L.A. as an association of libraries rather than of librarians. It was hopeless for the Association to embark on its ambitious schemes before the ground had been prepared by bringing the librarians themselves together. The official objectives of the old M.L.A., adopted at a meeting in Belfast in July, 1909, were, in themselves quite unexceptionable. They were:

1. To bring together those engaged in or interested in medical libraries and medical literature, and for the discussion of matters associated with their fostering and care.
2. To maintain an exchange for the distribution of duplicate books and periodicals.
3. To increase the facilities for reference work.
4. To encourage the study of medical history.
5. To issue publications dealing with library work.
6. To form a library union amongst those of the medical libraries between which the exchange of books can be arranged.

These were practically the same as the objectives which the Medical Section set before itself in 1947. It was, however, felt that undue prominence had been given to the subject of medical history, and the fourth aim was omitted from our programme. On the other hand our forerunners expressed no concern over the question of education and training for medical librarianship, a problem to which we attach the greatest importance and to which we have paid much attention. Apart from this notable omission, our predecessors of forty years ago anticipated all our projects and, furthermore, they had a wonderful scheme for a great union catalogue of the London medical libraries which still remains a dream. In spite of its unexceptionable objects and the support of Osler and other eminent medical men, the old M.L.A. did not long survive. At that time there were few medical libraries and fewer whole-time librarians. In 1947 we could not only profit by the mistakes of our predecessors but there was a very much greater potential membership.

The decision to find a place within the fold of the Library Association is one which few, if any, of us have regretted. I would remind you of the words printed on the cover of the first regular *Medical Directory*, that of 1845: "L'Union fait la Force". We believe in the essential unity of librarianship and we are proud to be a Section of the Association which is now celebrating the completion of 75 years of its great work. That is not to say that we are in agreement with all the views and policies of Chaucer House. Far from it! There are many things we should like to see done and which we hope to bring about by constitutional means, acting in close concert with our friends in the University and Research, and Reference and Special Libraries Sections. There are few politicians in the Medical Section and we do not pursue narrow sectional interests. We have many friends in the public libraries and we are glad to work in harmony with them in order to further the aims of the Library Association's Charter—which are to promote the science and art of librarianship in the widest sense; but it is so often forgotten that the number of public libraries in this country is very much less than the number of non-public and special libraries, and we feel that the tail has been wagging the dog for long enough.

Now to revert to the progress of the Section. Our first ordinary meeting was held at the National Institute for Medical Research on 2nd January, 1948. More than 70 members and guests took part in this meeting, which was addressed by Sir Charles Harington, Dr. G. Popjak, and Miss Wigmore, and we felt that we had got off to a flying start. Since that time the Section has held 32 meetings. On many occasions the attendance has exceeded 50 per cent of our total membership and I do not think that any other Section or Branch of the Association has met with such consistent support. At our second meeting, held at the Royal College of Surgeons on 18th March, 1948, we inaugurated the tradition of inviting distinguished medical men to talk to us from time to time on topics relevant to medical librarianship. On this occasion, Mr. Zachary Cope addressed us on the subject of "Some literary surgeons", and Mr. LeFanu spoke about the College Library.

As early as April, 1948, it was decided to apply for recognition as a full autonomous Section of the Library Association. The rapid growth of the Sub-Section and the highly specialized nature of its work made this step inevitable. Neither we nor the University and Research Section have had cause to regret the decision. We have always enjoyed the most friendly relations with the University and Research Section and we know that we can get on equally well with our younger brother, the Reference and Special Libraries Section. On several occasions we have held joint meetings with the other Sections, particularly on the occasion of the University and Research Section's week-end conferences, and we have been glad to act in concert in all matters affecting our mutual interests.

One of the most notable of our early meetings was that held at Chaucer House on 18th June, 1948, when Dr. John Fulton, the celebrated medical historian and bibliographer, gave us a paper which was published in the *Library Association Record* as "Notes on some American medical libraries".[1] In the course of his address, Dr. Fulton told us something about the crisis in the indexing of medical literature which had arisen following the decision to suspend publication of the Army Medical Library's *Index catalogue* and asked for our comments and suggestions. The Section Committee was able to submit certain recommendations regarding the cataloguing and indexing of medical literature which were gratefully acknowledged by the authorities of the Army Medical Library.

In November, 1948, the Section set up a special committee to consider the question of Subject Headings for Medical Libraries. The Committee produced a first draft which served as the basis for a discussion meeting held at Chaucer House on 27th October, 1949. The final Report of the Committee is now nearly ready. By the end of 1948 our membership had reached a hundred, and from 1st January, 1949, we enjoyed our new status as an independent Section of the Association.

From its very beginning the Section has taken a keen interest in the changes brought about in hospital libraries by the National Health Service Act, and has done all it could to foster their development. At the beginning of 1949 we were rather distressed by what we took to be an attempt on the part of some public libraries to enter into the medical field and to attempt to supply purely professional literature alongside the legitimate and wholly admirable service to hospital patients. There has been some confusion between libraries for patients and technical libraries for medical students and staff. The latter type of library we regard as our exclusive preserve: the work is one of the most highly specialized departments of librarianship and we would deplore any attempted penetration of public libraries into this field, both from the point of view of competency and of public welfare. In this con-

[1] Fulton, J. F. Notes on some American medical libraries. *L.A. Record*, 1948, 50, 174–180.

nexion I should like to quote from an editorial note which appeared in the *Library Association Record* in 1895:[1]

"It has recently come to our notice that in some libraries the current numbers of medical journals are placed in the reading room, thus bringing them within easy reach of the youth of both sexes. Were it not for the positive information we have upon the subject, we should be disinclined to believe that any librarian or library committee would sanction such an abuse of a public library. The public library movement has many enemies, and it would be a difficult objection to answer if the opponents of the Act could point out that library committees purveyed literature which, in the hands of young and ignorant people, is not only grossly indecent but dangerous. If such journals are taken at all, they should be kept under the jealous care of the librarian, or some responsible officer, and only given to adults. But in our opinion, no ordinary public library has any right to place journals which are intended solely for the use of the medical profession either on its tables or on its shelves."

With those sentiments the Medical Section is in entire agreement. Incidentally the same volume of the *Record* contains Miss Dorothy Taylor's paper on "Hospital libraries", read at the Cardiff meeting in September, 1895. This excellent paper was, in effect, an urgent plea for the Library Association to do something for this "rather an out-of-the-way corner of library work". That plea met with little response and it is only after the lapse of nearly half a century that the library profession has realized its responsibility in this matter. The question will, I think, arise whether the Medical Section should take any part in the work of patients' libraries, for although we are well content to leave the supply of books to the public libraries and to the British Red Cross and Order of St. John, there are certain aspects of bibliotherapy which have as yet received practically no attention in this country and which are more in the province of the medical librarian than of the general librarian.

In April, 1949, a Sub-Committee of the Section compiled a memorandum on Medical Libraries in Hospitals, which was printed in the *Lancet* of 3rd September, 1949. In connexion with this memorandum, which was also issued as a reprint, we compiled, with the willing help of more than thirty of the most eminent consultants and specialists in the various departments of medicine, a *Book list for hospital libraries*. About 300 copies of the Memorandum and *Book list* were distributed gratis on request to hospitals and other medical institutions in all parts of the world. Recently we have prepared a revised list of *Books and periodicals for medical libraries in hospitals* which has been published by

[1] Medical journals in public libraries. *Ibid.*, 1895, 7, 223.

the Library Association. In June, 1949, we had another very successful meeting at the National Institute for Medical Research, when we welcomed no less than three American friends—Miss Mildred Naylor, the indefatigable Manager of the American Medical Library Exchange, Dr. Henry R. Viets of the Boston Medical Library, and Dr. Sanford Larkey, head of the great William H. Welch Library at Johns Hopkins. To our great regret, Mrs. Eileen Cunningham, who should have been present, was detained at a Unesco conference in Paris.

In September, 1949, the Section joined forces with the University and Research Section to hold a week-end conference at Edinburgh. This was a most enjoyable meeting, at which Dr. Douglas Guthrie gave an address on "The evolution of medical education in Scotland" and visits were paid to the leading libraries of both Edinburgh and Glasgow. During 1949, we also had the pleasure of hearing addresses by the famous medical historian, Dr. Henry Sigerist, and by Professor R. H. Shyrock of Johns Hopkins University. One of our most memorable meetings was that held at the Wellcome Research Institution in connexion with the celebrations held to commemorate the Centenary of the Public Library Act. This took the form of a discussion on "The Role of libraries in the advance of medicine" which was opened by Sir Cecil Wakeley, President of the Royal College of Surgeons of England, and in which Dr. C. H. Kellaway, Dr. Hugh Clegg, Professor E. C. Dodds and many others distinguished in medicine and in librarianship took part.[1] This meeting was widely reported in the medical press and did a great deal to enhance the growing prestige of the Section. Here, I should like to record our gratitude to the many distinguished medical men who have given us encouragement and active support in many ways and especially to the medical editors who have spared precious space to report our activities. I think it is true to say that this is the first time in the history of our profession that a body of special librarians have had such contacts and have been able to make such an impact on the scientific world. The Section has, I think, done a great deal to awaken the medical profession to the vital necessity for adequate library services, without which they will find themselves drowned in their own literary secretions.

At the beginning of 1950, Mr. Barnard, the doyen of medical librarians in this country, whose admirable chairmanship had steered us so successfully through the first two years, resigned his office, and was succeeded by Mr. W. R. LeFanu. Mr. LeFanu's modesty is known to all of you. I will only say that we esteem him as a great librarian and bibliographer and respect him as a man. To find a worthy successor to

[1] Wakeley, Sir C., *et al*. The role of libraries in the advance of medicine. *L. A. Proc. Ann. Conf.*, London, 1950, pp. 50–52.

our first two chairmen was no easy task, but Liverpool—the home of one of the oldest and best medical libraries outside of London—has given us one in the person of Mr. Lee, whose masterly handling of the recent Liverpool conference was admired by all and augers well for the future. This is not a mutual admiration society, but I must also say how fortunate the Section is in having secured my very old friend and former colleague, Mr. Hipkins, as its Secretary.

We have seen that the most prominent of the declared aims of the Section were the establishment of an exchange system, the compilation of union lists and similar co-operative projects, and the encouragement of inter-library loans. I have already spoken about the List of Subject Headings for Medical Libraries. We had a Committee working on the compilation of a Union List of Medical Periodicals, but in view of the activities of Unesco and of the *World list* committees in this sphere, we felt that this project might well be suspended. Our other great project is the Exchange Service which has been in operation from the very beginning of the Section in 1947 under the capable direction of Mr. F. N. L. Poynter of the Wellcome Historical Medical Library.[1] There is no doubt that the Exchange has been one of the principal factors in the establishment of the Section on a firm basis. During the four years that the scheme has been in operation, many thousands of books and journals have passed through the depository at Euston Road and have found new homes. Without elaborate machinery or fuss of any kind, valuable consignments of books and journals have been transferred from one end of Britain to the other and even to darkest Africa. The Section owes a very great debt to Mr. Poynter, who has given so much of his time to this worthy object, and also to the many librarians and doctors who have helped by keeping up the flow of duplicate and unwanted items. Just what does go on in the basements of Wimpole Street, Lincoln's Inn Fields and the Euston Road cannot be revealed here, but one strongly suspects that some librarians are willing to connive at the robbery of the rich in order to help the poor.

The last and perhaps the most important of all our activities has been concerned with education and training for medical librarianship. We are witnessing a great expansion in the medical library field; new libraries are springing up, old ones are being enlarged, more and more demands are being made upon library staffs. This has led to a shortage of suitably trained staff and to a revaluation of exactly what is meant by medical librarianship. In the earliest days of its existence the Medical Section was, through its chosen representatives, given a voice in the revision of the Library Association's examination syllabus. For the

[1] Poynter, F. N. L. A duplicate exchange service for medical libraries. *L.A. Record*, 1950, 52, 41–43.

first time in the history of medical librarianship a detailed syllabus was drawn up and special examination papers were set as part of the final examination for the Fellowship of the Library Association. We have reason to believe that our syllabus and examinations have exerted a wide influence and many of their features are being copied both here and in other countries. Having established a syllabus and an examination, our next problem was to meet the demand for organized instruction. This was tackled in various ways. Our ordinary meetings were designed to give an airing to topics of practical importance to all members and at the same time give them the opportunity of visiting widely differing types of medical libraries. Secondly, we inaugurated a series of lecture meetings, which were purely didactic in their purpose and were adapted to the needs of the younger and less experienced members. The lectures were held at various appropriate libraries and were given by members of the Section having special experience and knowledge of the subject in hand. Ten or more lecture meetings of this kind have been held; they have been very well attended and have been of the greatest benefit not only to younger members but also to the lecturers, who have been stimulated to crystallize their ideas and to record their experience for the benefit of others. Two of the most valuable lectures—those of Mr. F. A. Tubbs on "The use of libraries" and of Mr. C. F. A. Marmoy on "Some special forms of medical literature"—have been published.[1,2] Several of our members have been stimulated to repay part of that debt which Francis Bacon said that every man owed to his profession by publishing valuable contributions to medical librarianship, history and bibliography. Contemporaneously with the official Section lectures, two courses of special lectures on medical librarianship have been given by Section members at the Northwestern Polytechnic, the first of five lectures and the second (which is still in progress) of thirty. This educational work will, I hope, be continued and extended. It is perhaps the most important thing we have to do, and I like to think that the Medical Section is leading the way back to the pure librarianship—not the librarianship of the high-flown theorist or the gadget-monger, but the real thing which is based upon a thorough grounding in the fundamental techniques and a profound knowledge of the literature with which one has to deal.

The Section initiated, and is taking the liveliest interest in, the organization of the First International Congress on Medical Librarianship which is to be held in London in July, 1953.

At the present time the 230 members of the Medical Section come

---

[1] Tubbs, F. A. The use of libraries. *St. Thos. Hosp. Gaz.*, 1951, 49, 208–216.

[2] Marmoy, C. F. A. Some special forms of medical literature. *L.A. Record*, 1951, 53, 354–362.

from 123 different libraries and institutions at home and abroad. Our members represent medical libraries of the ancient medical corporations, universities, colleges, government departments, hospitals, research institutions and the great chemical and pharmaceutical houses. No less than 30 of our members belong to the staffs of public or county libraries—a fact that rather puzzles some of us. We are not a closed shop, but we have never sought to add to our numbers by special drives or membership campaigns. We do not want members unless they share our ideals and are keen. We are proud of what we have done in the last four years and we look forward to greater achievements in the future.

From, *Library Association, Bournemouth Conference Papers and Discussion*, 1952, pp. 12–16.

# General References

THIS includes material used for general reference purposes in the preparation of this book, together with a selection of biographical sources, but excluding most of the obituary notices cited within chapters. Many of the items cited contain additional references, and others can be traced in *Library Science Abstracts*. Place of publication is London unless otherwise stated.

Abbott, Maude E., ed. *Classified and annotated bibliography of Sir William Osler's publications. . . . Second edition*, [etc.], Montreal, 1939.

*Annals of the Library Association, 1877–1960. Edited on behalf of the Library History Group by W. A. Munford*, 1965.

Ardagh, Philip. Sir William Osler as bibliophile and bibliographer. *Librarian*, 46, 1957, pp. 35–36.

Billings, John Shaw. *An autobiographical fragment, 1905. A facsimile copy of the original manuscript*, Bethesda, Md., 1965.

——. *Selected papers. . . . Compiled, with a life of Billings, by Frank Bradway Rogers*, Medical Library Association, 1965.

Brooks, Constance. *Antonio Panizzi, scholar and patriot*, Manchester, 1931.

[Brown, Samuel.] *Some account of itinerating libraries and their founder*, Edinburgh, 1856.

Browne, G. F., Bishop of Bristol. *Alcuin of York: lectures delivered in the Cathedral Church of Bristol in 1907 and 1908*, [etc.], 1908.

Carlton, Grace. *Spade work: the story of Thomas Greenwood*, 1949.

Central Council for the Care of Churches. *The parochial libraries of the Church of England*, [etc.], 1959.

Crone, John S. *Henry Bradshaw: his life and work*, Dublin, 1931.

Cushing, Harvey. *The life of Sir William Osler*, 2 vols., Oxford, 1925.

Cutter, William Parker. *Charles Ammi Cutter*, Chicago, 1931. (American Library Pioneers, III.)

Danton, Emily Miller, ed. *Pioneering leaders in librarianship. First series*, Chicago, 1953. (American Library Pioneers, VIII.)

Dawe, Grosvenor. *Melvil Dewey: seer, inspirer, doer, 1851–1931*, [etc.], New York, 1932.

Dee, John. *Autobiographical tracts of Dr. John Dee, Warden of the College of Manchester. Edited by James Crossley*, for the Chetham Society, 1951. (Chetham Society, O.S. 24, Miscellanies, Vol. 1.)

Dewey, Godfrey. Dewey, 1851–1951. *Library Journal*, 76, 1951, pp. 1964–1965.

Dowling, Basil. Sir Anthony Panizzi. *New Zealand Libraries*, 13, 1950, pp. 33–38.

Esdaile, A. J. K. *The British Museum Library: a short history and survey*, 1946.

Fagan, Louis. *The life of Sir Anthony Panizzi*, 2 vols., 1880.

Fletcher, Charlotte. The Reverend Thomas Bray, M. Alexandre Vattemare, and library science. *Library Quarterly*, 27, 1957, pp. 95–99.

Fry, W. G., and Munford, W. A., *Louis Stanley Jast: a biographical sketch*, 1966.

Garrison, Fielding Hudson. *John Shaw Billings: a memoir*, [etc.], New York, London, 1915.

Gibson, Strickland. E. W. B. Nicholson (1849–1912): some impressions. *Library Association Record*, 51, 1949, pp. 137–143.

Gjelsness, Rudolph H. William Warner Bishop, 1871–1955. *Libri*, 6, 1955, pp. 3–5.

Green, Evelyn K. Henry Benjamin Wheatley, D.C.L., F.S.A., (Born May 2nd, 1838, died April 30th, 1917). *The Indexer*, 4, 1964–65, pp. 115–116.

Greenwood, Thomas. *Edward Edwards, the chief pioneer of municipal public libraries*, 1902.

Hadley, Chalmers. *John Cotton Dana: a sketch*, Chicago, 1943. (American Library Pioneers, V.)

Heilbrun, Carolyn G. *The Garnett family*, 1961.

*Herbert Putnam, 1861–1955: a memorial tribute*, Washington, 1956.

Holley, Edward G. Neglect of the "greats": some observations on the problems of writing the biographies of American librarians. *Library Journal*, 88, 1963, pp. 3547–3551.

Horrocks, Sidney. Thomas Greenwood and his Library. *Manchester Review*, 8, Spring, 1959, pp. 269–277.

Houlette, William D. Parish libraries and the work of the Reverend Thomas Bray. *Library Quarterly*, 4, 1934, pp. 588–609.

Irwin, Raymond. The approach to a national library in England. *Library Association Record*, 64, 1962, pp. 81–93.

——. Does library history matter? *Library Review*, 128, 1958, pp. 510–513.

——. *The English library: sources and history*, 1966.

——. *The heritage of the English library*, 1964.

——. Studies in the history of libraries. I–XI. *Library Association Record*, 56, 1954, pp. 39–43, 117–121, 195–201, 283–288, 382–389; 57, 1955, pp. 90–97, 290–296, 464–470; 58, 1956, pp. 168–173, 413–419; 59, 1957, pp. 223–227. This material has largely been reproduced in the two above-mentioned books.

Kaser, David. William Warner Bishop: contributions to a bibliography. *Library Quarterly*, 26, 1956, pp. 52–60.

Keys, Thomas E. Sir William Osler and the medical library. Part I [–II]. *Bulletin of the Medical Library Association*, 49, 1961, pp. 24–39, 127–148.

Lydenberg, Harry Miller. *John Shaw Billings, creator of the National Medical Library and its catalogue; first director of the New York Public Library*, Chicago, 1924. (American Library Pioneers, I.)

Lydenberg, Harry Miller, and Keogh, Andrew, *eds. William Warner Bishop: a tribute*, New Haven, London, 1941.

McColvin, L. R. W. C. Berwick Sayers. *Library World*, 62, 1960–61, pp. 141–144.

McCrimmon, Barbara. Antonio Panizzi as administrator. *University of Illinois Library School, Occasional Papers*, No. 68, 1963.

Macleod, R. D. *The Anglo-American library associations*, 1958. (Library Association Pamphlet No. 19.)

——. Melvil Dewey and his famous school. *Library Review*, 135, 1960, pp. 479–484.

MacNalty, Sir Arthur Salusbury. Osler, the medical historian. *Proceedings of the Royal Society of Medicine*, 56, 1963, Supplement, pp. 3–9.

Marshall, John David, and others. *Books, libraries, librarians: contributions to library literature. Selected by John David Marshall, Wayne Shirley [and] Louis Shores*, Hamden, Conn., 1955.

Mearns, David C. Herbert Putnam, librarian of the United States; the Minneapolis years. *Wilson Library Bulletin*, 29, 1954, pp, 59–63.

Metcalfe, John. *Edward Edwards: his association with "New South Wales, its present state and future prospects"*, Sydney, 1952.

Minto, John. *A history of the public library movement in Great Britain and Ireland*, 1932. Among others, contains biographies of the following persons to whom chapters in this volume are devoted: F. T. Barrett, Sir E. A. Bond, J. P. Briscoe, J. D. Brown, Edward Edwards, R. Garnett, T. Greenwood, Minnie S. R. James, Sir John Y. W. MacAlister, T. Mason, E. W. B. Nicholson, J. J. Ogle, F. Pacy, H. R. Tedder, and W. H. K. Wright.

Mohrhardt, Foster. Dr. William Warner Bishop: our first international librarian. *Wilson Library Bulletin*, 32, 1957, pp. 207–215.

Moran, James. William Blades. *The Library*, 5th Ser., 16, 1961, pp. 251–266.

Morin, Georges. Un médecin bibliothécaire: Gabriel Naudé (1600–1653). *Paris-médical*, 1929, i, pp. 136–141.

Munford, W. A. *Edward Edwards, 1812–1886: portrait of a librarian*. 1963.

——. Edward Edwards in retrospect. *Library Review*, 146, 1963, pp. 90–93.

——. Edward Edwards reconsidered: (1) The man. [(2) The librarian and author.] *Library Review*, 133, 1960, pp. 310–313; 134, 1960, pp. 410–414.

——. Nicholson of the Bodleian. *Library Review*, 143, 1962, pp. 507–512.

——. Our library inheritance. *Library Review*, 130, 1959, pp. 101–106.

——. *Penny rate. Aspects of British public library history, 1850–1950*, 1951; (reprinted 1965).

——. Public libraries, 1850–1950. *Library Association Record*, 52, 1950, pp. 311–321.

——. *William Ewart, M.P.*, 1960.

Oldman, C. B., *et al. English libraries, 1800–1850. Three lectures at University College, London*, 1958. Contains, Sir Anthony Panizzi and the British Museum Library, by C. B. Oldman, pp. 5–32; George Birkbeck and mechanics' institutes, by W. A. Munford, pp. 33–59; Carlyle and the London Library, by Simon Nowell-Smith, pp. 59–78.

*Pietas Oxoniensis in memory of Sir Thomas Bodley, Knt., and the foundation of the Bodleian Library*, [Oxford], 1902.

Power, Sir D'Arcy. Sir Thomas Bodley's London house. *Bodleian Quarterly Record*, 8, No. 90, Summer, 1936

Poynter, F. N. L. William John Bishop, F.L.A., 1903–1961. *Medical History*, 5, 1961, pp. 306–308; portrait opposite p. 305.

Prothero, Sir George Walter. *A memoir of Henry Bradshaw, Fellow of King's College, Cambridge, and University Librarian*, 1888.

Rider, Fremont. *Melvil Dewey*, Chicago, 1944. (American Library Pioneers, VI.)

Rogers, Frank Bradway. John Shaw Billings: 1838–1913. *Library Journal*, 88, 1963, pp. 2622–2624.

Savage, Ernest A. Casual amateur in bibliography. *Library Association Record*, 65, 1963, pp. 361–365.

——. Edward Edwards and the Library Association. *Library World*, 54, 1952–53, pp. 132–136, 151–153. Comments on this article by W. A. Munford: Idol in the wood. *Ibid.*, pp. 167–168.

——. James Duff Brown after fifty years. *Library Review*, 135, 1960, pp. 489–495.

——. *A librarian's memories: portraits & reflections*, 1952.

——. Movements and men of the past in the Association. *Library Association Record*, 52, 1950, pp. 321–329.

Sayers, W. C. Berwick. The centenary of Melvil Dewey. *British Book News*, 136, 1951, pp. 749–753.

Shaw, Robert Kendall. *Samuel Swett Green*, Chicago, 1926.

*Sir John Young Walker MacAlister: a memorial for his family and friends*, 1926.

Smith, Charlotte Fell. *John Dee, 1527–1608*, [*etc.*], 1909.

Smith, George. Dr. Thomas Bray. *Library Association Record*, 12, 1910, pp. 242–260.

[Smith, Samuel.] *Public spirit illustrated in the life and designs of the Reverend Thomas Bray. . . . The second edition, revised*, 1808. (First edition, 1746.)

Stewart, James D. Brown's "Subject classification". *Review of Documentation*, 17, 1950, pp. 56–63.

——. James Duff Brown and the 'L.W.' *Library World*, 63, 1961–62, pp. 56–58.

Stych, F. S. The Thomas Bray Library from Sheldon in the Birmingham Reference Library. *Open Access*, 12, January, 1964, pp. 1–3.

Tedder, Henry R. E. W. B. Nicholson (Bodley's Librarian, 1882–1912): in memoriam. *Library Association Record*, 16, 1914, pp. 95–108; discussion of this paper by Falconer Madan, C. Madeley, T. W. Lyster and others, Vol. 15, 1913, pp. 630–633.

Thornton, John L. *The chronology of librarianship: an introduction to the history of libraries and book-collecting. . . . With an introduction by Ernest A. Savage*, 1941.

——. Dr. John Dee and his scheme for a national library. *Medical Bookman and Historian*, 2, 1948, pp. 359–362.

——. Steps in the development of the public library movement. *Library World*, 52, 1949–50, pp. 209–211.

*Trecentale Bodleianum. A memorial volume for the three hundredth anniversary of the public funeral of Sir Thomas Bodley, March 29, 1613*, Oxford, 1913.

Walmsley, Robert. Dr. Axon—Manchester bookman. *Manchester Review*, 10, 1964, pp. 138–154.

Watkins, S. H. A bibliography of W. J. Bishop. *Medical History*, 5, 1961, pp. 309–312.

Winser, Beatrice. *John Cotton Dana, 1856–1929*, Newark, New Jersey, 1930.

Wormald, Francis, and Wright, C. E., *eds. The English library before 1700. Studies in its history*, 1958.

# Index